AN EXPLORER'S GUIDE

Wyoming

Wyoming

Alli Rainey

with photographs by the author

The Countryman Press ✳ Woodstock, Vermont

FIRST EDITION

Copyright © 2010 by Alli Rainey

Wyoming: An Explorer's Guide

First Edition

ISBN: 978-0-88150-890-1

Cover photo by Alli Rainey
Interior photographs by the author unless otherwise specified
Maps by Erin Greb Cartography, © The Countryman Press
Book design by Bodenweber
Composition by PerfecType, Nashville, TN

Published by The Countryman Press, P.O. Box 748, Woodstock, VT 05091

Distributed by W. W. Norton & Company, Inc., 500 Fifth Avenue, New York, NY 10110

Printed in the United States of America

10 9 8 7 6 5 4 3 2 1

This book is for you, the explorer of Wyoming: I hope you learn to love this place as much as I do. Happy travels!

EXPLORE WITH US!

Welcome to the first edition of *Wyoming: An Explorer's Guide*. All attractions, activities, lodgings, and restaurants in this guide have been selected on the basis of merit. None is here as a paid advertisement. The organization of the book is simple, but the following points will help to get you started.

WHAT'S WHERE

In the beginning of this book, you will find an alphabetical listing with thumbnail sketches of special highlights and important information for travelers. Also, note that in general Wyoming is an extremely well-signed state, with hundreds of brown informational signs dotting its roadways to guide tourists to its plethora of attractions as painlessly as possible.

RATES

Please don't hold us or the respective innkeepers responsible for the rates listed as of press time in 2010. Some changes are inevitable. State and local room taxes (a 4 percent statewide tax plus an additional local tax of up to 6 percent) are not included in lodging prices unless specifically noted. Unless otherwise noted, all rates included are for double occupancy.

SMOKING

While Wyoming does not have a statewide smoking ban for public places (yet), Teton County and the cities of Laramie, Cheyenne, and Evanston do enforce bans on smoking in indoor public places. It's best to check up on local policies before you light up.

RESTAURANTS

In most sections please note a distinction between Dining Out and Eating Out. By their nature, restaurants listed in the Eating Out group are generally less expensive. See What's Where in Wyoming for more information on restaurants.

LODGING

Lodging establishments are selected for mention in this book based on merit; no business owner or innkeeper was charged for inclusion. See What's Where in Wyoming for more information on lodging.

KEY TO SYMBOLS

☘ The special-value symbol appears next to attractions, activities, lodgings, and restaurants that are either free (in the case of those types of attractions you might generally be charged for), or combine exceptional value with a reasonable price (or both).

✎ The kids-alert symbol appears next to lodgings, restaurants, and attractions that cater to children, or that children might find particularly interesting.

 ♿   The wheelchair symbol appears next to lodgings, restaurants, and attractions that are partially or completely handicapped accessible. While every effort has been made to ensure accuracy, it's best to double check with establishments before your arrival.

🐾   The dog-paw symbol appears next to lodgings that accept pets (usually with a reservation and a deposit) as of press time. Since campgrounds almost always allow pets, this symbol is not used for campgrounds.

"T"   The antenna symbol indicates a lodging (or other) establishment that offers WiFi access.

ORGANIZATION

In this book, you'll find Wyoming organized roughly north to south and west to east into six geographical regions. Within these major sections, you'll find each region further divided sensibly into chapters centered around one or two cities (or in a couple of cases, geographical features) and their surroundings, making it easy to find attractions close by no matter where you happen to be in the state. Please note that if a chapter has no entries in a particular category, that doesn't necessarily mean that none exist; it simply means that none have caught the eye (yet) of yours truly. As certain attractions fit in several categories, every attempt to provide helpful cross references has been made.

DINING PRICES

Average prices refer to a dinner consisting of an entrée, appetizer or dessert, and glass of wine or beer (tax and gratuities not included).

> Inexpensive: Up to $15
> Moderate: $15–30
> Expensive: $30–50
> Very Expensive: $50 or more

LODGING PRICES

The price range runs from low off-season rates to higher summer and holiday weekend rates.

> Very Inexpensive: Under $40 per night, double occupancy
> Inexpensive: $40–70
> Moderate: $70–100
> Expensive: $100–200
> Very Expensive: More than $200

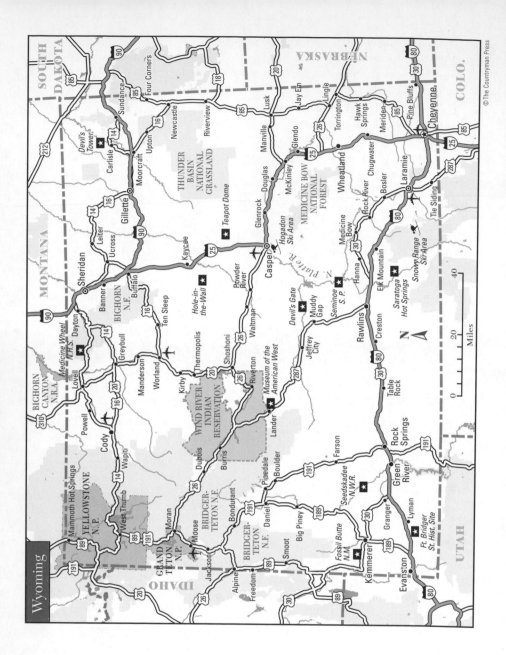

Wyoming

CONTENTS

MAPS

ACKNOWLEDGMENTS

U ltimately, this book would not have been possible to write without the inspiration provided by the incomparable state of Wyoming and all of the wonderful attractions and people found within it. Nor would this book have been possible without support from The Countryman Press.

INTRODUCTION

Welcome to the first edition of *Wyoming: An Explorer's Guide.* From the gorgeous and more familiar vistas of Yellowstone National Park and Grand Teton National Park to lesser-known but equally worthy travel destinations in my adopted home state of Wyoming, you'll find in these pages an honest effort to guide you to the most intriguing and awe-inspiring attractions and activities that Wyoming has to offer. As you make your journey through this state (or your lifelong journey, if it's your home), please alert me if you discover that I've left out something wonderful or amazing that should be included in the next edition, and I'll be sure to check it out and consider including it next time. But for now, let me start by introducing you to my favorite place on earth—the state of Wyoming.

Wyoming lays claim to both a rich natural history and an impressive record of human habitation. Long before explorers of European ancestry ever crossed its borders, humans inhabited the area now known as Wyoming—in fact, ancient people dwelled upon these lands more than 10,000 years ago, a testament to the lavish abundance of both flora and fauna that has long existed in this region, enabling people to live here despite often inhospitable weather conditions. Later, many tribes of American Indians called these lands home, including the Arapaho, Arikara, Bannock, Blackfeet, Cheyenne, Crow, Gros Ventre, Kiowa, Nez Perce, Sheep Eater, Sioux, Shoshone, and Ute.

Wyoming received its earliest visits from explorers in the first decade of the 19th century, when a man named John Colter discovered an area in 1807 that he deemed Colter's Hell. In 1872, this area became the world's first national park— Yellowstone National Park. Soon after the first European explorers passed through, Wyoming became favored stomping grounds for fur trappers and traders, who strove to meet the demand for beaver hats, which had become the latest fad in fashionable European society. As this demand waned in the middle of the century, the gold rush picked up, bringing a fresh onslaught of pioneers headed west on the Oregon Trail and other pioneer trails to seek their fortunes in Wyoming (and its northern neighbor, Montana), where gold had been found, or traveling through to California in pursuit of the gold there. Still others passed this way on journeys to claim a plot of the rich land rumored to be found in Oregon and thereabouts. Bands of Mormons came, too, traveling west on the Mormon Trail in an effort to escape religious persecution.

Conflicts between pioneers and Native Americans continued throughout the 19th century, as the struggle for land and resources grew, and the traditional ways of living for the American Indians came under siege from the combined effects of alcohol, new diseases, new people, and a new system of trading, among other stressors. Wyoming became the scene of some of the most horrific and bloody battles between American Indians and the encroaching settlers, with the ultimate result of the American Indians being forced onto reservations, for the most part, by the close of the 19th century. The vast herds of buffalo, too, that used to roam the area dwindled into virtual oblivion, unable to maintain their numbers in the face of the massive, wanton slaughtering of the herds undertaken by the newcomers.

Wyoming became a state in 1890. It developed a strong agricultural base, particularly in ranching for both sheep and cattle (though these two different types of ranching served as the basis for some historical conflicts as well), but also in growing crops. Wyoming also developed a strong economic dependence on the mineral extraction industry. The vast quantities of coal in Wyoming prompted the building of the transcontinental railroad across the southern part of the state in the mid- to late 19th century, leaving behind a legacy of interstate commerce in coal mining that still contributes to the state's economy today.

Throughout the 20th century and into the present time, Wyoming has continued to rely economically on both mining and agriculture. While mining holds the top position as the greatest economic contributor to the state's wealth, more of the state's residents make their livings off agriculture. In addition, Wyoming has undergone a gradual but significant shift in economic dependence on these traditional sources as tourism to the region has grown, taking a position as one of the state's top three industries. With so much focus on making Wyoming a friendly and worthy travel destination, not to mention the enormous quantity of diverse attractions, you can't go wrong in planning a visit.

If you've never been to Wyoming before, you're in for a true treat. Perhaps more than any other area of the country, Wyoming as a whole retains a strong, vibrant frontier spirit, embodied by the rugged, but for the most part welcoming, individuals who you'll undoubtedly encounter during your travels, as well as by the vast tracts of public lands contained within the state itself. Perhaps this vast inland sea of relatively untrammeled wild lands is what made me fall in love with Wyoming and choose it as my home, after years of feeling placeless and unable to answer the inevitable "Where are you from?" question that always comes up in standard introductory conversations. Born in New York City, I moved before I could even remember the place, spending my childhood in Seattle, Phoenix, and Boston. I moved west a year after finishing college, traveling for two months before settling in Colorado for a time. But it wasn't until I ventured up to Wyoming that I discovered a place where I really wanted to say I was from and call my home, a place that continues to wow and amaze me the more I explore and learn about it, from the stark beauty of its badlands and the colorful, sudden blooms of its spring wildflowers in its canyons and mountains, to the roughly 530,000 individuals (the smallest population of any state in the nation) scattered across its vast territory—Wyoming ranks ninth out of all of the states in area.

Enough about me and why I think Wyoming is such a wonderful place. For now, I will leave you to start your exploration, hoping that in Wyoming you will discover, as I have, a treasure trove of fantastic and wonderful opportunities that will leave you yearning to return again and again.

TOP 10 ATTRACTIONS BY REGION

For each top 10 list, the recommended attractions are not listed in any particular order—it was hard enough to choose only 10 attractions for each area. At the end of this section, you'll find two more top 10 lists: Wyoming's Top 10 Attractions/Activities Overall, and Wyoming's Top 10 Weirdest 'n' Wackiest Attractions. Just try to check off all of these attractions in one visit to Wyoming—I bet you'll have to come back more than once to actually see 'em all—and enjoy!

TOP 10 ATTRACTIONS IN YELLOWSTONE NATIONAL PARK AND GRAND TETON NATIONAL PARK

YELLOWSTONE

1. Canyon Visitor Education Center (*To See*—Visitor Centers, Yellowstone National Park)

2. Grand Loop Road (*To See*—Scenic Drives, Yellowstone National Park)

3. Grand Canyon of the Yellowstone (*To See*—Natural Wonders, Yellowstone National Park)

4. Old Faithful (*To See*—Natural Wonders, Yellowstone National Park)

5. Norris Geyser Basin Nature Trails (*To Do*—Hiking, Yellowstone National Park)

GRAND TETON

6. Craig Thomas Discovery and Visitor Center and/or Laurance S. Rockefeller Preserve Center (*To See*—Visitor Centers and Museums, Grand Teton National Park)

7. Menor's Ferry Historic District (*To See*—Historic Landmarks, Places, and Sites, Grand Teton National Park)

8. Grand Teton Multi-Use Pathway (*To Do*—Bicycling, Grand Teton National Park)

9. Climb the Grand Teton (*To Do*—Climbing, Grand Teton National Park)

10. Jenny Lake Scenic Cruise/Shuttle and Hidden Falls Trail (*To Do*—Unique Adventures and *To Do*—Hiking, Grand Teton National Park)

TOP 10 ATTRACTIONS IN NORTHWEST WYOMING

1. Buffalo Bill Historical Center (*To See*—Museums, Cody and Powell)

2. Cody Nite Rodeo (*To Do*—For Families, Cody and Powell)

3. Hot Springs State Park (*Green Space*—State Parks, Thermopolis and Worland)

4. Wyoming Dinosaur Center (*To Do*—For Families, Thermopolis and Worland)

5. Ten Sleep and all of its attractions/events (*To See*—Towns, Thermopolis and Worland)

6. Sinks Canyon State Park (*Green Space*—State Parks, Lander and Riverton)

7. South Pass City Historic Site (*To See*—Historic Landmarks, Places, and Sites, Lander and Riverton)

8. Explore one, two, or all three of Jackson Hole's ski resorts in winter or summer (see Grand Targhee Resort, Jackson Hole Mountain Resort, and Snow King Resort in *To Do*—Snow Sports, Jackson and Dubois)

9. National Elk Refuge and its associated attractions (*Green Space*—Wildlife Areas and Refuges, Jackson and Dubois)

10. Town Square shopping and dining (City Parks and Gardens and *Selective Shopping*, Jackson and Dubois).

TOP 10 ATTRACTIONS IN NORTHEAST WYOMING

1. Story and all of its attractions/events (*To See*—Towns, Sheridan and Buffalo)

2. Trail End State Historic Site and Kendrick Park (*To See*—Museums and *To Do*—For Families, Sheridan and Buffalo)

3. Medicine Wheel National Historic Landmark (*To See*—Historic Landmarks, Places, and Sites, Sheridan and Buffalo)

4. Bighorn Scenic Byway (*To See*—Scenic Drives, Sheridan and Buffalo)

5. Historic Occidental Hotel (*Lodging*—Hotels and Motels, Sheridan and Buffalo)

6. Campbell County Rockpile Museum (*To See*—Museums, Gillette and the Devils Tower Area)

7. Vore Buffalo Jump (*To See*—Historic Landmarks, Places, and Sites, Gillette and the Devils Tower Area)

8. Devils Tower National Monument (*To See*—A Natural Wonder, Gillette and the Devils Tower Area)

9. Coal Mine Tour (*To Do*—Unique Adventures, Gillette and the Devils Tower Area)

10. Keyhole State Park (*Green Space*—State Parks, Gillette and the Devils Tower Area)

TOP 10 ATTRACTIONS IN CENTRAL WYOMING

1. National Historic Trails Interpretive Center (*To See*—Museums, Casper and Douglas)

2. Independence Rock State Historic Site and Devils Gate (*To See*—Historic Landmarks, Places, and Sites/Natural Wonders)

3. Ayres Natural Bridge Park (*To See*—Natural Wonders, Casper and Douglas)

4. North Platte River and related attractions (*To Do*—Bicycling, Fishing, and Paddling/Floating, Casper and Douglas)

5. Bamboo Spa & Salon (*To Do*—Relaxation and Rejuvenation, Casper and Douglas)

6. Fort Laramie National Historic Site (*To See*—Historic Landmarks, Places, and Sites, Wheatland and Torrington)

7. Register Cliff/Oregon Trail Ruts (*To See*—Historic Landmarks, Places, and Sites, Wheatland and Torrington)

8. Table Mountain Vineyards (*To Do*—Wineries and Wine Tastings, Wheatland and Torrington)

9. Guernsey State Park (*Green Space*—State Parks, Wheatland and Torrington)

10. Chugwater Chili Cook-off and Chili Corporation (*Special Events/Selective Shopping*, Wheatland and Torrington)

TOP 10 ATTRACTIONS IN SOUTHWEST WYOMING

1. Pinedale and all of its attractions/events (*To See*—Towns, Evanston and Star Valley)

2. Fort Bridger State Historic Site (*To See*—Historic Landmarks, Places, and Sites, Evanston and Star Valley)

3. Historic Depot Square (*To See*—Historic Landmarks, Places, and Sites, Evanston and Star Valley)

4. Fossil Butte National Monument (*To See*—Natural Wonders, Evanston and Star Valley)

5. Bear River State Park/Greenway (*To Do*—Bicycling and *Green Space*—State Parks, Evanston and Star Valley)

6. The Great Divide Basin, Killpecker Sand Dunes, and Red Desert (*To See*—Natural Wonders, Green River and Rock Springs)

7. Green River (*To Do*—Fishing, Green River and Rock Springs)

8. Flaming Gorge National Recreation Area (*Green Space*—Recreation Areas, Green River and Rock Springs)

9. Coyote Creek Steakhouse and Saloon (*Where to Eat*—Dining Out, Green River and Rock Springs)

10. Wyoming's Big Show (*Special Events*, Green River and Rock Springs)

TOP 10 ATTRACTIONS IN SOUTHEAST WYOMING

1. Saratoga and all of its attractions/events (*To See*—Towns, Rawlins and Laramie)

2. University of Wyoming Art Museum, Geological Museum, and the American Heritage Center (*To See*—Museums, Rawlins and Laramie)

3. Wyoming Frontier Prison (*To See*—Historic Landmarks, Places, and Sites, Rawlins and Laramie)

4. Historic Downtown Laramie (*Selective Shopping*, Rawlins and Laramie)

5. Vedauwoo Recreation Area (*Green Space*—Recreation Areas, Rawlins and Laramie)

6. Wyoming State Museum (*To See*—Museums, Cheyenne)

7. Cheyenne Depot Museum (*To See*—Museums, Cheyenne)

8. Historic Governors' Mansion (*To See*—Historic Landmarks, Places, and Sites, Cheyenne)

9. Cheyenne Botanic Gardens (*To See*—City Parks and Gardens, Cheyenne)

10. Cheyenne Frontier Days (*Special Events*, Cheyenne)

WYOMING'S TOP 10 ATTRACTIONS/ACTIVITIES OVERALL

1. National parks and monuments, such as Yellowstone National Park

2. Informative and interactive history museums, such as the Buffalo Bill Historical Center (*To See*—Museums, Cody and Powell)

3. Western rodeos and celebrations, such as Cheyenne Frontier Days (*Special Events*, Cheyenne)

4. Scenic drives, such as the Wyoming Centennial Scenic Byway (*To See*—Scenic Drives, Jackson and Dubois)

5. State parks, such as Hot Springs State Park (*Green Space*—State Parks, Thermopolis and Worland)

6. Historic downtown shopping districts, such as Town Square (*To See*—City Parks and Gardens and *Selective Shopping*, Jackson and Dubois)

7. Historic sites, such as Independence Rock State Historic Site and Devils Gate (*To See*—Historic Landmarks, Places, and Sites/Natural Wonders, Casper and Douglas)

8. Numerous rivers and streams, such as the North Platte River and related attractions (*To Do*—Bicycling, Fishing, and Paddling/Floating, Casper and Douglas)

9. Incredible mountain ranges, such as the Big Horn Mountains (see Bighorn National Forest in *Green Space*—National Lands, Thermopolis and Worland)

10. Unique natural features, such as the Great Divide Basin, Killpecker Sand Dunes, and Red Desert (*To See*—Natural Wonders, Green River and Rock Springs)

WYOMING'S TOP 10 WEIRDEST 'N' WACKIEST ATTRACTIONS

Tired of the mainstream? Want to see some more offbeat or odd attractions? This list will get you started . . . try to check 'em all off!

1. Red Gulch Dinosaur Tracksite (*To See*—Natural Wonders, Thermopolis and Worland)

2. Two Castle Gardens (*To See*—Natural Wonders, Thermopolis and Worland, *and* Lander and Riverton)

3. Dry Creek Petrified Tree Environmental Education Area (*Green Space*—Wildlife Refuges and Areas, Sheridan and Buffalo)

4. Jackalope Square (Douglas in *To See*—City Parks and Gardens, Casper and Douglas)

5. Table Mountain Vineyards (*To See*—Wineries and Wine Tastings, Wheatland and Torrington)

6. Tri-State Monument (*To See*—Historic Landmarks, Places, and Sites, Evanston and Star Valley)

7. Periodic Geyser (*To See*—Natural Wonders, Evanston and Star Valley)

8. Two-bodied lamb, at the Fossil Country Frontier Museum (*To See*—Museums, Evanston and Star Valley)

9. Two-story outhouse, at the Grand Encampment Museum (*To See*—Museums, Rawlins and Laramie)

10. Shoes made from human skin, at the Carbon County Museum (*To See*—Museums in Rawlins and Laramie)

WHAT'S WHERE IN WYOMING

AGRICULTURE played an extremely important historic role in Wyoming's economic development. It continues to be a key component of Wyoming's economy today, both as a valuable cultural resource and as an essential contributor to the state's economic well-being. Chief agricultural endeavors include ranching—both cattle and sheep—as well as growing crops that include hay, grains like wheat and barley, and sugar beets.

AIRPORTS Wyoming has one international airport (Natrona County International Airport) centrally located near Casper, as well as a number of regional and municipal airports that offer commercial flights. You'll find the closest airport(s) offering commercial flights for each region listed in the Getting There section at the start of the chapter.

ANTIQUES Wyoming may not be known for its antiques, but you'll find antique shops here and there—many of which specialize in uniquely western antiques—throughout the state (look to the *Selective Shopping* section in some chapters for starters). You can also get your fix in September at the Northeast Wyoming Annual Antique Show (307-467-5524; http://www.hulett .org/Antiques.htm) in Hulett, among other annual events held around the state.

AREA CODE Wyoming has a single area code—307.

BEARS Many of the outdoor attractions listed in this work are home to bears—both grizzlies and black bears. Though seeing a bear can be quite a thrill, you need to remember at all times that bears are wild animals and that you should keep your distance and respect them as such. Educate yourself in advance about the area where you are going. Take proper precautions if you anticipate entering a bear habitat (usually, such areas are signed and have information about how you should behave). It is your responsibility to help keep bears wild by not habituating them to receiving food from human sources, including garbage.

BICYCLING Never heard of Wyoming as a cycling destination? Well, mark this place on your map, whether it's road riding or grinding on a mountain bike that lights your fire. Included in this guide you'll find a number of recommended rides or trails, most of them the short-'n'-sweet variety suitable for the novice or intermediate cyclist or tourist-on-a-bicycle who wants a brief, leg-stretching respite from traveling. However, more advanced mountain bikers should be aware that Wyoming's plethora of public lands—rife with dirt roads in varying conditions—coupled with a relative lack of regulations (though of course, mountain bikers should strive to maintain good ethics to keep it this way), can make for countless fun adventures. Likewise, expert road riders will delight in the relative lack of traffic on many of Wyoming's paved roadways. A good place to start your research into mountain biking, or any bicycling in Wyoming, for that matter, is Cycle Wyoming (http://www.cyclewyoming .org), a nonprofit organization with the aim of promoting cycling in the state.

BIRD-WATCHING Wyoming provides ample opportunities for bird-watchers, with nearly 400 species of birds in more than 40 families, from the state bird, the western meadowlark, to the national bird, the bald eagle. The Web site http://www.camac donald.com/birding/uswyoming.htm provides a fantastic starting place as a resource for bird-watching enthusiasts visiting the state. You'll find an array of places listed in various sections (especially Green Space) throughout this work that mention bird-watching opportunities.

BOATING The 20 reservoirs in Wyoming managed by the United States Bureau of Reclamation (USBR) make for popular boating locales. For the latest conditions and information, contact the Wyoming Area Office of the Great Plains Region of the USBR (307-261-5671, http://www.usbr.gov/gp/ wyao). In this guide, most of the listings in *To Do*—Boating provide information on water bodies (lakes and reservoirs) suitable for motorized watercraft in addition to human-powered craft. Listings for rivers—even

those that allow motorized watercraft—will be found in *To Do*—Fishing and *To Do*—Paddling/Floating, though they are usually cross-referenced at the end of the *To Do*—Boating section.

BUREAU OF LAND MANAGEMENT (BLM) LANDS The role of the BLM in Wyoming (307-775-6256; http://www.blm.gov/wy/st/en.html) is huge—with 10 area field offices around the state, not only does it manage more than 18 million acres of public lands, but also, it manages between 20 and 30 million acres of federal mineral estate, which produce much of Wyoming's mineral wealth annually. In addition, the BLM in Wyoming is responsible for the protection, management, and control of Wyoming's wild horse population, which is estimated at about 5,000; helps manage the Wyoming Wind Energy Project; and manages a portion of the 3,100-mile long Continental Divide National Scenic Trail, among other responsibilities. Find out more about what specific BLM lands have to offer for each region by looking under the *Green Space*—National Lands listing, or contact the BLM directly.

BUS SERVICE Greyhound (1-800-229-9424; http://www.greyhound.com) and Wind River Transportation (1-800-439-7118; http://www.wrtabuslines .com) provide bus service to various destinations in Wyoming. Several Wyoming cities, including Jackson and Cheyenne, have public bus services as well.

BYWAYS AND BACKWAYS Wyoming has no shortage of either of these, with a total of 14 officially designated Scenic Byways and Backways—10 Scenic Byways and 4 Scenic Backways, to be exact. Taking you away from the screaming diesels and dusty monotony of the four-lane interstates,

Wyoming's byways and backways offer the traveler the chance to take a breath, enjoy the scenery, and experience Wyoming at a slower pace reminiscent of times past. You'll find details about these fun side-adventures; as well as a number of additional scenic drives, in the *To See*—Scenic Drives sections of this book.

CAMPGROUNDS Many of the campgrounds listed in *Lodging*—Campgrounds in this guidebook lie on public lands, as it's my opinion that such camping adventures tend to be a little more outdoorsy and adventuresome (in keeping with that explorer's spirit) than staying at a full-service campground in a town or a city. In addition to those campgrounds listed, you should know that primitive camping is permissible on much of the public land in the state as well. Please note that often the dates given for when a campground is open mean that this is when a fee is charged to stay there and when all services (water, trash, camp hosts, and restrooms) are provided. Sometimes, free camping is permitted at these locations in the off-season so long as they are accessible, though no services are provided. For a free, comprehensive list of the state's campgrounds published annually in the *Wyoming Vacation Directory*, along with a free state map, visit the Wyoming Travel & Tourism Web site (http://www.wyomingtourism .org) and click on "Free Guide." Fill out the form, and you'll receive your guide and map in the mail within a couple of weeks.

CITIES Wyoming's state capital, Cheyenne, is also its largest city, with a population of about 56,000 people. Casper (about 50,000) and Laramie (about 30,000) are next on the list for biggest cities. Only eight Wyoming cities boast populations of more than 10,000 people.

CLIMATE With the second highest mean elevation of any state in the country at 6,700 feet above sea level, Wyoming has a semiarid but variable climate (above 6,000 feet temperatures seldom go above 100 degrees), due to its topographical diversity. Unless you love cold weather and snow sports, it's best to plan your travels for the late spring, summer, or early fall, when temperatures around the state are for the most part comfortable (between 60 and 80 for daytime highs). Just be aware that depending on where your travels take you and on the season when you visit, you could find yourself sweating up a storm, cursing the eternally blowing wind that plagues certain areas of the state, or dealing with a late spring or even summer snow- or hailstorm (I've been snowed on in every single month in Wyoming except for July). Average annual precipitation is a mere 12 inches, but certain locations get much more than this, of course.

COFFEE If you need a daily dose of java (as more than 50 percent of Americans do), never fear—you will find ample places throughout the state to meet your craving, and I'm not just talking the see-the-bottom-of-your-cup variety. Wyoming is up to date and ready to serve you your coffee—or your latté, espresso, or other specialty drink—from some great coffee shops and cafés you'll find highlighted throughout this book, as well as from those little drive-through huts that are popping up everywhere you look these days. In addition, Wyoming boasts several coffee roasters of its own, including Jackson's Cowboy Coffee (1-877-5COWBOY; http://www.cowboy coffee.com), and Laramie's Coal Creek Coffee Company (1-800-838-7737; http://www.coalcreekcoffee.com).

CONSERVATION GROUPS The Wyoming Outdoor Council (307-332-7031; http://www.wyomingoutdoor council.org) works "to protect and enhance Wyoming's wildlife through education and advocacy." You'll find additional links to Wyoming-based conservation groups, including Jackson Hole Alliance, The Nature Conservancy (Wyoming), and Wyoming Audubon, at http://www.wyomingoutdoor council.org/library/conservation.php.

COUNTIES Wyoming has 23 counties.

DUDE AND GUEST RANCHES Ranching is part of Wyoming's cultural and economic heritage, and it continues to play an important role in the state's culture and identity. For a unique insight into Wyoming's ranching, past and present, consider vacationing to one of Wyoming's dude and guest ranches, many of which offer both standard ranching experiences (such as horseback riding and cattle drives), as well as additional activities ranging from hunting and fly fishing to hiking and swimming. For more information, contact the Wyoming Dude and Guest Ranch Association (307-684-7157; http://www.wyomingdra.com).

EMERGENCIES Dial 911 statewide in case of emergency. In addition, contact information for regional medical facilities is provided in each chapter of this book.

ENTERTAINMENT If you're looking to catch the latest flick or perhaps see some live music, flip to the *Entertainment* section included in most of the chapters of this book. Here you'll find information on the area's cinemas, theaters, concert venues, and more. Also, don't forget to check the *Special Events* section for additional annual happenings in the region you're visiting.

EVENTS Like most states, Wyoming has so many annual events with such a wide variety that listing them all would easily fill this book—and more. In addition to those highlighted in the *Special Events* section of each area covered, you can find just what you're looking for by going to the Wyoming Tourism and Travel Web site (http://www.wyomingtourism.org). Click on "Events" to get started.

FARMERS' MARKETS You'll find fresh fare in season at a number of farmers' markets spread across Wyoming from Cheyenne to Cody. For more information or for locations of farmers' markets, contact the Wyoming Farmers' Marketing Association (307-777-6319; http://www.wyomingfarmers markets.org).

FISHING Wyoming is known internationally for its trout fishing, but it is also home to several species of bass, as well as 22 other species of game fish. You can obtain detailed information from the Wyoming Game and Fish Department (307-777-4600; http://gf.state.wy.us/fish), including regulations, licensing, and an incredibly informative, free, and helpful "Fishing Regulation Brochure." Wyoming has one free fishing day in early June every year; check with Wyoming Game and Fish to find out the current year's date. The Wyoming Fishing Network (http://www.wyomingfishing.net) is another great online resource for anglers planning a trip to this state. General regional recommendations for fishing in Wyoming can also be found in the ensuing chapters in the *To Do*—Fishing listings.

GAMBLING Gambling isn't legal in the state of Wyoming, except for on the Wind River Indian Reservation (see *To See*—Towns in Northwest

Wyoming: Lander and Riverton). You can gamble legally at the Wind River Casino (307-856-3964; http://500 nations.com/casinos/wyWindRiver.asp), 10369 Highway 789, Riverton.

GEOGRAPHY A roughly rectangular state that measures approximately 360 miles by 280 miles, Wyoming is the ninth largest state in the nation, covering almost 98,000 square miles. It is also the second highest state, with a mean elevation of 6,700 feet. In Wyoming, the Great Plains and the Rocky Mountains come together. In addition to these two geographic areas, Wyoming is home to a third region called the Intermontane Basins, which includes the Bighorn Basin, Powder River Basin, and Great Divide Basin, among others. These relatively flat stretches of land situated between Wyoming's mountain ranges receive little in the way of precipitation compared to their mountainous neighbors. Of particular interest is the Great Divide Basin, which runs along the continental divide and is covered in part by Wyoming's Red Desert. This area drains neither to the Atlantic nor to the Pacific, and the little rain that falls here is soaked up into the ground quickly. For more, see listing in *To See*—Natural Wonders in Southwest Wyoming: Green River and Rock Springs.

GEOLOGY If you are a geology aficionado, Wyoming will delight and amaze you to no end. Helpful signs along many state highways identify the type of rock adjacent to the road and its estimated dates of birth, piquing your interest and encouraging you to delve more deeply into the state's rich geological past of glaciers, volcanic action, tectonics, and erosion by wind and water. Whether you're interested in dinosaurs, mountains, badlands, canyons, mining, gemstones, or simply different types of minerals, in Wyoming, geological attractions and one-of-a-kind formations are plentiful. In addition to those geological attractions highlighted throughout this work, *Roadside Geology of Wyoming*, by Darwin R. Spearing and David R. Lageson (Mountain Press Publishing Company, 2003), $18, can help take your knowledge to the next level.

GOLF COURSES Wyoming has more than 50 golf courses to choose from around the state. For detailed information about all of the state's golf courses, contact the Wyoming State Golf Association (307-315-6105; http://www .wygolf.org) 100 N. Center Street, Suite 205, Casper, 82601. You'll also find contact information for golf courses listed in each chapter under *To Do*—Golf.

GUIDES AND OUTFITTERS If you need or want a guide for your adventure of choice, you'll find no shortage of services in Wyoming, whether you want to hire animals for a pack trip, discover great fishing spots, hunt for big game, raft whitewater, or backpack through the mountains. The Wyoming Outfitters and Guides Association (307-265-2376; http://www.wyoga.org) is good place to start the search for a qualified guide or outfitter that suits your needs.

HIGHWAYS Wyoming's major north south routes include US 89/189/191/287, which runs from Yellowstone National Park to I-80 (as US 189). US 191 and US 287 also reach I-80 farther east, while US 89 goes southwest into Idaho. I-25 runs from I-90 in Buffalo south into Colorado. The state's major east west routes include I-90 to US 14/16/20. I-90 heads northwest into Montana, but US 14/16/20 unite in Greybull to continue through Cody to Yellowstone. The central portions of Wyoming are linked east west by US 20, US 26, and US 287. Wyoming's major east west highway in the south is I-80.

HIKING Hiking opportunities abound in Wyoming. If you're visiting Wyoming specifically to hike, there are a number of detailed hiking guidebooks out there for you to choose from, depending on which area or areas of the state you plan to visit. With that in mind, the hikes covered in this book (in the *To Do*—Hiking section of each chapter) tend to highlight particularly noteworthy/educational attractions and/or are quick-and-easy leg stretching jaunts suitable for travelers. This means that the hikes included within these pages are, with a few notable and noted exceptions, suited for folks of any age and fitness level.

HISTORICAL MARKERS AND TRAILS You'll notice an abundance of historical markers alongside Wyoming's highways, so don't be shy—take a break from driving to stretch your legs and learn a little bit about the state's past. From mammoth hunts to the Oregon Trail, the state's history comes alive via these commemorative signs and plaques. Want to learn more? Order a copy of *A Few Interested Residents: Wyoming Historical Markers & Monuments,* by Mike Jording (M. Jord-

ing, 1992), $14.95, which provides a complete resource for history buffs interested in locating and learning about each marker and monument in detail.

HISTORY In addition to historical markers aplenty, Wyoming's history lives on in its historic sites, museums, historic houses, and of course, in the minds of its citizens. Throughout this work you will find fascinating facts, figures, and trivia relating to Wyoming's history, as well as descriptions of selected historical attractions in *To See*—Towns, *To See*—Museums, and *To See*—Historic Landmarks, Places, and Sites, among other places. For a more complete picture of this state's past, visit the Wyoming State Historical Society Web site (http://www.wyshs.org), where you will find society publications, recommended history books, photos, artwork, and more. Since its founding in 1953, the Wyoming State Historical Society has worked toward researching and preserving Wyoming's illustrious past.

HOT SPRINGS A number of user-friendly hot springs—including Hot Springs State Park in Thermopolis (307-864-2176; http://wyoparks.state.wy.us/Site/SiteInfo.asp?siteID=9), where you can soak, unbelievably, for free—invite the weary adventurer to Wyoming in for a soothing and refreshing break from traveling, or, in the case of many of those hot springs located in and around Yellowstone National Park, to look in awe from a distance (since they are scalding hot!). Look in *To Do*—Relaxation and Rejuvenation for selective information on hot springs in each region. For a complete list of Wyoming's hot and warm springs, visit Hot Springs Enthusiast (http://www.hotspringsenthusiast.com) and search the database for Wyoming.

HUNTING An abundance of big game—elk, mule deer, pronghorn, moose, and more—as well as smaller game, such as sage grouse, wild turkey, rabbits, and others, draw hunters to Wyoming every season. Nonresident big game hunting licenses are issued by a lottery system, and hunters must apply far in advance of the season in order to have a chance at a license, since demand always vastly exceeds supply. For details on hunting rules and regulations in Wyoming, please visit the hunting section of the Wyoming Game and Fish Department Web site, http://gf.state.wy.us/wildlife/hunting/index.asp (or call 307-777-4600).

INDIAN RESERVATIONS The sole Indian reservation in Wyoming is the 2.2 million-acre Wind River Indian Reservation north of Lander, home to members of the Northern Arapaho and Eastern Shoshone tribes. Reservation headquarters are located in Fort Washakie, which is also home to the graves of Chief Washakie and Sacajawea. The Wind River Indian Reservation has powwows and other events open to the public, as well as stores that cater to tourists. For more about the reservation, see *To See*—Towns in Northwest Wyoming: Lander and Riverton.

LEAVE NO TRACE The Leave No Trace Center for Outdoor Ethics (1-800-332-4100; http://www.lnt.org) is an educational, nonprofit organization dedicated to the responsible enjoyment and active stewardship of the outdoors by all people, worldwide. These seven principles of Leave No Trace are general guidelines for minimizing your impact on the land while you travel: plan ahead and prepare; travel and camp on durable surfaces; dispose of waste properly; leave what

you find; minimize campfire impacts; respect wildlife; and be considerate of other visitors. Detailed information on these principles, as well as other relevant information, can be found by calling or visiting the Web site.

LIBRARIES Need to check your email? That seems to be one of the primary functions of public libraries for travelers these days—though don't forget, libraries can be a great place to learn about local events and history, to catch up on the latest news, or just to relax and unwind with a great book. WYLDCAT: The Wyoming Libraries Database provides a helpful list of the state's libraries online at http://wyld.state.wy.us.

LICENSE PLATES Wyoming's distinctive license plates feature the legendary unrideable bucking bronco, Steamboat, as well as one of the state's amazing natural features, the Tetons. The Bucking Horse and Rider has been on the Wyoming license plate since 1936—the longest continuous use of any graphic on a license plate in the country. Its origins date back to 1918, when First Sergeant George N. Ostrom designed it to be the insignia worn by members of the Wyoming National Guard in World War I. It has since become a registered state and federal trademark for the State of Wyoming, and is a much-beloved symbol to Wyomingites. Wyoming's license plate has been selected Best License Plate by the Automobile License Plate Collectors Association three times: in 1972, 1978, and most recently, 2000.

The numbers on the left side of each place indicate the vehicle's county of registration. These numbers were originally assigned according the county's property valuation, but today, they no longer correlate accurately.

LODGING Lodgings described in this book are focused away from national-brand hotels and motels and more on each region's unique offerings, whether the area in question has bed and breakfasts, lodges, family-owned-and-operated budget motels, or some other sort of distinctive facilities. The reason behind this lies in the fact that you probably already know what to expect if you book reservations at a typical hotel or motel. In the places where you do find listings for more main-stream hotels and motels, you can assume that other sorts of more unique lodgings are slim to none for that par-ticular area, or that the mainstream hotel is unique in some way. For a free, detailed list of lodging options around the state published annually in the *Wyoming Vacation Directory*, visit the Wyoming Tourism Web site (http://www.wyomingtourism.org) or call Wyoming Travel & Tourism at 1-800-225-5996.

MAPS If you like to get topographi-cally intimate with the states in which you travel (or you just like looking at detailed maps), pick up a *Wyoming Atlas & Gazetteer* (DeLorme, $19.95, available at http://www.delorme.com), which will guide you to public and pri-vate lands, back roads and byways, and even ski areas and fishing spots—and much, much more.

MICROBREWERIES BrewPub-Zone.com (http://www.brewpubzone .com/States/Wyoming.html) lists 11 microbreweries for the state of Wyoming, including the award-winning Snake River Brewing Company (307-739-BEER; http://www.snakeriver brewing.com) in Jackson. With more than 200 national and international awards to its name after 15 years in business, a Snake River Brewery visit should be on tap for your Wyoming

vacation if you like sampling micro-brews (a hint for dark beer lovers: try the Zonker Stout). See *Where to Eat—Eating Out in Northwest Wyoming: Jackson and Dubois* for complete listing.

MILEAGE Please remember during your trip planning that all mileages given in this book are approximate and subject to a number of inaccuracies due to differences in odometers, source errors, or pilot errors—or all three (yikes!). That being said, the report of any gross inaccuracies you find would be greatly appreciated to avoid future misadventures by others, and if you do find yourself off in the middle of nowhere in the middle of the night, you might want to recheck your map and the directions—unless, of course, you planned it that way (which is always a possibility in Wyoming).

MUSIC Wyoming hosts musical events to meet the tastes of everyone, from classical chamber music to rock concerts, folk and bluegrass festivals to jazz. One of the biggest is Jackson Hole's Grand Teton Music Festival (307-733-3050; http://www.gtmf.org), still going strong after five decades, which features orchestral and chamber music as well as spotlight concerts (featuring tributes to particular artists, types of music, and so forth). Additional-al selected musical events are high-lighted in *Special Events* throughout this book, while musical venues can be found in the *Entertainment* sections.

NATIONAL FORESTS, GRASS-LANDS, AND RECREATION AREAS Wyoming became the first state ever to have a national forest in 1891 with the creation of the Yellow-stone Timberland Reserve, now known as Shoshone National Forest. Today encompassing almost 2.5 million acres in the northwest corner of the state adjacent to Yellowstone National Park, Shoshone National Forest is one of the largest of the 13 national forests in the Rocky Mountain region. In addition to Shoshone National Forest, Wyoming is also home to the Bighorn National Forest (north-central, 1.1 million acres), part of the Black Hills National Forest (northeast, 1.2 million acres), Bridger-Teton National Forest (west-central, 3.4 million acres), Medicine Bow National Forest (south, 1.6 million acres), and a small portion of Targhee National Forest (northwest); two national recreation areas, the Bighorn Canyon National Recreation Area (near Lovell in the north, 120,000 acres, one-quarter of which is in Wyoming) and the Flaming Gorge National Recreation Area (near Green River in the southwest, 201,000 acres, partially in Utah); and Thunder Basin National Grassland (northeast, 572,000 acres).

NATIONAL PARKS AND MONUMENTS Rack up two more firsts for Wyoming—first national park (Yellowstone National Park, established in 1872), and first national monument (Devils Tower National Monument, established in 1906). In addition to these, Wyoming is also home to Grand Teton National Park, just south of Yellowstone National Park; and Fossil Butte National Monument, near Kemmerer in the southwest.

PADDLING/FLOATING Kayaking, rafting, and canoeing enthusiasts will not be disappointed in Wyoming's offerings. Whether you're interested in a lazy day of rafting through the impressive Wind River Canyon outside of Thermopolis (where you can soak at Hot Springs State Park after your adventure, if you so wish), canoeing or

kayaking in Yellowstone National Park's lakes, or you want to bravely (or insanely) kayak some of the state's creeks swollen with snowmelt in the late spring or early summer, you'll find paddling adventures of all levels aplenty in Wyoming. In this book, for the most part you'll find information about instructional services and guided rafting adventures, as well as easy paddles and floats, listed in *To Do*—Paddling/Floating in each chapter. More experienced paddlers can learn more about Wyoming's waters by contacting the Jackson Hole Kayak Club (307-733-2471; http://jhkayakclub.org) or visiting Paddling.Net's Wyoming page on the Web (http://www.paddling.net/places/WY) for starters.

PUBLIC LANDS Wyoming contains more than 30 million acres of national lands, including two national parks, two national monuments, numerous national forests (see listing above), and about 18 million acres of land administered by the BLM; as well as state-owned lands including a dozen state parks, a state recreation area, and numerous state historic sites. See also National Forests, Grasslands, and Recreation Areas; Bureau of Land Management; and State Parks in this section.

REST AREAS The Wyoming Department of Transportation (WYDOT) has 34 rest areas throughout the state, located along interstates, primary, and secondary highways. For a downloadable brochure with a map showing all locations as well as other relevant information, go to http://www.dot.state .wy.us/wydot/travel/rest_area_ information.

RESTAURANTS Please note that due to the seasonal nature of tourism in Wyoming, many restaurants change their hours or close entirely in the off-season, accounting for the lack of business hours in some entries in this work. It's best to call ahead if your sights are set on a particular venue for the most up-to-date hours of operation. Also, you won't find fast-food or national chain restaurants listed in this work. If that's all (or most) of what a town has to offer, you'll probably have little trouble finding your way to them or knowing what they're all about.

RIVERS More than 20 rivers criss-cross Wyoming, including one nationally designated Wild and Scenic River, Clarks Fork of the Yellowstone River (for more about Wild and Scenic Rivers, visit http://www.rivers.gov), as well as scads of creeks and streams. These beautiful waterways provide fantastic recreational opportunities for fishermen, paddlers, rafters, and others. They also provide drinking water for residents in some areas of the state, such as the Laramie River, which is the largest provider of drinking water for residents of Laramie.

ROAD REPORTS The best resource for up-to-the-minute road conditions is the Wyoming Department of Transportation's (WYDOT) Road Report Web site (http://www.wyoroad.info) or hotline (511; 1-888-996-7623 or 307-772-0824). The site includes detailed information about closures, restrictions, and advisories, as well as images from live cameras around the state.

ROCK CLIMBING Wyoming has long been a hotspot for the nation's rock climbing community, with attractions that simply cannot be ignored, such as Devils Tower National Monument in the northeast, the Tetons in the northwest, and Vedauwoo in the southeast. More recently, the state's vast quantity of quality dolomite has drawn numerous sport climbers from

around the nation and the world. Due to its inherent danger, including a risk of injury or death, technical rock climbing (or ice climbing, for that matter) should not be attempted without proper instruction and solid knowledge of the safety skills necessary (after all, you wouldn't let someone drive a car without teaching them first, would you?). In this book, then, you'll find information in the *To Do*—Climbing sections about guiding services and climbing schools in each region (if any) that offer rock and/or ice climbing instruction, as well as a general write-up about notable nearby rock or ice climbing areas (where you might be able to witness some climbers in action, even if climbing isn't your thing).

ROCKHOUNDING Wyoming provides ample opportunities for the rock hound, with agate, bloodstone, fossils, jade, and petrified wood, among others, so just make sure to acquaint yourself with the rules and regulations of the appropriate landowner before you help yourself to its bounty. One great resource that details 75 rockhounding sites across the state is *Rockhounding Wyoming,* by Kenneth Lee Graham (Falcon, 1996), $12.95.

RODEOS With the Bucking Horse and Rider (BH&R) as a registered national and state trademark, and rodeo as its designated official state sport, it should not surprise you to discover that Wyoming—The Cowboy State—hosts rodeos year-round, with one or more rodeos occurring virtually daily throughout the summer season—in fact, the Cody Nite Rodeo (1-800-207-0744 or 307-587-5155; http://www.codystampederodeo.com) happens every night from June 1 through August 31. You'll also find selected rodeos around the state listed in the *Special Events* section of each chapter.

RV PARKS If you have a home on wheels, you probably already know some of the best resources for finding RV parks around the country—the Internet is rife with listings. A great place to start your search for a place to park and hook up is the Wyoming Campgrounds and RV Parks Web page (http://www.rvpark.com/wy.htm), which provides alphabetical listings by city or town, contact information, and sometimes, detailed information about RV parks statewide. See also Campgrounds in this section.

SHOPPING Wyoming might not top the lists as a national shopping destination, but that doesn't mean you won't find some shops to pique your interest if shopping happens to be your passion. Places like Jackson, Laramie, and Cody, among others, feature vibrant, historic downtown areas just packed with cute eclectic local shops and art galleries. And small towns here and there just might surprise you with some fun or truly artistic offerings or interesting antiques. Look to the *Selective Shopping* section included in some chapters for general or specific pointers about unique shopping opportunities in a particular region.

SNOW SPORTS If you plan to visit Wyoming in the winter, you'll find a number of snow sports to try your hand at, including snowshoeing, snowmobiling (or snow machining), skiing (cross-country and downhill), snowboarding, and more. Winter vacation packages (such as those offered in Yellowstone National Park or on some guest ranches, see listing above) can help take the pain out of planning a winter vacation to Wyoming, allowing you to just come and enjoy the snowbound fun.

SPEED LIMITS AND SEAT BELTS On the interstate, both day and night, the speed limit in Wyoming is 75 miles per hour, unless otherwise signed. On two-lane highways, the speed limit is 65 miles per hour, both day and night. Seat belts are required to be worn at all times by every occupant of the vehicle. Please be courteous—if you're driving exceptionally slow (say, 10 miles per hour below the speed limit), and traffic builds up behind you, make an effort to pull over safely and allow the other drivers to pass.

STATE CAPITAL Cheyenne is the capital of Wyoming.

STATE PARKS Wyoming has 12 state parks, a state recreation area, and numerous state historic sites, all of which fall under the jurisdiction of the Wyoming Division of State Parks and Historic Sites (307-777-6323; http://wyoparks.state.wy.us). You'll find many of these parks and sites listed under various To See and To Do entries throughout this book, as they include opportunities for camping, picnicking, fishing, hiking, learning, and much, much more. You can purchase annual daily use and camping permits in advance online at http://www.usedirect.com/cdweb, or by calling 1-877-WYO-PARK. You can also purchase a permit in person at a number of locations throughout the state. For a complete list, visit http://wyoparks.state.wy.us/Permits/agents.asp.

STATE THIS AND THAT Every state has them—those symbols, officially designated somethings, and nicknames that help define their identity. Some of Wyoming's include: nicknames—Equality State, Cowboy State, Big Wyoming; motto—Equal rights; state registered trademark—Bucking

Horse and Rider; state flower—Indian paintbrush; state mammal—bison; state bird—meadowlark; state tree—plains cottonwood; state gemstone—jade; state fish—cutthroat trout; state reptile—horned toad; state dinosaur—triceratops; and state sport—rodeo.

STATISTICS Wyoming is the ninth largest state in area (97,914 square miles, which is larger than all of the United Kingdom). The state ranks 50th in population, with about 530,000 residents (fewer than the amount of people who populate the city of Denver in its southern neighbor, Colorado). In Wyoming, there are 5 people per square mile (the national average is almost 80 per square mile). The highest point in Wyoming is Gannett Peak at 13,804 feet; the lowest is the Belle Fourche River at 3,100 feet. Wyoming became the 44th state to be admitted to the union on July 10, 1890.

TRAINS Wyoming's vast coal resources prompted the Union Pacific Railroad to construct a line across the southern part of the state in 1867–8, which largely accounted for the establishment of some of the state's first permanent settlements. Later, trains encouraged the development of tourism in the region. Today, trains are still used in Wyoming, mainly for the shipping of coal, agricultural products, and other goods made in Wyoming, as well as to bring in goods to the state from outside. For a detailed list of Wyoming's railroads (past and present), you can visit http://www.trainweb .org/wyomingrails/wyrr.html.

TRAVEL INFORMATION The best place to contact for overall travel information for the state of Wyoming is Wyoming Travel & Tourism (1-800-225-5996; http://www.wyomingtourism .org), which offers free vacation pack-

ets and a plethora of additional resources for travelers. For local and regional contacts to specific areas of the state, look to the Guidance sections of this book. Wyoming also has seven easily accessed information centers around the state: Frank Norris Jr. Travel Center (307-777-2883), I-25 at College Drive in Cheyenne, open daily; Bear River Travel Information Center (307-789-6540), I-80 East at Exit 6 in Evanston, open daily; Jackson Hole/Greater Yellowstone Information Center (307-733-3316), 532 North Cache in Jackson, open daily; Summit Information Center (307-721-9254), on I-80, 9 Miles east of Laramie at the Happy Jack exit, open mid-May to mid-October; Pine Bluffs Information Center (307-245-3695), along I-80 at the Pine Bluffs exit, open mid-May to mid-October; Sheridan Information Center (307-672-2485), located in Sheridan along I-90 at the Fifth Street exit, open daily; and the Sundance Information Center (307-283-2440), along I-90 at the Sundance Port-of-Entry exit, open mid-May to late September.

WEATHER The most reliable resource I've found for accurate weather forecasts is the National Ocean and Atmospheric Administration's National Weather Service (http://www.nws.noaa.gov). Just enter the city

and state name, and you'll have an up-to-date forecast and current conditions at your fingertips. The highest temperature recorded in Wyoming was 114 degrees Fahrenheit in Basin back in 1900; the lowest was minus 63 degrees Fahrenheit in Moran in 1933. See also Climate in this section.

WILDLIFE You're almost sure to see some of Wyoming's abundant wildlife while you're traveling around the state—even if you rarely get out of the car. It's not uncommon to see vast herds of pronghorn grazing adjacent to the interstates or mule deer crossing streets (at crosswalks, no less) en masse in the center of a Wyoming town. Bighorn sheep, bears, elk, moose, wild horses, and buffalo are also viewable from behind the glass of your automobile, if you're in the right place at the right time and possess a keen eye, as are many of Wyoming's other furred, scaled, and feathered residents. Of course, you up your chances of wildlife sightings dramatically if you plan to explore some of Wyoming's vast lands by foot, bicycle, or other non-motorized modes of transportation. For more details on Wyoming's wildlife, including the official state list of birds, mammals, reptiles, and amphibians in Wyoming, contact the Wyoming Game and Fish Wildlife Division (307-777-4600; http://gf.state .wy.us/wildlife/index.asp).

WILDLIFE REFUGES Seven national wildlife refuges encompassing 80,776 acres of land lie within Wyoming. In addition to those refuges highlighted in this book (usually under Wilder Places), detailed information about each national refuge, including directions, recreation opportunities, contact information, and more, can be found by clicking on "WY" at http:/ /www.fws.gov/refuges.

WILDERNESS AREAS Wyoming has 15 nationally designated wilderness areas, providing numerous recreation opportunities in pristine settings—so you need to be sure you know the rules and regulations governing each one, and the necessary outdoors skills, before you visit. As a general guideline, you should practice the principles of Leave No Trace (1-800-332-4100; http://www.lnt.org; see entry in this section) when visiting wilderness areas. You can find a complete list of Wyoming's wilderness areas by going to http://www.wilderness.net, clicking on "Find a Wilderness," and choosing Wyoming. You'll get a list of clickable links to all of Wyoming's designated wilderness areas, each of which yields detailed information about the area in question.

WILDFLOWERS Every spring brings with it a veritable explosion of multi-hued wildflowers to Wyoming's plains and mountains alike, from the brilliant red of the state flower, the Indian paintbrush, to the bright yellow arrowleaf balsamroot and deep indigo of lupine, among many others. You'll find many of these flowers—and other flora of the state—in the excellent book, *Plants of* *the Rocky Mountains,* by Linda Kershaw, Andy MacKinnon, and Jim Pojar (Lone Pine, 1998), $22.95. For those with an amateur interest in plants and flowers, this book will prove to be an indispensable resource, with its tremendous photography and keys to plants and flowers, as well as its well-written descriptions about each plant, including interesting trivia about historical uses and more. For a state-specific guide, pick up a copy of *Wildflowers of Wyoming,* by Diantha States and Jack States (Mountain Press Publishing Company, 2004), $19.

WINERIES AND WINE TASTINGS Believe it or not, you will find a few of these scattered around Wyoming. Look for this particular listing under the *To See*—Wineries and Wine Tastings section of each chapter.

WOMEN'S FIRSTS Wyoming's nickname, the Equality State, comes from the fact that Wyoming was the first state to grant women the vote in 1869. Louisa Gardner Swain became the first woman to cast her vote in the state in September of the following year. Wyoming was also the first state to grant women full citizenship in 1868, when it was still a territory; the first state to have a female governor (Nellie Tayloe Ross in 1925); and the first to allow female jurors (Laramie, 1870).

ZOOS Wyoming has no bona fide zoos of its own—but if animals are your area of interest, you'll find no shortage of them to see in this state. You'll find wildlife-related attractions usually listed under Green Space throughout this book. You can also just watch closely while you're riding in the car, and you'll probably see more wild animals than you're used to seeing anywhere else.

WHAT'S NEW IN WYOMING: AN EXPLORER'S GUIDE

While this is the first edition of Wyoming: An Explorer's Guide, you should know about some new listings appearing here that might be a little different from other Explorer's Guides you've seen:

The *To Do*—Climbing section highlights each region's well-known rock climbing (or ice climbing) area(s), as well as giving information about professional guiding services for novice climbers and information about indoor climbing facilities.

The *To Do*—Relaxation and Rejuvenation section includes listings for spas, yoga studios, and natural food stores, among other types of services that can help you, the road-weary traveler, find relaxation and rejuvenation for your body, mind, and spirit.

Yellowstone and Grand Teton National Parks

1

RESTROOMS

CANYON
VISITOR
EDUCATION
CENTER

YELLOWSTONE NATIONAL PARK

Whatever your Wyoming adventure plans might be, including world-famous Yellowstone National Park in your travel plans is virtually a must if you want to make your travels in Wyoming complete. While Idaho and Montana possess small portions of Yellowstone National Park within their boundaries—1.4 percent and 7.6 percent, respectively—Wyoming lays claim to a whopping 91 percent of this one-of-a-kind park's lands.

Yellowstone became the world's first national park in 1872, signed into existence by President Ulysses S. Grant in an effort to preserve and protect this natural wonderland for future generations of both humans and the park's wilder inhabitants. The Yellowstone area is filled with incredible natural phenomena, including not only mountains, lakes, and streams, but also an unsurpassed concentration of geothermal features. Approximately 10,000 of them are found within the park's 3,400 square miles. These features include hot springs, fumaroles (gas vents), mud pots, and perhaps the most famous of all geothermal features, geysers (of which the world-renowned Old Faithful is one). More than 300 geysers lie within the park's boundaries, accounting for roughly 75 percent of all the geysers in the world. These geysers fall within seven major geyser basins spread throughout the park, many of which feature interpretive trails that take you up close to the geysers to observe them in action.

A visit to Yellowstone and a stroll along its nature trails (see *To Do*—Hiking) will increase your knowledge of the how and why of geysers and other geothermal features (if I were a scientist, I'd try to explain how they work, but I'm sure I'd get at least a few facts twisted or turned about, so I'll leave that job to the experts at the park). You'll also likely be wowed by the spectacular scenery, from the forested mountainsides to the areas rapidly and spontaneously rejuvenating from the devastation of the 1988 fires—areas that can be explored more closely via the park's 1,200+ miles of trails or by paddling on one of its lakes. Yellowstone is packed so full of awe-inspiring sights that you'll be hard-pressed to learn about all of them during your visit, much less see them all with your own eyes. This is the reason behind the selective nature of the attractions included in this guide—to help you pick out some of the park's more incredible offerings to include on your itinerary. Despite Yellowstone's array of tourist-oriented sites, attractions, and activities, ranging from visitor centers to restaurants, historic sites to wayside exhibits, you might be surprised to learn that 97 percent of Yellowstone's lands remain undeveloped. In fact, the park forms the core of a much larger area—a 28,000-square-mile

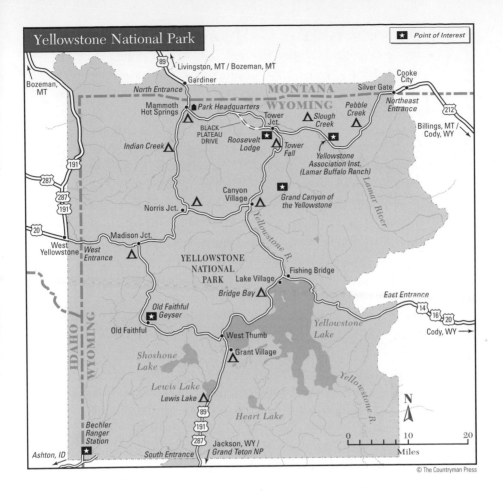

area—known as the Greater Yellowstone Ecosystem. This important area represents one of the largest, mostly intact temperate zone ecosystems remaining on the planet. Thus, in spite of all of the services geared toward human visitors, Yellowstone remains committed above all to protecting, sustaining, and preserving its natural features and its wild inhabitants, both living and nonliving alike. This mission accounts for the large number of rules and regulations governing the behavior of the park's human visitors—and their pets. Please be sure to familiarize yourself with these restrictions before you embark on your journey through one of the most wondrous wild areas you'll undoubtedly ever encounter.

GUIDANCE Xanterra Parks and Resorts (1-866-GEYSERLAND or 307-344-7311; http://www.travelyellowstone.com), P.O. Box 165, Yellowstone National Park, 82190. Xanterra is the primary, NPS-authorized, in-park concessionaire for Yellowstone. Xanterra provides camping, lodging, and dining reservations; general park information; auto and snowcoach tour reservations; and more. Xanterra does not charge a booking fee for its services.

THE WHY BEHIND THE RULES OF YELLOWSTONE

As a privileged visitor to the park, please make an effort to obey the park's rules and listen and respond to the rangers should they make a request. On one of my journeys through Yellowstone, a mother black bear and her cub appeared right on the roadway—undoubtedly a cool and amazing thing to witness. Unfortunately, the experience was marred by the disrespectful behavior of the drivers around me, who parked their vehicles all over the roadway, not even bothering to pull off to the side. This resulted in an enormous traffic jam, with traffic backed up both ways. Many people proceeded to get out of their cars and approach the bears, despite the ranger yelling at them not to do so and demanding that they return to their cars. This sort of disrespectful and frankly, downright dangerous, behavior compromises the safety of both visitors and the bears. Visitors could be charged by an angered bear—particularly one with a cub. In this case, the bear would then have to be considered aggressive, and action against it might have to be taken as a consequence, all because of tourists not listening to a ranger.

The point of this diatribe is that Yellowstone has its rules for a reason—including the rule that you must maintain a distance of at least 100 yards from bears, and at least 25 yards from all other wild animals, including bison. If you make an animal move or change its behavior due to your presence, you're too close and in violation of the park's rules. Do not stop in the road to view wildlife (unless the animal or animals are in the road, of course, in which case you should stay in your car and allow them to move off the roadway)—drive to the nearest pullout to avoid creating traffic problems. Additional rules to be aware of are the park's universal 45 mph speed limit (which they do enforce—I've seen many a tourist pulled over), the seasonal closure of many of the park's entrance roads during wintertime, the rule against putting or throwing any objects into the park's geothermal features (including yourself or any body part), and the rule that you must stay on trails, particularly in geothermal areas. Yellowstone National Park has a number of additional rules and regulations, some of which are covered in this chapter. Upon entering the park, you will receive literature that includes this information, so to avoid any problems, be sure to read it thoroughly before embarking on any adventures.

Yellowstone Association (406-848-2400; http://yellowstoneassociation.org), P.O. Box 117, Yellowstone National Park, 82190. The Yellowstone Association is a nonprofit organization that educates Yellowstone National Park visitors by offering trip planners, books, videos, and guided classes through Yellowstone Park via its field institute. This nonprofit has been serving the park and its visitors since 1933. The association runs eight stores throughout the park, situated in the visitor centers.

Proceeds from purchases directly benefit the park. See also Yellowstone Association Institute in *To Do*—Unique Adventures.

& **Yellowstone National Park** (307-344-7381; http://www.nps.gov/yell), P.O. Box 168, Yellowstone National Park, 82190-0168. Open all day every day **(but note that most entrance roads are seasonally closed to wheeled motor vehicle traffic);** $12 per individual (seven days) or $25 per vehicle (seven days), $50 annual pass (good for entrance into Grand Teton National Park as well). Unless you are visiting in June, July, or August, call ahead or check the park's Web site for the latest information on road closures. Most of the park's entrance roads are closed to wheeled vehicles seasonally, with the exception of US 89 from Gardiner, Montana, at the North Entrance to Silver Gate and Cooke City, Montana, near the Northeast Entrance (US 212). Please note that US 212 east of Cooke City is impassable to wheeled traffic during winter months (November through April). To confuse things even more, even if park entrances are open, you may not be able to travel around the park on all of its roads, particularly during spring and fall, as weather may cause closures. In addition, road construction can thwart your efforts as well. So what's a traveler to do? Plan ahead, map your route, and then contact the park or visit the park's Web site to ensure that your travel plans match up to the roads currently open for travel. From the Web site, simply download the year's free **"Yellowstone National Park Trip Planner"** for all of the latest information. You can also obtain a free **"Visitors Guide to Accessible Features"** brochure online. For details on snowmobile travel in the park, see *To Do*—Snow Sports.

Yellowstone Park Foundation (406-586-6303; http://www.ypf.org), 222 E. Main Street, Suite 301, Bozeman, MT 59715. As Yellowstone National Park's official fundraising partner, the Yellowstone Park Foundation works "in cooperation with the National Park Service to fund projects and programs that protect, preserve, and enhance the natural and cultural resources and the visitor experience of Yellowstone National Park."

GETTING THERE *By car:* Yellowstone National Park is accessed from the east via US 14/16/20, from the south via US 89/191/287, from the west via US 20, from the northeast via US 212 to the Northeast Entrance Road and from the north via US 89 to the North Entrance Road.

By plane: **Jackson Hole Airport** (307-733-7682; http://www.jacksonholeairport.com) is closest if you're entering from the south (Jackson/Grand Teton National Park), while **Yellowstone Regional Airport** (307-587-5096; http://www.flyyra.com) is closest if you're entering from the east (Cody).

By bus: A number of commercial bus services offer transportation to the park, especially during the summer season. Check with the **Jackson Hole Chamber of Commerce** (see Guidance in Northwest Wyoming: Jackson and Dubois) and the **Cody Country Chamber of Commerce** (see Guidance in Northwest Wyoming: Cody and Powell) for details on local bus services originating in Wyoming.

GETTING AROUND Unless you're paddling on one of the lakes, horseback riding, snowmobiling, on a guided tour, or hiking in the backcountry, you'll need to rely on your car (or a commercial bus tour) to get you around Yellowstone. Don't worry, you'll find plenty of places to stop and stretch your legs as you explore the sites and sights listed below

MEDICAL EMERGENCY Call 911; on-duty rangers provide emergency medical care.

Lake Clinic, Pharmacy, and Hospital (307-242-7241), in Lake Village; open daily in summer 8:30–8:30.

Mammoth Clinic (307-344-7965), next to Mammoth Post Office in Mammoth Hot Springs; open all year and daily in summer from 8:30–5.

Old Faithful Clinic (307-545-7325), by Old Faithful; open daily in summer from 7–7.

✳ To See

VISITOR CENTERS ♿ **Albright Visitor Center and Museum** (307-344-2263), at Mammoth Hot Springs, 5 miles south of North Entrance, at the northwest corner of the Grand Loop Road's upper loop. Open daily year-round, late fall through mid-April 9–5; mid-April through late May 9–6; late May through late fall 8–7. This visitor center (including a Yellowstone Association store), museum, and the surrounding red-roofed buildings were once home to Fort Yellowstone, a U.S. Cavalry post, back when the army ran the park. The buildings were turned over to the National Park Service when it was created in 1916. Today, they provide visitors with an excellent example of a turn-of-the-century army outpost on the outside, while on the inside providing up-to-date visitor information about the park, in addition to a museum. Among other displays, the museum features exhibits about the park's human past grouped by historical periods, from the time of the American Indians before 1800 to the founding and growth of the National Park Service. The museum also shows Yellowstone-themed films regularly during summertime and upon request during the off-season.

♿ ⚓ **Canyon Visitor Education Center** (307-344-2550) is less than .25 mile southeast of Canyon Junction in Canyon Village. Open daily 9–5 starting in early May; late May through early October 8–8. This new facility features interactive exhibits on the Yellowstone supervolcano, including audiovisual presentations and scientific data captured and brought to visitors in real time. Highlights include a 9,000-pound, illuminated, rotating globe that displays the planet's volcanic hotspots; a room-sized model of Yellowstone National Park that invites visitors to learn about the park's geology from both scientific and American Indian viewpoints; and one of the biggest lava lamps in the world (used to illustrate a scientific phenomenon, of course).

♿ **Fishing Bridge Visitor Center and Museum** (307-242-2450) is 1 mile east of the Grand Loop Road on the East Entrance Road. Open late May through late September 8–7. A National Historic Landmark, this stone visitor center was constructed in 1931. Its exhibits include wildlife displays, one of which was installed in 1931 and showcases Yellowstone's birds. The Fishing Bridge itself is a historic structure as well. The original bridge was built in 1902; the current bridge, in 1937. Despite its name, you can no longer fish from the Fishing Bridge—it has been closed to anglers since 1973 in response to declining cutthroat trout populations. Nonetheless, it's still a popular tourist place to stop, stroll, take pictures, and observe wildlife.

♿ **Grant Village Visitor Center** (307-242-2650) is in Grant Village, 1 mile from the Grant Village Junction off the S. Entrance Road on the shore of the West

Thumb of Yellowstone Lake. Open late May through late September 8–7. Named for Ulysses S. Grant, who signed the documentation that proclaimed Yellowstone America's first national park in 1872, this visitor center was constructed nearly 100 years later in prime grizzly habitat, making it rather controversial. Nonetheless, it stands, and it provides visitors with a comprehensive look at the 1988 fires, including a film shown regularly.

Madison Information Station (307-344-2821) is just south of Madison Junction at the Madison Picnic Area on the Grand Loop Road. Open late May through late September 9–6. This National Historic Landmark was built in 1929–30. It has served many purposes since then, as well as being left empty at times. Today, it welcomes visitors to explore its resources, which include park information, a bookstore, and exhibits. This is also the location of the **Junior Ranger Information Station** (see Junior Ranger Program below in *To Do*—For Families).

& **Old Faithful Visitor Center** (307-344-2750) is 16 miles south of Madison Junction off the Grand Loop Road, currently (as of 2009) situated in temporary quarters in Old Faithful Lodge. Open mid-April through late May 9–6; late May through early November 8–7; late November through early March, call or check Web site for hours (access via over-snow vehicles only). A brand-new facility (the Old Faithful Visitor and Education Center) is scheduled to open in 2010. If you're headed for this visitor center, you probably already have a specific attraction in mind! The center provides visitor information, including an award-winning film about geysers and predictions of geyser eruption times, as well as evening ranger-led talks in summer and winter.

& **West Thumb Information Station** (307-242-2650) is east of the junction between Old Faithful/S. Entrance Road and the Bridge Bay/Fishing Bridge/Lake Road in the West Thumb Geyser Basin. Open late May through late September, hours vary. The station provides visitor information and a bookstore. In winter, it serves as the **West Thumb Warming Hut,** where visitors can warm up from the chill outside while exploring Yellowstone's history or speaking with an interpretive guide. This structure also stands as a historical reminder of the park's early architectural style. Constructed in 1925, the log structure continues to serve its original purpose.

ᵒⱺᵒ **West Yellowstone Visitor Information Center** (406-646-7701; http://www .destinationyellowstone.com) is one block west of the park's West Entrance at the corner of Canyon Avenue and Yellowstone Avenue. NPS desk open mid-April through late May 8–4; late May through early November 8–8.

See also Norris Geyser Basin Museum and Information Station in *To See*—Museums; and Lake Ranger Station in *To See*—Historic Landmarks, Places, and Sites.

MUSEUMS Museum of the National Park Ranger, Norris (307-344-2812) is on the west side of the Grand Loop Road about 1 mile north of Norris Junction at the entrance to Norris Campground. Open late May through fall 9–5. Though you might never have thought about park rangers and the National Park Service (NPS) in depth before, a visit to this museum will surely pique your interest in these topics. Exhibits cover topics including the origination and development of not only park rangers, but also, the National Park Service (NPS), including an educational film. This museum is housed in the historic 1908 Norris Soldier Station, which was one of the park's original structures. Interestingly, this structure was later taken down and then rebuilt, using as much original building material as possible and recreating as much of the original floor plan as possible.

 ♿ **Norris Geyser Basin Museum and Information Station** (307-344-2812) is on the west side of the Grand Loop Road, .25 mile north of Norris Junction at the Norris Geyser Basin (see *To Do*—Norris Geyser Basin Nature Trails). Open late May through fall 9–6. An original log and stone structure constructed in 1929–30 houses this museum that introduces visitors to the geysers and geothermal features of Norris Geyser Basin. This architectural style became the archetype for many of the park's facilities built in the same time period.

See also Albright Visitor Center and Museum in *To See*—Visitor Centers.

HISTORIC LANDMARKS, PLACES, AND SITES Lake Ranger Station, in Lake Village on the Grand Loop Road, was one of the first ranger stations constructed in the park after the military turned control over to the NPS in 1916. Constructed in 1923, this log ranger station reflected an effort to establish structures that complemented rather than contrasted with the natural surroundings, as suggested by Steven Mather, the first NPS director. Additional historic ranger stations include the Northeast Entrance Ranger Station (a National Historic Landmark) and the Tower Ranger Station, which is a reconstruction of the 1907 soldier station that once stood in its place.

Lamar Buffalo Ranch Historic District, along the Northeast Entrance Road east of Tower Junction, is the location of an early 20th-century bison ranching operation that continued into the 1950s in an effort to preserve the park's bison population. Four of the ranch's structures are on the National Register of Historic Places, but the facilities are not open to the public. This area is now used by the NPS for its Expedition: Yellowstone! Program, an environmental education program for children in grades 4–8.

Nez Perce Creek Wayside, south of Madison Information Station and north of Fountain Paint Pot Nature Trail at Nez Perce Creek on the Grand Loop Road. At this wayside exhibit location, the Nez Perce Indians passed by in 1877 as they fled the encroaching U.S. troops during the five-month long Nez Perce War. This is part of the historic Nez Perce Trail, a National Historic Trail that follows the 1,170-mile journey taken by the Nez Perce from Wallowa Lake in Oregon to the Bear Paw Battlefield near Chinook, Montana.

Obsidian Cliff, 11 miles south of Mammoth Hot Springs or 8 miles north of Norris, is a National Historic Landmark that was long used by Indians for quarrying rock for use in projectile points. This unusually large outcropping of obsidian rises 150–200 feet above the creek below and features the glassy, crystal-free rock that makes excellent projectile points. Projectile points from this cliff's rock have been found as far east as Ohio. In addition to its historic significance and value as a quarry, in the 1920s Obsidian Cliff became one of the park's first places to establish a wayside exhibit to help visitors learn more about the park's resources while driving through.

Roosevelt Arch marks the park's northern entrance, on the North Entrance Road in Gardiner, Montana. Constructed in 1903, this stone arch was dedicated by President Teddy Roosevelt, who placed its cornerstone. Today this historic structure continues to welcome visitors to the park year-round as it has for more than a century.

See also Albright Visitor Center and Museum, Fishing Bridge Visitor Center and Museum, and West Thumb Information Station in *To See*—Visitor Centers; Museum of the National Park Ranger and Norris Geyser Basin Museum in *To See*—Museums; and Lake Yellowstone Hotel, Mammoth Hot Springs Hotel, Mammoth Hotel Dining Room, Old Faithful Inn, Old Faithful Lodge, and Roosevelt Lodge in *Lodging/Dining*.

SCENIC DRIVES Blacktail Plateau Drive departs the Grand Loop Road heading one way east of Mammoth Hot Springs (about halfway to Tower-Roosevelt), rejoining the Grand Loop Road near the Petrified Tree (see *To See*—Natural Wonders). The drive takes you away from the main road and through less-trafficked terrain of the Blacktail Deer Plateau, yielding you the opportunity to see wildlife and enjoy scenery away from the regular route. This road is also open to mountain bikes (two-way traffic).

Grand Loop Road forms the park's major road as a figure eight and is accessible from all five park entrances. Traveling all 142 miles of this road will take you past virtually all of the park's major natural attractions, as well as providing you with access to campgrounds, picnicking facilities, visitor centers, visitor services, scenic views, and wildlife viewing opportunities. All of the other short and scenic drives listed here are accessible from the Grand Loop Road.

Firehole Canyon Drive is a one-way road that departs from the Grand Loop Road just south of the Madison Information Station, rejoining it a bit farther south. The drive takes you along the Firehole River (see *To Do*—Fishing) to view the scenic 40-foot Firehole Falls. The area is a popular place to swim in the heat of summer, but there are no lifeguards, so you must use caution.

&. **Firehole Lake Drive** is a one-way road that leaves the Grand Loop Road north of the **Midway Geyser Basin** (north of Old Faithful), rejoining the road farther north across from the Fountain Paint Pot Nature Trail (see *To Do*—Hiking). The road leads you past the **Great Fountain Geyser,** which features regular eruptions towering 100 feet in height and lasting for up to an hour in length. You will see a number of additional geothermal features along this road, including **Firehole Spring, Surprise Pool, Firehole Lake,** and **Pink Cone Geyser,** among others. All of these geothermal features are handicapped accessible.

THE SPECTACULAR 308-FOOT HIGH LOWER FALLS OF THE GRAND CANYON OF THE YELLOWSTONE

North Rim Drive is a one-way road that begins at the Grand Loop Road junction in Canyon Village and deposits you back on the Grand Loop Road south of Canyon Village. You can also take a spur road off the one-way road to **Inspiration Point**. This scenic point gives you a tremendous view of

the Grand Canyon of the Yellowstone (see *To See*—Natural Wonders). Also along the one-way road, you can stop at Grand View and Lookout Point for views of the canyon's Lower Falls.

& **South Rim Drive** is an out-and-back road to **Artist Point,** accessible off the Grand Loop Road just south of Canyon Village. The drive includes a view of the spectacular 308-foot high Lower Falls of the **Grand Canyon of the Yellowstone** (see *To See*—Natural Wonders). You can also stop to view the 109-foot Upper Falls along this road. Artist Point affords you a scenic overlook of the Grand Canyon of the Yellowstone.

& **Upper Terrace Drive** is a one-way road leaving the Grand Loop Road just south of **Mammoth Hot Springs,** returning you to the road just next to your starting point. Closed in winter, the road is suitable for passenger cars only. It takes you past the multicolored, sculpture-like limestone terraces, giving you a quick view of their beauty and uniqueness. You can also access the Mammoth Hot Springs Nature Trails (see *To Do*—Hiking) from here if you'd like to take a closer look.

See also John D. Rockefeller Jr. Memorial Parkway in *To See*—Scenic Drives in Grand Teton National Park.

NATURAL WONDERS **American bison** are viewable along the Grand Loop Road throughout the park; please observe the 25-yard minimum distance required by law for your own safety and that of these wild animals. More than 3,000 American bison live in Yellowstone National Park today, and visitors often see them along the roadside. You may be surprised to learn, then, that by the turn of the 20th century, the number of bison remaining in the park totaled fewer than 50. The remarkable comeback of the bison came about through human efforts (see Lamar Buffalo Ranch Historic District in *To See*—Historic Landmarks, Places, and Sites). The buffalo continue to survive here in the only area of the lower 48 states that has sustained a bison population nonstop since prehistoric times. Be aware that though they may appear somewhat like cattle, bison are truly wild animals, making them unpredictable. They are also huge—males weigh almost a ton, while females are *only* 1,000 pounds or thereabouts—not exactly the sort of creature you'd want to make angry!

YOU'LL SEE AMERICAN BISON ALONG THE GRAND LOOP ROAD THROUGHOUT THE PARK

Bears make their homes by the hundreds in Yellowstone National Park, both the American black bear and the more formidable grizzly bear; please observe the 100-yard minimum distance required by law for your own safety and that of these wild animals. *Do not feed the bears.* Not at all like the friendly Yogi Bear encountered in the fictional Jellystone Park, Yellowstone's bears, while probably accustomed, in varying extents, to the presence of humans, are wild animals that can be extremely dangerous, and they should be treated as such. If you see a bear, keep your distance, respect the animal's space, and report the sighting to the nearest ranger station.

Grand Canyon of the Yellowstone, observable from the Canyon Village area, continues north with the Yellowstone River flowing through it to the Tower-Roosevelt Area. Originally carved out by massive erosive forces more than 10,000 years ago, this canyon of soft, yellowish, volcanic stone features gorgeous falls, plus a wild environment tucked between canyon walls that tower 800–1,000 feet above the Yellowstone River, which continues to erode the canyon today. See also North Rim Drive and South Rim Drive in *To See*—Scenic Drives.

OLD FAITHFUL

Ġ **Old Faithful** is at the southwest corner of the bottom loop of the Grand Loop Road. Probably the most recognized of Yellowstone's attractions, this geyser erupts every 45 to 90 minutes, making it the most frequently erupting of all of Yellowstone's large geysers—one of the major facts that accounts for its popularity. You might feel like you're at a circus or theatrical production while you wait for the geyser to erupt, due to the stage-like setting complete with ample seating to accommodate the crowds gathered to watch it, not to mention the proliferation of buildings and services surrounding it. Nonetheless, when Old Faithful bursts forth with a fury, spewing scalding hot water 100–180 feet into the air, you'll probably forget about all of the development and distractions. For a bit more solitude, you can also take a hike or bike ride on the paved, 1.5-mile trail (handicapped accessible) to the **Morning Glory Pool,** which includes views of other geothermal features including **Castle Geyser** and **Crested Pool.** Hikers (but not bikers) can continue on the unpaved trail to **Biscuit Basin** from here. See also Old Faithful Visitor Center in *To See*—Visitor Centers.

Petrified Tree is east of the Tower-Roosevelt area just off the Grand Loop Road. A 20-foot portion of this petrified redwood tree stands upright, where it has stood since it grew some 50 million years ago. Volcanic activity fossilized the specimen, and you can read about this process in depth at the display area. More specimens of petrified trees, which together make up the world's most concentrated known area of petrified trees, can be viewed along the **Specimen Ridge Trail,** accessible from **Tower Fall** (see below), as well as at several points along the Northeast Entrance Road east of Tower Junction.

Tower Fall is just south of Tower Junction on the Grand Loop Road. This waterfall is distinctive due to its multihued, jagged towers of eroded volcanic rock that frame the actual 132-foot waterfall made by Tower Creek. A short, .5-mile hike down steep switchbacks takes you up closer for a more intimate view of this inspirational setting.

Wolves were successfully reintroduced to the park in 1995 after a human-caused absence that lasted at least 25 years and was probably more like 50 years. Please observe the 25-yard minimum distance required by law for your own safety and that of these wild animals. That being said, you're not likely to get that close, even if you should catch a glimpse of one of these magnificent predators—but some lucky park visitors are treated to the sight of Yellowstone's wolves each year. Wolves represent a critical piece in putting back together the somewhat shattered ecological balance in the park, considered by some to embody a microcosm of the predator-prey imbalances caused by human actions that persist outside of the park.

Yellowstone Caldera, forming the central portion of the park, is a 28-mile by 47-mile caldera, making it one of the world's largest. A caldera is a volcanic crater that results from either a massive eruption or the collapse of a volcano's cone. Formed by the former some 600,000 years ago, the Yellowstone Caldera continues to reverberate with the aftereffects of that event to this day, as evidenced by Yellowstone's extensive geothermal features. Yellowstone Lake (see below) fills a large portion of the caldera with its waters.

Yellowstone Lake is huge. The Grand Loop Road follows its shoreline for some 30 miles of its southeastern portion, which represents a mere fraction of its 110 miles of total shoreline. The lake is also deep—390 feet at its deepest spot. It is roughly 20 miles by 14 miles in area. These statistics make it one of the largest alpine lakes on the planet. Visitors enjoy numerous activities centered on Yellowstone Lake, including fishing, boating (motorized), paddling, bicycling, hiking, swimming, and picnicking, among others.

See also Obsidian Cliff in *To See*—Historic Landmarks, Places, and Sites; *To See*—Scenic Drives; Lone Star Geyser Road in *To Do*—Bicycling; *To Do*—Hiking; Shoshone Lake in *To Do*—Paddling/Floating; and *To Do*—Relaxation and Rejuvenation.

✳ To Do

BICYCLING Yellowstone National Park allows bicycles on park roads, in parking areas, and on certain designated roads (mostly closed to motor vehicle traffic), including those listed below. Bicycles are available for rent from Xanterra Parks and Resorts (see Guidance, above) in the Old Faithful area of the park. Bicycles are not permitted on any park trails or off-road, backcountry areas. Cyclists must obey all traffic rules. Use caution on roadways, as most do not have shoulders, and many are narrow and winding, making it difficult for autos to see cyclists. Advance planning is strongly advised for those considering a bicycling adventure in Yellowstone. For more details on the park's bicycling regulations and opportunities, visit the Web site, click on "Plan Your Visit," "Things To Do," and then "Bicycling," or call the park and request the "Bicycling in Yellowstone National Park" brochure. A number of commercial outfitters are NPS licensed to provide bicycle tours in the park, including Jackson, Wyoming-based **Teton Mountain Bike Tours** (1-800-733-0788 or 307-733-0712; http://www.tetonmtbike.com), among others. See also Teton Mountain Bike Tours in *To Do*—Cycling in Northwest Wyoming: Jackson and Dubois.

Bunsen Peak Road, departing from Grand Loop Road just south of Mammoth and north of Upper Terrace Drive, is a 6-mile route that is designated for bicycle travel. You can combine Bunsen Peak Road with the section of abandoned road-way starting in Gardiner that parallels the Yellowstone River to the park's entrance (5 miles), among other options, to lengthen your bicycle outing in this area of the park.

Fountain Freight Road leaves Grand Loop Road just south of the Nez Perce Creek Wayside (see *To See*—Historic Landmarks, Places, and Sites). Appropriate for mountain bikes, this route follows an auto road for 1.5 miles along the Firehole River, and then continues for about 5.5 miles on an old service road, taking you by Goose Lake and **Grand Prismatic Spring,** the park's largest hot spring. The trail then rejoins Grand Loop Road at the **Midway Geyser Basin**.

Lone Star Geyser Road leaves Grand Loop Road just south of Old Faithful at the **Kepler Cascades**, a 125-foot, easily accessible waterfall. This route takes you on a 2-mile journey up to the **Lone Star Geyser**. The geyser erupts roughly every three hours, so if you bring a picnic lunch and have some patience (or are just lucky with your timing), you can probably catch it in action.

Riverside Trail leaves the West Entrance Road at the park entrance and rejoins it 1.4 miles later, providing a nice, albeit short, ride along the Madison River away from automobile traffic.

See also Blacktail Plateau Drive in *To See*—Scenic Drives; and Old Faithful in *To See*—Natural Wonders.

BOATING Yellowstone National Park allows motorized boating on both Lewis Lake and Yellowstone Lake, except for the South, Southeast, and Flat Mountain Arms. If you're bringing your own boat to Yellowstone, advance planning is a necessity. Obtain a copy of "Yellowstone National Park Boating Regulations" either online (click "Plan Your Visit," "Things to Do," and then "Boating") or by calling the park. Bridge Bay, south of Lake Village on Grand Loop Road, serves as the park's central location for motorized boating. Here you'll find a boat launch and marina, where **Xanterra Parks and Resorts** (see Guidance) rents out motorized boats (first-come, first-served). Xanterra also offers guided fishing boats, but it's best to call in advance for reservations. See also Yellowstone Lake Scenicruises in *To Do*—Unique Adventures.

See *To Do*—Paddling/Floating for details on the use of nonmotorized watercraft in Yellowstone National Park.

BOATING IS JUST ONE OF THE MANY RECREATIONAL ACTIVITIES AVAILABLE AT ENORMOUS YELLOWSTONE LAKE

FISHING Yellowstone National Park is home to a number of prime fishing destinations, including Yellowstone Lake (see *To See*—Natural Wonders), **Heart Lake, Lewis Lake, Shoshone Lake,** and smaller lakes; as well as a number of rivers and streams, including the rivers listed briefly below. Yellowstone's fishing season opens the Saturday of Memorial Day weekend and closes after the first

Sunday in November. Fishing in Yellowstone requires a park permit. Anglers ages 16 and up must pay for the privilege to fish ($15 for a three-day permit; $20 for a seven-day permit; or $35 for an annual permit). Children 15 and under can fish without a permit under direct adult supervision (so long as the adult has a valid fishing permit), or can obtain a free permit signed by a responsible adult to fish without direct adult supervision. Permits can be purchased at visitor centers, ranger stations, and general stores throughout the park. No state fishing license is required. In an effort to preserve ecosystems and protect native fish species, Yellowstone also has a number of special rules and regulations in place regarding fishing practices. These can be found in the "Fishing Regulations" handbook, available either online, by calling the park, or obtainable during a park visit.

Firehole River flows from south of Old Faithful, paralleling Grand Loop Road north to its confluence with the Gibbon River and the Madison River. This much-loved, pristine stream is renowned among anglers for its healthy populations of brook, brown, cutthroat, and rainbow trout, as well as its scenic qualities.

Gardner River flows from a lake on Joseph Peak east of Mammoth first north, then south, then wraps around north again at Indian Creek Campground, where it flows north along North Entrance Road to its confluence with the Yellowstone River. Species of fish include brook, brown, cutthroat, and rainbow trout.

Gibbon River flows from northwest of Norris along Grand Loop Road to its confluence with Firehole River to form Madison River at the Madison area. The mostly spring-fed Gibbon River has brook, brown, and rainbow trout, as well as Montana grayling and mountain whitefish.

Lewis River flows from Lewis Lake south along South Entrance Road to the park's border and its confluence with the Snake River. Fish species include brook, brown, cutthroat, mackinaw, and rainbow trout.

Yellowstone River, the park's largest and most distinctive river, flows from its origins in the mountains southwest of the park northward into the Southeast Arm of Yellowstone Lake. The river continues to flow north from the **Fishing Bridge** (which has been closed to fishing since 1973), angling east through the **Grand Canyon of the Yellowstone** (see *To See*—Natural Wonders) at Canyon Junction, before heading northwest to Gardiner, Montana. In the park, the portion of the river south of Yellowstone Lake is remote and difficult to access. North of the lake, the Upper Yellowstone, or the portion before the Grand Canyon between Fishing Bridge and Canyon Village, runs right along Grand Loop Road. This portion's species of game fish is primarily cutthroat trout. The Lower Yellowstone, or the area between Tower Junction and Gardiner, Montana, is accessible via the **Yellowstone River Trail** and several spur trails off Grand Loop Road, such as the **Blacktail Creek Trail.** This section's game fish species include brook, brown, cutthroat, and rainbow trout.

See also Yellowstone Lake in *To See*—Natural Wonders; Shoshone Lake in *To Do*—Paddling; and Snake River in *To Do*—Fishing in Grand Teton National Park.

FOR FAMILIES ✐ **Junior Ranger Program** materials are available at park visitor centers (see *To See*—Visitor Centers); $3 per child. Designed for children ages 5–12 (and their families, of course), this fun-filled program features a 12-page activity book (one for younger children and one for older children) for kids to complete in order to earn a Junior Ranger badge. Activities include attending a ranger-led talk (held throughout the summer season; stop in at a visitor center or ranger station for a schedule), taking a hike on one of Yellowstone's many trails, and much more. Kids will also find a number of age-appropriate, interactive, Yellowstone-oriented activities on the Web to prepare them for their travels to the park. Just go to the main Web site and click on "For Kids," and you're on your way. See also Madison Information Station in *To See*—Visitor Centers.

✒ **Yellowstone for Families** (406-848-2400; http://www.yellowstoneassociation .org/institute). Offered early June through late August, Monday through Friday or Friday through Tuesday; about $700 double occupancy/$1,000 single occupancy, plus about $400 per child (make reservations in advance). Given by the Yellowstone Association Institute (see Unique Adventures, below), these four-day learning and lodging programs, recently chosen by *Good Morning America* as the Best Summer Family Camp in America, are specially designed for families with children ages 8–12 in mind. Spend four days and four nights exploring Yellowstone with a naturalist guide, who will lead the family on easy hikes of up to 3 miles while educating everyone about the surrounding natural wonders. Children will have the chance to become junior rangers (see listing above). Programs for families with older children and family programs in wintertime are available as well.

✒ **Young Scientist Program** materials can be purchased at the Canyon Visitor Education Center or the Old Faithful Visitor Center (see *To See*—Visitor Centers); $5 per participant. This program allows children ages 5 and older to learn more about the science behind Yellowstone National Park through fun, age-appropriate materials. Materials for ages 5–9 are only available at Old Faithful, while the packets for ages 10–13 and ages 14 and up are available at both locations. Activities include conducting field research and investigative work at the visitor center. Upon successful completion of the program, graduates receive either a Young Scientist keychain or a Young Scientist patch. Adults are welcome to become Young Scientists, too!

See also Xanterra Parks and Resorts in *To Do*—Horseback Riding; Old West Dinner Cookout, Xanterra Parks and Resorts, and Yellowstone Lake Scenicruises in *To Do*—Unique Adventures; and Lake Lodge Cabins, Bear Paw Deli, and Roosevelt Lodge and Cabins in *Lodging/Dining*.

HIKING ♿ **Fountain Paint Pot Nature Trail** is accessible from Grand Loop Road about midway between Madison and Old Faithful. This .5-mile, easy, interpretive trail is handicapped accessible only with assistance. You'll walk on one of Yellowstone's cool boardwalks for much of your journey as you pass by numerous geothermal features. These include **seven geysers**—Twig, Jet, Fountain, Morning, Clepsydra, Spasm, and Jelly Geysers—as well as bubbling mud pots, steaming and hissing fumaroles, and hot springs, among others. This cluster of geysers features regular spouters, so you'll likely catch at least one of them in action during your trek. As always, you must stay on the trail for your safety, and please don't throw anything into any of the geothermal features or put your hands (or any other body part) in the water.

Mammoth Hot Springs Nature Trails are accessible from a parking area adjacent to Upper Terrace Drive (see *To See*—Scenic Drives) as well as from a parking area farther toward North Entrance on North Entrance Road. This network of

A DISTINCTIVE LIMESTONE TERRACE AT
MAMMOTH HOT SPRINGS

trails provides you with a variety of distances, depending on where your wanders take you and your time constraints. You'll tour through the distinctive limestone terraces, viewing the unique formations that differ from geothermal areas in the rest of the park. Interpretive signs help explain the geothermal processes that contribute to the formation of these intriguing travertine terraces. As always, you must stay on the trail for your safety, and please don't throw anything into any of the geothermal features.

&. **Mud Volcano Loop Nature Trail**, accessible from the east side of Grand Loop Road northwest of Fishing Bridge. A portion of this .7-mile interpretive trail is handicapped accessible. This trail takes you on an easy, if somewhat steep, stroll through some of the park's murkiest, muddiest geothermal features. Though the mud in the mud pots and pools may appear to be boiling or simmering, the bubbles are actually just from volcanic gases escaping from beneath the earth's surface. That doesn't mean that they're not hot, though! You'll see a variety of goopy wonders, including a mud geyser (that has not been observed to erupt for more than a century), cauldrons, pots, and the **Mud Volcano.** As always, you must stay on the trail for your safety, and please don't throw anything into any of the geothermal features.

&. **Norris Geyser Basin Nature Trails** are accessible from Grand Loop Road near the Norris area. Portions of this area's various trails are handicapped accessible. For a short journey, you can stroll through the Porcelain Basin on a .75-mile interpretive trail, partly a boardwalk, which loops you past a number of geothermal features in an otherworldly setting. You'll see the colorful hues of heat-loving microorganisms in pools and streams, passing by **Constant Geyser** and the small but distinctive **Whale's Mouth,** a deep blue, calm, and cavernous little pool so clear and still that you can actually see the whale's mineral *teeth* jagging in and out below the water's surface. A longer, 1.5-mile journey along a part-boardwalk, part-dirt trail takes you through the geothermal features in the more forested Back Basin. This area is home to the world's largest geyser, **Steamboat Geyser,** which erupts rarely, but when it does, shoots water 300 to 400 feet into the air. As always, you must stay on the trail for your safety, and please don't throw anything into any of the geothermal features.

Storm Point Trail is accessible from East Entrance Road 3 miles east of the Fishing Bridge, from the turnout next to Indian Pond. If you've just driven in from Cody through the East Entrance, Storm Point provides you with a great chance to get out of the car, stretch your legs, and get a good look at your surroundings. This 2-mile loop trail takes you along the shore of Indian Pond, through a forest, then out to rocky Storm Point, where you may observe the marmots who live there in action. The trail then loops you along the lakeshore and back through a forested area, with the potential to see bison, moose, and waterfowl, among other wildlife.

See also Old Faithful, Petrified Tree, and Tower Fall in *To See*—Natural Wonders; and Fountain Freight Road and Riverside Trail in *To Do*—Bicycling.

HORSEBACK RIDING *&* **Guided horseback rides** are available through **Xanterra Parks and Resorts** (see Guidance). Corrals are located at Mammoth Hot Springs, Canyon Village, and Roosevelt Lodge. Numerous departure times daily at each location from late May through early September, (opening date and closing date varies with location), $37 per person for a one-hour ride; $56 per person for a two-hour ride. Ages 8–11 must be accompanied by an adult and be at least 4 feet tall. It's recommended to make reservations in advance. Each location and length of ride features an opportunity to view a piece of Yellowstone from a uniquely different vantage point than most visitors will ever have.

Yellowstone National Park allows private horse owners to ride their horses in the park, but you should be sure to make your arrangements in advance to ensure compliance with all rules and regulations. Overnight horse trips are not allowed before July 1, due to potentially wet trail conditions and general preparedness issues. Horses are not allowed in the developed campgrounds, but they are allowed in certain backcountry campgrounds. For information and assistance in planning an overnight trip with horses, visit the Web site for free copies of Yellowstone's "Backcountry Trip Planner" and "Horsepacking Information," and/or call the Backcountry Office (307-344-2160).

See also Old West Dinner Cookout in *To Do*—Unique Adventures.

PADDLING/FLOATING **Yellowstone National Park** allows paddling and floating of nonmotorized watercrafts on many of its lakes, including Yellowstone Lake (see *To See*—Natural Wonders), Lewis Lake, and Shoshone Lake (see below). Paddling/floating on all of the park's rivers and streams is strictly prohibited, with the sole exception being the channel between Lewis Lake and Shoshone Lake. You must purchase a permit ($5 for seven days, or $10 annually; also valid in Grand Teton National Park) in person for each nonmotorized watercraft. Permits can be purchased at Bridge Bay Ranger Station, Canyon Visitor Center, Grant Village Visitor Center, Lewis Lake Campground, Lake Ranger Station, Mammoth Visitor Center, and South Entrance. Xanterra Parks and Resorts (see Guidance) offers rental boats at Bridge Bay Marina.

Several commercial outfitters are also permitted by the NPS to guide paddling trips in Yellowstone National Park, including **Snake River Kayak and Canoe School** (1-800-529-2501; http://www.snakeriverkayak.com); see full listing in Northwest Wyoming: Jackson and Dubois.

Shoshone Lake, located north of Lewis Lake and accessible by nonmotorized watercrafts via a channel, is the largest backcountry lake in the continental United States. For paddlers looking for an incredible adventure in

THE WHALE'S MOUTH AT THE NORRIS GEYSER BASIN

an unbelievably scenic setting, this lake should be high on the list. Numerous backcountry campsites dot the lake's shore, making point-to-point travel via paddled vessels a popular way to explore this pristine, remote water body. You can even hike to the Shoshone Geyser Basin, northwest of the lake, via trails accessible from the lakeshore. July and August are the best times to plan a trip to Shoshone Lake, as it can still be partially covered by ice in June. Due to the remote nature of this lake and the lack of rapid rescue services for the backcountry, a paddle in Shoshone Lake must involve careful advance planning (or the assistance of a professional guide service) to ensure a safe and successful adventure.

See also O.A.R.S. Snake River Rafting and Jackson Lake Kayaking in *To Do—Unique Adventures in Grand Teton National Park.*

RELAXATION AND REJUVENATION **Yellowstone National Park** obviously has an abundance of geothermal features, including a huge number of hot springs. Soaking in the springs is strictly off limits to park visitors—and probably, most of the park's hot springs would scald the skin off your body in seconds or sicken you due to their extreme alkalinity or acidity, as well as the presence of potentially health-damaging algae and bacteria. You are not allowed to swim, bathe, or soak in any of the park's thermal waters that originate from thermal sources only. That being said, the park does have a few places where swimming or soaking in geothermally warmed waters is allowed, though somewhat grudgingly. Popular swimming/soaking thermal areas include the swimming area on the Firehole River (see

A SKIN-SCALDING GEOTHERMAL FEATURE
AT THE FOUNTAIN PAINT POT AREA

To See—Scenic Drives), an area of the Madison River at the Madison Campground, and the Boiling River—a popular location near Mammoth Hot Springs where a hot spring enters the Gardner River.

SNOW SPORTS **Cross-country skiing** is a popular winter activity in Yellowstone National Park, with miles and miles of trails to choose from. For the most part, these trails are ungroomed, and thus you must possess the proper equipment and knowledge to make your trip a safe one. Talking with a park ranger about your plans is necessary for your safety, as he or she can update you on the latest weather conditions, forecasts, and the condition of the trails or terrain you're interested in skiing—trails are sometimes closed due to severe weather or for wildlife protection. If you go into the backcountry, bringing a USGS map and a compass (and the knowledge of how to use them properly) is recommended. A number of NPS-licensed concessionaires, including Xanterra Parks and Resorts (see Guidance) offer guided cross-country skiing and snowshoeing adventures in the park during wintertime. For a full list of winter business concessionaires, visit http://www.nps.gov/yell/plan yourvisit/wintbusn.htm. See also Old Faithful Snow Lodge in *Lodging/Dining*— Lodges.

Snowmobiling has long been a popular winter pastime in Yellowstone National Park, though in recent years, it has received national attention due to the purported ill effects of snowmobiles on the park's ecosystem—namely pollution. As of winter 2009, the current plan in place allows up to 720 commercially guided snowmobiles daily in Yellowstone and up to 78 snowcoaches. All of Yellowstone's roads, except for the North Entrance Road and Northeast Entrance Road, are usually opened to snowmobiles and other over-snow vehicles (such as snowcoaches) from mid-December through mid-March. Visitors wishing to tour the park via over-snow travel in a motorized vehicle (snowmobile or snowcoach) must hire a commercial guide. For a list of NPS-licensed concessionaires, call the park or visit http://www.nps.gov/yell/planyourvisit/wintbusn.htm.

Snowshoeing, like cross-country skiing, is a great way to enjoy the wintry beauty of Yellowstone National Park. You can even join a ranger for a free, ranger-led snowshoeing tour (snowshoes are available for rent, or bring your own). Check the park Web site or call the park for the latest winter schedule of events. For more details about snowshoeing, read the above listing on cross-country skiing. See also Old Faithful Snow Lodge in *Lodging/Dining*—Lodges.

See also Yellowstone in a Day in *To Do*—Unique Adventures; and Mammoth Hot Springs Hotel and Cabins and Old Faithful Snow Lodge and Cabins in *Lodging/Dining*.

UNIQUE ADVENTURES ℰ **Old West Dinner Cookout,** run by Xanterra Parks and Resorts (see Guidance); leaves from Roosevelt Lodge. Offered daily early June through late August with various check-in times. The Old West Dinner Cookout includes a 12-ounce steak dinner cooked out cowboy style, with your choice of an accompanying wagon ride to the cookout spot ($55 per adult; $45 per child ages 5–11), a one-hour horseback ride ($66 per adult; $56 per child ages 8–11), or a two-hour horseback ride ($80 per adult; $70 per child ages 8–11). Reservations are required. You can also take a **stagecoach ride,** offered daily with various departure times from early June through August, at Roosevelt Lodge ($10 per adult; $8 per child ages 2–11). See also Roosevelt Lodge and Cabins in *Lodging/Dining*.

& ℘ **Ranger-Led Programs**, run by Yellowstone National Park (see Guidance) can involve active participation from you, such as a guided interpretive hike into an area otherwise not accessible to the public; as well as presentations in the form of a lecture, film, slide show, or other such event. Many of these activities are handicapped accessible. They can range from 20 minutes to three hours or longer, depending on the program, and most of them are free. For a current schedule, visit the Web site, call the park, or check at a visitor center during your visit. See also Snowshoeing in *To Do*—Snow Sports.

ℰ **Xanterra Parks and Resorts** (see Guidance) offers a number of unique Yellowstone National Park adventures in additional to those detailed in this section. Adventures include interpretive bus/van tours (including Yellowstone in a Day, listed below), Historic Yellow Bus tours, boating (including Yellowstone Lake

Scenicruises detailed below), walking tours, and photography workshops. Most of these activities require advance reservations, and many of them can be combined into package deals that include lodging. Contact Xanterra or visit Xanterra's Web site for more information.

ᔑ **Yellowstone Association Institute** (406-848-2400; http://www.yellowstone association.org/institute), P.O. Box 117, Yellowstone National Park, 82190. Run by the Yellowstone Association (see Guidance), this educational institute provides you with a number of opportunities for a more in-depth learning experience at Yellowstone National Park. Choose from a wide variety of programs, including field seminars, backcountry courses, lodging and learning programs, and private tours. For more information about all of the programs, call to request a course catalog, or download the course catalog from the Web site. See also Yellowstone for Families in *To Do*—For Families.

Yellowstone in a Day, by Xanterra Parks and Resorts (see Guidance and listing above), is one of a number of auto tours offered by this concessionaire in the park. Departs daily late May through mid-August from Gardiner, Montana (tour runs from 7:45–6:15) or Mammoth Hotel (tour runs from 8–6); $70 per adult, $35 per child 8–15, under 8 free (Gardiner); $68 per adult, $34 per child 8–15, under 8 free (Mammoth). The Yellowstone in a Day tour takes you in a circle around the outer loop of the park's Grand Loop Road, with stops at a number of the park's major attractions, including Old Faithful and the Grand Canyon of the Yellowstone (see *To See*—Natural Wonders). A stop for lunch is made at Old Faithful, but lunch is not included in the fee. In wintertime, Xanterra and several other licensed concessionaires offer tours of the park in a snowcoach (a heated, over-snow vehicle).

ᔑ **Yellowstone Lake Scenicruises,** operated by Xanterra Parks and Resorts (see Guidance), departs from the marina at Bridge Bay. Open late May through mid-September; $14.25 per adult, $9 per child 2–11, children under 2 free. This one-hour boat tour offers you the opportunity to see some of the park's majesty and wonder from the waters of Yellowstone Lake. It's also short enough to keep squirmy, small children more entertained (or at least contained) than some of the lengthier outings available. See also Yellowstone Lake in *To See*—Natural Wonders.

See also Mammoth Hot Springs Hotel and Cabins and Old Faithful Snow Lodge and Cabins in *Lodging/Dining;* and O.A.R.S. Snake River Rafting and Jackson Lake Kayaking, Teton National Park Tours, and Teton Science Schools Wildlife Expeditions: Grand Teton Expeditions in *To Do*—Unique Adventures in Grand Teton National Park.

✴ Lodging/Dining

All of Yellowstone National Park's lodging and dining facilities are run by Xanterra Parks and Resorts (1-866-GEYSERLAND (866-439-7375) or 307-344-7311; http://www.travelyellow stone.com, see also in Guidance). Because the lodging and dining facilities are typically grouped together in Yellowstone, they are organized alpha-betically as such below—lodging establishment first, and then nearby dining facilities. **Campgrounds** are listed at the end of this section.

Please note that all park lodging accommodations are nonsmoking, do not have Internet access, and also do not have televisions, radios, or air conditioning. The dining facilities, be they fine dining or fast food (or somewhere in between) feature American/western fare for the most part, including steaks, prime rib, pork, chicken, fish, and salads at the finer establishments; and burgers, pizzas, sandwiches, pastas, and salads at the more casual eateries. Most restaurants offer either a children's menu or a kiddie meal. For detailed menus from each establishment, visit the Xanterra Web site. Breakfast and lunch are first-come, first-served throughout the park. Some dining facilities accept dinner reservations and some do not; see below for details. Dress for all dining establishments is casual.

Canyon Village

LODGING & **Canyon Lodge and Cabins** are located in Canyon Village, the largest and most centrally located lodging complex in the park. **Cascade Lodge** and **Dunraven Lodge** are open late May through mid-September (expensive); **Western Cabins** late May through mid-September (expensive); and **Frontier Cabins** (moderate) and **Pioneer Cabins** (moderate) late May through August. Lodge rooms contain western-themed décor, private baths, and typically have two double beds. Western Cabins include two queen beds, full private baths, and spacious, modern living quarters (no telephones). The smaller Frontier and Pioneer Cabins are not handicapped accessible, featuring simpler accommodations that include private baths (sink, toilet, and shower only).

DINING & **Canyon Cafeteria,** open late May through August, offers quick, cafeteria-style eating for breakfast (6:30–11), lunch (11:30–3), and dinner (4:30–9:30). Moderate.

& **Canyon Lodge Deli,** open (late May through late September), offers fast food, light meals, and snacks daily

from 11–9:30, except for its final month of the season, when it closes at 6. Moderate.

& **Canyon Lodge Dining Room**, open late May through mid-September, offers a sit-down, family-restaurant atmosphere, serving a breakfast buffet (7–11), lunch buffet (11:30–2:30), and dinner (5–10), which includes a full salad bar. Moderate to expensive; no reservations accepted.

Grant Village

LODGING & **Grant Village's** lodging complex is open late May through late September (expensive). This is a modern lodge built in the early 1980s, with all of the amenities you'd expect from such a facility. Each of the 100 rooms divided between the lodge's two, 6-story buildings has a private bath, some with bathtubs, and some with just a shower.

DINING & **Grant Village Dining Room,** open late May through late September, offers sit-down dining with a view of Yellowstone Lake, serving a breakfast buffet (6:30–10), lunch (11:30–2:30), and dinner (5–10). Expensive; reservations are required for dinner.

The Lake House, open early June through late September, offers a breakfast buffet (6:30–10), no lunch service, and dinner (5–9), which features pizza and pasta dishes. This restaurant also has a view of Yellowstone Lake. Moderate; no reservations accepted.

Lake Village

LODGING & **Lake Lodge Cabins** are open early June through late September. The **Western Cabins** feature spacious motel-style accommodations, modern furnishings, usually two beds, and a private bath (expensive). The more basic **Pioneer Cabins,** constructed in the 1920s, provide a basic cabin accommodation along with a private bath (inexpensive). Families fit right in here and can enjoy easy access to the **Lake Lodge Cafeteria** for mealtime convenience (see listing below).

& **Lake Yellowstone Hotel and Cabins** are open mid-May through early October. The original portion of this historic structure was completed in 1891, with additions added later. It underwent complete renovation in 1990. This startlingly yellow hotel provides the most comfortable and luxurious hotel room accommodations in Yellowstone—there's even a presidential suite (very expensive). Rooms are available in both the hotel proper (very expensive) and the hotel annex (expensive). Visitors can also opt for lodging in the **Frontier Cabins** near the hotel, which feature simple and comfortable, recently renovated accommodations (expensive). For a free historic tour of the hotel, call Xanterra Parks and Resorts for tour times.

DINING & **Lake Hotel Deli,** open late May through early October,

LAKE YELLOWSTONE HOTEL AND CABINS

10:30–9, offers soups, salads, and sandwiches to eat or to go. Inexpensive.

& **Lake Hotel Dining Room,** open mid-May through early October, serves breakfast (6:30–10), lunch (11:30–2:30), and dinner (5–10). This is the fanciest fare you'll find in all of Yellowstone National Park, served complete with views of Yellowstone Lake. Expensive to very expensive; reservations highly recommended.

& **Lake Lodge Cafeteria,** open early June through late August, serves breakfast (6:30–10; continental only 10–10:30), lunch (11:30–2:30), and dinner (4:30–9:30). Also open late August through late September for breakfast (7–10; continental only 10–10:30) and dinner (5–10) only. Lakeview eating in a casual, family-friendly atmosphere is what you'll find at this cafeteria. Inexpensive to moderate.

Mammoth
LODGING & **Mammoth Hot Springs Hotel and Cabins** are open early May through early October and mid-December through mid-March. Situated within view of the famous terraces of the area (see *To Do*—Hiking), this historic hotel, built in 1911, features a variety of rooms with assorted amenities. Suites (very expensive) top the charts for luxury, including two queen beds in a private bedroom plus a separate living area with cable television. Hotel rooms usually include two double beds and come either with a private bath (expensive) or shared bath (moderate). **Hot Tub Cabins** come with (what else?) a private, six-person hot tub along with a queen bed and private bath (very expensive). **Frontier Cabins** usually have two double beds and a private bath (expensive). **Budget Cabins** usually have two double beds and a shared bath (moderate). Visiting Yellowstone in winter? Be sure to ask about **Winter Getaway** packages.

DINING & **Mammoth Hotel Dining Room,** open early May through early October, serves breakfast (6:30–10), lunch (11:30–2:30), and dinner (5–10); late December through early March, serves breakfast buffet (6:30–10), lunch (11:30–2:30), and dinner (5:30–8). The dining room offers sit-down family dining with a view of **Fort Yellowstone's** former officers' quarters and parade grounds. This is still the location of the park headquarters today. Dinner reservations recommended in wintertime only. Expensive.

& **Terrace Grill,** open mid-May through mid-October, serves breakfast, lunch, and dinner; call or stop by for current hours. Fast-food favorites are what you'll find here, from ice cream cones and burgers to breakfast sandwiches and biscuits and gravy. The grill does serve salads and soups, too, for those in search of healthier fare. Inexpensive.

Old Faithful
LODGING & & **Old Faithful Lodge Cabins** are located in the Old Faithful area of the park, a National Historic District. Open mid-May through late September. The rustic cabins, some with private baths (**Frontier Cabins,** expensive) and some with shared baths (**Budget Cabins,** inexpensive), provide you with a more economical option when compared to most accommodations in the park.

& **Old Faithful Inn** is open May through September. Constructed in 1903–4, the inn is a National Historic Landmark. It is one of the few remaining log hotels in the United States. A vast lobby highlighted by an enormous stone fireplace welcomes visitors to this special place. There are also an espresso cart and a bar on the mezzanine level, in case you need some java. You can choose your level of luxury. Options include suites, semi-suites,

and premium rooms (very expensive); rooms with private baths (expensive); rooms without private baths (moderate); two-room units with private baths (very expensive); and two-room units without private baths (expensive). Since this is the park's most popular and well-known lodging facility, you should make reservations at least half a year in advance.

& **Old Faithful Snow Lodge and Cabins** are open early May through mid-October and mid-December through mid-March. The park's newest lodging facility, completed in 1999, features award-winning, modern, western-style lodge accommodations, complete with exposed wooden beams, high ceilings, and plenty of comfortable common areas where guests can congregate or relax. Rooms in the lodge include private baths (very expensive). **Frontier Cabins** (moderate) and **Western Cabins** (expensive) are also available. The Snow Lodge also has cross-country ski and snowshoe rentals. Visiting Yellowstone in winter? Be sure to ask about **Winter Getaway** packages.

DINING & & **Bear Paw Deli,** at the Old Faithful Inn, open early May through late August, 10:30–7:30 (ice cream served until 9); late August through early October, 11–7. Fast-food, deli-style treats are perfect for grab-'n'-go meals—or to get the kids a special after-dinner treat. Inexpensive.

& **Geyser Grill,** at the Old Faithful Snow Lodge, is open daily mid-April through early November and mid-December through mid-March; 8–9 from late May through mid-August with shortened hours at other times. You'll find typical fast-food fare here, from burgers and salads to sandwiches and soups, along with some breakfast options. Inexpensive.

&. **Obsidian Dining Room,** at the Old Faithful Snow Lodge, is open early May through mid-October for breakfast/breakfast buffet (6:30–10:30) and dinner (5–10; no reservations accepted); mid-December through mid-March for breakfast/breakfast buffet (6:30–10) and dinner (5–9:30; reservations required) Moderate to expensive.

&. **Old Faithful Inn Dining Room,** open early May through early October, serves breakfast (a la carte 6:30–10, buffet until 10:30), lunch (11:30–2:30), and dinner (buffet or a la carte, 5–10). Enjoy a fabulous feast in this one-of-a-kind setting, with seating for 300 surrounding the old stone fireplace with its historic painting of Geyser Basin. Expensive; dinner reservations suggested.

&. **Old Faithful Lodge Cafeteria and Bake Shop,** cafeteria open mid-May through mid-September. for lunch (11–4:30) and dinner (4:30–9), bake shop open mid-May through late August, 7 AM–10 PM and late August through late September, 7 AM–8 PM. You'll find standard cafeteria fare here (sandwiches, pasta, salads, hot entrées), plus some extras at the bakeshop (fried chicken, cinnamon buns, deli sandwiches, and other goodies). Inexpensive to moderate.

See also Old Faithful Inn, above.

Roosevelt

LODGING &. ✐ 🍴 **Roosevelt Lodge and Cabins** are open early June through early September. Perfect for families or for those who like the idea of a sit-down dinner among newfound friends, these rustic cabins bring people together for dinner in the central lodge. **Frontier Cabins** (expensive) include modern amenities like running water, two double beds, and private baths, while the **Roughrider Cabins** (inexpensive) give you a roof overhead

and woodstove heating, plus access to shared baths.

DINING &. ✐ **Roosevelt Lodge Dining Room,** open early June through early September, serves breakfast (7–10), lunch (11:30–3), and dinner (4:30-9). Family-style dining with a cowboy twist is what you'll find at this rustic lodge setting. No reservations accepted. Expensive. See also Old West Dinner Cookout in *To Do— Unique Adventures.*

See also Flagg Ranch Resort in Grand Teton National Park: *Lodging/Dining.*

CAMPGROUNDS Please note: Yellowstone National Park allows no camping anywhere in the park except in designated campgrounds.

&. **Xanterra Parks and Resorts** (see Guidance) runs five developed campgrounds in the park, all of which are handicapped accessible, with sites that can be reserved in advance. Individual sites (except for the RV campground) are limited to six people (or one family with dependent children), and to one vehicle with one towed unit. These include Bridge Bay Campground (open late May through mid-September; $18.50); Canyon Campground (open early June through early September; $18.50); Fishing Bridge RV Park (RVs only; open mid-May through late September; $35 for up to four adults, extra $1 per night for each additional adult); Grant Campground (open late June through late September, $18.50); and Madison Campground (open early May through late October; $18.50).

&. **Yellowstone National Park** runs seven developed first-come, first-served campgrounds (all of which are handicapped accessible) and some 300 backcountry campsites. Developed campgrounds include Indian Creek

Campground (open mid-June through mid-September; $12); Lewis Lake Campground (open mid-June through early November; $12); Mammoth Campground (open year-round; $14); Norris Campground (open mid-May through late September; $14); Pebble Creek Campground (open mid-June through late September; $12); Slough Creek Campground (open late May through late October; $12); and Tower Fall Campground (open mid-May through late September; $12).

Backcountry camping requires a Backcountry Use Permit ($20), which must be obtained in person no sooner than 48 hours before the start of your adventure in the backcountry. Backcountry camping is only permitted in specified backcountry campsites. You can obtain a Backcountry Use Permit at most visitor centers and ranger stations. For a $20 reservation fee, you can reserve some backcountry campsites in advance of your trip by mail or in person only. For a Backcountry Reservation form, call 307-344-2160; write to Backcountry Office, P.O. Box 168, Yellowstone National Park, WY 82190; or download the form from the park's Web site.

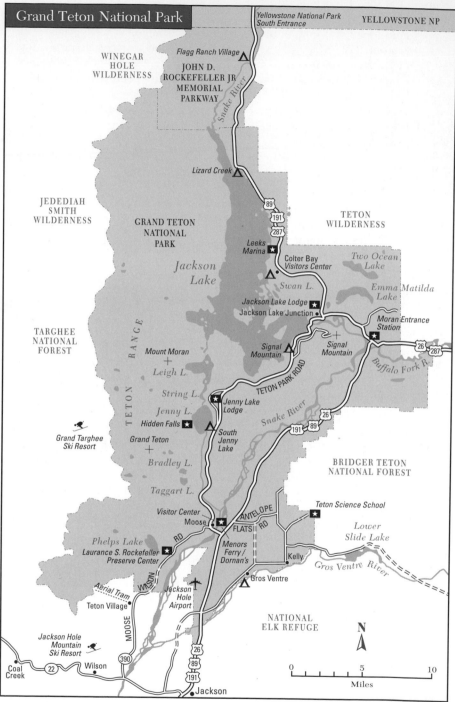

Grand Teton National Park

YELLOWSTONE NP

Yellowstone National Park
South Entrance

WINEGAR
HOLE
WILDERNESS

Flagg Ranch Village

JOHN D.
ROCKEFELLER JR
MEMORIAL
PARKWAY

Snake River

Lizard Creek

JEDEDIAH
SMITH
WILDERNESS

89
191
287

TETON
WILDERNESS

GRAND TETON
NATIONAL
PARK

Leeks
Marina

*Jackson
Lake*

Two Ocean
Lake

Colter Bay
Visitors Center

Swan L.

Emma Matilda
Lake

Jackson Lake Lodge
Jackson Lake Junction

Moran Entrance
Station

26   287

TARGHEE
NATIONAL
FOREST

Mount Moran
+

Signal
Mountain

Signal
Mountain

Buffalo Fork R.

Leigh L.

TETON PARK ROAD

String L.

Jenny Lake
Lodge

Jenny L.

Snake River

26

Hidden Falls

South
Jenny
Lake

191   89

Grand Targhee
Ski Resort

Grand Teton
+

Bradley L.

BRIDGER TETON
NATIONAL FOREST

Taggart L.

Teton Science School

*Lower
Slide Lake*

Visitor Center
Moose

ANTELOPE
FLATS   RD

Phelps Lake

Laurance S. Rockefeller
Preserve Center

Menors
Ferry /
Dornan's

Kelly

Gros Ventre River

Gros Ventre

RD

WILSON

Aerial Tram

Teton Village

Jackson
Hole
Airport

NATIONAL
ELK REFUGE

N

Jackson Hole
Mountain
Ski Resort

MOOSE

390

26
89
191

Coal
Creek

22

Wilson

0   5   10
Miles

Jackson

© The Countryman Press

GRAND TETON NATIONAL PARK

Defined by its most striking feature—the incredibly distinctive Teton Range (see *To See*—Natural Wonders)—Grand Teton National Park (GTNP) is genuinely a wilderness lover's playground, with copious opportunities to hike, fish, paddle, climb, bicycle, view wildlife, and more. Created in 1929, the park expanded in 1950 to encompass most of its current area, which includes nearly 500 square miles of land. Within its boundaries lie seven morainal lakes and more than 100 backcountry lakes, a large portion of the Snake River, the Teton Range, the recently added 1106-acre Laurance S. Rockefeller Preserve, numerous species of wildlife, and a human history that includes American Indians, ranchers, and conservationists.

When compared with Yellowstone National Park, Grand Teton National Park has fewer visitor-oriented services and sites, providing an alternative option for those seeking a less cattle-like vacation experience or needing a break from the teeming crowds usually encountered (at least during the summer season) at Yellowstone's most famed attractions. That being said, you'll find plenty of visitor services at Grand Teton National Park to make your visit a pleasant one: With 4 million human visitors a year, the park aims to serve and educate its human tourists as well as caring for and protecting its abundance of wild areas and residents. To this end, you'll find that Grand Teton National Park publishes a free, helpful, and educational brochure for almost every recreational opportunity in the park. Picking up a copy of the appropriate brochure(s) on your way into the park before you pursue your activity of choice will educate and inform you about it, while also familiarizing you with the regulations and precautions you are responsible for knowing. You'll also find helpful information at the park's six distinctive visitor centers (see *To See*—Visitor Centers and Museums), each of which focuses on a different aspect (or aspects) of all that Grand Teton National Park has to offer.

Two of these centers—the Craig Thomas Discovery and Visitor Center and the Laurance S. Rockefeller Preserve Center—are recent, 21st-century additions to the park's offerings, bringing park visitors a whole new level of interactive exhibits that use the latest technology combined with sustainable architecture. Another new addition for the 2009 season, the Grand Teton Multi-Use Pathway (see *To Do*—Bicycling, below), added an 8-mile paved trail to the park, allowing visitors a more intimate experience of this area of the park. Like all trails in Grand Teton National Park (and Yellowstone National Park), this trail is off-limits to pets. Pets

THE TETON RANGE IN WINTER

must always be leashed, and can basically only go where cars can go in these parks, for the greater good of all.

Grand Teton National Park is linked to its more famous and well-traveled northern neighbor, Yellowstone National Park, by the John D. Rockefeller Jr. Memorial Parkway (US 89/191/287; see *To See*—Scenic Drives in Grand Teton National Park). In addition to the lands contain within its borders, Grand Teton National Park also manages the section of the John D. Rockefeller Jr. Memorial Parkway south of the Yellowstone's southern border and north of GTNP's northern boundary, and the corridor that surrounds it, as a recreation area.

GUIDANCE Grand Teton Association (or GTA, 307-739-3403; http://www .grandtetonpark.org), P.O. Box 170, Moose, 83012. Formed in 1937, this organization is responsible for running all of GTNP's stores. Materials sold are selected on the basis of educational and/or interpretive value, and proceeds benefit the park. You can also purchase Grand Teton merchandise online, including helpful trip planning materials.

Grand Teton Lodge Company (1-800-628-9988 or 307-543-2811; http://www .gtlc.com), P.O. Box 250, Moran, 83013. This NPS-authorized concessionaire can help organize and book the details of your stay in GTNP, including lodging, dining, and most recreational activities.

♿ **Grand Teton National Park** (307-739-3300; http://www.nps.gov/grte), P.O. Drawer 170, Moose, 83012-0170. Open all day every day; $12 per individual (seven days) or $25 per vehicle (seven days), $50 annual pass (good for entrance into Yellowstone National Park as well); $5 per person per day mid-December through April 30, good only for Grand Teton National Park entry. Some roads are closed seasonally, as are many visitor services. Most visitor services are open May through October. For free, updated information about handicapped accessible park attractions, download the **"Grand Teton Accessibility"** brochure, available online.

You'll also find the park's current schedule of events, included handicapped-accessible events, in the park's newspaper, the *Teewinot* (available online as well).

Grand Teton National Park Foundation (307-732-0629; http://www.gtnpf.org), P.O. Box 249 Moose, 83012 or 25 S. Willow, Suite 10, Jackson, 83001. Founded in 1997, GTNPF works in partnership with Grand Teton National Park to provide financial support for programs and projects which enhance, preserve, and protect Grand Teton National Park's treasured cultural, historic, and natural resources. A shining example of GTNPF's efforts is the new (2007) **Craig Thomas Discovery and Visitor Center** (see *To See*—Visitor Centers and Museums).

Jenny Lake Ranger Station (307-739-3343), located at the Jenny Lake Visitor Center (see *To See*—Visitors Centers and Museums), is open 8–5 mid-May through early September. This is the place to stop for information if your GTNP travel plans include backpacking and/or climbing.

See also The Murie Center in *To See*—Historic Landmarks, Places and Sites; and Teton Science Schools Wildlife Expeditions: Grand Teton Expeditions in *To Do*—Unique Adventures.

GETTING THERE *By car:* Grand Teton National Park is accessed from the north and south via US 89/191/26, and from the east via US 26/287.

By plane: **Jackson Hole Airport** (307-733-7682; http://www.jacksonholeairport.com). Grand Teton Lodge Company (see Guidance) meets most commercial flights and offers transportation to lodging within the park.

By bus: **Alltrans, Inc.** (1-800-443-6133 or 307-733-3135; http://www.jacksonhole alltrans.com), P.O. Box 96, Jackson, 83001. This commercial bus service provides shuttle service from the Jackson Hole Airport to various locations in Grand Teton National Park from June through September and December through March. It's best to make reservations in advance. See also *To Do*—Unique Adventures.

GETTING AROUND Unless you're hiking, climbing, horseback riding, paddling, or something of the sort, you'll need your car or the help of a tour-bus service to get from destination to destination within the park's boundaries.

MEDICAL EMERGENCY Call 911 in the park or 307-739-3300 for the NPS dispatch.

Grand Teton Medical Clinic (307-543-2514 or 307-733-8002 after hours), near the gas station at Jackson Lake Lodge (see *Lodging*—Lodges); open mid-May through mid-October, 10–6.

See also St. John's Medical Center in Medical Emergency in Northwest Wyoming: Jackson and Dubois.

✳ To See

TOWNS Moose is situated at GTNP's southern entrance, at the junction of Teton Park Road and Moose-Wilson Road. This is the location of park headquarters and the Craig Thomas Discovery and Visitor Center (see listing below).

VISITOR CENTERS AND MUSEUMS ♿ **Colter Bay Visitor Center and Indian Arts Museum** (307-739-3594), 25 miles north of Moose on US 89/191/287 on the shore of Jackson Lake. Open early May through late May 8–5, early June through early September 8–7, early September through early October 8–5; closed early October through early May. In addition to visitor information, this location includes an impressive collection of Indian artifacts collected by David T. Vernon and donated by the Rockefeller family. During the summer, guided tours, craft demonstrations, and more are available in addition to exhibits. This location also has a bookstore, an auditorium, and backcountry permits for purchase. See also Teton National Park Tours in *To Do*—Unique Adventures.

✦ ♿ **Craig Thomas Discovery and Visitor Center** (307-739-3399; http://www.gtnpf.org/projects.php), at the junction of Moose-Wilson Road and Teton Park Road (go 12 miles north of Jackson via US 191/26/89, then west on Teton Park Road). Open year-round, early April through late May 8–5, early June through early September 8–7, early September through late October 8–5, early November through late March 9–5, closed Christmas Day. A stunning example of a public-private partnership between GTNP and the Grand Teton National Park Foundation (see Guidance), this state-of-the-art visitor center began wowing visitors when it opened its doors in August 2007. With beautiful, sustainable architecture and interactive exhibits (including children's exhibits) that integrate the latest technological advances, this visitor center has set the standard for the 21st century visitor center, lifting it to the level of a true discovery center. This is a must-see and the best possible point of entry for anyone visiting Grand Teton National Park. It's also the takeoff point for many park activities (such as interpretive walks and talks), as well as a place to get maps, park information, and backcountry camping and boat permits. A bookstore is located here, and a post office is nearby.

♿ **Flagg Ranch Information Station** (307-543-2327), 2.5 miles south of the Yellowstone National Park boundary and 40 miles north of Moose on US 89/191/287. Open early June through early September 9–3 (with possible lunchtime closure); closed early September through early June. In addition to visitor information, this station has a bookstore as well as exhibits about Greater Yellowstone and about John D. Rockefeller Jr., for whom the road connecting Grand Teton and Yellowstone was named (see *To See*—Scenic Drives).

♿ **Jenny Lake Visitor Center** is 8 miles north of Moose on Teton Park Road at South Jenny Lake. Open mid-May through late May 8–5, early June through early September. 8–7, early September through late September 8–5; closed late September through mid-May. Along with general visitor information, this visitor center includes exhibits on geology and natural features, as well as a bookstore.

CRAIG THOMAS DISCOVERY AND VISITOR CENTER

♿ **Laurance S. Rockefeller Preserve Center** (307-739-3654), situated on Moose-Wilson Road 4 miles south of Moose. Open 8–6 late May through early September, 8–5 early September through late September. This is the latest (2008) addition to Grand Teton National Park's visitor centers and a model of both a successful public-private partnership and sustainable architecture. With green technologies including solar power and composting toilets, this structure is the National Park System's first platinum-level Leadership in Energy and Environmental Design (LEED)-certified building. This lovely structure now serves as the starting point, complete with interactive exhibits, for visitors to this area of the park, the **Laurance S. Rockefeller Preserve,** a 1,106-acre parcel donated by Laurance S. Rockefeller and estimated to be worth $160 million. From the preserve, visitors can explore some 8 miles of newly created

LAURANCE S. ROCKEFELLER PRESERVE CENTER

trails year-round (including a .3-mile handicapped accessible trail) through this new (2007) addition to the park. The center does not issue permits, nor does it have a store. What it does have is all of the information you need for exploring the preserve, plus fantastic views of the **Teton Range** (see *To See*—Natural Wonders).

See also Mural Room in *Lodging/Dining:* Jackson Lake Junction Area.

HISTORIC LANDMARKS, PLACES, AND SITES Menor's Ferry Historic District is located .5 mile north of Moose on Teton Park Road. A short, self-guided trail (less than .5 mile long) takes you back in time to the area's homesteading era, exploring former rancher Bill Menor's cabin and country store. If the Snake River's waters are high enough, you can even take a ride on a replica of the ferry that Menor used to operate. You can also visit the historic and lovely **Chapel of the Transfiguration,** a place of worship. See also Teton National Park Tours in *To Do*—Unique Adventures.

The Murie Center (307-739-2246; http://www.muriecenter.org), P.O. Box 399, Moose, 83012; physical location is 2 miles west of Moose on the Snake River. The Murie Center, in partnership with Grand Teton National Park, engages people to understand and to commit to the enduring value of conserving wildlife and wild places. A former dude ranch, this National Historic Landmark served for a time as the headquarters for The Wilderness Society. Since 1997, the nonprofit Murie Center has been steward of the former ranch, launching a renovation project in 2001 to restore the ranch's 18 cabins. This is a lovely place to hold a meeting or seminar.

CHAPEL OF THE TRANSFIGURATION

See also Grassy Lake Road in *To Do*—Bicycling; and Jackson Lake Lodge and Jenny Lake Lodge in *Lodging/Dining*.

SCENIC DRIVES Jenny Lake Scenic Drive is a one-way road that leaves Teton Park Road at North Jenny Lake Junction, roughly paralleling it for about 3 miles to rejoin it just north of South Jenny Lake Junction. The route takes you along the shores of Jenny Lake, passing by **Jenny Lake Lodge** (see *Lodging/Dining*) and **String Lake** (see *To Do*—Fishing).

John D. Rockefeller Jr. Memorial Parkway is a scenic road connecting Yellowstone National Park with Grand Teton National Park. It starts at the southern border of Grand Teton National Park, leading you north along the shores of Jackson Lake to Yellowstone's South Entrance and along S. Entrance Road to the West Thumb of Yellowstone Lake. This scenic corridor takes you through classic forested terrain, past lakes, rivers, and streams.

Teton Park Road loosely parallels US 89/191 for 22 miles as it journeys from Moose Junction in the south to Jackson Lake Junction in the north. This alternate route takes you closer to the Teton Range (see Natural Wonders), as well as passing by Jenny Lake and the south end of Jackson Lake. To take a 45-mile scenic loop drive, you can start from Moose Junction, Jackson Lake Junction, or Moran Junction, and drive Teton Park Road in combination with US 89/191. Teton Park Road is also a popular place for road bicycling.

Signal Mountain Summit Road is an out-and-back, roughly 5-mile jaunt leaving from the northern portion of Teton Park Road to the east (a few miles south of Jackson Lake Junction). This drive takes you to the summit of Signal Mountain, yielding tremendous views of the Tetons and their surroundings.

See also Grassy Lake Road in *To Do*—Bicycling.

NATURAL WONDERS The Teton Range runs north and south, west of Teton Park Road and US 89/191/John D. Rockefeller Jr. Memorial Highway (see *To See*—Scenic Drives). This breathtaking mountain range rises dramatically from the valley of Jackson Hole. The uplift was caused by a fault that continues to push the mountains upward today. Part of the Rocky Mountains, these represent the youngest members of the range and some of its most distinctive, with their rough and jagged cragginess making for an incredibly scenic backdrop, not to mention a playground for hikers and rock climbers. The tallest mountain in the range is the majestic Grand Teton, which at 13,770 feet rises more than 7,000 feet above the valley floor (see also *To Do*—Climbing).

THE TETON RANGE

Wildlife viewing in Grand Teton National Park rivals Yellowstone National Park, at least in terms of opportunities to see all sorts of flora and fauna in their natural environments. Animals that call this area home include moose, otters, elk, mule deer, antelope, coyotes, muskrats, beavers, marmots, American bison (see American bison in *To See*—Natural Wonders in Yellowstone National Park), and bears (see Bears in *To See*—Natural Wonders in Yellowstone National Park), among others. In addition, numerous birds, including bald eagles, are found within the park. Some key rules for safe wildlife watching include maintaining a distance of 300 feet from all large animals, avoiding disrupting or disturbing any animal, and never feeding any animal. If an animal responds to your presence, you're too close. For more information about wildlife viewing, you can visit that section of the park's Web site (which includes key wildlife viewing areas and a downloadable list of park mammals). Another option is to participate in a wildlife-oriented **Ranger-Led Activity** (see *To Do*—Unique Adventures), which are listed regularly in the park's newspaper that you can pick up at one of the visitor centers (or download online). See also Teton National Park Tours and Teton Science Schools Wildlife Expeditions: Grand Teton Expeditions in *To Do*—Unique Adventures.

See also Laurance S. Rockefeller Preserve Center in *To See*—Visitor Centers and Museums.

✷ To Do

BICYCLING Grand Teton National Park has no designated bike paths, though bicycling is a popular activity in the park. Bicyclists must follow all rules and regulations, including remaining only on paved and unpaved roads that are open to autos (except for the Grand Teton Multi-Use Pathway; see below). Bikes are not allowed on footpaths or in the backcountry. Bicyclists are subject to all traffic laws. The park offers a (downloadable) brochure, "Grand Teton Bicycling," that explains more rules and regulations.

& **Grand Teton Multi-Use Pathway** goes from the border of Dornan's Spur Ranch Cabins (see *Lodging/Dining*) in the south to South Jenny Lake in the north, paralleling Teton Park Road. Open daily sunrise to sunset from whenever the snow melts until whenever it's covered by snow. This new (2009), 8-mile paved trail is

GRAND TETON MULTI-USE PATHWAY

not only for bicycles, but also for hikers and inline skaters. The trail brings park users closer to an area of the park previously less accessible. Potentially, more segments will be added to this pathway in the future, depending on how this new addition impacts the park on a number of levels.

Grassy Lake Road (FR 3261/261) is a 52-mile road that goes west from Flagg Ranch, (see *Lodging/Dining*), skirting along the boundary between Yellowstone National Park and Grand Teton National Park before hitting the Idaho border and continuing in that state to Ashton. Closed in winter, the winding, hilly road is suitable for mountain bikes, taking you past a number of lakes and streams, some of which are accessible via Forest Service spur roads as well, (FR 026 and 027 lead to **Lake of the Woods**). Grassy Lake Road follows a trail historically used by American Indians.

River Road is a 15-mile dirt road situated in between Teton Park Road and US 89/191. The road can be accessed in the north from just south of the Signal Mountain Road turnoff on Teton Park Road, or in the south from the road linking Moose to Moose Junction. River Road parallels the Snake River as it flows through a choice wildlife habitat area (be respectful of wild animals should you encounter them, keeping your distance and leaving them in peace for your safety and theirs).

See also *To See*—Scenic Drives; and Jenny Lake Lodge, Colter Bay Village, and Dornan's Spur Ranch Cabins in *Lodging/Dining*.

BOATING Grand Teton National Park allows motorized boating on Jackson Lake (see listing below), as well as Jenny Lake (motors 10hp and below only). You must purchase a permit ($20 for seven days, or $40 annually; also valid in Yellowstone after check-in at ranger station) for each motorized watercraft (which must already have state registration as well). The park publishes a brochure on boating that is available for downloading online or by calling the park, as well as a helpful list of boating concessionaires (including **guided fishing trips, floating guides, kayaking guides, sailboat tours,** and more) on the Web site's "Boating" page. All boaters should read both the brochure and the Web page to familiarize themselves with the park's rules before planning a boating outing in the park. See also Jenny Lake Scenic Cruise/Shuttle in *To Do*—Unique Adventures.

Jackson Lake is located west of the northern part of Teton Park Road and south of Flagg Ranch along the John D. Rockefeller Jr. Memorial Parkway. Jackson Lake is Grand Teton National Park's largest lake. In addition to boating, the lake is popular for water skiing and swimming, as well as fishing (species include brown, cutthroat, and mackinaw trout). If you don't own your own motorboat, or you don't want to bring it with you, you can rent a motorboat from a number of NPS-licensed concessionaires, including the Colter Bay Marina (1-800-628-9988 or 307-543-3100) and the marina at Signal Mountain Lodge (307-543-2831; see listing in *Lodging/Dining*), among many others. See also O.A.R.S.' Jackson Lake Kayak/Snake River Rafting Combo Trip in *To Do*—Unique Adventures.

See also Jenny Lake Scenic Cruise/Shuttle in *To Do*—Unique Adventures.

See *To Do*—Paddling/Floating for details on the use of nonmotorized watercraft in Grand Teton National Park.

CLIMBING Grand Teton National Park (307-739-3343 (summer) or 307-739-3309 (winter); http://www.tetonclimbing.blogspot.com), see Jenny Lake Ranger

Station in Guidance. Rock climbing and mountaineering are popular activities in the park, but neither should be undertaken without proper training and experience. The park's bookstores sell several rock climbing guidebooks, and more information (such as updated route conditions) can be found at the Web site above as well as online at the park's "Climbing" page. An additional "Mountaineering" brochure is available for download or at the park. If you're new to rock climbing or you'd like to try it out, Grand Teton National Park licenses two concessionaires to guide in the park (listed below).

Exum Mountain Guides (307-733-2297; http://www.exumguides.com), South Jenny Lake, P.O. Box 56, Grand Teton National Park, Moose, 83012. In business for eight decades, Exum knows the Tetons inside and out. Even if you've never rock climbed before in your life, Exum can prepare you safely and have you successfully ascending Grand Teton (the biggest of them all) in four short days of instruction. The Four-Day Grand Teton package (from $785 per person) includes two days of instruction prior to attempting the Grand Teton, and then the Classic Grand Teton two-day climb. Exum also offers kids' climbing camps and private family climbing days, as well as guided climbing on other Tetons and other rock features in the surrounding environs.

Jackson Hole Mountain Guides (1-800-239-7642 or 307-733-4979; http://www.jhmg.com), P.O. Box 7477, 165 N. Glenwood Street, Jackson, 83002. For more than four decades, Jackson Hole Mountain Guides (JHMG) has been serving visitors to Grand Teton National Park and the surrounding area. JHMG offers a four-day Grand Teton ascent package (from $1,295 per person) that requires no prior climbing experience (you spend a full day learning the ropes before you attempt to climb the Grand). In addition, JHMG offers rock climbing outings (including single-day climbs, from $275 per person) on the other Tetons and on rock formations in the surrounding area. JHMG also offers walk-up guide services (no technical rock climbing) from $225 per person. JHMG's Kids Rock! ($100 per person for three or more participants) program, designed for kids under 12 and their parents, gets families out rock climbing together right in the middle of Grand Teton National Park.

See also Grand Teton Climbers' Ranch in *Lodging/Dining*.

FISHING Grand Teton National Park includes a number of lakes, rivers, and streams that provide anglers with great opportunities for catching native game fish, mainly trout. These include **Jackson Lake** and **Jenny Lake** (see *To Do*—Boating), among others (see below for a few more suggestions). The park requires anglers to possess a valid state fishing license, and fishing in the park is subject to state laws and regulations (for details, including current licensing fees, go to http://gf.state.wy.us/fish/fishing/index.asp). The park publishes an informative brochure about fishing as well, which includes specific rules and regulations and the opening and closing dates for seasons on the park's waters—many of which are open year-round. The angler is responsible for knowing all of the current rules and regulations.

Leigh Lake, north of Jenny Lake and String Lake and west of Teton Park Road, is open to fishing year-round and has cutthroat and mackinaw trout.

Snake River flows from the mountains northeast of the park through the southern portion of Yellowstone National Park before entering Jackson Lake near the park's northern boundary, then continuing south through the park after exiting the lake at the Jackson Lake Dam near Jackson Junction. The river then flows south through the valley of Jackson Hole as well. Special regulations apply to fishing the Snake River in the park. The river's game fish species in Grand Teton include brook and cutthroat trout. In the more remote Yellowstone portion of the river, accessible via the S. Boundary Trail and the Snake River Trail, species also include brown and mackinaw trout as well as mountain whitefish. See also Snake River in *To Do*—Paddling/Floating.

String Lake, just north of Jenny Lake and west of Teton Park Road, is open to fishing year-round and has cutthroat and mackinaw trout.

Two Ocean Lake, east of the John D. Rockefeller Jr. Memorial Parkway north of Jackson Lake Junction, is open to fishing year-round and has cutthroat trout.

See also Grand Teton National Park in *To Do*—Boating; Signal Mountain Lodge in *Lodging/Dining*—Lodges; and Flagg Ranch Resort and Triangle X Ranch in *Lodging/Dining*.

FOR FAMILIES ✐ **Junior Ranger Program,** materials available at visitor centers (see *To See*—Visitor Centers and Museums) or online, $1 donation per child. Children of all ages can earn a Young Naturalist patch and take a pledge to be a junior ranger by completing the array of activities detailed in "The Grand Adventure" (stop at a visitor center to pick up a schedule). Kids must attend at least one ranger-led talk in the park (see *To Do*—Unique Adventures), and go on one hike, watch an informational video, or attend one additional park program (listed regularly in the park's paper, the *Teewinot*). Additional activities involve learning about the park's history, wildlife, geology, and more. Kids can also get started learning about Grand Teton by visiting the park's Web site (see Guidance) and clicking on "For Kids."

See also Craig Thomas Discovery and Visitor Center in *To See*—Visitor Centers and Museums; Grand Teton National Park in *To Do*—Boating; *To Do*—Climbing; Flagg Ranch Resort in *To Do*—Horseback Riding; Snake River in *To Do*—Paddling/Floating; and O.A.R.S.' Jackson Lake Kayak/Snake River Rafting Combo Trip and Teton Science Schools Wildlife Expeditions: Grand Teton Expeditions in *To Do*—Unique Adventures.

HIKING Grand Teton National Park (see Guidance) has an excellent brochure available (downloadable online as well as at the park) with details about day hikes in the park, some of which have their own specific brochures as well. A selected few of these are listed below.

♿ **Colter Bay Lakeshore Trail**, accessible from the Colter Bay Visitor Center, is a 2-mile round-trip easy hike along the shores of Jackson Lake through ideal wildlife habitat, providing you with the potential to see trumpeter swans, waterfowl, moose, elk, otters, and beavers, among other inhabitants. The trail is handicapped accessible for .3 mile where it leaves from the marina, along the eastern shore of Jackson Lake. You'll also have great views of the mountains. Additional trails, including the 3-mile round-trip Heron Pond and Swan Lake Trail, are accessible from this area as well; request a brochure at the visitor center for details.

Hidden Falls Trail, accessible from the Cascade Trailhead Dock on the west side of Jenny Lake, is a 1-mile round-trip, steep hike up to Hidden Falls, providing incredible scenic vistas of the lakes below. Those in search of a longer outing can continue up the **Cascade Canyon Trail**, which leads to more trails, including the trail to Solitude Lake. You can access the Hidden Falls trailhead via a boat shuttle (see Jenny Lake Scenic Cruise/Shuttle in *To Do*—Unique Adventures), by hiking a 2-mile portion of the 3.3-mile round-trip **String Lake Trail** (park in the String Lake Parking Lot off Jenny Lake Scenic Drive) or by hiking a 2-mile portion of the 6.6-mile round-trip **Jenny Lake Trail**, accessible from the Jenny Lake Ranger Station off Jenny Lake Scenic Drive. Both of these lake trails are fun, relatively flat outings that wrap around the lakes. These two trails are connected as well, if you want a really long hike. In addition, the **Leigh Lake Trail** (see *To Do*—Fishing) is a spur trail off the String Lake Trail, traveling along the eastern shoreline of Leigh Lake.

  Jenny Lake Trail, accessible from the Jenny Lake Ranger Station off Jenny Lake Scenic Drive, is a 6.6-mile round-trip, relatively easy path around Jenny Lake. A portion of the trail is handicapped accessible. For more information, see Hidden Falls Trail, above.

Lunch Tree Hill Trail, accessible from Jackson Lake Lodge, is an easy, .5-mile round-trip self-guiding trail with interpretive signs to help you learn more about your surroundings. In its short distance, the trail takes you to the top of the hill, where you'll enjoy a scenic overlook of the valley below, the lakes, and the Teton Range.

JENNY LAKE

  String Lake Trail, accessible from the String Lake Parking Lot off Jenny Lake Scenic Drive, is a 3.3-mile round-trip, relatively easy trail around String Lake. A portion of the trail is handicapped accessible. For more information, see Hidden Lake Trail, above.

See also Laurance S. Rockefeller Preserve Center in *To See*—Visitor Centers and Museums; Menor's Ferry Historic District in *To See*—Historic Landmarks, Places, and Sites; and Grand Teton Multi-Use Pathway in *To Do*—Bicycling.

HORSEBACK RIDING Grand Teton National Park permits private horseback riding and overnight camping with stock, subject to a number of limitations, rules, and regulations. For details and assistance in planning a horse trip, start by contacting the park and requesting the "Saddle and Pack Stock" brochure (or simply download it from the Web site).

✍ **Flagg Ranch Resort** (1-800443-2311 or 307-543-2861; http://www .flaggranch.com), 2 miles south of the border of Yellowstone National Park and 5 miles north of the border of Grand Teton National Park along the John D. Rockefeller Jr. Memorial Parkway. Call for current rates. Flagg Ranch is one of several NPS-licensed concessionaires offering horseback rides to park visitors. Rides last one hour, two hours, a half-day, or a full day. Rides depart hourly during the summer season. Children ages 8 and older are welcome. See also Flagg Ranch Resort in *Lodging/Dining.*

See also Colter Bay Village, Jackson Lake Lodge, Jenny Lake Lodge, and Triangle X Ranch in *Lodging/Dining.*

PADDLING/FLOATING Grand Teton National Park allows paddling and floating of human-powered and nonmotorized watercraft on a number of its water bodies, including Jackson, Jenny, Phelps, Emma Matilda, Two Ocean, Taggart, Bradley, Bearpaw, Leigh, and String Lakes, as well as on the Snake River (see below for details) starting 1,000 feet below the Jackson Dam. Watercraft are prohibited on all other rivers and streams in the park. You must obtain a permit for each nonmotorized watercraft ($10 for seven days; $20 annually; also valid in Yellowstone after check-in at ranger station). Before engaging in any private paddling or floating, be sure to read through the park's "Boating" brochure, available online or by calling the park. A number of NPS-licensed concessionaires rent out hand-propelled crafts such as rowboats, canoes, kayaks, and dories (see Jackson Lake in *To Do*—Boating; Jenny Lake Scenic Cruise/Shuttle in *To Do*—Unique Adventures; and Dornan's Spur Ranch Cabins and Signal Mountain Lodge in *Lodging/Dining*).

Snake River is a popular river to float and paddle, starting from 1,000 feet below the Jackson Lake Dam, near the Jackson Lake Junction. Though the river's lack of rapids makes it a relatively easy float in technical terms, floaters and paddlers should be experienced, as they must remain alert and attentive due to the high number of logjams and channel systems encountered, as well as the river's frequently changing flow rates and water depths. Before engaging in any private paddling or floating, be sure to read through the park's brochure "Floating the Snake River," available online or by calling the park. You can also book a relaxing scenic float of one of the river's calmest sections from an NPS-licensed concessionaire (see GTNP Web site for a full list), including **Solitude Float Trips** (1-888-704-2800 or 307-733-2871; http://www.solitudefloattrips.com), which charges $55 per adult and $35 per child 6–12 for a 10-mile trip. See also Grand Teton National Park in *To Do*—Boating; Snake River in *To Do*—Fishing; O.A.R.S.' Jackson Lake Kayak/Snake River Rafting Combo Trip and Teton Science Schools Wildlife Expeditions: Grand Teton Expeditions in *To Do*—Unique Adventures; and Dornan's Spur Ranch Cabins, Flagg Ranch Resort, Jackson Lake Lodge, Signal Mountain Lodge, and Triangle X Ranch in *Lodging/Dining.*

RELAXATION AND REJUVENATION Huckleberry Hot Springs are accessible via an easy trail from Flagg Ranch Resort (see *Lodging/Dining*), 2 miles south of the border of Yellowstone National Park. Not technically in either park, these primitive hot springs bubble out of the ground too hot for soaking (140 degrees), but then blend with the cooling waters of Polecat Creek, flowing into several primitive pools that are more comfortable for human skin.

SNOW SPORTS Cross-country skiing and snowshoeing offer the park's winter visitors a great way to explore the park's natural wonder and beauty when it's dressed in its annual shroud of white. Before embarking on a winter journey, be sure to educate yourself by obtaining a copy of the park's "Cross-country Skiing & Snowshoeing" brochure, available online or by stopping at a visitor center. The brochure details the safety information and regulations that you need to know before taking part in these activities. In some years, a number of trails are groomed and marked for cross-country skiers and snowshoers, including 14 miles of Teton Park Road (see *To See*—Scenic Drives), which is machine groomed for both skiers and snowshoers/hikers (check the Web site for the latest information on trail marking/grooming). From this road, you can potentially access a number of skier-groomed trails, including Jenny Lake Trail (see *To Do*—Hiking) and Signal Mountain Road (see *To See*—Scenic Drives), among others. You can even join a ranger for a **guided snowshoe hike** December through March ($5 per adult and $2 per child donation requested), departing from the Craig Thomas Discovery and Visitor Center (307-739-3399; see Guidance). Several NPS-licensed concessionaires provide guided cross-country skiing, backcountry skiing/snowboarding, and snowshoeing trips, including **Rendezvous Backcountry Tours** (1-877-754-4887 or 307-353-2900; http://www.skithetetons.com). You can rent cross-country skis or snowshoes from Dornan's Spur Ranch Cabins (see *Lodging/Dining*), and enjoy the terrain as a guest at Triangle X Ranch (see *Lodging/Dining*).

Snowmobiling in GTNP has undergone the same sort of recent scrutiny and resulting regulations as Yellowstone National Park (see Snowmobiling in *To Do*—Snow Sports in Yellowstone National Park for details). However, snowmobiles are permitted in GTNP without a commercial guide, as of 2009 ($20 per snowmobile for a seven-day permit good for entrance into Yellowstone National Park as well). The park has a helpful, updated brochure that contains all pertinent regulations, available at the Web site or from visitor centers. See also Triangle X Ranch in *Lodging/Dining*.

UNIQUE ADVENTURES 🦌 ♿ **Jenny Lake Scenic Cruise/Shuttle** (307-734-9227; http://www.jennylakeboating.com), open 10–4 May 15–31 and September 8–30; open 8–6 June 1 through July 5 and August 16 through September 7; and open 7–7 July 6 through August 15. Shuttles leave every 15 minutes and scenic tours are scheduled daily from mid-June through early September (call or stop by for schedule); cruises are $15 per adult, $7 per child ages 7–12, children 6 and under free; round-trip shuttles are $10 per adult, $5 per child ages 7–12, children 6 and under free; one-way rates also available. Jenny Lake Boating provides a one-hour scenic cruise around Jenny Lake, or a scenic shuttle boat ride across the lake to the **Cascade Trailhead Dock** (see also Hidden Falls Trail in *To Do*—Hiking). You can also

JENNY LAKE SCENIC CRUISE/SHUTTLE

rent a canoe or kayak here for $15/hour. See also Jackson Lake Lodge in *Lodging/Dining.*

⚓ **Outdoor Adventure River Specialists (O.A.R.S.) Snake River Rafting and Jackson Lake Kayaking** (1-800-346-6277; http://www.oars.com), trips depart Sunday and Friday, early June through mid-December from the Signal Mountain Public Boat Launch Ramp. This three-day, two-night trip is $644 per adult, and $541 per child (ages 4 and up); make reservations in advance. For an intimate view of Grand Teton National Park, you can't beat this trip. You'll paddle sea kayaks on Jackson Lake, and then test your mettle whitewater rafting a portion of the Snake River, all under the direction of experienced guides from O.A.R.S. In business for more than 30 years, O.A.R.S. provides some of the most top-quality river guides in the world. O.A.R.S. also offers a four- to six-day **Yellowstone and Grand Teton National Park Explorer Trip,** among the many additional guided trips available in its portfolio.

See also Grand Teton National Park and Jackson Lake in *To Do*—Boating and Snake River in *To Do*—Paddling/Floating.

♿ 🐾 **Ranger-Led Programs**, run by Grand Teton National Park (see Guidance) can involve active participation from you, such as a guided interpretive hike; as well as presentations in the form of a lecture, film, slide show, or other such event. Many of these activities are handicapped accessible. They can range from 20 minutes to three hours or longer, depending on the program, and most of them are free. For a current schedule, call the park, visit the Web site, or check at a visitor center during your visit for a current schedule of events. See also Cross-country skiing and snowshoeing in *To Do*—Snow Sports.

Teton National Park Tours (1-800-443-6133 or 307-733-4325; http://www.gray linejh.com), available Monday, Wednesday, and Saturday from early June through early September, $100 per person; make advance reservations (online or by calling). No children under 8. Enjoy a full-day sightseeing tour of Grand Teton National Park, complete with stops for wildlife viewing (see *To See*—Natural Wonders), Menor's Ferry Historic District (see *To See*—Historic Landmarks, Places, and Sites), and Colter Bay Visitor Center and Indian Arts Museum (see Guidance), among other stops. Grayline of Jackson Hole also offers guided bus tours of Yellowstone National Park, as well as private tour options for both parks.

🐾 *⚓* **Teton Science Schools Wildlife Expeditions: Grand Teton Expeditions** (1-888-945-3567 or 307-733-1313; http://www.tetonscience.org/index.cfm?id =expeditions_gtnp), 700 Coyote Canyon Road, Jackson, 83001. Offering a variety of educational wildlife expeditions year-round, from $69–199 per adult and $49–159 per child 6–12. Join the experts at Teton Science Schools for a half- or full-day adventure of wildlife viewing (see *To See*—Natural Wonders) and sometimes more, depending on which expedition you pick. Options include sunrise/sunset wildlife-viewing expeditions, paddling or floating the Snake River, plus wildlife viewing, full-day wildlife viewing, park tours, or even a Wildlife, Art, and Sleigh Expedition. Teton Science Schools also offers similar expeditions for Yellowstone National Park, as well as multiday wildlife-viewing expeditions for both parks.

See also Menor's Ferry Historic District in *To See*—Historic Landmarks, Places, and Sites; *To Do*—Climbing; Snake River in *To Do*—Paddling/Floating; and Dornan's Spur Ranch Cabins, Flagg Ranch Resort, and Triangle X Ranch in *Lodging/Dining.*

✳ Lodging/Dining

Many of Grand Teton National Park's lodging and dining facilities are run by Grand Teton Lodge Company (307-543-2811; http://www.gtlc.com, see also in Guidance), while others are independently run. Because the lodging and dining facilities within the park are typically grouped together in specific areas of the park, they are organized alphabetically as such below—lodging establishments first, and then nearby dining facilities (or in several inseparable cases, both together). Unless a separate number is listed for the dining establishment, contact the related lodge for more information or reservations. Please note that while some accommodations provide telephones, televisions are not allowed in guest rooms in GTNP. **Campgrounds** are listed at the end of this section. For more ideas of where to stay and dine while visiting GTNP, look to the listings for Jackson in the *Lodging* and *Where to Eat* sections in Northwest Wyoming: Jackson and Dubois.

Colter Bay Village

LODGING ♿ 🍴 🐾 **Colter Bay Village** (1-800-628-9988 or 307-543-3100; http://www.gtlc.com/lodge CBV.aspx). At Colter Bay Village, you'll find a number of different accommodations to choose from. These include 166 rustic log cabins, including some built by homesteaders (late May through late September; inexpensive to expensive); tent cabins, with log walls and canvas roofs (late May through late August; inexpensive); and RV camping with hookups (late May through late September; inexpensive). Colter Bay Village has a wide range of visitor services, including a marina, grocery store, horse corrals, a service station, gift shops, and two restaurants (see *Dining*). See also Grand Teton Lodge Company in Campgrounds.

DINING ♿ **John Colter Café Court** is located in Colter Bay Village and open June through early September, offering snack bar fare (both Mexican and American) and boxed lunches daily. Inexpensive to moderate.

♿ 🍴 🐾 **Leek's Pizzeria** (307-543-2494) is situated about a mile north of Colter Bay Village off US 191/26/89, near the lakeshore with a lovely view of the Tetons. Open 11–10 late May through early September. Creative pizzas (such as Thai chicken or Teton cheese steak) with an abundance of toppings form just part of the menu here. Other options include sandwiches, calzones, and salads. You can eat either inside or outdoors on the deck. A green restaurant run by environmentally conscientious Signal Mountain Lodge (see below in Jackson Lake Junction Area), Leek's also offers local microbrews and organic ice cream as well as a children's menu. Moderate.

♿ **Ranch House Restaurant and Bar**, located in Colter Bay Village, is open daily for breakfast, lunch, and dinner from late May through late September (call for current hours). Here you'll find hearty American fare, including steaks and prime rib. Expensive.

Flagg Ranch Village

LODGING/DINING ♿ 🍴 🐾 🐾 **Flagg Ranch Resort** (1-800-443-2311 or 307-543-2861; http://www.flaggranch .com), just south of the border of Yellowstone National Park along the John D. Rockefeller Jr. Memorial Parkway. Open mid-May through mid October and mid-December through mid-March; expensive, but children 17 and under stay with parents for free. Pets are $10 extra per night. You'll stay in a log-cabin room with either two queen beds or one king bed, as well as a private bath, coffeemaker, telephone, and patio. Flagg Ranch is licensed by NPS to provide a number of additional activities, including scenic float and whitewater rafting trips on the Snake River, camping, horseback riding (see also Flagg Ranch Resort in *To Do*—Horseback Riding and in Campgrounds), all-day interpretive park tours of both parks, and guided fishing trips. The resort also has a relaxing **dining room** that serves three meals daily plus an **espresso bar and pub**, as well as a grocery store, gift shop, and gas station. See also Huckleberry Hot Springs in *To Do*—Relaxation and Rejuvenation.

Jackson Lake Junction Area
LODGING ♿ **Jackson Lake Lodge** (1-800-628-9988 or 307-543-3100; http://www.gtlc.com/lodgeJac.aspx), near Jackson Lake Junction. Open mid-May through early October. Very expensive. This National Historic Landmark serves visitors as a full-service resort, with 37 rooms available in the main lodge, as well as an additional 348 luxurious guest cottages on both sides of the main lodge. Set atop a bluff overlooking Jackson Lake, you'll find all of the comforts for a relaxed and elegant vacation here, including a large, heated, outdoor swimming pool; easy access to guided activities like horseback rides, scenic lake cruises, and float trips on the Snake River, among others; and several on-premises restaurants (see *Dining*, below).

🐾 **Signal Mountain Lodge** (307-543-2831; http://www.signalmtnlodge.com), on the shores of Jackson Lake. Open early May through mid-October; expensive to very expensive. Pets are $15 extra per night. Choose from one- or two-room cabins; motel-style lodge rooms; one- or two-room bungalows; lakefront retreat suites, overlooking Jackson Lake with stunning mountain views; or a three-room cabin. In addition to lodging, Signal Mountain Lodge is licensed by NPS to provide a

number of additional activities, including Snake River float trips, boat rentals (motorized and nonmotorized), guided sailboat trips, and guided fishing trips. Signal Mountain Lodge is a proud member of the Environmental Protection Agency's (EPA) National Environmental Performance Track Program. In addition to the restaurants listed below, Signal Mountain Lodge also has several gift shops and a camp store. See also listing in Campgrounds.

DINING ♿ **Blue Heron Lounge,** located at Jackson Lake Lodge and open mid-May through early October, serves cocktails and snacks. It also features live entertainment.

Deadman's Bar, located at Signal Mountain Lodge, serves appetizers (from the Trapper Grill, see below) and drinks, including a popular blackberry margarita. Open early May through mid-October

♿ **Mural Room,** (307-543-3463; http://www.gtlc.com/dineJac.aspx), located at Jackson Lake Lodge, is open mid-May through early October, serving breakfast (7–9:30), lunch (11:30–1:30), and dinner (5:30–9; reservations recommended), daily in an elegant, fine-dining setting with views of the Tetons, as well as 80 feet of murals painted by masterful artist Carl Roters (docent tours also available). Enjoy the finest Rocky Mountain cuisine in an unforgettable setting. Expensive.

♿ **The Peaks Restaurant,** located at Signal Mountain Lodge, is open early May through mid-October for dinner. A rustic fine-dining experience awaits here that's sure to please the discerning palate. Regional specialties and sustainable cuisine are the theme here, with entrées that include elk, bison, organic beef, and trout. Vegetarian options are available. Expensive.

Pioneer Grill, located at Jackson Lake Lodge, is open 6 AM–10:30 PM mid-May through early October. This café serves lighter, over-the-counter fare for breakfast, lunch, and dinner. Inexpensive to moderate.

Pool Snack Bar, located at Jackson Lake Lodge and open mid-May through early October, serves sandwiches, pizzas, and salads. At sunset, it offers an all-you-can-eat western BBQ (reservations required) complete with live entertainment. Inexpensive to moderate.

☛ ᐃ **Trapper Grill,** located at Signal Mountain Lodge, is open early May through mid-October for breakfast, lunch, and dinner. A full menu for every meal, including a full children's menu, guarantees that even the pickiest eater will find something that pleases them at the Trapper Grill. Specialty sandwiches, salads, burgers, and full entrées are complemented by a great list of tempting desserts. Vegetarian options are available. Breakfast offers everything you'd expect, from hearty omelets to lighter fare. Moderate.

Jenny Lake Area
LODGING/ DINING ᐃ **Grand Teton Climbers' Ranch** (307-733-7271 June 1 through September 30 only; http://www.americanalpineclub.org/gtcr), 3 miles south of Jenny Lake on Teton Park Road. Open early June through early September; very inexpensive. Run by the American Alpine Club, a nonprofit climbing conservation and education organization, the Climbers' Ranch has provided climbers and their families with an affordable lodging option since 1970 (nonclimbers are welcome, too). The accommodations are dormitory style in small cabins sleeping four to eight people. Guests must bring their own sleeping bags, food, pillows, gear, cook-

ing equipment, and personal items. The ranch has a cooking area, hot showers, and toilets, as well as a small lounge and mountaineering library.

ᐃ **Jenny Lake Lodge** (1-800-628-9988 or 307-733-4647; http://www.gtlc.com/lodgeJen.aspx), along Jenny Lake Scenic Drive (see *To See*—Scenic Drives). Open late May through early October, very expensive. This top-rated, historic 1920s lodge includes 37 private cabins tucked into a lovely, forested setting near Jenny Lake. To make your western vacation experience more authentic, the décor follows a western theme, and you'll find nary a radio or television in your cabin—though you can request a phone. Included in your nightly rate is breakfast, a prix fixé, five-course gourmet dinner, horseback riding, and bicycling. Even if you are not staying as an overnight guest, you are welcome to enjoy a **fine dining** experience (including an award-winning wine list) at Jenny Lake Lodge (serving breakfast, lunch, and dinner); reservations are required for breakfast and dinner. See also Grand Teton Lodge Company in Campgrounds.

Moose
LODGING ☛ **Dornan's Spur Ranch Cabins** (307-733-2522 (cabins) or 733-2415 (main number); http://www.dornans.com), located off Teton Park Road between Moose and Moose Junction, before crossing the Snake River (12 miles from Jackson). Open year-round; expensive to very expensive. This family-owned resort features 8 one-bedroom and 4 two-bedroom riverside duplexes, each of which has a fully equipped kitchen and a large living/dining area. While small, this resort offers numerous amenities, including gas pumps; the award-winning **Wine Shoppe** offering **monthly wine tastings;** a grocery store and **deli;** cross-country ski and snowshoe rentals;

Adventure Sports (307-733-3307), which rents out canoes, kayaks, and mountain bikes in summer; and two restaurants (see below). See also Grand Teton Multi-Use Pathway in *To Do*—Bicycling.

DINING ✒ **Pizza Pasta Company,** run by Dornan's, is open 11:30–3 Monday through Friday and 11:30–5 Saturday and Sunday, plus Monday nights in summer season at 6 for the **Hootenany** (limited menu), which includes live entertainment and is open to the public. This restaurant serves a variety of pizzas, salads, pasta, sandwiches, and more. It has a children's menu as well. Moderate.

🍴 ✒ **Moose Chuckwagon,** run by Dornan's, is open from the first Saturday in June through Labor Day for breakfast (7–11), lunch (12–3), and dinner (5–8). This family-style restaurant has been serving up all-you-can-eat hearty western fare since 1948. Enjoy Wyoming beef from Dornan's own butcher shop, aged perfectly and cooked over an open fire in cast-iron Dutch ovens, along with a salad bar and more. Breakfast features famous all-you-can-eat sourdough pancakes, while lunch abounds with salads and sandwich choices. Moderate.

Triangle X Ranch
LODGING/ DINING ✒ **Triangle X Ranch** (307-733-2183; http://www.trianglex.com), 2 Triangle X Ranch Road, Moose, WY. Open mid-May through late October and late December through March; very expensive. Triangle X is a working dude ranch. During the summer, this family-owned and -operated ranch offers inclusive, dude ranch style vacations priced by the week (in summer season), which include lodging, meals, ranch activities, and horseback riding. The ranch also offers a number of activities not

included in the basic rate, including guided hunting and fishing trips, pack trips, scenic floats on the Snake River, snowmobiling, and cross-country skiing. In winter, guests must stay a minimum of two nights. From mid-May through early June and late August through late October, guests must stay a minimum of four nights. Rates are reduced (but still very expensive) during these times.

CAMPGROUNDS ♿ **Flagg Ranch Campground** (1-800-443-2311 or 307-543-2861; http://www.flaggranch.com), located 2 miles south of the border of Yellowstone National Park and 5 miles north of the border of Grand Teton National Park along the John D. Rockefeller Jr. Memorial Parkway. Open late May through late September, $50 (RV site), and $25 (tent site). This concessionaire-operated campground takes reservations (recommended, especially in summer months). See also Flagg Ranch Resort in *Lodging/Dining*.

♿ **Grand Teton Lodge Company** (1-800-628-9988 or 307-543-2811; http://www.gtlc.com/campgrounds.aspx), P.O. Box 250, Moran, 83013. This concessionaire operates several first-come, first-served campgrounds in the park, including **Colter Bay Campground** (open late May through late September; $19); **Gros Ventre Campground** (open early May through mid-October; $19); and **Jenny Lake Campground** (open mid-May through late September; $19).

Grand Teton National Park (see Guidance) has a number of designated **backcountry campsites** and backcountry camping zones. Backcountry camping is extremely popular and requires a permit. Advanced reservations ($25 service fee) are highly recommended, and must be made during the reservation period (January 1 through May 15) online, by faxing 307-739-3438, or by writing Grand Teton National Park, Permits Office, P.O. Drawer 170, Moose, 83012. Only a third of the sites can be reserved in advance, leaving two-thirds available for walk-in reservations. Walk-in permits (free) are available at Colter Bay Visitor Center and Craig Thomas Discovery and Visitor Center (see *To See*—Visitor Centers and Museums), and at the Jenny Lake Ranger Station (see Guidance). More information is available on the Web site, including the downloadable "Backcountry Trip Planner."

Signal Mountain Lodge (307-543-2831; http://www.signalmtnlodge.com) runs two first-come, first-served campgrounds on the shores of Jackson Lake: **Lizard Creek Campground** (open early June through late August; $18) and **Signal Mountain Campground** (open early May through mid-October; $20).

See also Colter Bay Village in *Lodging/Dining*.

Northwest Wyoming

2

CODY AND POWELL

I n Cody, the Old West lives on, and legends and local lore about Buffalo Bill and his contemporaries abound—with good reason. Born in Iowa, not only was William F. "Buffalo Bill" Cody (1846–1917) instrumental in the founding of Cody in 1896, but also, in his day, he was one of the most recognized and revered figures of the American West. The creator of the famous Wild West show, which toured the country and even went overseas (1883–1913), Cody was a figure of not merely national, but rather, international renown. Today's Cody maintains a strong bond with its historical namesake, with many of its attractions directly affiliated with Buffalo Bill, and many more indirectly connected in one way or another.

Cody isn't all about the Old West and the frontier days, though. In addition to calling itself the Home of Buffalo Bill, of equal import is the moniker Gateway to Yellowstone Park. On your way to or from this one-of-a-kind national park, you'll also find plenty of opportunities to explore and enjoy the vast tracts of incredible public lands surrounding Cody, whether on horseback, guided by an expert from one of the area's many guest and dude ranches, or on foot, by boat, or on wheels, depending on your preferred mode of travel. Coming back to civilization, you'll find that downtown Cody is a veritable paradise for shoppers in search of Western and Native American-themed souvenirs to remind them of their adventures, as well as being home to a number of great eateries (that even include a sushi bar!).

Cody's neighboring city, Powell, lies a scant 25 miles north and east. Named for noted scientist and explorer John Wesley Powell, Powell lies in a rich agricultural area, made so by the irrigation system that virtually created the town. Originally settled by workers brought to the area to create and implement a flood irrigation system for the Powell Valley, Powell and its environs today continue to rely heavily on agriculture, but with the added benefit of the recreational opportunities resulting from the Shoshone Irrigation Project, which include fishing, wildlife viewing, hunting, and more. Powell is also home to Northwest College (see *Special Events*).

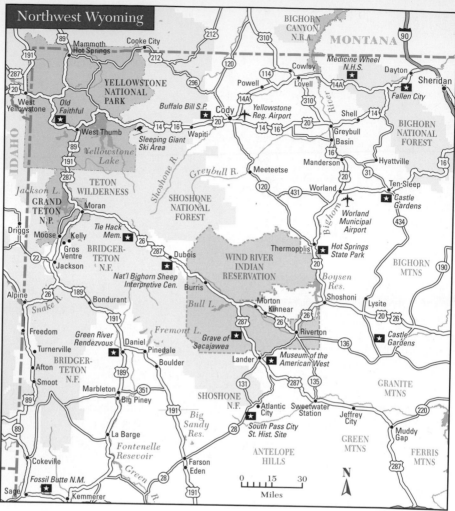

Northwest Wyoming

© The Countryman Press

GUIDANCE Cody Country Chamber of Commerce (307-587-2777; http://www
.codychamber.org), 836 Sheridan Avenue, Cody, 82414.

East Yellowstone Valley Chamber of Commerce (307-587-9595; http://www
.yellowstone-lodging.com), P.O. Box 21, Wapiti, 82450.

Park County Travel Council (1-800-393-2639 or 307-587-2297; http://www.yellow
stonecountry.org), Buffalo Bill's Cody/Yellowstone Country, P.O. Box 2454, Cody,
82414.

Powell Valley Chamber of Commerce (1-800-325-4278 or 307-754-3494;
http://www.powellchamber.org), 111 S. Day Street, Powell, 82435.

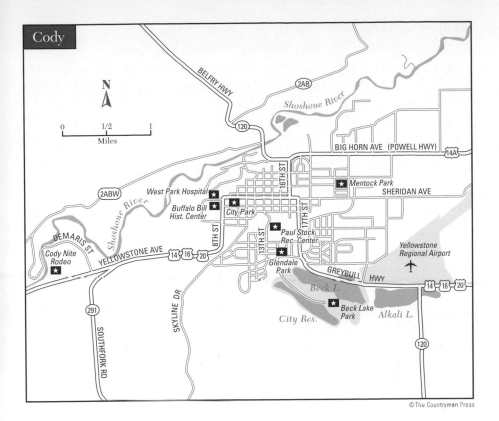

GETTING THERE *By car:* US 14/16/20 runs through Cody from east to west, while WY 120 runs through Cody from north to south. Powell is 25 miles northeast of Cody on US Alternate 14.

By plane: **Yellowstone Regional Airport** (307-587-5096; http://www.flyyra.com) is on the east side of Cody.

GETTING AROUND Both Cody and Powell have nice downtown shopping and dining areas that are perfect for strolling on foot, but you'll need to get back in your car to explore some this region's outlying attractions. In Cody, footsore travelers can also catch a ride on the handicapped-accessible **COLT! (Cody Over Land Transit)** from June through September, Monday through Saturday; $2 per person for unlimited all-day rides. The bus circles town once every 45 minutes, covering most of the city's most popular attractions. Go to http://www.codytrolley tours.com/Shuttle.cfm for a current bus schedule, or call 307-527-7043.

MEDICAL EMERGENCY Dial 911.

ExpressCare Clinic (307-754-7708), 450 Mountain View, Powell.

Powell Valley Hospital (307-754-2267), 777 Avenue H, Powell.

Urgent Care Clinic (307-587-7207), 424 Yellowstone Avenue, Cody.

West Park Hospital (1-800-654-9447 or 307-527-7501), 707 Sheridan Avenue, Cody.

✳ To See

TOWNS Meeteetse is a place where the Old West stays alive. The town still boasts wooden boardwalks, hitching rails, and water troughs along its streets. Formerly the home of Butch Cassidy, Meeteetse was also the site of the first cattle ranching operation in the Big Horn Basin, which was established by Otto Franc in 1879. Today's Meeteetse is a charming blend of well-kept turn-of-the-century structures combined with modern amenities. For more information: **Meeteetse Tourist Information Center** (307-868-2454; http://www.meeteetsewy.com), 1947 State Street, P.O. Box 238, Meeteetse, 82433.

MUSEUMS ⊛ **Buffalo Bill Dam Visitor Center** (307-527-6076; http://www .bbdvc.com), 6 miles west of Cody on US 14/16/20. Open 8–6 Monday through Saturday, 10–6 Sunday, May and September; 8–8 Monday through Friday, 8–6 Saturday, 10–6 Sunday, June through August; free. Interpretive displays and exhibits tell the story of the dam's engineering and construction as well as the natural history of the surroundings. You'll also find gorgeous views of Shoshone Canyon, Buffalo Bill Reservoir, and an impressive overlook of the dam. A self-guided audio tour is available for purchase as well ($4). See also Buffalo Bill State Park in *Green Space*—State Parks.

✑ ⅋ ⊛ **Buffalo Bill Historical Center** (307-587-4771; http://www.bbhc.org), 720 Sheridan Avenue, Cody. Open 10–5 daily April and mid-September through October; 8–6 daily May through September 15; 10–5 Thursday through Sunday, November through March; closed Thanksgiving, Christmas, and New Year's Day; $15 per adult, $13 per senior (65-plus), $13 per student (13–17 or 18-plus with college ID), $10 youth (5–10), children under 5 free, or $45 per family (one or two adults and their dependent children under 17). Admission covers two consecutive days of access to all five museums. One of Wyoming's top attractions, the Buffalo Bill Historical Center (BBHC) is actually a collection of five world-renowned museums and a research library, meaning that you should allot at the very least an entire day to exploring the treasure trove of exhibits held within its walls. These include the **Buffalo Bill Museum,** which celebrates and records the personal and public life of the legendary William "Buffalo Bill" Cody (1846–1917), from whom the town of Cody took its name; the **Plains Indian Museum,** which not only displays Indian objects, but also places them in context and interprets their historical, cultural, and current significance for visitors; the **Cody Firearms Museum,** home to the world's most complete collection of American firearms; the **Draper Museum of Natural History,** the center's newest museum, which strives to educate visitors about geology, wildlife, and human presence in the Greater Yellowstone region via interactive and engaging exhibits; the **Whitney Gallery of Western Art,** where you'll see original paintings and sculptures by artists past and present renowned for their abilities to capture the spirit and rugged beauty of the West; and the **Harold McCracken Research Library** (see also Buffalo Bill Historical Center and Cody Trolley Tours in *To Do*—Unique Adventures).

🦫 **Homesteaders Museum** (307-754-9481), 133 S. Clark Street, Powell. Open 10–4 Tuesday through Friday, 10–2 Saturday, mid-April through May 1; 10–5 Tuesday through Friday, 10–2 Saturday, early May through December; free. A collection of Indian artifacts, old tools, antique farm equipment, photographs, geological exhibits, and other pertinent memorabilia walks you through the history of the settlement of Powell and the Big Horn Basin.

🦫 **Meeteetse Museum** (307-868-2423); 1947 State Street, Meeteetse. Open 10–5 Monday through Saturday (summer), 10–4 Monday through Friday (winter); donations gladly accepted. It's suggested to call ahead for current hours. This museum includes exhibits on ranching, as well as a mount of one of the largest grizzlies ever known to come from the Yellowstone ecosystem. In the same location is the **Charles J. Belden Museum of Western Photography** (307-868-2264), which features photographs of early 20th-century life on the Pitchfork Ranch.

Museum of the Old West and Old Trail Town (307-587-5302; http://www .museumoftheoldwest.org), 1831 DeMaris Drive, (2 miles west of Cody off US 14/16/20), Cody. Open daily 8–8 mid-May through September; $6 per adult, $5 per senior, $2 per child 6–12. **Old Trail Town** features a collection of 26 historically significant structures dating from the late 19th to early 20th century, along with 100 horse-drawn vehicles. The **Museum of the Old West** contains numerous American Indian artifacts, plus a collection of items from Wyoming's frontier days. Highlighted here are some of the area's most notorious and flamboyant personalities from the past, making for a fun and informative visit.

Old West Miniature Village and Museum (307-587-5362; http://www .tecumsehs.com/museum.htm), 142 W. Yellowstone Avenue, Cody. Open daily 8–8 June through August, 9–6 May and September; by appointment in off-season; $5 per adult, $3 per child; children under 6 free. For a historically accurate bird's-eye view of the Old West at its wildest, this incredible collection of hand-carved figures suspended in action will not disappoint. From battles to buffalo hunts, you'll find it all captured here, along with artifacts from the Old West and items available for purchase at Tecumseh's Trading Post.

HISTORIC LANDMARKS, PLACES, AND SITES 🦫 **Meeteetse Bank Museum** (307-868-2423); 1033 Park Avenue, Meeteetse. Open by appointment; donations gladly accepted. Built from sun-dried bricks in 1900 for the banking firm of Hogg, Cheeseman, and McDonald, this historic structure is now listed on the National Register of Historic Places.

See also Meeteetse in *To See*—Towns; Museum of the Old West and Old Trail Town in *To See*—Museums; Pahaska Teepee in *Lodging*—Lodges; and Buffalo Bill's Irma Hotel in *Lodging*—Hotels and Motels.

CITY PARKS AND GARDENS ♿ **Beck Lake Park**, 2401 14th Street, Cody, features 2 miles of paved trails around two reservoirs, plus handicapped-accessible fishing piers, boating access, picnic tables, and great opportunities for wildlife viewing.

🐾 ♿ **Cody City Park**, located at 908 Sheridan is one of more than 20 parks in Cody managed by Cody's Parks and Recreation Department. At City Park, you'll find playgrounds, picnic areas, barbecue grills, a band shell for Cody's summer concert series, a tennis court, miniature golf, and restrooms. For a full, download-able map of Cody's parks, go to http://www.cityofcody.net/downloads/17/196.pdf. See also Homesteader Park in *To Do*—Snow Sports: Ice-skating.

SCENIC DRIVES Beartooth Scenic Byway runs for 64 miles on US 212 from Cooke City, Montana to Red Lodge, Montana, with much of the drive in Wyoming. Closed seasonally, it's easily accessed in Wyoming from WY 296, the Chief Joseph Scenic Byway (see below). This highway has been acclaimed the most beautiful highway in America by a number of people, due to the incredible scenery and unique natural features in the surrounding Gallatin National Forest, Shoshone National Forest, and Custer National Forest. Completed in 1936, this highway provides passers-through with the opportunity to witness the transforma-tion of the terrain outside from a green, subalpine forest to a true alpine environ-ment as they climb into the **Beartooth Range,** a mountain range with more than 20 peaks higher than 12,000 feet and numerous glaciers. Tremendous wildlife viewing prospects and recreational activities abound along this drive, including camping, fishing, hiking, picnicking, and bicycling for experienced road riders who want a high-altitude challenge.

Buffalo Bill Cody Scenic Byway is 27.5 miles long, stretching from 24 miles east of Cody at the border of Shoshone National Forest (see *Green Space*—National Lands) on US 14/16/20 (Yellowstone Highway) to the eastern border of Yellow-stone National Park. This drive begins at the border of the 2.4-million-acre Shoshone National Forest and follows the North Fork of the Shoshone River as it turns and twists through the rugged terrain of the Wapiti Valley, showcasing tower-ing formations of conglomerate rock and offering abundant opportunities for wildlife viewing, fishing, hiking, camping, and picnicking, as well as access to more than 10 historic guest lodges, including Pahaska Teepee (see *Lodging*—Lodges).

Chief Joseph Scenic Byway runs for 47 miles on WY 296, starting at its intersec-tion with WY 120 north of Cody and ending at its intersection with US 212 (Beartooth Scenic Byway, see above). A drive along the Chief Joseph Scenic Byway leads you through some of the land through which Chief Joseph and the Nez Perce Indians fled as they battled defensively in the late 1870s against soldiers, civilians, and even other Indians. Spectacular natural features include the Clarks Fork of the Yellowstone River (see *To See*—Fishing) and views of **Sunlight Basin** and **Sunlight Gorge.** Recreational opportunities include wildlife viewing, fishing, hiking, picnicking, and camping, among others.

NATURAL WONDERS See *To See*—Scenic Drives and Clarks Fork of the Yel-lowstone River in *To Do*—Fishing.

✳ To Do

BICYCLING 🐾 **Paul Stock Nature Trail** is accessible via River View Drive in Cody. Take the whole family for a fun, easy spin along this 1.3-mile, wide, gravel trail that parallels the Shoshone River just outside of downtown Cody. This moder-ate ride winds above the cottonwood-lined banks of the river, with side trails leading down for a closer look. See Cody City Park in *To See*—City Parks and Gardens for information on obtaining a map of Cody's city parks and paths (including this one), or stop in at the Cody Chamber of Commerce (see Guidance) for a map of local mountain bike trails.

See also Beck Lake Park in *To See*—City Parks and Gardens; Beartooth Scenic Byway in *To See*—Scenic Drives; Cedar Mountain in *To Do*—Climbing; Beartooth Loop National Recreation Trail in *To Do*—Hiking; and *Green Space*.

BOATING See Beck Lake Park in *To See*—City Parks and Gardens; Deaver Reservoir and Newton Lakes in *To Do*—Fishing; Buffalo Bill State Park in *Green Space*—State Parks; and Bureau of Land Management in *Green Space*—National Lands. .

CLIMBING **Cedar Mountain,** on the south side of US 14/16/20 just west of Cody, is home to some of the finest bouldering (climbing on boulders without ropes) in the United States. Some 1,000 sandstone boulder problems ranging from the easiest to double-digit grades pepper the side of the mountain (with more in the Sphinx area across the road). Like all rock climbing, bouldering should not be undertaken without proper training and equipment. Pick up a copy of the guidebook, written by the owner of The Beta Coffeehouse (see *Where to Eat*—Eating Out), either there or at Core Mountain Sports. Cedar Mountain is also a popular place for hikers and bicyclists.

✒ **Core Mountain Sports** (1-877-527-7354; http://www.coremountainsports.com), 1019 15th Street, Cody. At Core, you can try your hand at bouldering before you head outside on the indoor climbing wall. Core also offers guided rafting trips down the Shoshone River (see *To Do*—Paddling/Floating) and guided fishing trips, as well as climbing, paddling, and floating gear for sale. Core also serves as the Cody headquarters for Jackson Hole Mountain Guides (see below).

Ice climbing opportunities of the finest caliber begin in Cody as early as October and last as late as April. Hundreds of waterfalls in the South Fork Canyon of the Shoshone River (see *To Do*—Fishing) freeze up and form climbs, so if ascending frozen waterfalls is one of your favorite pastimes, Cody will not disappoint. For more information about ice climbing, as well as about current conditions (in season), visit http://www.coldfear.com or http://www.codyice.com, or call Sunlight Sports (307-587-9517) or the climbers' hostel, Bison Willy's (307-587-0629; http://www.bisonwillys.com;

BOULDERING ON CEDAR MOUNTAIN

see also *Lodging*—Other Options). See also Jackson Hole Mountain Guides (below) and Waterfall Ice Roundup in *Special Events*.

Jackson Hole Mountain Guides (307-250-0763; http://www.jhmg.com), inside Core Mountain Sports (see above). If you're new to rock climbing or need a refresher course, you can hire a guide here. JHMG takes students out to local Cody crags for half- ($110–195) or full-day ($160–375) climbing courses. Guided ice climbs are offered in winter. JHMG also offers a guided day hike to **Heart Mountain** ($250 for one person, $50 for each additional person). Reservations are recommended for all guide services.

Shoshone Canyon, west of Cody on US 14/16/20, is not only home to Cedar Mountain, but also, to dolomite and granite sport climbing.

See also Bureau of Land Management in *Green Space*—National Lands.

FISHING **Clarks Fork of the Yellowstone River** (307-527-7125; http://gf.state .wy.us/fish), located northwest of Cody along WY 292, WY 296, and US 212 in the Shoshone National Forest (see *Green Space*—National Lands). This river is known for its rainbow trout, mountain whitefish, brook trout, Yellowstone and Snake River cutthroat trout, grayling, brown trout, and some rainbow-cutthroat trout hybrids. The 22.5-mile portion of the river that is nationally designated as **Wild and Scenic** (Wyoming's only such river) runs through the awe-inspiring **Clarks Fork Canyon,** with its dramatic, upsweeping cliffs rising more than 1,000 feet above the canyon floor. Wildlife species abound here, including moose, mountain goats, marmots, and more. See also Shoshone River in *To Do*—Paddling/Floating.

Deaver Reservoir (307-527-7125; http://www.usbr.gov/gp/recreation/bbrrec2 .htm), 3 miles northwest of Deaver off WY 114. Open for fishing year-round; no entrance fee required. This 800-acre reservoir's fish species include catfish, trout, and walleye. The area also has picnic tables, boating (10hp or less), and wildlife viewing opportunities, and permits primitive camping (but no drinking water is available).

&. **Newton Lakes** (307-527-7125; http://www.usbr.gov/gp/recreation/bbrrec3.htm), 5 miles northwest of Cody off WY 120. Open for fishing year-round; no entrance fee required. Known for its trophy trout fishing accessible via both boat and shore-line, this area also features picnicking, swimming, wildlife viewing, and tube float-ing. No drinking water is available, and no overnight camping is permitted.

Shoshone River (307-527-7125; http://gf.state.wy.us/fish). The North Fork of this river flows from Yellowstone Lake in Yellowstone National Park east along US 14/16/20 west of Cody in the Shoshone National Forest (see *Green Space*— National Lands) to the Buffalo Bill Reservoir (see *Green Space*—State Parks), eventually merging with the Bighorn River in Bighorn Lake (see Bighorn Canyon National Recreation Area in *Green Space*—Recreation Areas in Thermopolis and Worland). It is closed from Buffalo Bill Reservoir up to and including Newton Creek from April 1 through July 1 in order to protect spawning runs of rainbow trout and Yellowstone cutthroat trout. Species include brook trout, brown trout, mountain whitefish, rainbow trout, rainbow-cutthroat hybrids, and Yellowstone cutthroat trout. The South Fork starts high in the Absaroka Mountains in the Shoshone National Forest, and then flows along WY 291 southwest of Cody to Buffalo Bill Reservoir. Species include brook trout, brown trout, rainbow trout, mountain whitefish, and Yellowstone cutthroat trout. Many marked fishing access sites lie along the roads paralleling both forks of this river. See also Paul Stock Nature Trail in *To Do*—Bicycling and Shoshone River in *To Do*—Paddling/Floating.

See also Beck Lake Park in *To See*—City Parks and Gardens; Beartooth Scenic Byway, Buffalo Bill Cody Scenic Byway, and Chief Joseph Scenic Byway in *To See*—Scenic Drives; Core Mountain Sports in *To Do*—Climbing; *Green Space*; and Absaroka Mountain Lodge in *Lodging*—Lodges.

FITNESS CENTERS ✔ ♿ **Paul Stock Aquatic and Recreation Center** (307-587-0400; http://www.cityofcody-wy.gov/parks_recreation.cfm?id=31), 1402 Heart Mountain Street/P.O. Box 2200, Cody. Open 5:30 AM–10 PM Monday through Thursday (pool open until 8 PM), 5:30 AM–8 PM Friday (pool open until 7:45 PM), 8 AM–6 PM Saturday (pool open noon–5:45), and noon–6 Sunday (pool open noon–5:45); $6 per adult (Park County resident), $10 per adult (nonresident), $4 per student (resident ages 16+), $3 per child (resident), $5 per child/student (nonresident). Part of the **Cody Quad Center,** which includes the Victor J. Riley Arena and Community Events Center (see *To Do*—Snow Sports: Ice-skating), this full-scale recreation center includes a pool (with waterslide), exercise machines, hot tub, wet steam room, walking/jogging track, weights, racquetball courts, childcare options (extra fee for nonresidents), and more.

FOR FAMILIES ✔ **Cody Nite Rodeo** (1-800-207-0744 or 307-587-5155; http://www.codystampederodeo.com), Cody. Nightly at 8 (gates open at 7), June 1 through August 31; $18 per adult, $8 per child ages 7–12; children 6 and under free. Entertaining visitors to Cody for more than 70 years, the Cody Nite Rodeo features numerous PRCA-sanctioned rodeo events such as saddle bronc riding, team roping, and barrel racing, among others.

✔ ♞ **Cody Gunfighters** (307-587-4221; http://www.codygunfighters.com), on the porch of Buffalo Bill's Irma Hotel (see *Lodging*—Other Options Cody), at 6 PM Monday through Saturday, June through September; free. Every night during the summer, you can watch reenactments of famous gun battles and shootouts by infamous characters of the Old West, as well as related historic presentations, courtesy of the Cody Gunfighters.

See also Buffalo Bill Historical Center in *To See*—Museums; Cody City Park in *To See*—City Parks and Gardens; Paul Stock Nature Trail in *To Do*—Bicycling; Core Mountain Sports in *To Do*—Climbing; Paul Stock Aquatic and Recreation Center in *To Do*—Fitness Centers; Bill Cody Ranch, Cedar Mountain Trail Rides, and Ishawooa Outfitters in *To Do*—Horseback Riding; Shoshone River in *To Do*—Paddling/Floating; Ice-skating in *To Do*—Snow Sports; Absaroka Mountain Lodge, Pahaska Teepee, and Shoshone

CODY NITE RODEO

Lodge Guest Ranch in *Lodging*—Lodges; Cody KOA Campground in *Lodging*—Campgrounds; Buffalo Bill Chuckwagon Show and Dan Miller's Cowboy Music Revue in *Entertainment*; and Buffalo Bill Cody Stampede Rodeo in *Special Events*.

GOLF Olive Glenn Golf and Country Club (307-587-5551; http://www.olive glenngolf.com), 802 Meadow Lane Avenue, Cody, 18 holes.

Powell Golf Club (307-754-7259; http://www.powellgolfclub.com), 600 WY 114, Powell, 18 holes.

HIKING Beartooth Loop National Recreation Trail (#619), in the Shoshone National Forest (see *Green Space*—National Lands) can be accessed via three trailheads—Hauser Lake Trailhead, Gardner Lake Trailhead, and Dollar Lake Trailhead (accessible via 4WD or ATV only)—all of which are just off US 212 northwest of Cody (Beartooth Scenic Byway in Wyoming, see *To See*—Scenic Drives). Even hiking just a short portion of this 14.4-mile trail will bring you a little bit closer to the beautiful scenery of the rugged **Beartooth Mountains.** With little elevation change, this trail makes for relatively easy walking, allowing you to really enjoy the fresh mountain air and views of the surrounding mountains. Motorized vehicles, horses, and mountain bikes are also permitted on much of this trail.

Trout Creek Nature Trail is located in Buffalo Bill State Park (see *Green Space*—State Parks) near the group camping area of the North Shore Campground. Take a .25-mile stroll through a riparian area located on the west side of Trout Creek along the Shoshone River, observing the unique features characteristic of this type of habitat. Also at Buffalo Bill State Park, you'll find **Eagle Point Trail** (handicapped-accessible), a short and easy jaunt located within the Eagle Point Day Use Area.

See also Beck Lake Park in *To See*—City Parks and Gardens; Beartooth Scenic Byway, Buffalo Bill Cody Scenic Byway, and Chief Joseph Scenic Byway in *To See*—Scenic Drives; Paul Stock Nature Trail in *To Do*—Bicycling; Cedar Mountain and Jackson Hole Mountain Guides in *To Do*—Climbing; and *Green Space*.

HORSEBACK RIDING ⚘ 🐾 **Bill Cody Ranch** (1-800-615-2934 or 307-587-2097; http://www.billcodyranch.com), 2604 Yellowstone Highway, Cody. Open mid-May through early October; $50 per person for a two-hour morning or evening ride. With more than 70 horses on hand, this dude ranch offers expert horseback rides through beautiful terrain. Other ride options include half-day rides ($80 per person) and all-day cookout rides ($140 per person). Lodging (very expensive; no minimum stay required) and dining (expensive) are also available on this lovely ranch situated halfway between Cody and Yellowstone National Park.

⚘ **Cedar Mountain Trail Rides** (307-527-4966 or 307-587-7313), 12 Spirit Mountain Road or at Cody KOA Campground (see *Lodging*—Campgrounds), Cody. Open June through August. You can choose from a ride as short as an hour or go for a day—or longer. Specialties include guided fishing and wildlife viewing forays. Call for current rates and to make reservations.

⚘ **Ishawooa Outfitters** (1-888-801-9250 or 307-587-9250; http://www.ishawooa outfitters.com), Cody. For families and other travelers who wish they'd planned a

multiday pack trip ahead of time but didn't, Ishawooa is usually able to accommodate last-minute requests for overnight pack trips, departing on the following
morning ($300 per person per day; two-day minimum). Ishawooa also guides fish-
ing trips. See also McCullough Peaks Herd Management Area in Wilder Places—
Wildlife Refuges and Areas.

See also *Green Space*—National Lands; and Absaroka Mountain Lodge, Pahaska
Teepee, and Shoshone Lodge Guest Ranch in *Lodging*—Lodges.

PADDLING/FLOATING ✄ ⚓ **Shoshone River** (see *To Do*—Fishing), outside of
Cody, offers some of the finest whitewater in the state of Wyoming. For the less-
experienced paddler, Cody has several guiding services that can help you plan a
safe and fun family adventure on the river. These include **River Runners** (1-800-
535-7238; http://www.riverrunnersofwyoming.com), 1491 Sheridan Avenue, Cody;
offering three daily departures June 1 through August 30 ($28 per adult and $24
per child under 13; reservations recommended), and **Wyoming River Trips** (1-
800-586-6661 or 307-587-6661; http://www.wyomingrivertrips.com), Buffalo Bill
Village-Holiday Inn Complex and 233 US 14/16/20 (by Wal-Mart), offering two or
three daily departures from May 1 through August 30 ($27 per adult and $25 per
child under 13; reservations recommended); handicapped-accessible trips available
as well. See also Core Mountain Sports in *To Do*—Climbing.

See also Newton Lakes in *To Do*—Fishing; and *Green Space*.

RELAXATION AND REJUVENATION Here. **Yoga for the Well Spirit** (307-
899-3147; http://www.hereyogacody.com), 2532 E. Sheridan Avenue, Cody. Open
year-round with classes Monday through Saturday; price varies according to class.
Call or visit the Web site for a current schedule of classes. Yoga is taught in the
Iyengar and Power yoga traditions. Beginners are welcome.

Whole Foods Trading Co. (307-587-3213), 1239 Rumsey Avenue, Cody. Open
9:30–5:30 Monday through Saturday. Not affiliated with the national grocer of a
similar name, this independent natural foods store carries organic products as well
as supplements, books, and related accessories.

11th Street Spa (307-527-7123; http://www.11thstreetspa.com), 1208 11th Street,
Cody. This full-service day spa offers hair care (cuts, colors, weaves, perms), nail
care (manicures, pedicures, artificial nails), tanning, waxing, ear piercing, facials,
and a wide range of massage treatments ($50–65 per hour), all for reasonable
rates.

See also Paul Stock Aquatic and Recreation Center in *To Do*—Fitness Centers.

SNOW SPORTS Cross-country skiing and snowshoeing opportunities can be
found throughout this region in wintertime. In addition to many miles of
ungroomed trails, you'll find a number of groomed and marked trails. These
include the **Wood River Valley Ski Touring Park** (307-868-2603; http://www
.meetrec.org/wrski/wrski.html), 22 miles southwest of Meeteetse in the Shoshone
National Forest (see *Green Space*—National Lands), with roughly 15 miles of
groomed and backcountry trails open daily October through April; free (donations
gladly accepted). See also *To Do*—Hiking; Sleeping Giant Ski Area (below);
Bureau of Land Management in *Green Space*—National Lands; and Pahaska
Tepee in *Lodging*—Lodges.

Ice Fishing is possible on many of this region's frozen lakes and ponds come wintertime. For ideas about where to go, see listings in *To Do*—Boating and *To Do*—Fishing.

§ **Ice-skating** can be found in Cody at the **Victor J. Riley Arena and Community Events Center** (307-587-1681; http://www.codyicearena.com), 1400 Heart Mountain Street, P.O. Box 1902. Open October through March for public skating; hours vary, please call or check Web site for current schedule. In off-season (March through October), this space is used for special events. In Powell, **Homesteader Park** (307-754-5711; http://www.powellrec.com), 501 Homesteader Court, is open for ice-skating daily in season from 11 AM–10 PM, with skate rentals/concessions open 1–5 Friday and Sunday and 11–5 Saturday.

Sleeping Giant Ski Area (307-587-3125; http://www.yellowstonerec.com), Yellowstone Recreations Foundation, 348 Yellowstone Highway/P.O. Box 400, Cody; located 48 miles west of Cody on US 14/16/20. One of America's oldest ski resorts, Sleeping Giant has been around since 1936-7, but just reopened its doors for the 2009–10 ski season after several years of not operating. Standout attractions include ample natural snowfall, great temperatures, and little wind. Snowboards are permitted on all trails. Lifts: one rope tow and one double chair lift. Trails: 17 trails—20 percent beginner, 40 percent intermediate, 40 percent advanced. Vertical drop: 900 feet. Facilities: The area has a heated day lodge with a snack bar. Ski school: Offers lessons for all ages and ability levels. Cross-country skiing is available as well. Rates: Please call for current rates. See also Pahaska Tepee in *Lodging*—Lodges.

Snowmobiling is popular in this region, with incredible trail systems found throughout the region's national forests (see *Green Space*—National Lands), as well as close proximity to snowmobiling in Yellowstone National Park (see *To Do*—Snowmobiling in Yellowstone National Park). For detailed trail reports, call 307-777-6560 or go to http://wyotrails.state.wy.us/snow, the Wyoming Snowmobile Trails Web site, which also provides information about rules, rental agencies, trails around the state, and more.

See also Ice Climbing in *To Do*—Climbing and *Green Space*—National Lands.

UNIQUE ADVENTURES Buffalo Bill Historical Center and Cody Trolley Tours (307-587-4771; http://www.bbhc.org/tours/trolleyTours_01.cfm), 720 Sheridan Avenue, Cody. Open June 1 through late September; $32 per adult/senior, $18 children 6–17, price includes admission to the center. Spice up your visit to the Buffalo Bill Historical Center (see *To See*—Museums) with this interpretive, one-hour, 24-mile trolley tour that spotlights historical sites, geological sites, wildlife, and more, complete with hands-on objects of interest and two live narrators.

WINERIES AND WINE TASTINGS 🍷 **Juniper** (307-587-4472; http://www.junipershop.com), 30 Pearson Avenue, Cody. Open 11–6, Tuesday through Saturday. Tucked away in an industrial complex on the north side of Cody, Juniper seems an unlikely place for a wine bar. As you wend your way away from town and through the sheet-metal buildings, you might wonder if you're headed in the right direction. Don't worry—you are! Once you walk through the door of this elegant escape, you'll feel like you're jumping through a magical hatchway into a chic world of artisan-made arts and crafts. Browse through the store's eclectic collection, and then meander back to the wine bar to taste whatever's on today's printed menu. Samples range from $2 to $5 per taste. You'll receive not only a write-up of the wines on tap, but also, a separate sheet to make your own tasting notes. Knowledgeable staff people will help guide you to the wines you might enjoy, and they will also help you shop for wines to take home with you when you're done tasting.

✴ Green Space

STATE PARKS 🐾 ♿ **Buffalo Bill State Park** (307-587-9227; http://wyoparks .state.wy.us/Site/SiteInfo.asp?siteID=3), 47 Lakeside Road, Cody. Open 24 hours year-round for day use ($4/resident; $6/nonresident) and May 1 through September 30 for camping ($10/resident; $17/nonresident; reservations taken for some sites). Located about 9 miles west of Cody on US 14/16/20 (Yellowstone Highway), Buffalo Bill State Park provides visitors with an array of recreational opportunities including camping, hiking, fishing, windsurfing, boating (three boat ramps), wildlife viewing, scenic vistas, picnicking, and bicycling, to name a few. Surrounded by mountains and including **Buffalo Bill Reservoir,** with its 40 miles of shoreline, the park is an outdoor-lover's paradise. The lake, with its 8,000 acres of surface area, contains brown trout, cutthroat trout, mackinaw trout, and rainbow trout, with easy access from roads along the shoreline. The park also has two campgrounds—**North Shore Bay Campground** and **North Fork Campground.** See also Buffalo Bill Dam Visitor Center in *To See*—Museums and Trout Creek Nature Trail in *To Do*—Hiking.

NATIONAL LANDS Bureau of Land Management (BLM) (307-578-5900; http://www.blm.gov/wy/st/en/field_offices/Cody.html), 1002 Blackburn Avenue, Cody. The Cody Field Office manages 1.1 million acres of public lands and 1.5 million acres of federal mineral estate in this region. Much of the lands administered by the BLM are open to recreational pursuits, including bicycling, boating, camping (both primitive and developed; most developed campgrounds are handicapped accessible), fishing, hiking (portions of the 3,100-mile long **Continental Divide National Scenic Trail** pass through sections of Wyoming's BLM land; see http://www.cdtrail.org for details), horseback riding, paddling, rock climbing, wildlife viewing (including wild horses), and snow sports, including snowmobiling and cross-country skiing. BLM lands tend to be the most unregulated of public lands, meaning that most typical outdoor recreational pursuits are allowed on most BLM lands, guided by the dictates of Leave No Trace (1-800-332-4100 or 303-442-8222; http://www.lnt.org) outdoor ethics. To find out additional general information about the BLM lands in this region, including maps, developed campgrounds, and other recreational pursuits, contact the field office. See also *Lodging*—Campgrounds.

BUFFALO BILL RESERVOIR

Shoshone National Forest (307-527-6921; http://www.fs.fed.us/r2/shoshone), 203A Yellowstone Avenue, Cody. Created in 1891 as the Yellowstone National Reserve, Shoshone National Forest enjoys not only the distinction of being America's first national forest, but also, one of the largest national forests in the Rocky Mountain Region. The forest encompasses more than 2.4 million acres of land, stretching from the northern border of Wyoming south to Lander and bordering Yellowstone National Park on the west. This forest includes portions of the Absaroka and Beartooth Mountain Ranges in the area surrounding Cody, as well as part or all of five designated wilderness areas. Recreational opportunities abound, including hiking, fishing, camping, picnicking, horseback riding, wildlife viewing, boating, snowmobiling, and more. See also *Lodging*—Campgrounds.

WILDLIFE REFUGES AND AREAS McCullough Peaks Herd Management Area is located between 12 to 27 miles east of Cody along US 14/16/20. This BLM-managed (see *Green Space*—National Lands) Herd Management Area (HMA), one of a number in Wyoming, is home to an estimated 450 wild horses. Encompassing nearly 110,000 acres, the HMA also contains the McCullough Peaks Wilderness Study Area. Even if you don't see any of the horses, be sure to bring your camera along to take some photos of the desolate, yet somehow strikingly beautiful, badlands of the Wilderness Study Area, and stop at the **Wild Horse Interpretive Site** along US 14/16/20 several miles before the intersection with WY 32 to learn a little more about Wyoming's herds. See also Ishawooa Outfitters in *To Do*—Horseback Riding; and Bighorn Canyon National Recreation Area in *Green Space*—National Lands in Thermopolis and Worland.

OTHER WILD PLACES ⚲ **Ralston Reservoir Facilities** (307-527-7125; http://www.usbr.gov/gp/recreation/bbrrec4.htm), 15 miles northeast of Cody off US 14 Alternate, free. A walkway and bridge provide visitors with access to tremendous wildlife viewing opportunities, particularly wetland species and waterfowl including sandhill cranes, pelicans, and ducks. This area has no overnight camping, restroom facilities, or drinking water.

✳ Lodging

BED AND BREAKFASTS

Cody

Angel's Keep (1-877-320-2800 or 307-587-6205; http://www.angelskeepbandb .com), 1241 Wyoming Avenue. Billed as the most fun you've ever had in church, Angel's Keep offers its guests lodging in a 1930s church just four blocks from downtown Cody. Rate includes a gourmet country breakfast and fresh-baked cookies served daily. Moderate to expensive.

⁍ **The Lambright Place** (1-800-241-5310 or 307-527-5310; http://www .lambrightplace.com), 1501 Beck

Avenue. Constructed in 1924 for Cody Mayor P. E. Markham, this beautiful B&B has three guest rooms that come with queen-sized beds and private baths, as well as a separate bunkhouse that sleeps five (a queen-sized bed and three single beds). You can enjoy a hearty breakfast served in the dining room or grab a speedy breakfast if you're rarin' to go. Expensive.

⁍ **The Mayor's Inn Bed & Breakfast** (1-888-217-3001 or 307-587-0887; http://www.mayorsinn.com), 1413

Rumsey Avenue. Sleep in the very same house—or rather, mansion—that was built from 1905–9 for Cody's first elected mayor, Frank L. Houx. Moved to its present location in 1997 and restored to its full historical splendor with modern amenities, this B&B offers five guest rooms (including a detached carriage house behind the main building) that come with a full breakfast included. Moderate to very expensive. See also *Where to Eat—Dining Out.*

🍴 ☃ Robin's Nest Bed & Breakfast (1-866-723-7797 or 307-527-7208; http://www.robinsnestcody.com), 1508 Alger Avenue. Getting away from the hustle and bustle of Cody's downtown is easy if you stay at the Robin's Nest, where two blocks make a world of difference. Stepping inside this B&B brings you in touch with the West through numerous vintage photographs, Indian weavings, and other such trappings, many of which are available for purchase. Dogs are welcome but arrangements must be made in advance. Three guest rooms all include private baths and a full breakfast. Expensive.

Powell

Aspen House B&B (307-754-2468; http://www.aspenhousebnb.com), 783 Road 12, Powell. In a rural area 4 miles from Powell, you'll find this new B&B, which has two bedrooms (shared bath). Enjoy beautiful views plus easy access to nearby attractions in a peaceful, away-from-it-all setting. A complete breakfast is included, and a complete supper can be requested (extra charge). Moderate.

LODGES

Cody

𝄓 Absaroka Mountain Lodge (307-587-3963; http://www.absarokamtlodge.com), 1231 Yellowstone Highway.

Open mid-May through September; expensive. Built in 1910, Absaroka's historic lodge offers a central gathering place for the activities you'll find available here, which include horseback riding, trout fishing (specializing in fly fishing), and more. Sleep in one of 18 cabins, with varying amenities. Adults and children (6 and up) can also saddle up for a number of horseback riding adventures (starting at $55 for two and one-half hours) offered here daily. The lodge's restaurant serves breakfast (7–9, daily) and dinner (6–8, closed Sunday); moderate to expensive.

♿ Pahaska Teepee (1-800-628-7791 or 307-527-7701; http://www.pahaska.com), 183 Yellowstone Highway. Included on the National Register of Historic Places, Buffalo Bill's original 1904 hunting lodge today offers visitors rustic, cabin-style accommodations (beware: no television included!) near Yellowstone National Park's East Entrance. Pahaska offers guided trail rides (June through August), fishing trips, overnight trips, and more. Also on the premises you'll find a restaurant, gift shop, and an antique bar that dates back to 1872. Pahaska Teepee also has a 12-mile (20-km) groomed cross-country skiing trail system connecting the lodge with the Sleeping Giant Ski Area (see *To Do—Snow Sports*). In addition, the lodge offers snowmobile rentals and guided snowmobile excursions through the East Entrance of Yellowstone National Park. See also Buffalo Bill Cody Scenic Byway in *To See—Scenic Drives.* Moderate to very expensive.

𝄓 Shoshone Lodge Guest Ranch (307-587-4044; http://www.shoshonelodge.com), 349 Yellowstone Highway (46 miles from Cody and 3 miles from Yellowstone National Park's East Entrance). Open May through mid-October. Lodge activities include horseback riding (from $35/one hour;

children 6 and up are welcome), pack trips, and hunting. Meals are available for moderate prices in the main lodge, and children can play on the on-premises playground. Reserve a one-, two- or three-bedroom log cabin—rustic on the outside, modern on the inside, each with a private bath. Inclusive vacation packages are available. Expensive. The lodge has a restaurant that serves breakfast and dinner (open to the public; moderate).

HOTELS AND MOTELS
Cody
Buffalo Bill's Irma Hotel (1-800-745-4762 or 307-587-4221; http://www .irmahotel.com), 1192 Sheridan Avenue. Named in honor of Buffalo Bill Cody's youngest daughter, the Irma was constructed in 1902 out of local building materials, including sandstone quarried from nearby Beck Lake (see *To See*—City Parks and Gardens). Listed on the National Register of Historic Places, today's Irma Hotel gives you the best of both worlds, offering rooms with modern amenities in a one-of-a-kind historical setting—if you want, you can even reserve Buffalo Bill's own suite. Centrally located in downtown Cody just off the main drag, the Irma makes for a great place to start your exploration of the Old West. Moderate to expensive. Also on the premises, you can dine at the **Irma Restaurant Grill,** where you'll find tasty western fare served for breakfast, lunch, and dinner (expensive). See also Cody Gunfighters in *To Do*—For Families and Cody Wild West Days in *Special Events*.

CAMPGROUNDS ✿ ⅙ BLM Campgrounds (see Bureau of Land Management in *Green Space*—National Lands) in this region include the first-come, first-served, five-site **Hogan and Luce Campground** (open May 1

BUFFALO BILL'S IRMA HOTEL

through December 14; free), located 18 miles north of Cody off WY 120, then 5 miles west on County Road (CR) 7RP to signed left turn for trailhead, 1 mile to campground. You should also know that in general, primitive camping is permitted on most BLM lands unless otherwise marked. See also Five Springs Falls Trail in *To Do*—Hiking.

"↑" ✐ **Cody KOA Campground** (1-800-562-8507; http://www.codykoa .com), 5561 Greybull Highway, Cody. Seasonal. Whether you're looking for a deluxe RV site, a cabin/lodge, or a simple place to pitch your tent, you'll find it here—and more. This KOA comes complete with an activity director ready to help you plan your stay in Cody, whether you want to go horseback riding, visit Yellowstone National Park, or go whitewater rafting. Inexpensive to expensive.

⅙ **Shoshone National Forest** (see Wilder Places—Forests) has three ranger districts in this region with more than 20 seasonal developed campgrounds. The Clarks Fork Ranger District (307-527-6921) has eight first-come, first-served campgrounds, and one that accepts advance reservations (1-877-444-6777 or http://www.recreation.gov), near Cody (along US 212 and WY 296), with daily fees ranging from $10–20. The Wapiti Ranger District (307-527-6921) has six first-come, first-served campgrounds and three that accept advance reservations (four handicapped accessible) near Cody (along US 14/16/20), with daily fees ranging from free to $20. The Greybull Ranger District (307-527-6921) has three first-come, first-served campgrounds west of Meeteetse, all of which are free of charge. Camping season (meaning services like water and trash pickup) generally opens Memorial Day and runs through the end of September, though camping is permitted in some campgrounds during the off-season. In addition to the developed campgrounds, dispersed camping (free) is permitted throughout much of the forest. Visit the Web site or call the associated ranger office for maps and information.

See also Beartooth Scenic Byway, Buffalo Bill Cody Scenic Byway, and Chief Joseph Scenic Byway in *To See*—Scenic Drives; Deaver Reservoir in *To Do*—Fishing; and Buffalo Bill State Park in *Green Space*—State Parks.

OTHER OPTIONS
Cody
🐾 🐕 ¡¡ **Bison Willy's** (307-587-0629; http://www.bisonwillys.com), 1625 Alger Avenue. This is the best deal you will find for lodging in Cody. Enjoy dormitory-style lodging at its finest, complete with a kennel for Fido, plus a full kitchen, laundry, barbecue, and more, all within walking distance of Cody's bustling downtown. Very inexpensive to inexpensive.

Cody Lodging Company (1-800-587-6560 or 307-587-6000; http://www.codyguesthouses.com), 1102 Beck Avenue. An assortment of cozy getaways from cottages to vacation homes is available for booking through Cody Lodging Company, as well as bed and breakfast accommodations.

See also Bill Cody Ranch in *To Do*—Horseback Riding.

¡¡ **Cross Five Retreats** (1-888-587-2764 or 307-587-2764; http://www.crossfiveretreats.com), Cody. Unwind in the private comfort of your own unique, fully furnished retreat in one of these new (2010) Cody vacation rental properties. Choices include the Coop (a two-bedroom, one-bathroom home that sleeps up to 6, complete with a fire pit and private backyard), Little Blue (a cozy two-bedroom, one-bathroom cottage that sleeps up to 4), and Daddy's Ranch (a historic property with 360-degree mountain views and absolutely luxurious accommodations that can sleep up to 12 people). Very expensive.

✳ Where to Eat

EATING OUT
Cody
Adriano's Italian Restaurant (307-527-7320), 1244 Sheridan Avenue. Open for lunch and dinner; call for current hours/days. Enjoy homemade pasta, salads, and other genuine Italian specialties . . . yup, right here in the heart of the Old West. It may be a little lacking in décor department, but the authenticity of the food makes up for it. Moderate.

The Beta Coffee House (307-587-7707), 1132 12th Street. Open early morning to early evening year-round; hours/days vary according to season. Just off the main drag and across the street from the Irma Hotel (see

Lodging—Hotels and Motels) sits the finest coffee joint in town. Run by avid rock climbers Mike and Meg Snyder (look for portraits of both Snyders in action on the walls), the Beta serves not only coffee, tea, smoothies, and specialty drinks, but also fantastic baked goods and homemade soup in winter. Enjoy the rotating exhibitions of artwork by local and regional artists or grab a seat on the couch and flip through a magazine while you sip your brew. Inexpensive.

The Breadboard (307-527-5788), 1725 17th Street. Open daily for three meals. For a quick, freshly prepared lunch, stop in at The Breadboard, where a huge selection of sub sandwiches is sure to make your mouth water, from the meatiest of meaty to vegetarian options. Soups, espresso, and bagels are also on the menu. Inexpensive.

✎ ❦ **Granny's Restaurant** (307-587-4829), 1550 Sheridan Avenue. Open 24 hours. Perfect for families, this restaurant serves hearty breakfasts all day long as well as lots of other classic American diner fare. An extensive menu virtually guarantees that everyone will find something that suits their tastes, while those on a budget will appreciate the moderate prices. Inexpensive to moderate.

❦ **Our Place** (307-527-4420), 148 Yellowstone Avenue. Open daily for breakfast and lunch/brunch. Serving up old-fashioned, hearty American breakfasts—and 25-cent coffee—is what Our Place is all about. Sit down and enjoy a delicious breakfast or lunch in this unassuming but oh-so-popular eatery on the western side of town. Inexpensive.

❦ **Shiki** (307-527-7116), 1420 Sheridan Avenue. Open daily for lunch and dinner (only dinner on Saturday); closed Sunday in winter. Yes, it's amazing—a genuine sushi bar and Japanese restaurant in Cody. Better yet, it's actually quite good, with fresh fish flown in several times each week, resulting in creative sushi specials that tantalize. If raw fish isn't your thing, plenty of other (cooked) options are available. Moderate to expensive.

❦ **Silver Dollar Bar** (307-527-7666; http://www.codysilverdollarbar.com), 1313 Sheridan Avenue. Open daily for lunch and dinner; happy hour 5 PM–7 PM Monday through Friday. Pull up a barstool and order the Silver Dollar Burger—you won't be disappointed. Or else choose from an array of appetizers (yes, they serve Rocky Mountain oysters), salads, wraps, and more, accompanied by a drink from the full bar. The Dollar also has pool tables and live music (9 PM–1:30 AM) every Friday and Saturday night. Inexpensive to moderate.

See also Shoshone Lodge Guest Ranch in *Lodging*—Lodges and Buffalo Bill Chuckwagon Show in *Entertainment*.

THE BETA COFFEE HOUSE: CODY'S PREMIER COFFEE SHOP

Cody

Cassie's Supper Club and Dance Hall (307-527-5500; http://www.cassies.com), 214 Yellowstone Avenue. Open 11 AM–10 PM daily. A Cody fixture since 1922, Cassie's is the place in Cody to go for a delicious, aged to perfection, and cut-to-order steak or prime rib, served with a relish tray, homemade bread, and soup of the day or fresh garden salad, as well as your choice of baked potato, steak fries, rice, or pasta. Other menu items include seafood and chicken selections. Three levels of dining space, three bars, and a large dance floor incorporate parts of the club's original structure and décor. West the Band—which includes among its members Cassie's' owner, operator, and head chef, Steve Singer—plays Friday and Saturday nights starting at 10 PM throughout the year. Expensive.

The Mayor's Inn Dinner House (307-587-0887; http://www.mayorsinn dinnerhouse.com), 1413 Rumsey Avenue, Cody. Located with the historic Mayor's Inn Bed & Breakfast (See *Lodging*), this elegant restaurant serves dinner Thursday through Saturday, with seating beginning at 5 (reservations appreciated). Entrée selections can include buffalo rib eye steak, wild sockeye salmon, and roasted duckling. Delectable appetizers and desserts and an extensive selection of wine and spirits make this a perfect choice for a romantic meal. Expensive.

Proud Cut Saloon (307-527-6905), 1227 Sheridan Avenue. Open daily for lunch and dinner. Known for its knowledge of beef, the Proud Cut is a great place to sit down for a fine prime rib or steak dinner. Also on the menu, you'll find chicken, fish, hamburgers, and ribs. Expensive.

The Terrace (307-587-5868), 525 W. Yellowstone Avenue. Open for dinner 4–11 Monday through Saturday (bar open until midnight). This recent (2009) arrival on the Cody fine dining scene offers an edge-of-town dining experience in an open space pleasantly divided by simple screens. The bar has 21 beers on tap (and many more in bottles). Friendly servers will help you decide which tantalizing meal to devour, with choices including lamb, seafood, chicken, and pork. Creative salads, appetizers, and desserts round out the menu. Moderate to expensive.

Wyoming's Rib and Chop House (307-527-7731; http://www.ribandchop house.com), 1367 Sheridan Avenue. Open daily for lunch and dinner. Here you'll find fantastic Western fare ranging from buffalo steaks to beef, chicken, seafood, and salads. What it may lack in décor, it makes up for in delicious food and attentive service. Moderate to expensive. There's also a location in Sheridan at 5 E. Alger Street. (307-673-4700).

See also Bill Cody Ranch in *To Do*— Horseback Riding; and Buffalo Bill's Irma Hotel in *Lodging*—Other Options.

✳ Entertainment

Americandream Drive In (307-754-5133), 1070 Road 9, Powell.

Big Horn Cinemas (307-587-8001 (movie line) or 307-587-8009 (box office); http://www.bighorncinemas.net), 2525 Big Horn Avenue, Cody.

✐ **Buffalo Bill Chuckwagon Show** (1-888-587-2090 or 307-587-2090; http://www.buffalobillchuckwagon.com /The_Show.html), 610 Yellowstone Avenue, Cody. Shows at 6 PM, May through September; $19.95 per adult, $9.95 per child ages 6–11, 5 and under

5 eat for free. Saddle up for some cowboy grub while you enjoy some good (tasteful) Old West hoots and laughter during an evening of cowboy entertainment. Reservations recommended.

Cody Theater (307-587-2712), 1171 Sheridan Avenue, Cody.

♪ **Dan Miller's Cowboy Music Revue** (307-272-7855; http://www.cowboymusicrevue.com), at the Cody Theater. Shows at 8 PM Monday through Saturday, May through September; $12. This family entertainment show features cowboy poetry and comedy along with plenty of music—gospel, country, and bluegrass.

Park Drive In Theater (307-587-7177), 3127 Big Horn Avenue, Cody.

Vali Twin Cinema (307-754-4211), 204 N. Bent Street, Powell.

See also Cody City Park in *To See*— City Parks and Gardens; Cody Nite Rodeo and Cody Gunfighters in *To Do*—For Families; Silver Dollar Bar in *Where to Eat*—Eating Out; and Cassie's Supper Club in *Where to Eat*—Dining Out.

✷ Selective Shopping

Big Horn Galleries (307-527-7587; http://www.bighorngalleries.com), 1167 Sheridan Avenue, Cody. Call for current store hours. Enjoy viewing fine western paintings and sculptures by some of today's best artists at this gallery. Many pieces are by local artists of renown, both living and deceased. This shop also holds seasonal art shows.

Open Range Images (307-587-8870; http://www.openrangeimages.com), 1201 Sheridan Avenue, Cody. Call for current store hours. Didn't quite get the shot you were hoping for during your visit to the West? Perhaps Open Range has just what you were looking for to remind you of your journey. Here you'll find a selection of vivid images captured by some of the finest western photographers of both yesterday and today.

Sheridan Avenue in Cody, along with the surrounding side streets, is absolutely packed with a wide variety of stores and shops guaranteed to please the avid shopper. From fine art to folk art, Western wear to designer clothing, you'll find ample shopping opportunities during a walk through downtown Cody.

Sierra Trading Post (307-578-5802; http://www.sierratradingpost.com/lp2/cody-outlet-store.html), 1402 Eighth Street, Cody. Open 9–5 Monday through Saturday, 11–5 Sunday. The bargain-hunting outdoor enthusiast will be hard-pressed to leave Sierra without a full shopping bag. Everything from fishing gear and climbing gear to down jackets and hiking boots can be found here, usually at deep discounts.

Wyoming Buffalo Company (1-800-453-0636; http://www.wyomingbuffalocompany.com), 1270 Sheridan Avenue, Cody. Call for current store hours. You'll find a full-range of western-themed products here, with a particular focus on buffalo, venison, elk, and antelope.

THE CODY THEATER, HOME TO DAN MILLER'S COWBOY MUSIC REVUE

SIERRA TRADING POST IS A HAVEN FOR THE BARGAIN-HUNTING OUTDOOR ENTHUSIAST

See also Old West Miniature Village and Museum in *To See*—Museums; Juniper in *To See*—Wineries and Wine Tastings; and Whole Foods Trading Co. in *To Do*—Relaxation and Rejuvenation.

✳ Special Events

February: **Waterfall Ice Roundup** (307-527-4326; http://www.southfork ice.com), Cody: Ice climbers from around the world gather annually on Presidents' Day Weekend to celebrate the fantastic ice climbing in the South Fork of the Shoshone. See also Ice climbing in *To Do*—Climbing.

May: **Cody Wild West Days** (1-866-754-4320 or 307-587-4221; http:// www.codywildwestdays.com), Cody: The **Buffalo Bill Top Notch Horse Sale** (a horse auction) takes place in front of the Irma Hotel (see *Lodging*—Hotels and Motels); other events include barrel racing and a ranch rodeo.

June: **Plains Indian Museum Powwow** (307-587-2297; http://www.bbhc .org/events/powwow.cfm), Cody: An annual competition that draws dancers and drummers from around North America to compete for more than $25,000 in cash and prizes.

♪ *July:* **Buffalo Bill Cody Stampede Rodeo** (1-800-207-0744 or 307-587-5155; http://www.codystampederodeo .com), Cody: For more than 85 years, the Buffalo Bill Cody Stampede Rodeo has been a major annual happening— a four-day extravaganza complete with parades, rodeos, fireworks, and family entertainment. See also Cody Nite Rodeo in *To Do*—For Families.

July: **Yellowstone Jazz Festival** (307-587-2777; http://www.tctwest.net/ ~yellowstonejazz), Cody: This two-day annual event attracts great jazz musicians and performers each year, with some free performances and some requiring ticket purchase.

July: **Park County Fair** (307-754-5421; http://www.parkcountyfair.com), Powell: See a traditional county fair with a 4-H competition, carnivals, livestock, food, exhibits, and more.

September: **Buffalo Bill Art Show** (1-888-598-8119 or 307-587-5002; http:// www.buffalobillartshow.com), Cody: This fine art show of contemporary, western-themed art, includes an art auction and the Quick Draw, in which artists have one hour to complete a piece of artwork.

Year-round: **Northwest College** (1-800-560-4692; http://www.northwest college.edu), 231 W. Sixth Street, Powell: NWC holds student art shows, concerts, athletic events, and more; call or check online for current schedule.

THERMOPOLIS AND WORLAND

From Cody and Powell, you can easily head south and east to explore the rest of the Bighorn Basin, an area distinguished by fertile valleys giving way to rolling badlands, which then sweep up into the gorgeous Bighorn Mountains. The relative lushness and abundance of this area of Wyoming has made it a natural choice for human habitation since prehistoric times (though the climate was surely different back then), as well as for dinosaurs and other prehistoric creatures long before humanity's arrival. This means that you'll find ample opportunities to explore Wyoming's wealth of dinosaurs and other fossils here, as well as petroglyphs, pictographs, and other relics and artifacts left by the humans who made this area their home in the past. You'll also find modern human history to explore, from stories of the pioneers who settled this land to those of the American Indians that they largely displaced in doing so.

Today, the cowboy spirit lives on in the Bighorn Basin, where folks still ranch to make a living and cattle wander through the Bighorn National Forest (see *Green Space*—National Lands) to graze during certain times of the year, reminiscent of the bison that once made such forests their homes. It's not entirely uncommon to see horses hitched outside at the bar or cowboys and cowgirls stomping into the post office to pick up their mail after a long day in the saddle. If you time your visit right, you can catch a rodeo or two and dance in the streets to the sounds of western music, or perhaps (with a little more advance planning on your part) even experience life on a working ranch (see Blazing Saddles, LLC and Horseworks Wyoming in *To Do*—Horseback Riding) or join in an Outlaw Trail Ride (see *Special Events*) yourself.

But dinosaurs and cowboys are not all you'll find in the Thermopolis and Worland area. You'll also find an abundance of public lands providing additional recreational opportunities, as well as unsurpassed scenery and ample locations to experience solitude in nature. Start by exploring, hiking, fishing, sightseeing, and/or rock climbing (or at least watching rock climbers climb!) in Ten Sleep Canyon (see *To See*—Natural Wonders). Check out the tremendous fishing, hiking, wildflower- and wildlife-viewing opportunities throughout the rest of the Bighorn National Forest (see *Green Space*—National Lands). The Bighorn Canyon National Recreation Area (see *Green Space*—Recreation Areas) near Lovell offers boating, sightseeing, kids' activities, and more. If you're visiting in winter, you won't want to miss out on the area's incredible snowmobile trails and cross-country skiing opportunities (see *To Do*—Snow Sports).

For the more urban at heart, some uniquely western shopping experiences await the curious traveler to both cities (see *Selective Shopping*), as do abundant opportunities for relaxation and rejuvenation—especially at Hot Springs State Park (see *Green Space*—State Parks) and its surrounding amenities. This region also hosts a food, wine, and art show (see Hot Springs County Wine, Food, and Fine Arts Festival in *Special Events*), plus the chance to catch some quality live music here and there, particularly in the tiny town of Ten Sleep (see *To See*—Towns) at the Big Horn Mountain Stage Company (see *Entertainment*) and the Nowoodstock Music Festival (see *Special Events*).

With its vast tracts of public lands, along with two cities and several smaller settlements offering a complete range of visitor services, you'll find plenty to keep you busy—and pampered, should you so choose—during a visit to this gorgeous and sparsely populated area of the state.

GUIDANCE Thermopolis–Hot Springs Chamber of Commerce and Visitor Information Center (1-877-864-3192; http://www.thermopolis.com), 220 Park Street, Thermopolis, 82443. Open 8–5 Monday through Friday (summer), 9–5 Monday through Friday (winter).

Worland–Ten Sleep Chamber of Commerce and **Worland–Ten Sleep Visitors Council** (307-347-3226; http://www.worlandchamber.com and http://www.tensleepworlandwyoming.com) 120 N. 10th Street, Worland, 82401.

GETTING THERE *By car:* Thermopolis and Worland are both on US 20, which runs north and south. Worland can be accessed from the east via US 16. Thermopolis can also be accessed from the northwest via WY 120.

By plane: **Worland Municipal Airport** (307-347-8977; http://www.cityofworland.org/airport.htm) is on the south side of Worland.

GETTING AROUND Strolling around town on foot is a great way to explore Worland and Thermopolis, as well as the smaller towns in this region. You'll have to get in your car to go between both cities (they're about 30 miles apart), as well as to explore many of the area's outlying attractions.

MEDICAL EMERGENCY Dial 911.

Hot Springs County Memorial Hospital (307-864-3121; http://www.hscmh.org), 150 E. Arapahoe Street, Thermopolis.

North Big Horn Hospital (307-548-5200), 1115 Lane 12, Lovell.

South Big Horn County Hospital (307-568-3311), 388 S. US 20, Greybull.

Washakie Medical Center (307-347-3221), 400 S. 15th Street, Worland.

✳ To See

TOWNS Basin, founded in 1896, is the county seat for Big Horn County. A quiet, western town known as the Lilac City, Basin bustles with activity every August when it hosts the Big Horn County Fair (see *Special Events*). For more information: **Basin Area Chamber of Commerce** (307-568-3055; http://www.basincc.com), 407 W. C Street, P.O. Box 883, Basin, 82410. This chamber also serves the smaller nearby towns of **Burlington, Hyattville, Manderson,** and **Otto.**

Greybull is just 8 miles north of Basin at the junction of US 14/16 and US 310. Just north of town, visit **The Museum of Flight and Aerial Firefighting** (307-765-4322; http://www.tctwest.net/~flight), which features a large collection of old planes, a visitor center, and a gift shop (call for current hours; expansion is planned). You'll also find another museum, a shopping district, and more. For more information: **Greybull Area Chamber Of Commerce** (1-877-765-2100 or 307-765-2100; http://www.greybull.com), 521 Greybull Avenue, Greybull, 82426.

Lovell (The Rose City) and the surrounding smaller communities of **Byron, Cowley, Deaver,** and **Frannie** serve as gateways to the Bighorn Canyon National Recreation Area (see *Green Space*—Recreation Areas) and the **Pryor Mountains,** as well as providing visitors with ample recreational and sightseeing opportunities (some of which are listed below). Lovell itself is known for its colorful rose gardens in both public parks and on the grounds of private residences. For those who love the mountains, this area of Wyoming is sure to delight. For more information: **Lovell Chamber of Commerce** (307-548-7552; http://www.lovellchamber.com), 287 E. Main Street, Lovell, 82431.

Shell is a tiny hamlet, with a population of about 50, which serves as the gateway to Shell Canyon and Shell Falls. It takes its name from the fossilized shells found in abundance in Shell Creek. For more information: **A Little About Shell, Wyoming** (307-765-9319; http://www.allaboutshell.com), 2735 Beaver Creek Road, Shell, 82441.

Ten Sleep. A little western town with a big western heart, Ten Sleep lies just outside the mouth of Ten Sleep Canyon, through which runs the Cloud Peak Scenic Byway (see *To See*—Scenic Drives). Ten Sleep hosts a number of great annual events (See *Special Events*). For more information stop in at the new (2009) **Ten Sleep Visitors Center** at 424 S. Second Street (see also Guidance and Ten Sleep Museum in *To See*—Museums).

MUSEUMS ✿ **Greybull Museum** (307-765-2444), 325 Greybull Avenue, Greybull. Open year-round with hours/days varying seasonally (call for current hours); free. Exhibits include artifacts and items from Greybull's pioneer and American Indian history, as well as fossils from nearby dinosaur dig sites.

✿ **Hot Springs County Museum and Cultural Center** (307-864-5183; http://www.hschistory.org), 700 Broadway Street, Thermopolis. Open 9–5 Monday through Saturday, Memorial Day through Labor Day; 9–4 Monday through Saturday, Labor Day through Memorial Day; $4 per adult, $2 per senior (over 60), and $2 per child ages 5–12, children under 5 free. Annual family pass costs $20. The museum documents the history of the settlers in the Thermopolis area (1880–1930) with an extensive collection of artifacts from that time period. Also on exhibit are a large collection of American Indian artifacts, a log cabin from a Wyoming ghost town, some 8,000 historical photos, and a one-room schoolhouse. The museum store sells not only books related to local/Wyoming history, but also jewelry and other fine souvenirs made by local craftspeople and artists.

✂ ✿ **Ten Sleep Museum** (307-366-2759). 436 Second Street, Ten Sleep. Call for this season's hours; open Memorial Day weekend through November 1; free. This museum features a mishmash of historical items of local significance collected in one place, including humorous photos of pioneer days and artifacts from Ten Sleep's history. Nearby find lovely **Vista Park** with a playground and picnicking facilities, where many events (such as the Nowoodstock Music Festival, see *Special Events*) are held.

 ♿ ☙ **Washakie Museum and Cultural Center** (307-347-4102; http://www .washakiemuseum.org/), 2200 Big Horn Avenue, Worland. Call for current hours. A 25,000-square-foot facility, the magnificent new (May 2010) Washakie Museum and Cultural Center features strikingly beautiful architecture that draws the eye to its presence along the city's main street. Stop in for a closer look, and learn all about the geography and human history of the surrounding Bighorn Basin. Exhibits include details on its incredible archaeological sites, as well as more recent human history. This lovely community gem also hosts numerous cultural events throughout the year, including visual performing arts, conventions, book signings, and more. Check the Web site or stop by for a current calendar of events.

FIRST WASHAKIE COUNTY CHURCH

See also Wyoming Dinosaur Center and Dig Sites in *To Do*—For Families.

HISTORIC LANDMARKS, PLACES, AND SITES ☙ **First Washakie County Church** (307-366-2241; http://www.circlejchristiancamp.org), at the Circle J Christian Camp & Retreat Center, 3338 US 16, Ten Sleep. Situated in the mouth of beautiful Ten Sleep Canyon (see *To See*—Natural Wonders), this church is on the National Register of Historic Places. It was constructed in 1904 and moved to its present site in 1975. Visitors are welcome to stop and read about this historic site as well as take photos. The ranch also offers camping and dormitory accommodations in conjunction with its ministries (youth, adult, and family). Contact Circle J for more information about scheduling and suggested donations.

☙ **Legend Rock Petroglyph Site** (307-864-2176; http://wyoparks.state.wy.us/Site/ SiteInfo.asp?siteID=20), 30 miles northwest of Thermopolis. Open sunrise to sunset daily; free. Check with staff at the State Bath House at Hot Springs State Park (see *Green Space*—State Parks) to get a gate key and a permit (photo ID required) before driving to Legend Rock (they will give you precise directions, too). After parking at the end of the road, follow a trail a short distance down into a gully and then up a small rise to view this beautiful display of ancient artwork up close. Etched into the cliff faces at Legend Rock are some 300 American Indian petroglyphs, including kokopellis, birds, buffalo, rabbits, humans, and numerous other animals. Their precise origins are unknown, but they provide a window into the past and are considered sacred by American Indians today. As you view the petroglyphs, you'll find that it's hard to imagine just how much intricacy and precision the carving of these images required—especially when you compare them to the latter-day graffiti that some people have added to the mix. Please do your part

AMERICAN INDIAN PETROGLYPHS AT
LEGEND ROCK PETROGLYPH SITE

and don't add any marks or touch the petroglyphs (or anything else, for that matter). Not only does it mar things for future visitors, but also, it can be a felony. Feel free to take photographs, but leave only footprints.

🦌 ♿ ✍ **Medicine Lodge Archaeological Site** (307-469-2234; http://wyo parks.state.wy.us/Site/SiteInfo.asp?site ID=21), 6 miles north of Hyattville via WY 31 to Cold Springs Road. Open year-round for day-use (free) and camping ($10/resident, $17/nonresident; some sites take reservations). Visitor center open May 1 through September 29. This area has drawn human visitors to set up camp for more than 10,000 years. Archaeological study has revealed more than 60 cultural levels of continuous human occupation at this site, with numerous artifacts, pictographs, and petroglyphs recovered. You can still view a plethora of pictographs and petroglyphs along with helpful interpretive signs. This site includes handicapped-accessible pit toilets and a concrete trail. Medicine Lodge also offers fishing, tremendous wildlife viewing opportunities in both the site and the surrounding wildlife habitat management area (see Medicine Lodge Wildlife Habitat Management Area in *Green Space*—Wildlife Refuges and Areas), mountain biking, playground equipment, and a self-guided nature trail, among other attractions. See also Red Gulch/Alkali National Back Country Byway in *To See*—Scenic Drives.

See also Pioneer Square in *To See*—Historic Landmarks, Places, and Sites; WY 434 in *To See*—Scenic Drives; Hot Springs State Park in *Green Space*—State Parks; Nature Conservancy's Tensleep Preserve and Ten Sleep Fish Hatchery in *Green Space*—Wildlife Refuges and Areas; Best Western The Plaza Hotel in *Lodging*—Hotels and Motels; Dirty Sally's in *Where to Eat*—Eating Out; and Big Horn Mountain Stage Company in *Entertainment*.

PIONEER SQUARE

CITY PARKS AND GARDENS ♿
Pioneer Square. Located along Worland's main street, Big Horn Avenue, Pioneer Square commemorates the spot where Charles H. "Dad" Worland put in a stage stop in 1900. Lovely sculptures capture the spirit of the pioneer days, while ample grass, shade trees, and benches make this a great spot for a picnic.

See also Basin and Lovell in *To See*—Towns; Ten Sleep Museum in *To See*—Museums; and Hot Springs State Park in *Green Space*—State Parks.

SCENIC DRIVES Cloud Peak Skyway Scenic Byway, about 65 miles on US 16, starting west of Buffalo and ending near the base of Ten Sleep Canyon on the other side of Powder River Pass. Offering travelers the only close-up view of the highest peak in the Bighorn Mountains, **Cloud Peak** (13,167 feet), this drive features gorgeous views of the Bighorn National Forest (see *Green Space*—National Lands), Cloud Peak Wilderness, and the breathtaking limestone and dolomite cliffs of Ten Sleep Canyon (see also *To See*—Natural Wonders). Many pullouts and side roads afford you the chance to step out of the car, picnic, view wildlife (moose are often seen along this route), or gain access to numerous fishing and camping areas (see Bighorn National Forest in *Lodging*—Campgrounds).

Red Gulch/Alkali National Back Country Byway, 32 miles on BLM 1111 and BLM 1109 between US 14, just north of Hyattville and 4 miles west of Shell and WY 31. Allow two to three hours for this historic 32-mile drive through red canyons and mesas. Few signs of humanity, save fences and roads, make for a feeling of emptiness and isolation as you pass sweeping vistas, sandstone buttes, and tall cairns atop hills marking an American Indian/pioneer days trail system. Do not drive this road in wet or inclement conditions. A high-clearance, two-wheel drive vehicle (don't try to bring an RV through) suffices, but be prepared for slow going in certain areas and be sure to have a spare tire in good condition, since there are no services along the drive. Consider stopping at Medicine Lodge Archaeological Site (see *To See*—Historic Landmarks, Places, and Sites) and the BLM's Red Gulch Dinosaur Tracksite (see *To See*—Natural Wonders). See also Bureau of Land Management in *Green Space*—National Lands.

WY 434, either 20 or 80 miles, one way, on WY 434. Turn south at the west side of Ten Sleep off US 16 and enter rolling brush and grasslands for a few miles, passing the monument for the **Spring Creek Raid** at around mile 7. At mile 16, the scenery changes as the road drops into a gorgeous valley. Lush and green in spring and early summer, the vegetation contrasts beautifully with the brilliant red soil and sandstone buttresses reminiscent of Utah's similar formations. The pavement ends at around 20 miles, but the idyllic scenery continues if you're willing to keep going on a well-maintained gravel road, passing by the enormous **Mahogany Butte**. At this point or somewhere not too far beyond it, you can choose to end your journey and simply turn around, or you can continue on through more rolling hills to the tiny town of Lysite (70.5 miles from Ten Sleep) or the town of Moneta (79.5 miles from Ten Sleep), which lies on US 20/26. Be sure to have a full tank of gas, since the towns of Big Trails and Nowood are simply small clusters of homes or ranches. The latter portion of this road is not maintained (read: covered in snow and often impassable) from October through April.

See also Medicine Wheel Passage Scenic Byway in *To See*—Scenic Drives in Northeastern Wyoming: Sheridan and Buffalo.

NATURAL WONDERS 🐾 ♿ **Castle Gardens Scenic Area** is accessible by traveling about 3 miles west of Ten Sleep on US 16, and then turning south onto a signed dirt road and following signs for about 6 miles. Open year-round; free. Managed by the Bureau of Land Management's Worland Field Office (see *Green Space*—National Lands) Castle Gardens features sandcastle-like eroded towers and ribs of sandstone set in an isolated, windswept landscape replete with wildflowers in spring and early summer, when lilies, prickly pears, and scarlet globemallows carpet the ground. Accessible via a decent dirt road suitable for two-wheel drive autos when not wet or snowy, this magical destination has a desert canyon feel, with its juniper and sagebrush. This area is great for hiking, wildlife watching, and picnicking. Primitive camping is permitted at this area, but water and trash pickup are not available.

& ♂ 🐾 **Red Gulch Dinosaur Tracksite** (307-347-5100; http://www.wy.blm.gov/rgdt), 5 miles south on the Red Gulch/Alkali National Back Country Byway (BLM Road 1109; see also *To See*—Scenic Drives). Open dawn through dusk, free. The BLM's Red Gulch Dinosaur Tracksite leads you back to prehistoric times through helpful interpretive signs along a wooden boardwalk that deposits you directly onto the surface in which the dinosaur tracks lie. Though at first they are hard to discern, once the eye is clued in to what to look for, tracks spring up from the stone surface all around, allowing one to walk in the footsteps left by a number of as-yet-undetermined species of three-toed dinosaurs from the middle Jurassic period, some 160–180 million years ago. You can even keep small, invertebrate fossils for your personal collection if you find any at the site. See also Red Gulch/Alkali National Back Country Byway in *To See*—Scenic Drives and Bureau of Land Management in *Green Space*—National Lands.

Ten Sleep Canyon, via US 16 east of the small town of Ten Sleep (see *To See*—Towns), along the Cloud Peak Skyway Scenic Byway (see also *To See*—Scenic Drives). Despite the road running through it, the canyon still retains a wild flavor that can best be appreciated by pulling off the road and stretching your legs, or better yet, staying overnight in one of a number of Bighorn National Forest campgrounds along the way (see also *To Do*—Camping and *Green Space*—National Lands) and spending a few days exploring the canyon. If you don't have the time for that, consider driving up the old highway (open June 16 through November 16; known by locals as Sweet 16), which parallels the paved highway but gives you the chance to get a feel for the true beauty of this magical place. Best visited in late May through June, when the wildflowers bloom in an abundant explosion of yellows, purples, pinks, and whites, US 16 can be closed due to inclement weather in the winter months. This canyon is also a popular rock-climbing destination of national renown, but no commercial guide services are currently available. Rock climbers are often visible from the road scaling the sheer cliffs above—just be sure to pull over if you want to watch. See also Salt Lick Trail in *To Do*—Hiking.

TEN SLEEP CANYON IS A POPULAR DESTINATION FOR EXPERIENCED TECHNICAL ROCK CLIMBERS

Wind River Canyon, 4 miles south of Thermopolis on US 20, is one of the most stunning canyons that you can drive through in Wyoming. The canyon is a geological wonderland with its enormous walls of dolomite and limestone that dominate the scenery. Located on the Wind River Indian Reservation (see sidebar in Northwest Wyoming: Lander and Riverton), this canyon's recreational opportunities include fishing and rafting (special permit required; see listing in *To Do—Fishing*).

See also WY 434 in *To See—Scenic Drives* and Hot Springs State Park in *Green Space—State Parks*.

✳ To Do

BICYCLING See Medicine Lodge Archaeological Site in *To See—Historic Landmarks, Places, and Sites*; Bighorn National Forest and Bureau of Land Management in *Green Space—National Lands*; Bighorn Canyon National Recreation Area in *Green Space—Recreation Areas*; and The Hideout and the Snowshoe Lodge at Flitner Ranch in *Lodging—Lodges*.

BOATING See Hot Springs State Park in *Green Space—State Parks*; Bighorn National Forest in *Green Space—National Lands*; and Bighorn Canyon National Recreation Area in *Green Space—Recreation Areas*.

CLIMBING See Ten Sleep Canyon in *To See—Natural Wonders*; and Gottsche Public Fitness & Wellness Center in *To Do—Fitness Centers*.

FISHING Bighorn River (307-777-4600; http://gf.state.wy.us/fish/fishing/index .asp) begins at the Wedding of the Waters area (a fishing access point), where the Wind River exits the Wind River Canyon (see *To See—Natural Wonders*) just south of Thermopolis and changes its name to the Bighorn River. From there, it flows north along US 20/WY 789 to Greybull, where it continues north to empty into Bighorn Lake, in the Bighorn Canyon National Recreation Area (see *Green Space—Recreation Areas*). Species include brown trout, channel catfish, cutthroat trout, rainbow trout, sauger, and walleye. Numerous signed access points can be found all along US 20/WY 789 from the Wedding of the Waters to Greybull.

Wind River Canyon (307-332-7207), 4 miles south of Thermopolis on US 20. Located on the Wind River Indian Reservation (see sidebar in Northwest Wyoming: Lander and Riverton), this easily accessed canyon and its surrounding environs are home to some of the finest brown and rainbow trout fishing available in the state. A special permit is required to fish here; contact the Wind River Reservation Fish and Game Department at the above number for details. Another option is to contact the Wind River Visitors Council (1-800-645-6233; http://www .wind-river.org), which can advise you of local stores that sell licenses and provide you with an information packet including guiding services and outfitters.

See also Medicine Lodge Archaeological Site in *To See—Historic Landmarks, Places, and Sites*; Wind River Canyon Whitewater and Fly Fishing in *To Do—Paddling/Floating*; *Green Space*; and The Hideout and the Snowshoe Lodge at Flitner Ranch in *Lodging—Lodges*.

FITNESS CENTERS ⅙ ☙ **Gottsche Public Fitness & Wellness Center** (307-864-2145; http://www.gottsche-rehab.com), 148 E. Arapahoe Street, Thermopolis.

Open 5:30 AM–7:30 PM Monday through Thursday, 5:30 AM–6:30 PM Friday, and 7:00 AM–12:00 PM Saturday; $5 per person. This nonprofit, 10,000-square-foot fitness and wellness center offers classes (spinning, yoga, senior-oriented fitness) along with exercise facilities and equipment. A new (2009) youth-oriented wellness area includes a climbing wall, air hockey, plyometric training, and more. Massages are also available here.

See also The Star Plunge in *To Do*—For Families; Hellie's Tepee Pools in *To Do*—Relaxation and Rejuvenation; and Days Inn Hot Springs Convention Center in *Lodging*—Hotels and Motels.

FOR FAMILIES ✐ 🐾 Dairyland Ice Cream and Sweet Spot Miniature Golf

(307-864-2757), 510 E. Park Street, Thermopolis. Open April through September, Monday through Saturday 11–10; Sunday 1–10; $3 per person. Play 18 holes and then treat the kids to an ice cream or even a full meal at this perennially popular hangout spot near the entrance to Hot Springs State Park (see *Green Space*—State Parks).

✐ ♿ The Star Plunge

(307-864-3771), 115 Big Springs Drive, Hot Springs State Park, Thermopolis (see *Green Space*—State Parks). Open 9–9 every day; $10 per person; $5 per child 5 and under. Enjoy the healing mineral waters in whatever style you fancy at this water park. Waterslides and diving boards entertain the young (or young at heart), while the serious fitness fanatic can partake of the exercise classes or weight room. Feel like just relaxing? Then make an appointment for a massage or a tanning bed, or simply soak away your troubles in the soothing waters.

✐ 🐾 Wyoming Dinosaur Center and Dig Sites

(307-864-5522; http://www.wyodino.org), 110 Carter Ranch Road, Thermopolis. Open 8–6 every day (summer), 10–5 every day (winter, except Thanksgiving, Christmas, and New Year's Day); $10 per adult, $5.50 per child ages 4–13 and seniors 60-plus, children under 3 are free. More than 200 exhibits await exploration at the dinosaur center, including interactive exhibits, 10 full-sized mounted dinosaur skeletons, and many smaller fossils and displays. Hourly tours of actual dinosaur dig sites take place from 9–4 in the summer season, allowing you to take a closer look at the actual places where dinosaur fossils have been unearthed (for an additional fee). For an unforgettable dino experience, during the summer season adults, families, or just the kids alone (ages 8–12) can partake in real-life dinosaur digs at the sites (advance reservations required, please call for details and current prices). The museum store contains an extensive array of dinosaur- and fossil-related gifts.

See also Ten Sleep Museum in *To See*—Museums; Medicine Lodge Archaeological Site in *To See*—Historic Landmarks, Places, and Sites; Red Gulch Dinosaur Tracksite in *To See*—Natural Wonders; Gottsche Public Fitness & Wellness Center in *To Do*—Fitness Centers; Blazing Saddles, LLC in *To Do*—Horseback Riding; Float Trips by Eagle RV Park and Campground and Wind River Canyon Whitewater in *To Do*—Paddling/Floating; Hellie's Tepee Pools in *To Do*—Relaxation and Rejuvenation; Hot Springs State Park in *Green Space*—State Parks; Bighorn Canyon National Recreation Area in *Green Space*—Recreation Areas; Best Western The Plaza Hotel and Days Inn Hot Springs Convention Center in *Lodging*—Hotels and Motels; and *Where to Eat*—Eating Out.

GOLF **Canyon Valley Resort** (307-366-2768; http://www.canyonvalleyresort .com); 126 Old Maid Gulch, Ten Sleep, 9 holes.

Foster Gulch Golf Club (307-548-2445) 925 Lane 13, Lovell, 9 holes.

Green Hills Municipal Golf Course (307-347-8972; http://www.cityofworland .org/golf.htm), 1455 Airport Road, Worland, 18 holes.

Legion Town and Country Club (307-864-5294), 141 Airport Road, Thermopolis, 9 holes.

Midway Golf Club, (307-568-2255), 4053 Golf Course Road, Basin, 9 holes.

HIKING **Five Springs Falls Trail** involves a short, easy (less than 1 mile) nature trail that departs from the parking area at Five Springs Falls Campground (see Five Springs Falls Campground in *Lodging*—Campgrounds). As your vehicle climbs the hill up to the campground, the scenery changes from arid desert to a lush, green canyon filled with trees and plant life. In addition to the falls tumbling down a narrow, granite canyon, scenic attractions include sweeping views of the surrounding mountain ranges—the Bighorns, Pryors, and Absarokas—as well as the opportunity to view wildlife including mule deer and elk.

Gooseberry Badlands Scenic Overlook and Interpretive Trail is located on BLM lands 25 miles west of Worland. Go south on US 20/26 from Worland, then turn right onto WY 431 (see also Bureau of Land Management in *Green Space*— National Lands). The startling scenery encountered at this area—a collection of oddly sculpted rock formations including arches, spires, and mushrooms, together with soil that changes colors with the seasons—makes for an intriguing place you'll learn more about while hiking the 1.5-mile interpretive trail.

High Point Lookout, in Bighorn National Forest (see *Green Space*—National Lands), is located east of Ten Sleep just off US 16 (Cloud Peak Skyway Scenic Byway, see *To See*—Scenic Drives) before **Powder River Pass** (look for signs). A hike to the High Point Lookout offers a spectacular panoramic view of the Bighorn Mountains. After leaving your vehicle at the parking area, follow a well-marked, moderately steep trail as it winds through a heavy evergreen forest and gorgeous dolomite boulders. A 15-minute hike brings you to the tower, which was once manned all summer long by an individual or couple hired by the National Forest Service to watch for fires. This is a great, remote spot for picnics and views, though the cliffs nearby mean that small children should be watched closely. Also stop at **Saint Christopher's in the Bighorn Chapel for Travelers.** Located on the same road as the High Point Lookout Tower, this rustic, humble outdoor chapel lies about .25 mile off the highway. Episcopalian services are held on Sundays during the summer; check the sign on US 16 for details.

Salt Lick Trail is located at the mouth of Ten Sleep Canyon (see *To See*—Natural Wonders) on the north side of US 16 on BLM land (see *Green Space*—National Lands). Park by the large black sandstone boulder to begin your journey—there's also a public outhouse here for your convenience. A short, steep, trail takes you up to the towering sandstone walls above. This will get your heart pumping, so take your time and enjoy the views. From here, you can turn around and head back down for a total hike of less than 2 miles, or else meander on a trail around the large sandstone formation to lengthen your journey.

See also Legend Rock Petroglyph Site and Medicine Lodge Archaeological Site in *To See*—Historic Landmarks, Places, and Sites; *Green Space*; and The Hideout and the Snowshoe Lodge at Flitner Ranch in *Lodging*—Lodges.

HORSEBACK RIDING Big Horn Mountain Adventures (307-366-2676), located at Canyon Valley Resort (see *To Do*—Golf) offers half-day and full-day rides in the Ten Sleep area June through August, as well as multiday pack trips and outfitting services in autumn. Call for current rates.

🐾 🐎 **Blazing Saddles, LLC** (307-272-0874; http://www.mahoganybuttepasofinos .com), 3348 Road 82, Ten Sleep. Open seasonally for trail rides in the beautiful country around WY 434 (see *To See*—Scenic Drives); $40/hour per rider (ages 6 and up), or $50 for a two-hour ride. Rides take place on private land and are scheduled around the ranch's work. This is not a guest ranch; it is a real working cattle, sheep, and horse ranch, but the owners generously will offer their time (when possible) and knowledge of the land and their horses to guide visitors on horseback rides.

Horseworks Wyoming (1-877-807-2367 or 307-867-2525; http://www.horseworks wyoming.com), 3809 Grass Creek Road, Thermopolis. For serious students of ranching and horsemanship, Horseworks offers inclusive three- and four-week internship programs every summer ($2,500/three weeks). Enrollment is limited; apply early.

See also Bighorn National Forest and Bureau of Land Management in *Green Space*—National Lands; and The Hideout and the Snowshoe Lodge at Flitner Ranch in *Lodging*—Lodges.

PADDLING/FLOATING 🎐 🐎 🐾 **Float Trips by Eagle RV Park and Campground** (1-888-865-5707 or 307-864-5262; http://www.eaglervpark.com/river %20float%20trips.htm), 204 US 20, Thermopolis. Tube rental is $7 per tube for a two-and-one-half- to three-hour float, includes transportation up river to put-in point; $5 per tube for a group of six or more people. Reservations recommended. Get downright intimate with the beautiful Bighorn River by seeing it close up as you float in your inner tube—a perfect way to while away a summer day, and to get a little closer to nature while you're at it. You can also grab a site at the campground (open year-round; $20, tent site; $30.50, RV site; $40, camping cabin). This privately owned RV park and campground gives you easy access to attractions around Thermopolis in addition to providing more than 100 large shade trees, a playground, and a pet walk area.

🐾 **Wind River Canyon Whitewater and Fly Fishing** (1-888-246-9343 or 307-486-2253 (off-season booking); http://www.windrivercanyonraft.com), 210 US 20, Suite 5, Thermopolis. Trips run Memorial Day through Labor Day. This is the only outfitter permitted to guide rafters through the Wind River Canyon (see *To See*—Natural Wonders). Paddle exciting whitewater and potentially view wildlife for a half day ($45 per person, depending on trip choice) or a whole day ($90, lunch included). Also available is a scenic float trip, with no whitewater ($30 per person). Reservations are recommended. Children are permitted, but the age limit depends on the water level, so call in advance. Also available through this outfitter are guided fishing trips in Wind River Canyon; call for details. See also Wind River Canyon in *To Do*—Fishing.

RELAXATION AND REJUVENATION ⬟ **CÁRÁ** (307-347-6457), 716 Big Horn Avenue, Worland. Open Tuesday through Friday 11–6 and later by appointment. Enjoy a full range of top-quality salon and spa services here, plus on-premises chiropractic treatments by Myers Chiropractic (307-921-9890). Massages, pedicures, manicures, waxing, piercing, facials, and hairstyling are all delivered with expertise by the qualified staff at this caring establishment.

✿ ৬ **Hellie's Tepee Pools** (307-864-9250; http://www.tepeepools.com), Hot Springs State Park, Thermopolis. Open daily 9–9; $10 per person, $5 per child under 5, $8 per senior. Indoor-outdoor pools, water slides, saunas, spas, and an on-site water therapist are featured at this water park. Also available are water aerobics classes.

Nature's Corner (307-864-3218), 530 Broadway Street, Thermopolis. Open 8:30–5:30 Monday through Saturday (coffee bar open until 5). You'll find vitamins, supplements, Chinese medicine, herbs, reference books, natural foods, and more here, along with a helpful, knowledgeable staff. This store also carries interesting gifts and candles. At the back of the store, the **Crow Bar** serves coffee and smoothies, among other treats.

See also Gottsche Public Fitness & Wellness Center in *To Do*—Fitness Centers; The Star Plunge in *To Do*—For Families; Hot Springs State Park in *Green Space*—State Parks; Best Western The Plaza Hotel and Days Inn Hot Springs Convention Center in *Lodging*—Hotels and Motels; and Fountain of Youth RV Park in *Lodging*—Campgrounds.

SNOW SPORTS ✿ **Big Horn Mountain Resorts** (1-888-BIG-HORN or 307-366-2424; www.thebighorn.com), on US 16 (Cloud Peak Skyway Scenic Byway, see *To See*—Scenic Drives) east of Ten Sleep before Powder River Pass in the Bighorn National Forest (see *Green Space*—National Lands). This charming, family-friendly ski resort is nestled in the Big Horn Mountains on the shores of Meadowlark Lake. It reopened for business in 2009-10, as did its companion lodging/dining properties, Meadowlark Lake Resort and Deer Haven Resort. Call or check the Web site for updated snow conditions, reservations, hours, and pricing.

Cross-country skiing and **snowshoeing** are popular in this area in winter, particularly around the Powder River Pass off the Cloud Peak Skyway Scenic Byway (see *To See*—Scenic Drives) in the Bighorn National Forest (see *Green Space*—National Lands). Visit http://www.fs.fed.us/r2/bighorn/recreation/winter for downloadable trail brochures and updated trail conditions. See also Bighorn Canyon National Recreation Area in *Green Space*—Recreation Areas.

Ice fishing is possible on many of this region's frozen lakes and ponds come wintertime. For ideas about where to go, see listings in *To Do*—Boating and *To Do*—Fishing.

NATURE'S CORNER IN THERMOPOLIS CARRIES A WIDE RANGE OF NATURAL HEALTH PRODUCTS AND FOODS

Snowmobiling is popular in this region with almost 400 miles of trails found throughout the Bighorn National Forest (see *Green Space*—National Lands). You'll find numerous places to access the trails that make up the Bighorn Mountain/North Central Wyoming trail system (almost 350 of which are groomed snowmobile trails) along the scenic drives through the Big Horn Mountains (see *To See*—Scenic Drives). For detailed trail reports, call 307-777-6560 or go to http://wyotrails.state.wy.us/snow, the Wyoming Snowmobile Trails Web site, which also provides information about rules, rental agencies, trails around the state, and more. You can also plan a full-scale snowmobiling vacation with The Hideout and the Snowshoe Lodge at Flitner Ranch (see *Lodging*—Lodges).

See also Bighorn National Forest and Bureau of Land Management in *Green Space*—National Lands.

UNIQUE ADVENTURES Dinosaur Safaris, Inc. (1-800-367-7457; http://www.dinosaursafaris.com), Shell. Dig season is usually open July and August; reservations required; $100 per adult per day, $50 per child ages 16–18, children 10–15 free, no children under 10 permitted unless by special permission. Dig with experts for a day—or a few—for dinosaur bones and other fossils on this private, active dig site. Dinosaur Safaris provides you with the proper tools and training, educates you about the types of dinosaur fossils you'll likely encounter, teaches you about casting fossil(s) you unearth (so that you can take away a permanent reminder of your findings), and provides you with lunch and transportation to and from the dig site.

🐾 🐶 "T" **Wayfaring Traveler Llama Ranch** (307-762-3536; http://www.tctwest.net/~wtr), 1100 Lane 38, Burlington (east of Cody just off US 14/16/20). For the simplest llama trekking experience, renting a llama (which comes with a prepared lunch for two) will run you $45 for the day (add $25 for a human guide to come along with you) if you wish to hike to the top of nearby Table Mountain to take in the scenic Bighorn Basin below. The Wayfaring Traveler Llama Ranch offers a number of more involved llama rentals and excursions, as well as additional adventure packages. It also has a guesthouse available for rent (moderate; pets are $5 extra/night), with the option of one, two, or three vegetarian meals daily (inexpensive).

WINERIES AND WINE TASTINGS See Hot Springs County Wine, Food, and Fine Arts Festival in *Special Events*.

✳ Green Space

NATIONAL LANDS Bighorn National Forest (307-347-5105 (Worland) or 307-548-6541 (Lovell); http://www.fs.fed.us/r2/bighorn), east of Lovell (US 14 Alternate), Greybull (US 14), and Worland (US 16). The Bighorn National Forest encompasses more than 1 million acres of land, including the 189,000-acre Cloud Peak Wilderness Area. It is also home to the headwaters of the Bighorn River (see *To Do*—Fishing), from which it took its name. This national forest provides an abundance of recreational opportunities, including boating, camping, fishing, hiking (more than 1,500 miles of trails), horseback riding, bicycling, snowmobiling, wildlife viewing, and more. See also *Lodging*—Campgrounds.

Bureau of Land Management (BLM) has the Worland Field Office (307-347-5100; http://www.wy.blm.gov/wfo/index.htm), 101 S. 23rd Street, managing more

STATE PARKS

&. 𝒹 🦞 **Hot Springs State Park** (307-864-2176; http://wyoparks.state.wy.us/ Site/SiteInfo.asp?siteID=9), 538 N. Park Street, Thermopolis. Open sunrise to sunset daily; free. Restrooms closed October through April. Located near the center of the state, Hot Springs State Park is one of Wyoming's top attractions, as well as being the most defining aspect of Thermopolis' town character and amenities. Wyoming's unique **State Bath House** (open 8–5:30 Monday through Saturday, noon–5:30 Sunday and summer holidays, closed winter holidays; free), run by the state park, allows you to soak in the 104-degree mineral waters for 20 minutes at a time, indoors or outside. Just sign in at the desk. Following a soak, showers are available free of charge as well. Also available nearby are a number of private facilities that charge for the use of the mineral waters due to their steam rooms, waterslides, and other services, including lodging (see The Star Plunge in *To Do*—For Families; Hellie's Tepee Pools in *To Do*—Relaxation and Rejuvenation; and Best Western The Plaza Hotel and Days Inn Hot Springs Convention Center in *Lodging*—Hotels and Motels). Stroll along the **Terrace Walk** after soaking and read about the source of the healing waters—**Big Spring**—which bubbles out of the ground at a steaming hot 135 degrees. You'll also learn about the human history of the waters, as Indians knew of them and their healing properties long before the State Bath House ever came into being. In addition to its healing waters, this park is home to the **Hot Springs State Park bison herd,** the state's central herd, with nearly 30 animals. The bison can usually be viewed roaming within the boundaries of their pasture in the park (please stay in your car while viewing, since bison are wild animals and can be dangerous). Picnic tables, shade trees, and three playgrounds are available at the park, but no overnight camping is allowed. The park also has a boat ramp on the Bighorn River, a fishing pier, a swinging bridge over the river with great views, 6.2 miles of handicapped-accessible trails for strolling, and lovely flower gardens. See also Legend Rock State Petroglyph Site in *To See*—Historic Landmarks, Places, and Sites and Gift of the Waters Pageant in *Special Events*.

than 2 million acres of public lands and mineral estate in this region. Much of the land administered by the BLM is open to recreational pursuits, including bicycling, boating, camping (see Five Springs Falls Campground in *Lodging*—Campgrounds), fishing, hiking, horseback riding, paddling, rock climbing, wildlife viewing, and snow sports, including snowmobiling and cross-country skiing. BLM lands tend to be the most unregulated of public lands, meaning that most typical outdoor recreational pursuits are allowed on most BLM lands, guided by the dictates of Leave No Trace (1-800-332-4100 or 303-442-8222; http://www.lnt.org) outdoor ethics. To find out additional information about the BLM lands in this region, including maps, developed campgrounds, and other recreational pursuits, contact the field office.

RECREATION AREAS 🐾 ♿ ✇ **Bighorn Canyon National Recreation Area** (307-548-2251; http://www.nps.gov/bica), Bighorn Canyon Visitor Center located at 20 US 14 Alternate E., Lovell. Open 8–6 Memorial Day through Labor Day and 8:30–4:30 Labor Day through Memorial Day; entry fee to recreation area is $5 per vehicle or $30 for an annual pass. This national recreation area encompasses more than 70,000 acres of land in Wyoming and Montana, including 60-mile-long **Bighorn Lake.** Popular activities include hiking, fishing, boating, year-round camping, wildlife viewing, cross-country skiing/snowshoeing, bicycling and more. Boats are available for rent during the summer season at the Ok-A-Beh Marina, located within the recreation area. You might even glimpse wild horses from the BLM's **Pryor Mountain Wild Horse Range** along WY 37 in the recreation area. The Bighorn Canyon Visitor Center (free) has a wheelchair-accessible nature trail with a reflection pond. Kids (and their families) can participate in the Bighorn Canyon's **Junior Ranger Program** by completing the activities listed in several fun and educational booklets available for purchase ($1 apiece) at the visitor center. Upon completion of the program, children earn a Junior Ranger badge.

WILDLIFE REFUGES AND AREAS Duck Swamp Interpretive Area is located about 3 miles north of Worland on WY 433, on the east side of the road. At this 81-acre Bighorn River oxbow marsh/lake, managed by the Bureau of Land Management (see *Green Space*—National Lands), you'll discover an environment replete with wildlife, particularly waterfowl. Bird species include great blue herons, kingfishers, and numerous ducks, while beavers and muskrats are a common sight as well. Hike a 1-mile interpretive loop trail to learn more about the area. Restrooms, drinking water, and picnic facilities are available, but overnight camping is not permitted.

Medicine Lodge Wildlife Habitat Management Area (307-469-2234; http://gf.state.wy.us/accessto/Whmas/medicine.asp), 6 miles north of Hyattville via WY 31 to Cold Springs Road. This area surrounds the Medicine Lodge Archaeological Site (see *To See*—Historic Landmarks, Places, and Sites), encompassing more than 12,000 acres. Managed by the Wyoming Game and Fish Department, this area was purchased in 1972 in an effort to protect winter grazing lands for the Big Horn Mountains' elk herds, among other species. Accessible to the public via the archaeological site, the habitat management area allows great opportunities for viewing wildlife, including elk, mule deer, beaver, jackrabbits, marmots, porcupines, and bobcats, among many others.

Nature Conservancy's Tensleep Preserve (307-366-2671; http://www

DUCK SWAMP INTERPRETIVE AREA

.nature.org), 101 Rome Hill Road (east of Ten Sleep via US 16 to Rome Hill Road/WY 436). Open May through October; advance reservations required, contact the preserve for details. The Ten Sleep Preserve lies along 12 miles of the stunningly hued sandstone cliffs that rise above Canyon Creek. With eight plant communities and abundant wildlife, including 120 species of birds as well as mountain lions, black bears, mule deer, elk, and spotted bats, the preserve works to educate visitors while protecting the environment contained within its 9,000 acres. Hiking trails, a lodge, a tent

TEN SLEEP FISH HATCHERY

camp, and a learning center all enable visitors to become better acquainted with all the preserve has to offer, from pictograph viewing to wildlife viewing.

Ten Sleep Fish Hatchery (307-366-2404; http://gf.state.wy.us/fish/culture/tensleep.asp), 9 miles east of Ten Sleep on WY 435 (off US 16). Open 8–5 daily; free. Constructed in 1939, this historic hatchery is situated near the confluence of Ten Sleep Creek and Leigh Creek. A self-guided tour helps you find your way around the gorgeous grounds.

Wigwam Rearing Station (307-366-2217; http://gf.state.wy.us/fish/culture/wigwam.asp), 4 miles east of Ten Sleep on US 16. Open 8–5 daily; free. Situated on the grounds of a former dude ranch at the mouth of Ten Sleep Canyon (see *To See*—Natural Wonders), this fish rearing station welcomes visitors to its idyllic 420 acres to learn more about how fish are raised.

See also Hot Springs State Park in *Green Space*—State Parks.

✳ Lodging

BED AND BREAKFASTS
Worland
❝↑❞ ☗ ☀ **C's B & B** (307-347-9388), 1000 Howell Avenue. Located within walking distance of Worland's downtown area, this quiet, 1954 ranch-style home in a residential neighborhood has two rooms (shared bath). In addition to breakfast (included), other meals are available upon request (extra). Moderate to expensive.

LODGES
Shell
❝↑❞ **The Hideout and the Snowshoe Lodge at Flitner Ranch** (1-800-354-

8637; http://www.thehideout.com), Shell. Open year-round; reservations required. Along with private cabins and gourmet ranch dining three meals a day (drinks included), this 300,000-acre ranch offers numerous additional activities including mountain biking, horseback riding, fishing, trap shooting, and guided hiking—all as part of the inclusive vacation package. Winters bring loads of snow to the Big Horn Mountains, making for tremendous snowmobiling opportunities. The ranch provides easy access to the nearly 400 miles of trails that make up the

Bighorn Mountain/North Central Wyoming trail system (almost 350 of which are groomed snowmobile trails). Very expensive.

HOTELS AND MOTELS
Greybull
♦ ❦ ⁅¶⁆ **A Maverick Motel** (307-765-4626; http://www.greybull.com/rest lodge/adpages/AMaverikMotel/index.html), 625 N. Sixth Street. Almost like having your own cottage, every room at A Maverick Motel has its own kitchenette. The motel also features a free **Mini Western and Ranch Antique Museum** with more than 550 items on display. Pets are permitted in all rooms, and continental breakfast is included in rates from June 1 through September 1. Inexpensive; weekly and monthly rates available.

Ten Sleep
& **Log Cabin Motel** (307-366-2320), 314 Second Street. Clean and affordable, the Log Cabin Motel has one, two, and three-bedroom accommodations, some with kitchenettes. You'll enjoy easy access to all of the shops and restaurants situated on Ten Sleep's main street (Second Street). Inexpensive.

Thermopolis
⁅¶⁆ & ✐ **Best Western The Plaza Hotel** (1-888-919-9009 or 307-864-2939; http://www.bestwesternwyoming.com), 116 E. Park Street in Hot Springs State Park (see *Green Space—State Parks*). Children 16 and under stay free with their parents. Yes, it has the name of a mainstream hotel, but due to its location in Hot Springs State Park, plus the historic nature of its structure (built in 1918 and renovated in 1999), it is a noteworthy lodging accommodation with plenty of local character. The hotel has 18 standard rooms and 18 two-room suites (some with wood-burning fireplaces), plus

mineral soaking tubs, a pool, and a complimentary breakfast. Expensive.

& ⁅¶⁆ ❦ **Coachman Inn Motel** (1-888-864-3854 or 307-864-3141; http://www.coachmanmotel.com), 112 US 20 South. Pets are $5 extra. All of the rooms in this small, privately owned motel come with a microwave and refrigerator. Continental breakfast is included, and the motel's grounds include large trees and lots of green grass. Moderate.

❦ ⁅¶⁆ ✐ & **Days Inn Hot Springs Convention Center** (1-800-DAYS-INN or 307-864-3131; http://www.thermopolis-hi.com), 115 E. Park Street in Hot Springs State Park (see *Green Space—State Parks*). Children 17 and under stay free with their parents; pets are $15 extra. Yes, it too has the name of a mainstream hotel, but this privately owned and operated establishment has several unique offerings for guests. Not only can you soak in the hot mineral water piped directly to its mineral soaking tubs, but also, you can take advantage of an athletic club with two floors and an outdoor swimming pool (in season). What else? On-premises massages, a big-game wildlife display in the **Safari Club Lounge,** and fine dining at the **Safari Club Restaurant** (serving dinner seven nights a week; expensive) . . . and the list goes on. Moderate to expensive.

⁅¶⁆ ❧ **Roundtop Mountain Motel** (1-800-584-9126; http://www.roundtopmotel.com), 412 N. Sixth Street. Recently renovated log cabins and motel rooms are available at this privately owned establishment situated within walking distance of Hot Springs State Park (see *Green Space—State Parks*). Hang out after the day's excursions on the large redwood deck—you can even throw some meat on the barbecue and enjoy a cookout. Moderate.

See also Float Trips by Eagle RV Park

and Campground in *To Do*—Paddling/Floating; and Fountain of Youth RV Park in Campgrounds.

CAMPGROUNDS &. **Bighorn National Forest** (see *Green Space*—National Lands) has more than 30 developed campgrounds, some handicapped accessible, mainly located along the Cloud Peak Skyway Scenic Byway, the Bighorn Scenic Byway, and the Medicine Wheel Passage Scenic Byway (see *To See*—Scenic Drives and *To See*—Scenic Drives in Northeast Wyoming: Sheridan and Buffalo). For a comprehensive map and description of campgrounds, visit the Web site. These campgrounds are operated by a private concessionaire, and they charge fees from mid-May through mid-September. Some accept reservations (1-877-444-6777 or http://www.recreation .gov), though many are first-come, first-served. Expect to pay $10–20 per night for most sites. For more details on campgrounds in specific areas, contact the Tongue Ranger District (307-674-2600), the Medicine Wheel/Paintrock District (307-548-6541 in Lovell; 307-765-4436 in Greybull), or the Powder River District (307-684-7806 in Buffalo; 307-347-5105 in Worland). In addition to the developed campgrounds, dispersed camping (free) is permitted throughout much of the forest.

&. **Five Springs Falls Campground** is located 22 miles east of Lovell on US 14 Alternate (access road not recommended for recreational vehicles of more than 25 feet in length). Open year-round; $7. This 19-site, first-come, first-served Bureau of Land Management (see *Green Space*—National Lands) campground is managed by the Cody Field Office. You should also know that in general, access to campgrounds is limited to the summer season, and that primitive camping is permitted on most BLM

lands (14-day limit) unless otherwise marked. See also Castle Gardens Scenic Area in *To See*—Natural Wonders and Five Springs Falls Trail in *To Do*—Hiking.

&. "ǀ" **Fountain of Youth RV Park** (307-864-3265; http://www.fountainof youthrvpark.com), 250 US 20 North, Thermopolis. Open year-round; reservations recommended. Under new ownership since 2005, this campground boasts its own private hot springs mineral pool on the premises, free to all guests for swimming and soaking. Shady sites promise a comfortable place to park and camp, while a cafeteria serves up meals if you don't feel like cooking. The owners of this campground also run the **Fountain of Youth Inn** (307-864-2321) in Thermopolis. Inexpensive to moderate.

"ǀ" **Ten Broek RV Park and Cabins and Horse Hotel** (307-366-2250), 98 Second Street, Ten Sleep. Open April through October. Situated on the west side of Ten Sleep, this campground features grassy areas and mature shade trees. It also has cabins and a bunkhouse (sleeps 12) available, as well as a horse boarding facility. Very inexpensive to inexpensive.

🐾 &. **Worland Campground** (307-347-2329; http://www.worlandcamp ground.info), 2313 Big Horn Avenue, Worland. Open year-round. Both tent campers and RVs are welcome here at this clean campground located on the east side of Worland. Plenty of shade trees and grassy sites offer ample room to spread out. Very inexpensive.

See also First Washakie County Church and Medicine Lodge Archaeological Site in *To See*—Historic Landmarks, Places, and Sites; Float Trips by Eagle RV Park and Campground in *To Do*—Paddling/Floating; and Bighorn Canyon National Recreation Area in *Green Space*—Recreation Areas.

Burlington

See Wayfaring Traveler Llama Ranch in *To Do*—Unique Adventures.

Hyattville

Diamond S Retreat (307-469-2204; http://personal.tctwest.net/~kr/), off WY 31 outside Hyattville (north of Ten Sleep). A large country cabin situated in an amazing setting perfect for fly fishing, hiking, wildlife viewing, or just relaxing, Diamond S sleeps up to seven people in its rustic, comfortable, hand-made pine log beds. The cabin is fully furnished and comes with a full-service kitchen (but no television or phone, to help preserve that sense of truly getting away from it all). Reservations are required. Expensive.

Ten Sleep

See Big Horn Mountain Resort in *To Do*—Snow Sports and Ten Broek RV Park & Cabins & Horse Hotel in Campgrounds.

Worland

⁰¡⁰ **Herzberg Hideaway Country Guest House** (307-347-2217; http://www.herzbergguesthouse.com), 1365 Airport Road. For a different sort of home-away-from-home experience, rent this charming, two-story, 1930s adobe home nestled 3 miles south of Worland on an acre of wooded land. This lodging is for adults only (up to five people), and a minimum stay of two nights is requested. A barn for horses or llamas is available by pre-arrangement. Moderate to expensive.

✳ Where to Eat

EATING OUT

Greybull

✎ **Wheels Inn Restaurant and Gift Shop** (307-765-2456), 1336 N. 6th Street (or US 16, the main street through town). Open 24 hours, this restaurant specializes in what seems to be Wyomingites' unofficial favorite dessert—homemade pie. Grab yourself a slice anytime, day or night, or sit down for a full meal. A salad bar is available daily, and a buffet is served every Sunday. As an added attraction, the Wheels Inn Restaurant has a **50-foot dinosaur mural.** Moderate.

Shell

⁰¡⁰ ✎ **Dirty Annie's Country Store** (307-765-2304; http://www.dirtyannies.com), 1669 US 14. Open three meals a day; call for current hours. If you've never had a lamb burger, you can try one out at Dirty Annie's for lunch or dinner—the lamb is raised by 4-H participants from Shell. Regular burgers are also available, along with a full menu of American favorites (and Mexican options, too). This is also a great place to stop for some old-fashioned, hand-dipped hard ice cream. Let the kids explore the store's authentic sheep wagon while you stretch your legs and browse the shopping area before beginning your journey up the Bighorn Scenic Byway (see *To See*—Scenic Drives in Northeastern Wyoming: Sheridan and Buffalo). Moderate.

Ten Sleep

🌸 ✎ **Crazy Woman Café** (307-366-2700), 125 Second Street. Open daily for breakfast, lunch, and dinner. Home-style cooking is the menu here, with burgers, sandwiches, salads, and steaks. Save room for a delicious slice of freshly baked, homemade pie. Inexpensive.

✎ **Dirty Sally's** (307-366-2500; http://www.tctwest.net/~kmoore/), 124 Second Street. Open daily; hours vary according to season. If you like ice cream, no visit to Ten Sleep would be complete without a stop at Dirty Sally's. Not only is the store (a historic structure itself) filled to the brim with souvenirs and items of local interest, but also, it serves the best ice cream in town in quantities so vast that you won't believe your eyes. Try a waffle cone (made right in the shop) with two scoops—go ahead, you deserve it. Inexpensive.

☝ **Ten Sleep Saloon and Restaurant** (307-366-2237), 211 Second Street, Ten Sleep. Open for lunch and dinner; call for current hours/days. A family-friendly restaurant (with eat-in or take-out Chicago-style pizza) accompanies the standard western bar you'll find here. Inexpensive to moderate.

See also Big Horn Mountain Stage Company in *Entertainment*.

Thermopolis

☝ **Pumpernicks Family Restaurant** (307-864-5151; http://www.pumper nicksfamilyrestaurant.com), 512 Broadway, Thermopolis. Open daily for breakfast, lunch, and dinner; closed Sundays in winter. Have a seat on the enclosed patio if the weather permits, and then take some time perusing the large menu at this family-run restaurant—unless it's Friday or Saturday night. So long as you're a meat eater, the prime rib special is all you need to satisfy your hunger. Deli sandwiches are recommended as well. Be sure to save room for a slice of one of Verna's homemade pies, brownies, or carrot cake. Inexpensive to moderate.

See also Dairyland Ice Cream and Sweet Spot Miniature Golf in *To Do—For Families*; and Nature's Corner in *To Do—Relaxation and Rejuvenation*.

Worland

☝ **Brass Plum** (307-347-8999), 1620 Big Horn Avenue. Open for breakfast and lunch Monday through Saturday. This café-style restaurant serves up family-style, hearty breakfast and lunch fare in a comfortable environment. Outdoor patio seating is available when weather permits. Inexpensive.

☝ **Habanero Mexican Grill** (307-347-4222), 1608 Big Horn Avenue.

Open daily for lunch and dinner. Big portions mean good value here, where you get to watch your burrito being created from start to finish, telling them which toppings to add before they roll it up into one delicious wrapped-up feast. Inexpensive.

DINING OUT

Greybull

Lisa's Fine Food and Spirits (307-765-4765; http://www.lisasfinefoods .com), 200 Greybull Avenue. Open for three meals a day; call for current hours. Serving up delicious and creative entrées with a Southwestern flair, as well as native Wyoming favorites (think steak), for more than a decade, Lisa's is a favorite both with locals and passers through. Southwestern specialties include enchiladas and fajitas, while steaks are available prepared in a variety of ways. The menu also includes pastas, stir-fries, and heart-healthy options. Expensive.

Thermopolis

See Days Inn Hot Springs Convention Center in *Lodging*—Hotels and Motels.

✳ Entertainment

☙ **Big Horn Mountain Stage Company** (307-366-6848; http://www.big hornmountainstage.com), 201 Second Street, Ten Sleep. Hours vary according to the day and the season. This historic building, constructed in 1903, has been completely renovated, yet retains its historic flair, complete with an unusual pressed-copper ceiling. Step into an old-fashioned general store complete with barrels of hard candy and all sorts of cool gifts and local souvenirs, or grab a brew and some wood-fired pizza out in the beer garden. Perhaps best of all, the stage company hosts talented musicians frequently, especially throughout the summer months, including local sensation Jalan Crossland (http://www.jalancrossland .com).

Cottonwood Twin Cinemas (307-347-8414), 401 Robertson Avenue, Worland.

The Ritz Theatre (307-864-3118), 309 Arapahoe Street, Thermopolis.

✳ Selective Shopping

Bighorn Quilt Shop (1-877-586-9150; http://www.bighornquilts.com); 529 Greybull Avenue, Greybull. Open 9–5 Monday through Saturday. For those who love to sew, this store is a must. Here, you'll find all your fabric supplies and patterns, plus completed quilts for sale, along with gifts, books, magazines, and more.

See also Hot Springs County Museum and Cultural Center in *To See*—Museums; Wyoming Dinosaur Center and Dig Sites in *To Do*—For Families; Nature's Corner in *To Do*—Relaxation and Rejuvenation; Dirty Sally's in *Where to Eat*—Eating Out; Big Horn Mountain Stage Company in *Entertainment*; and Gift of the Waters Pageant in *Special Events*.

✳ Special Events

April: **Hot Springs County Wine,**

Food and Fine Arts Festival (307-864-3192): This annual celebration of all three (wine, food, and art) includes a juried art competition and a silent auction.

June: **Days of 49,** Greybull: The annual local celebration includes a barbecue, rodeo, parade, western street dance, and more.

July: **Fourth of July Parade, Ten Sleep Rodeo, and Street Dance,** Ten Sleep: The whole town comes out to celebrate during this annual two-day bash, featuring fireworks, a rodeo, dancing, live entertainment, food, and more.

July to August: **Big Horn County Fair** (307-568-2968, http://www.big horncountyfair.com), Basin: This is a traditional county fair running from the end of July into August.

August: **Nowoodstock Music Festival** (http://www.nowoodstock.com), Ten Sleep: A three-day outdoor music festival featuring local musicians and special guests. See also Ten Sleep Museum in *To See*—Museums.

August: **Outlaw Trail Ride** (http://www.rideoutlawtrail.com), Thermopolis: A weeklong, 100-mile trail ride through the Bighorn Basin brings participants in touch with the Old West; advance reservations required.

August: **Gift of the Waters Pageant,** Thermopolis: Taking place the first full weekend of August annually, this Indian ceremony reenacts the legend of the hot springs being given to Wyoming; you'll also find many vendor booths in Hot Springs State Park (see *Green Space*—State Parks).

August: **Washakie County Fair and Parade,** Worland: Enjoy a traditional county fair and events.

TEN SLEEP RODEO

LANDER AND RIVERTON

L ander is a growing Wyoming hotspot that thrives on a unique blend of cowboy culture, students, and environmental activism. The fact that Lander serves as the national headquarters for the National Outdoor Leadership School (NOLS; see *To Do*—Unique Adventures) probably has a lot to do with this trend. NOLS brings in numerous outsiders to Lander regularly as they filter through the town on their way to their outdoor educational experiences—and many of them keep on coming back, or end up staying in Lander and making it home. Hence Lander's mix that includes traditional Wyomingites such as ranchers, farmers, and cowboys, as well as the granola contingent—folks who sport the finest in outdoor tech wear, pursue outdoor recreational activities with abundant enthusiasm, and possess extensive knowledge of the environmental impact of humans on the natural world. As a result of this somewhat unusual combination of people making up the local population, you'll find amenities and services geared toward both crowds in Lander.

Not to be forgotten are the other peoples who have strong traditional ties and histories associated with this area—namely, American Indians. Wyoming's sole Indian reservation, the 2.2-million-acre Wind River Indian Reservation, lies in this region. In addition to the Indian artifacts and histories documented at many of the museums and historical attractions throughout this region, the reservation itself is home to several museums that endeavor to chronicle the past of the reservation's two distinctively different tribes—the Eastern Shoshone and the Northern Arapaho (see Fort Washakie in *To Do*—Towns). The Eastern Shoshone received the reservation—their cultural and traditional homeland—through the Fort Bridger Treaty, negotiated by the great leader, Chief Washakie, in 1868. They thereby became America's sole Indian tribe to actually remain on their traditional homelands—every other tribe in this region and elsewhere was placed on a reservation that did not include its original and familiar lands. Such was the fate of one of the Eastern Shoshone's historic enemies, the culturally distinctive Northern Arapaho, who joined them on the Wind River Reservation in 1878 in what was supposed to be a temporary arrangement—but which nonetheless became a permanent one. The two tribes have struggled to live together on this land ever since, attempting to find harmony while still retaining their unique cultural histories and traditions.

Lander's northeastern neighbor, Riverton, is located on the Wind River Indian Reservation. This town of nearly 10,000 people is home to a regional airport with daily flights to and from Denver. In addition to Wind River Heritage Center (see

To See—Museums) and a nice downtown shopping area, you'll find a plethora of inexpensive motel-style lodging options in Riverton, as well as a Wal-Mart and at least two handicapped-accessible, privately run campgrounds (see *Lodging*—Campgrounds). Riverton also has seven city parks and 8 miles of paths maintained by the parks department.

Recreational opportunities in this area of Wyoming range from snowshoeing and snowmobiling in winter to rock climbing and hiking in summer. Here you'll find the state's highest mountain, Gannett Peak (13,804 feet), situated on the Continental Divide in the Wind River Mountains of the Shoshone National Forest (see *Green Space*—National Lands). An abundance of adventures awaits you in these mountains, whether you choose to explore them yourself, or perhaps under the guidance of an instructor from the National Outdoor Leadership School (NOLS; see *To Do*—Unique Adventures). Some of the state's most well-known rock climbing destinations—Sinks Canyon and Wild Iris (see *To Do*—Climbing) among them—can be found within a half-hour drive of Lander, accounting for the annual International Climbers' Festival hosted by the town (see *Special Events*). In winter, Lander serves as the southern terminus of the state's acclaimed Continental Divide Snowmobile Trail (see *To Do*—Snow Sports), which stretches northwest past Dubois, ultimately reaching its northern terminus in West Yellowstone, Montana. Free or inexpensive camping is easy to find in both Lander and Riverton.

GUIDANCE Lander Chamber of Commerce (1-800-433-0662 or 307-332-3892, http://www.landerchamber.org), 160 N. First Street, Lander, 82520.

Riverton Chamber of Commerce (1-800-325-2732 or 307-856-4801, http://www.rivertonchamber.org), 213 W. Main Street, Riverton, 82501.

Wind River Visitors Council (1- 800-645-6233; http://www.wind-river.org, also http://www.windrivercountry.com), P.O. Box 925, Lander, 82520. Provides visitor information on all towns, plus Indian reservation.

GETTING THERE *By car:* US 287 leads to Lander from the northwest and the southeast. WY 28 reaches Lander from the southwest. WY 789 reaches Riverton and Lander from the north and south and is the main road connecting the two cities. US 26 reaches Riverton from the east and west.

By plane: **Riverton Regional Airport** (307-856-1307; http://www.flyriverton.com) is located on the west side of town.

GETTING AROUND Both Lander and Riverton are small enough that walking around the downtown area (and much of the town) is a great way to see each place. The cities are 25 miles apart, so you'll have to get in your car to travel between them, as well as to many of this area's outlying attractions.

MEDICAL EMERGENCY Dial 911.

Lander Valley Medical Center (307-332-4420; http://www.landerhospital.com), 1320 Bishop Randall Drive, Lander.

Riverton Memorial Hospital (307-856-4161; http://www.riverton-hospital.com), 2100 W. Sunset Drive, Riverton.

✳ To See

TOWNS **Hudson** is a small town about 10 miles northeast of Lander on WY 789, just on the border of the Wind River Indian Reservation. It has a handful of eclectic shops and restaurants, as well as a gas station.

Shoshoni is situated at the junction of US 20/26, 22 miles northeast of Riverton. Here you'll find several motels and service stations, as well as restaurants, an old-fashioned drugstore serving malts and shakes, and a city park that allows overnight camping.

MUSEUMS ✿ ♿ ✐ **Museum of the American West** (307-335-8778; http://www .amwest.org), 1445 W. Main Street, Lander. Open 9–5 Monday through Friday, 1–4 Saturday, May 16 through October 31; free. At the time of publication, this museum was still in its development phase. Ultimately, the Museum of the American West aims to include the Lander Children's Museum (see listing in For Families), the Pioneer Museum, the Pushroot Living History Village, and the Native Americans of the Central Plains and Rockies Museum and an adjoining living history display, all in the same location. This will provide visitors with a wonderfully extensive and informative historical destination that will include places of interest for the whole family. The museum also offers self-guided tours and guided tours as well as American American powwow dance exhibitions and occasional concerts.

WIND RIVER INDIAN RESERVATION

You'll find the headquarters of the **Wind River Indian Reservation,** Wyoming's sole Indian reservation, northwest of Lander on US 287 in **Fort Washakie.** Established in 1868, the reservation is home to two tribes—the Northern Arapaho (307-332-6120 or 307-856-3461; http://www.northern arapaho.com) and the Eastern Shoshone (307-332-3532; http://www.eastern shoshone.net). Having once served as a U.S. military post, Fort Washakie is home to many historic buildings and is listed on the National Register of Historic Places. Fort Washakie is also home to the **graves of Sacajawea and Chief Washakie.** The towns of **Ethete, Arapahoe,** and **St. Stephens** to the east of Fort Washakie are mainly home to members of the Northern Arapaho tribe. You'll find the **Northern Arapaho Cultural Museum** (307-332-2660) at the old **St. Michael's Mission** in Ethete, and the **North American Indian Heritage Center** at **St. Stephen's Mission** in Arapahoe (307-856-7806). To take advantage of the tremendous fishing opportunities on the reservation—including more than 1,000 miles of streams and more than 250 lakes—you'll need a permit from the Tribal Fish and Game Department, which you'll find at the old Bureau of Indian Affairs building in Fort Washakie (307-332-7207), open regular business hours. Both tribes hold annual powwows that are open to the public (see *Special Events*). See also Wind River in *To Do*—Fishing.) Other towns on the reservation include **Crowheart, Kinnear,** and **Pavillion.**

RIVERTON MUSEUM

❧ Riverton Museum (307-856-2665; http://www.wyoming.com/~rivmus/ default.shl), 700 E. Park Avenue, Riverton. Open 10–4 Tuesday through Saturday; free. Housed in a historic building that served as the Riverton Methodist Church from 1916–1960, the museum maintains a collection of items and artifacts detailing the pioneer history of the local area.

❧ Wind River Heritage Center (307-856-0706), 1075 S. Federal Boulevard, Riverton. Open 10–6 Monday through Saturday; donations gladly accepted. The central attraction of this local history museum is the Jake Korell Wildlife Collection. This collection includes life-sized displays of local and regional wildlife positioned in active, realistic settings, giving the visitor a sense of the area's ecological diversity. Also included in the exhibits are animal traps dating to the early 1800s, as well as additional fur-trade era artifacts. Additionally, you'll find an extensive gift shop here with jewelry and other artwork made by members of the Northern Arapaho and Eastern Shoshone tribes that call the Wind River Indian Reservation home. The center hosts dancing demonstrations and lectures throughout the year.

See also Fort Washakie in *To See*—Towns; and Atlantic City Mercantile in *To See*—Historic Landmarks, Places, and Sites.

HISTORIC LANDMARKS, PLACES, AND SITES Atlantic City Mercantile (307-332-5143), 100 E. Main Street, Atlantic City; 2 miles off WY 28 (look for signs to Atlantic City). Open year-round; call for current hours/days. Listed on the National Register of Historic Places, this historic structure, constructed in 1893, hearkens back to this area's booming gold rush days. Back in the late 19th and early 20th centuries, both Atlantic City and nearby South City served as destinations for those willing to seek their fortunes in this part of Wyoming's high country. The mercantile served not only as a place for locals to stock up on supplies, but also as one of the town's social centers where people could catch up on the latest news and gossip from around the town. The store closed in 1929 after the death of its original owner, Lawrence Giessler. It remained closed until 1964, when it was purchased by a new owner and reopened as a bar. Since then, it has remained open, though its ownership and functions have changed over the years.

HISTORIC BUILDINGS AT SOUTH PASS CITY HISTORIC SITE, ONE OF THIS REGION'S MAIN HISTORICAL ATTRACTIONS

Castle Gardens (307-332-8400; http://www.wy.blm.gov/lfo/cultural/castlegardens .htm) is roughly 45 miles east of Riverton; take WY 136 (Gas Hills Road) about 35 miles to a left turn (signed), proceed about 6 miles to a right turn (signed), and proceed about 5 miles to the site. This drive—particularly the last few miles—is best made in summer months, when the dirt road has had an ample opportunity to dry out. At Castle Gardens, you'll be swept into the area's prehistoric past via the impressive array of petroglyphs found carved into the rocks here. Unlike pictographs, or paintings on the rocks, petroglyphs are actually carved into the rocks' surfaces, often a laborious process for the carver. The petroglyphs at Castle Gardens feature shields and warriors bearing shields, among other distinctive artwork, and many were colored with dyes after being carved into the stone. A footpath takes you among the petroglyphs, but please only look and don't touch—they've already seen more than their fair share of damage from vandals throughout the years. Managed by the Lander Field Office of the Bureau of Land Management, Castle Gardens is listed on the National Register of Historic Places (see also Bureau of Land Management in *Green Space*—National Lands).

South Pass is located 10 miles southwest of South Pass City and about 45 miles southwest of Lander on WY 28. This National Historic Landmark proved to be the key to unlocking westward travel for pioneers along the Oregon Trail. The easiest passage through the Rocky Mountains, South Pass witnessed the flood of emigrants traveling by wagon train through this barren country from 1843 through 1912. Today, South Pass still serves as a key travel route, but trust me—unless you need to, you do NOT want to travel this route at any time of year except for summer. I've witnessed some of the most treacherous and terrible driving conditions of my entire life along WY 28 over South Pass, including a brilliant combination of pea soup fog, horizontal sleet, snow-covered roads, and high winds—in May. Just imagine enduring such conditions in a covered wagon without a well-marked highway dotted with reflectors to guide your way! See also Bureau of Land Management in *Green Space*—National Lands.

&. ❦ **South Pass City Historic Site (307-332-3684;** http://wyoparks.state.wy.us/ Site/SiteInfo.asp?siteID=22), 125 South Pass Main, several miles off WY 28 (35 miles south of Lander). Exhibits are open daily 9–6 May 16 through September 30, grounds open year-round sunrise to sunset; $2 per adult (resident), $4 per adult (nonresident). This is a must-see site for anyone interested in the gold rush or just the general history of pioneers in this area. A fully restored gold rush town allows you intimate access into some 30 structures, which feature period furnishings and plenty of interpretive materials to guide your way. Stroll through town and take it in, learning about the strike that originally brought people to the area in 1867, as well as the unique

SOUTH PASS CITY HISTORIC SITE

characters who left long-term legacies for the generations to come. Additional attractions at this site include an operational general store with items for sale, a 3-mile hiking trail along Willow Creek, and access to the Continental Divide National Scenic Trail, which runs right through town. To complete your South Pass experience, stop at the former mining towns of **Miner's Delight** and **Atlantic City,** which can be accessed via the same area of WY 28, before journeying over South Pass (see above). Want to stay nearby? Try Miner's Delight Bed and Breakfast in nearby historic Atlantic City (see *Lodging*—Bed and Breakfasts). See also Bureau of Land Management in *Green Space*—National Lands and Gold Rush Days in *Special Events*.

See also Fort Washakie in *To See*—Towns; Riverton Museum in *To See*—Museums; Blue Spruce Inn and Delfelder Inn Bed and Breakfast in *Lodging*—Bed and Breakfasts; and Gannett Grill in *Where to Eat*—Eating Out.

CITY PARKS AND GARDENS **Lander City Park** (307-332-4647), 405 Fremont Street. Open year-round; free. Lander's city park should be a model for all small towns in America. You can stay and camp for up to three days in the shade of giant cottonwood trees next to a pleasant, gurgling stream. The park also has picnic tables, flush toilets, and large grassy areas, as well as a playground, baseball diamond, and in winter, an ice-skating rink. I've spent many a night camping in this park, and though local kids might cruise through looking for excitement, they rarely find anything going on here besides sleeping campers.

See also Shoshoni in *To See*—Towns.

SCENIC DRIVES **Red Canyon Overlook,** located 24 miles south of Lander on WY 28, offers a beautiful view of the stunning Red Canyon. This striking landscape is managed by the BLM (see *Green Space*—National Lands), except for the centrally located Red Canyon Ranch, which is owned and managed by The Nature Conservancy (http://www.nature.org).

See South Pass in *To See*—Historic Landmarks, Places, and Sites; Louis Lake in *To Do*—Boating; Sinks Canyon State Park in *Green Space*—State Parks; and BLM Campgrounds in *Lodging*—Campgrounds.

NATURAL WONDERS See Castle Gardens in Historic Landmarks, Places, and Sites; Popo Agie Falls Trail in *To Do*—Hiking; Sinks Canyon State Park in *Green Space*—State Parks; and Wind River Canyon in *To See*—Natural Wonders in Northwest Wyoming: Thermopolis and Worland.

RED CANYON OVERLOOK IN WINTER

✷ To Do

BICYCLING **Baldwin Creek Road-Squaw Creek Road Loop** is a 10.6-mile ride best done on a road bike; it starts on the west end of Lander's Main Street. From there, you'll head left (west) on Baldwin Creek Road for 5.3 miles, climbing gradually out of town and then winding through sparsely inhabited lands, with some BLM- and state-owned lands on the south side of the road (great for mountain biking). After 5.3 miles, the road angles sharply southeast (left), looping as it becomes Squaw Creek Road. Continue your journey through undulating, winding terrain for another 5.2 miles before you reach the intersection with Sinks Canyon Road (WY 131). From there, you can complete the loop by following Sinks Canyon Road to 9th Street. Go left on 9th Street, and then left on Main Street, and pedal back to your starting point—or stop in at one of the restaurants on Main Street to refuel. For a longer ride, you can tack on an out-and-back journey along Sinks Canyon Road to Sinks Canyon State Park (see *Green Space*—State Parks) by turning right instead of left off Squaw Peak Road. It's about 6 miles to the park's entrance from the intersection of Squaw Peak Road and Sinks Canyon Road.

& **Wyoming Heritage Trail** is a rails-to-trails project that takes you from Riverton to Shoshone, with about 5 miles paved with asphalt and the remaining 17 miles of trail featuring rather rough terrain. You'll have to do a little searching to find the trailhead, since it's not well marked (unless things have changed recently). Stop in at the Riverton Chamber of Commerce (see Guidance) for the latest information. Basically, you'll be heading northeast through town on a paved surface until you reach the edge of Riverton—and then, you're on your way through the wilder, wackier terrain of Wyoming's wetlands and prairies, which can be rocky and rutted at times. You'll probably enjoy total solitude, unless you count the jackrabbits, antelope, mule deer, birds, and other fauna you'll potentially encounter as you ride. Bring plenty of water, food, and an adventuresome spirit on this ride. The trail terminates in the tiny town of Shoshoni (see *To See*—Towns). Hikers and four-wheelers also enjoy this trail, as do snowmobilers and cross-country skiers in winter.

See also Wild Iris Mountain Sports in *To Do*—Climbing; Popo Agie Falls Trail in *To Do*—Hiking; *Green Space*; Louis Lake Lodge in *Lodging*—Lodges; and BLM Campgrounds in *Lodging*—Campgrounds.

BOATING Louis Lake, in the Shoshone National Forest (see *Green Space*—National Lands) southwest of Lander, is accessible by taking Sinks Canyon Road southwest out of town, through Sinks Canyon State Park (see *To See*—Natural Wonders), and then up the canyon, where it changes into Louis Lake Road (also called The Loop Road), switchbacks up Fossil Hill, and leads you back to this remote yet accessible alpine lake—a beautiful drive. Situated nearby is Louis Lake Lodge (see *Lodging*—Lodges), which provides you with an array of services, including boat rentals if you don't have your own boat with you. Close to the border of the **Popo Agie Wilderness,** the lake is a great place to start a boating or fishing adventure. You can easily access numerous other nearby lakes, including **Fiddlers Lake,** where boating is also permitted. In addition, this area is rife with trails great for hiking, cross-country skiing, snowmobiling, and more. See also Popo Agie River in *To Do*—Fishing.

See also Boysen State Park in *Green Space*—State Parks and Shoshone National Forest in *Green Space*—National Lands.

CLIMBING Exum Mountain Guides (307-733-2297; http://www.exumguides .com), South Jenny Lake, P.O. Box 56, Grand Teton National Park, Moose, 83012.

Exum teaches rock climbing classes (from $155 per person per day and up) at both Wild Iris and Sinks Canyon State Park (see *Green Space*—State Parks), near Lander.

Jackson Hole Mountain Guides (1-800-239-7642 or 307-733-4979; http://www .jhmg.com), P.O. Box 7477, 165 N. Glenwood Street, Jackson, 83002. JHMG teaches full-day (from $160 per person) and half-day (from $110 per person) classes at a number of Lander-area crags, including Sinks Canyon State Park (see *Green Space*—State Parks) and Wild Iris.

Wild Iris Mountain Sports (1-888-284-5968 or 307-332-4541; http://www.wildiris climbing.com), 333 Main Street, Lander. Open daily; call for current hours. For all the information you might need about rock climbing at nearby **Wild Iris** (located a half-hour's drive south of Lander off WY 28) or other popular climbing areas around Lander, this store (or its Web site) is the place to go. You can find updated crag and trail conditions (for hikers and cyclists), as well as all of the outdoor-related supplies and information you need.

See also Elemental Training Center in *To Do*—Fitness Centers; NOLS in *To Do*—Unique Adventures; Sinks Canyon State Park in *Green Space*—State Parks; Bureau of Land Management and Shoshone National Forest in *Green Space*—National Lands; and International Climbers' Festival in *Special Events*.

FISHING **Popo Agie River** (307-332-7723; http://gf.state.wy.us/fish/fishing/ index.asp), pronounced Puh-*poh* zha, (meaning headwaters in Crow Indian), lies mainly in the Shoshone National Forest (see also *Green Space*—National Lands). The Popo Agie has three forks: the North Fork, flowing from the Wind River Mountains through the North Fork Canyon northwest of Lander; the Middle Fork, flowing from the Wind River Mountains through Sinks Canyon southwest of Lander; and the Little Popo Agie River, flowing from the Wind River Mountains through Little Popo Agie Canyon south of Sinks Canyon. The Middle and North

THE MIDDLE FORK OF THE POPO AGIE RIVER, FLOWING THROUGH SINKS CANYON

Forks meet just north of Lander, along with Baldwin Creek, Squaw Creek, and several other creeks. The Little Popo Agie joins them around Hudson, northeast of Lander along WY 789. The river then flows northeast a few more miles to its confluence with the Little Wind River, which empties into the Wind River shortly thereafter in Riverton. The North Fork's species include brook trout, hybridized Yellowstone cutthroat, rainbow trout, and mountain whitefish in its upper reaches, giving way to brook trout, brown trout, burbot, mountain whitefish, rainbow trout, and sauger in the midway and lower portions. The Middle Fork's species include arctic grayling, golden trout, Snake River cutthroat trout, and Yellowstone cutthroat trout in the upper reaches, with brown trout, brook trout, mountain whitefish, and rainbow trout throughout. The Little Popo Agie's species include brook trout, golden trout, and Snake River cutthroat trout in the upper regions, with brown trout, burbot, rainbow trout, and sauger throughout. See also Popo Agie Falls Trail in *To Do*—Hiking and Sinks Canyon State Park in *Green Space*—State Parks.

Wind River (307-332-7723; http://gf.state.wy.us/fish/fishing/index.asp; and 307-332-7207 for the section on the Wind River Indian Reservation managed by the Tribal Fish and Game Department), flows from its origins on Togwotee Pass northwest of Dubois alongside US 26/287, and then roughly parallels US 26 through the Wind River Indian Reservation to its confluence with the Little Wind River in Riverton. From there, it turns northeast, flowing roughly parallel to US 26/WY 789 into Boysen Reservoir (see *Green Space*—State Parks), and then flows north out of the reservoir through the Wind River Canyon (see *To See*—Natural Wonders in Thermopolis and Worland), where it changes names to the Bighorn River (see *To Do*—Fishing in Thermopolis and Worland) just south of Thermopolis. Species include brook trout and rainbow trout, as well as walleye and sauger in the Wind River Canyon vicinity. To fish on the reservation, a special tribal permit is required. Upon purchasing the permit, you can also ask for information about access points on the reservation.

See also Fort Washakie in *To See*—Towns; Louis Lake in *To Do*—Boating; NOLS in *To Do*—Unique Adventures; Boysen State Park in *Green Space*—State Parks; Bureau of Land Management and Shoshone National Forest in *Green Space*—National Lands; Louis Lake Lodge in *Lodging*—Lodges; BLM Campgrounds in *Lodging*—Campgrounds; and Sweetwater River in Central Wyoming: Casper and Douglas.

FITNESS CENTERS 🛥 **Elemental Training Center** (307-332-0480; http://www.elementalgym.com), 134 Lincoln Street, Lander. Open daily; hours vary according to season; $8 per person. This serious training facility features top-notch exercise equipment plus drop-in classes, personal training, and an indoor rock-climbing wall.

Teton Athletic Club (307-856-5424; http://www.tetonac.com), 911 Flag Drive, Riverton. Open 5:30 AM–9:30 PM Monday through Thursday, 5:30 AM–8:30 PM Friday, 7–4 Saturday, noon–6 Sunday; call for current drop-in rates. This full-service fitness center has exercise equipment, fitness classes, racquetball courts, and more.

FOR FAMILIES 🖉 **Lander Children's Museum** (307-332-1341; http://www.landerchildrensmuseum.org), 445 Lincoln Street. Open 10–1 Tuesday through Friday; $3 per person ages 3 and up. Geared toward children ages 3–12, the Lander Children's Museum offers an array of hands-on exhibits designed to stimulate children's innate curiosity about the world around them. Learning becomes fun through interactive exhibits that provide children with ample opportunities to explore not only the disciplines of math and science, but also, art, music, reading and more. The Lander Children's Museum is scheduled to move at some point in the future to the campus of the Museum of the American West (see *To See*—Museums).

See also Lander City Park in *To See*—City Parks and Gardens; Ice-skating in *To Do*—Snow Sports; Boysen State Park and Sinks Canyon State Park in *Green*

Space—State Parks; Louis Lake Lodge in *Lodging*—Lodges; Owl Creek Kampground and Sleeping Bear Ranch RV Park and Campground in *Lodging*—Campgrounds; and Silver Spur Lanes in *Entertainment*.

GOLF Lander Golf Club (307-332-4653; http://www.landergolfclub.com), 1 Golf Course Drive, Lander, 18 holes.

Renegade Golf Course (307-857-0117), 12814 US 26 West, Riverton, 9 holes.

Riverton Country Club (307-856-4779; http://www.rivertoncountryclub.net), 4275 Country Club Drive, Riverton, 18 holes.

HIKING Popo Agie Falls Trail, in the Shoshone National Forest (see *Green Space*—National Lands) south of Lander, can be accessed by going south on Sinks Canyon Road from Lander, and then proceeding through Sinks Canyon State Park (see *Green Space*—State Parks) to Bruce's Parking Area. From there, start your hike by crossing the footbridge over the Middle Fork of the Popo Agie River and turning left (west). The 3-mile round-trip features a moderate gain in elevation as it takes you through forests, passing granite outcrops, and then through an open area with great views of the canyon below and behind you. Finally, you'll reach the falls themselves. In spring and early summer, they can appear as roaring cascades up to 60 feet in height, with pools where local teenagers often can be seen frolicking. By mid- to late summer and early fall, the falls usually have dwindled in size and scope, though they are still lovely. In winter, viewing the falls can be just as awesome as seeing them in the tumultuous raging beauty of the spring thaw. You'll likely have the place all to yourself while you observe the white and deep-blue hues of the frozen falls set against the bleak and harsh winter landscape. This trail is very popular not only for hikers, but also for trail runners, mountain bikers, and horseback riders. See also Popo Agie River in *To Do*—Fishing.

See also South Pass City Historic Site in *To See*—Historic Landmarks, Places, and Sites; Wyoming Heritage Trail in *To Do*—Bicycling; Louis Lake in *To Do*—Boating; Wild Iris Mountain Sports in *To Do*—Climbing; NOLS in *To Do*—Unique Adventures; *Green Space*; Louis Lake Lodge in *Lodging*—Lodges; and BLM Campgrounds in *Lodging*—Campgrounds.

HORSEBACK RIDING See Popo Agie Falls Trail in *To Do*—Hiking; NOLS in *To Do*—Unique Adventures; Bureau of Land Management and Shoshone National Forest in *Green Space*—National Lands; and Louis Lake Lodge in *Lodging*—Lodges.

PADDLING/FLOATING See NOLS in *To Do*—Unique Adventures; Boysen State Park in *Green Space*—State Parks; and Louis Lake Lodge in *Lodging*—Lodges.

RELAXATION AND REJUVENATION ❧ **Kathleen Chopping, CMT** (307-332-4696), 159 N. Second Street, Lander. Open by appointment; call for current rates. Qualified hands knead your troubles and tensions away to the sounds of gentle music. Professional and experienced, this is one of the finest massage therapists you will find anywhere.

Graham's Gluten-Free Foods (307-857-6155; http://www.grahamsglutenfree .com) 414 E. Main Street, Riverton. Open 10–5:30 Monday, 8:30–5:30 Tuesday through Thursday, 8:30–4 Friday, closed Saturday, 11–5:30 Sunday This wonderful natural foods store carries a large inventory of not just gluten-free foods, but also, all sorts of quality organic and whole foods as well as supplements, vitamins, books, and gifts. Their organic, gluten-free soup and salad bar is open 11–2 Sunday through Friday.

Pelle Bella Day Spa (307-856-7374; http://www.pellebella.net); 213 S. Broadway, Riverton. Call in advance to make an appointment. This day spa offers a full-range of skin treatments, including facials, peels, exfoliations, and LED light treatments.

SNOW SPORTS Continental Divide Snowmobile Trail (http://www.sled wyoming.com) is a 365-mile trail roughly paralleling the Continental Divide that runs from Lander in the south to West Yellowstone, Montana in the north, running northwest through areas around Pinedale, Dubois, Togwotee Pass, and Yellowstone National Park. The trail passes over the divide four times, and it also gives you access to hundreds of miles of side trails, both groomed and ungroomed, along its way. Consistently ranked as one of the nation's premier snowmobiling destinations by enthusiasts of the activity, the trail features incredibly remote and scenic terrain as well as an array of visitor services spread out along its length. See also Louis Lake in *To Do*—Boating; and Louis Lake Lodge in *Lodging*—Lodges.

Cross-country skiing opportunities are virtually limitless in this region, with miles and miles of trails for the both the fit and seasoned skier as well as the novice to explore. You'll find 6 miles (10 km) of groomed trails accessible near South Pass (see *To See*—Historic Landmarks, Places, and Sites), south of Lander. In town, Freewheel Ski and Cycle (307-332-6616), 378 W. Main Street, offers ski rentals and can give you advice about where to ski in the area, as can Wild Iris Mountain Sports (see *To Do*—Climbing). See also Lander Golf Course in *To Do*—Golfing.

Ice fishing opportunities can be found in this region, particularly at Boysen Reservoir (see *Green Space*—State Parks). Also look for opportunities at smaller mountain lakes in the Wind River Mountains (see Shoshone National Forest in *Green Space*—National Lands).

🦌 🛹 **Ice-skating** on rinks, as well as on frozen lakes and ponds, provides a fun diversion and a great workout. Test your skill on the blades in this region at Lander City Park (see *To See*—City Parks and Gardens), which has a regulation hockey rink open to the public during wintertime (skate rentals available for a small fee). See also Louis Lake Lodge in *Lodging*—Lodges.

Snowmobiling opportunities in this region are incredible, including the trail by which all others can be judged, the Continental Divide Snowmobile Trail (see above). In addition to this showpiece, you'll find an array of side trails, both groomed and ungroomed, throughout the region. For detailed trail reports, call 307-777-6560 or go to http://wyotrails.state.wy.us/snow, the Wyoming Snowmobile Trails Web site, which also provides information about rules, rental agencies, trails around the state, and more. If you want to rent a snowmobile or hire a guide, you'll find a number of outfitters in this region, including Louis Lake Lodge (see *Lodging*—Lodges), near Lander, among others. Many of the area's guest ranches provide snowmobiling packages in the winter as well.

Snowshoeing is a great way to explore this region's abundance of developed trails in wintertime. You'll find plenty to keep you busy and warm in the Shoshone

National Forest (see *Green Space*—National Lands), as well as in Sinks Canyon State Park (see *Green Space*—State Parks) and in lands managed by the Bureau of Land Management (see *Green Space*—National Lands). See also Louis Lake in *To Do*—Boating; Popo Agie Falls Trail in *To Do*—Hiking; Cross-country skiing in *To Do*—Snow Sports; and Louis Lake Lodge in *Lodging*—Lodges (snowshoe rentals available).

See also *Green Space* and Louis Lake Lodge in *Lodging*—Lodges.

UNIQUE ADVENTURES Lander Llama Company (307-332-5624; http://www .llamahiking.com), 2024 Mortimore Lane, Lander. Hire a llama to do the work of ferrying your loads while you hike alongside this beast of burden in the Wind River Mountains, Absaroka Mountains, or Wyoming's Red Desert (see *To See*—Natural Wonders in Southwest Wyoming: Green River and Rock Springs). You'll start your llama rental experience with a mandatory three- to four-hour introductory course (for first timers) to backpacking with a llama ($25 per adult; free for children), which you can schedule anytime before your trip. Then rent a pair of llamas (you must rent at least two llamas, as they are social animals) for a minimum of three days ($100 per day for the first pair of llamas; $50 per day for each additional llama). The llamas come with their packs and gear; transporting the llamas to and from the trailheads will cost you extra (cost dependent on trailhead locations). Sound too complex? Then consider taking a guided trip, where experienced llama handlers lead you and the llamas through Wyoming's lovely terrain for anywhere from three days to a week ($630–1,575 per person). Either way, you must call in advance to make reservations, so you can consider all of your options then. See also The Bunk House in *Lodging*—Bed and Breakfasts.

WINERIES AND WINE TASTINGS See Wild West Winter Carnival in *Special Events*.

✳ Green Space

STATE PARKS ⟁ ✎ **Boysen State Park** (307-876-2796; http://wyoparks.state.wy .us/Site/SiteInfo.asp?siteID=2), accessible via US 20/WY 789 north of Shoshoni and just south of Wind River Canyon, and via points off US 26 west of Shoshoni (see *To See*—Towns). Open year-round for both day use ($4/resident, $6/nonresident) and camping ($10/resident, $17/nonresident), with limited facilities in the winter. The almost jarring visual dissonance created by Boysen Reservoir results from the presence of such an enormous body of water—nearly 20,000 acres—covering an area that at one point probably featured mainly arid prairies. The first damming of the Wind River took place here in 1908 under the directorship of a Danish immigrant, Asmus Boysen. That dam ceased operations in 1925. The present dam was built in 1951. Today, visitors enjoy easy access from a number of points to the reservoir's abundance of water-oriented recreational opportunities, including not only boating (five boat ramps), but also water skiing, swimming, and fishing (species include brown trout, crappie, cutthroat trout, ling, perch, rainbow trout, sauger, and wall-eye, among others). Additional recreational opportunities include playgrounds, bicycling, hiking, camping (11 campgrounds, some can be reserved), picnicking, and wildlife viewing. The marina is near the entrance of Wind River Canyon just off US 20 (watch for signs). See also Wind River in *To Do*—Fishing.

NATIONAL OUTDOOR LEADERSHIP SCHOOL

National Outdoor Leadership School (NOLS) (1-800-710-NOLS; http://www
.nols.edu), 284 Lincoln Street, Lander. One of the nation's top outdoor educational institutions, NOLS runs a wide variety of courses both in Wyoming
and around the world throughout the year covering an array of outdoor dis-
ciplines. Courses—including some that count for college credits—range in
length from 10 days to an entire school semester, and can include such
activities as backpacking, skiing, rock climbing, paddling, camping, environmental education, caving, snowboarding, horsepacking, and more. Many
courses do not require that you have any previous experience in the disci-
pline taught. Courses in Wyoming include Absaroka Backpacking, a 30-day
hiking/fly-fishing course open to ages 16 and up ($3,765 per person); Wind
River Wilderness—the original NOLS course—a 30-day hiking/fly-fishing
adventure open to ages 16 and up ($3,850 per person); and Rock Climbing, a
21-day course that takes place in the Wind River Range and is open to ages
16 and up ($3,965 per person); among other course offerings. Contact NOLS
for a complete course catalog and additional information about the applica-
tion process.

NATIONAL OUTDOOR LEADERSHIP SCHOOL HEADQUARTERS IN LANDER

&. ♪ ⚘ **Sinks Canyon State Park** (307-332-3077; http://wyoparks.state.wy.us/Site/SiteInfo.asp?siteID=12), 3079 Sinks Canyon Road, Lander. Open sunrise to sunset year-round for day use (free) and camping ($10 resident/$17 nonresident); visitor center open 9–6 Memorial Day through Labor Day. This park's biggest attraction gave the canyon its name. On your first visit, drive right by the signs marking The Rise and start your exploration of the park at The Sinks, which is accessible via hiking a short trail by the visitor center. A walk down the trail brings you to the remarkable cave complex known as The Sinks, where the Popo Agie River (see *To Do*—Fishing) plunges down into a latticed network of limestone caverns beneath the surface, disappearing entirely from sight until it resurfaces .25 mile down-canyon in a placidly bubbling pool known as the Rise, having worked its way through the underground tunnels back to the surface. The Rise is home to enormous trout that visitors feed by purchasing fish food from a nearby dispenser—but alas, no fishing is permitted at the Rise, which accounts for their enormity, no doubt! In addition to the Sinks and the Rise, Sinks Canyon State Park provides visitors with opportunities for bicycling (on-road only), camping, hiking (1-mile and 4-mile trails depart from the suspension bridge at the Popo Agie Campground), picnicking, playing on playground equipment, fishing, wildlife viewing (with Rocky Mountain bighorn sheep sometimes seen right along the road), and rock climbing, among other popular endeavors. See also Baldwin Creek Road-Squaw Creek Road Loop in *To Do*—Bicycling; and Popo Agie Falls Trail in *To Do*—Hiking.

NATIONAL LANDS Bureau of Land Management (BLM) (307-332-8400; http://www.wy.blm.gov/lfo/index.htm), Lander Field Office, 1335 Main Street, Lander. The BLM manages 2.5 million acres of public lands and 2.7 million acres of federal mineral estate in this region. Of particular interest to history aficionados exploring BLM land are the historic sites around South Pass, including South Pass City, Atlantic City, and Miner's Delight, as well as Castle Gardens (see *To See*—Historic Landmarks, Places, and Sites). Much of the land administered by the BLM is open to recreational pursuits, including bicycling, boating, camping (see *Lodging*—Campgrounds), fishing, hiking, horseback riding, paddling, rock climbing, wildlife viewing (including wild horses) and snow sports, including snowmobiling and cross-country skiing. BLM lands tend to be the most unregulated of public lands, meaning that most typical outdoor recreational pursuits are allowed on most BLM lands, guided by the dictates of Leave No Trace (1-800-332-4100 or 303-442-8222; http://www.lnt.org) outdoor ethics.

THE "SINKS" IN SINKS CANYON STATE PARK

Shoshone National Forest (307-332-5460; http://www.fs.fed.us/r2/shoshone), Washakie Ranger District, 333 E. Main Street, Lander. Created in 1891 as the Yellowstone National Reserve, Shoshone National Forest enjoys not only the distinction of being America's first national forest, but also, one of the largest national forests in the Rocky

Mountain Region, encompassing more than 2.4 million acres stretching from the northern border of Wyoming south to Lander and bordering Yellowstone National Park on the west. In this area of Wyoming, this land includes the southern Wind River Mountains. Recreational opportunities include bicycling, boating, camping, fishing, hiking, horseback riding, rock climbing, off-road vehicle travel (ATVs and snowmobiles), snow sports, hunting, wildlife viewing, and more. See also *Lodging*—Campgrounds.

✳ Lodging

BED AND BREAKFASTS

Atlantic City

🦟 **Miner's Delight Inn Bed and Breakfast** (1-888-292-0248 or 307-332-0248; http://www.minersdelightinn.com), 290 Atlantic Road. You'll enjoy a true old-time gold rush experience by staying in one of this B&B's three hotel rooms or one of its five historic log cabins (no televisions or Internet included). Situated in a historic 1895 former log hotel and surrounded by the historic setting of Atlantic City—once the site of a flourishing gold rush town, but now a mere ghost of its former incarnation—this lodging lies conveniently close to another former boomtown: South Pass City Historic Site (see *To See*—Historic Landmarks, Places, and Sites). The lodging also provides you with convenient access to the area's abundant snowmobiling and cross-country skiing opportunities, should you happen to stay in wintertime. Moderate.

Lander

✐ 🐾 **Baldwin Creek Bed and Breakfast** (307-332-7608; http://www.wyomingbandb.com), 2343 Baldwin Creek Road. You can enjoy the beauty of Red Butte Canyon on the outskirts of Lander while also enjoying convenient access to town at this B&B. Town proper is a short drive or bike ride away (see Baldwin Creek Road to Squaw Creek Road Loop in *To Do*—Bicycling), but you will enjoy the peace and quiet of this 34-acre country retreat, with access to literally thousands of acres of state lands just outside your door. Accommodations are in one of four cabins or two guest rooms in the main house, all with private bathrooms. Lodging rates include early morning coffee, a full breakfast served daily, and even afternoon treats. Moderate.

✐ ⁙ **The Bunk House** (307-332-5624; http://www.wyomingadventure.com/fbunkhouse.html), 2024 Mortimore Lane. The Bunk House is located at the headquarters of the Lander Llama Company (see *To Do*—Unique Adventures). The rustic lodgepole lodging can sleep up to five people, and you'll also find an equipped kitchenette and a shower bath. You can see all of the llamas just outside the doors and windows, making it a fun spot for families—particularly if your kids like animals. Guests enjoy a complimentary, make-it-yourself breakfast each morning, which includes homemade cinnamon rolls. Moderate to expensive.

✐ ⁙ 🐾 **Cottage House of Squaw Creek** (307-332-5003; http://www.squawcreekranch.com), 72 Squaw Creek Court. This log cabin on Squaw Creek, 4 miles from Lander, is situated on a working ranch—a working llama and miniature horse ranch, that is! The private cabin can sleep up to six people, and includes a fully equipped kitchen, private bath, laundry facilities, a wood-burning stove, a TV/VCR, and phone, among other amenities. Rent either as a B&B or as a guest house (no breakfast included). Expensive.

Riverton

ⁱᵀⁱ **Delfelder Inn Bed and Breakfast** (1-888-856-6002 or 307-856-6002; http://www.delfelderinn.com), 222 S. Broadway. If you're a history lover, you'll love staying in the Delfelder Inn, one of the oldest homes in Riverton that still stands. Constructed in 1906, this lovely Victorian house features off-street parking, a large yard, and easy access to the town—a mere two blocks' walk from the door. Inside, you'll find a sun porch, dining room, and four well-appointed, differently themed guest rooms, some with private baths, and some with shared baths. A full breakfast is served in the morning. Moderate to expensive.

LODGES

Lander

ℐ **Louis Lake Lodge** (1-888-422-2246 or 307-330-7571; http://www.louis lake.com), 1800 Louis Lake Road. This remote and rustic lodge, accessible via Sinks Canyon Road to Louis Lake Road southwest of Lander, provides a wonderful, wholesome place for a family vacation. The lodge, situated in the Shoshone National Forest (see *Green Space*—National Lands), provides year-round recreational opportunities, including horseback riding, canoeing, fishing, and hiking in summertime; and snowmobiling, cross-country skiing, and snowshoeing (the lodge is on the groomed Continental Divide Snowmobile Trail; see *To Do*—Snow Sports). You'll stay in a one- or two-room cabin, or a room in the lodge, all with no electricity. Most cabins share a common bathhouse. The lodge also welcomes campers. You can rent canoes, motorized fishing boats, horses, human guides, and snowmobiles by the hour, half-day, or full day. Moderate to

expensive. See also Louis Lake in *To Do*—Boating.

HOTELS AND MOTELS

Riverton

🐾 ⁱᵀⁱ 🌸 **Paintbrush Motel** (1-800-204-9238 or 307-856-9238; http://www .paintbrushmotel.com), 1550 N. Federal Boulevard. This family-owned and -operated motel features everything a traveler needs, with none of the fancy extras that mean higher prices. Modern, clean rooms have refrigerators, microwaves, and coffeemakers. Inexpensive.

CAMPGROUNDS ♿ **BLM Campgrounds** (see Bureau of Land Management in *Green Space*—National Lands) in this area are first-come, first-served. The Lander Field Office manages **Cottonwood Campground** ($6), accessible by taking US 287/WY 789 east of Jeffrey City to BLM 2411 (Green Mountain Road), and then going south for 11 miles to the campground (on the east loop of Green Mountain Road). Green Mountain Road is also a good mountain biking loop (31 miles total). **Wild Horse Point Picnic Area** is on the east loop of Green Mountain Road as well, 17 miles from US 287. The Lander Field Office also manages two campgrounds near South Pass—**Atlantic City Campground** (handicapped accessible; $6) on the west side of the road to Atlantic City just 1 mile south of WY 28, and **Big Atlantic Gulch Campground** ($6), located on Fort Stambaugh Loop Road, .25 mile from its intersection with Atlantic City Road Great roads for mountain biking are accessible from both of these campgrounds.

ⁱᵀⁱ *ℐ* **Owl Creek Kampground** (307-856-2869; http://www.campowlcreek .com), 11124 US 26/WY 789 (5 miles northeast of Riverton). This environmentally conscious, full-service campground welcomes both RV travelers and tent campers. It has an on-premises convenience store and a playground for the kids. Also available for rent are hooked-up trailers. Very inexpensive to inexpensive.

⚲ **Shoshone National Forest** (see National Lands—*Green Space*) camping in this region includes six developed first-come, first-served campgrounds ($5–10), mostly in the area southwest of Lander in and around Sinks Canyon, including **Sinks Canyon Campground,** accessed by taking Sinks Canyon Road southeast out of Lander and through Sinks Canyon State Park, then watching for signs to the campground. Dispersed camping (free) is also available. Contact the forest for more information.

🐾 ⁇ ⚲ ⁇ **Sleeping Bear Ranch RV Park and Campground** (1-888-757-2327 or 307-332-5159; http://www .sleepingbearrvpark.com), 7192 WY 789/US 287. Not just a spot for RVs, this cool campground 9 miles south of Lander also has a cabin rental available. The campground additionally includes a playground and family-oriented evening activities/entertainment in summertime. Tent campers are also welcome here. Very inexpensive to inexpensive.

⚲ 🐾 ⁇ **Wind River Campground/Riverton RV Park** (1-800-528-3913 or 307-857-3000; http:// www.rvwyoming.com), 1618 E. Park Avenue, Riverton. This full-service RV Park also allows tent camping and has plenty of shade trees for its 60 sites (38 pull-throughs). Enjoy clean restrooms and on-site laundry facilities. Very inexpensive.

See also Shoshoni in *To See*—Towns; Lander City Park in *To See*—City Parks and Gardens; and Boysen State Park and Sinks Canyon State Park in *Green Space*—State Parks.

OTHER OPTIONS

Lander

🐾 ⁇ **Outlaw Cabins** (307-332-9655; http://www.outlawcabins.com), 2415 Squaw Creek Road. Two private, handcrafted log cabins resting near Squaw Creek accommodate guests at this location. One of the cabins was constructed from downed wood on the surrounding ranch's property. A local sheriff constructed the other cabin in the 1890s— but the inside is brand spanking new, with all of the modern amenities you'd expect to find. Both cabins include a queen-sized bed as well as a loft perfect for children, with two twin beds. Guests enjoy the fixings for breakfast already stocked in the cabins' kitchens, including coffee, cereal, cocoa, tea, and so forth. Moderate to expensive.

See also Cottage House of Squaw Creek in Bed and Breakfasts.

Riverton

See Owl Creek Kampground in *Lodging*—Campgrounds.

✳ Where to Eat

EATING OUT

Lander

Asian Cuisine (307-335-7171), 140 N. Seventh Street. Open for lunch and dinner; call for current hours/days. This little tucked-away gem features finely prepared (what else?) Asian cuisine, including Indian, Chinese, Thai, and more. Comfortable, welcoming décor and helpful, attentive service complement the delicious entrées. Moderate.

🐾 ⁇ **Gannett Grill** (307-332-8228; http://www.landerbar.com), 126 Main Street. Open daily for lunch and dinner; call for current hours. Situated in the historic **Coalter Block,** the Gannett Grill provides the best deal in town for good food at great prices. Whether you're in search of a giant burger with all the fixings, or you prefer a salad, this is the place to go. The Gannett doesn't skimp in either department—salads are served in a veritable trough of a bowl, with fresh, crispy greens, ample toppings, and soft pita triangles. Add in some grilled chicken to the Green and Greener; it's awesome. Burgers feature a half-pound of beef, organic if you choose, topped with a variety of condiments ranging from grilled mushrooms to jalapeno peppers. The Gannett also does pizza, appetizers, sandwiches, and specials that are usually quite tasty as well. The outdoor deck is a popular hangout in warmer months, and the adjacent **Lander Bar** is one of the most hopping nightspots in town. The Gannett Grill is connected by an outdoor deck to the more upscale Cowfish (see listing in Dining Out). Moderate.

✒ **Tony's Pizza** (307-332-3900), 637 Main Street. Open daily for lunch and dinner; hours vary according to season. Recently remodeled and enlarged, this is the locals' favorite place to go for a pizza dinner. Tony's offers pizzas in both basic flavors and pies that are more creative, depending on what you're in the mood for. You can also opt for a cheesy stromboli, a veggie bread-bowl salad, a pasta creation, or a chicken dish, among other menu selections. In warmer weather, the roof deck is one of the most happening places in the town of Lander, as folks flock to share drinks and meals while perched above the main drag. Inexpensive to moderate.

Wildlflour Bakery and Espresso (307-332-9728), 545 W. Main Street. Open 7–5:30 Monday through Friday, 7–2 Saturday. Bagels, breads, and other baked goods made from scratch are in the spotlight here. You'll also find specialty coffees, plus made-to-order sandwiches, wraps, soups, and salads. Eat-in or take out. Inexpensive.

See also Silver Spur Lanes in *Entertainment*.

Riverton

✒ **The Bull Steak House** (307-856-4728), 1100 W. Main Street. Open for lunch and dinner; call for current hours/days. Where the locals go, The Bull Restaurant serves up steaks and other down-home fare in good-sized portions for both lunch and dinner. The restaurant features reasonable prices on entrée selections that include chicken and seafood as well as beef. Lunches, served on weekdays, include three daily specials in addition to the normal menu. The restaurant also has a special seniors' menu and a children's menu. Moderate to expensive.

See also Graham's Gluten-Free Foods in *To Do*—Relaxation and Rejuvenation.

DINING OUT

Lander

Cowfish (307-332-8227; http://www .landerbar.com), 128 Main Street. Open daily for lunch and dinner; call for current hours. Situated in the historic Coalter Block of buildings, the Cowfish itself is housed in an elegantly renovated 1888 structure. Here you'll find delicious new American cuisine, including not only creative full entrées (featuring—what else?—beef and fish, with some chicken and pastas thrown in for good measure), but also savory salads, appetizers, and desserts. Fish tacos are always a tasty choice, but you'll probably be happy with most anything you order in this stylish, hip hangout. The Cowfish is connected by an outdoor deck to the more casual **Gannett Grill** and Lander Bar (see listing in Eating Out). Expensive.

The Hitching Rack (307-332-4322), 785 E. Main Street. Open for lunch and dinner Monday through Saturday. This well-respected Lander establishment specializes in one thing—steaks, cooked to perfection, however you prefer them. This is the place where locals go to impress their dates, in the true tradition of wowing them with a pricey steak dinner. The cozy ambiance complements the delicious, melt-in-your-mouth entrées, which don't disappoint in either taste or size. Desserts are yummy too—if you have any room left after your dinner. Expensive.

Riverton

⚓ **QT's Restaurant** (307-856-8100), 900 E. Sunset Boulevard. Open three meals a day. This family-style fine dining establishment is located inside Riverton's Holiday Inn. Here you'll find well-prepared, traditional American food, with dinner entrée selections including beef, seafood, chicken, and more. If you're staying at the hotel, your kids 12 and under eat for free from the children's menu, making it easy on the pocketbook while satisfying for the belly. In summertime, the restaurant is open early for breakfast (6 AM) and late for dinner (10 PM), making it a surefire option for off-hours dining needs. Moderate to expensive.

See also The Bull Steak House in Eating Out.

✳ Entertainment

Acme Theater (307-856-3415 (movie information) or 307-856-9589 (office); http://www.gabletheaters.com/acme.htm), 312 E. Main Street, Riverton.

Gem Theater (307-856-3415 (movie information) or 307-856-9589 (office); http://www.gabletheaters.com/gem.htm), 119 S. Third East, Riverton.

Grand Theater (307-332-3300 (movie information) or 307-332-4437 (office); http://www.gabletheaters.com/grand.htm); 250 Main Street, Lander.

Lander Community Concert Association (307-332-8253; http://www.landerconcerts.org); P.O. Box 647, Lander. This nonprofit organizes an annual series of concerts (autumn through spring) featuring a variety of nationally and internationally acclaimed musical acts of all genres. Check online or call for a current schedule.

⚓ **Silver Spur Lanes** (307-332-5830), 1290 W. Main Street, Lander. This bowling alley also has a fast-food restaurant that serves burgers, hot dogs, and chili.

See also Museum of the American West and Wind River Heritage Center in *To See*—Museums; Sleeping Bear Ranch RV Park and Campground in *Lodging*—Campgrounds; and Gannett Grill in *Where to Eat*—Eating Out.

✳ Selective Shopping

The Golden Buffalo (307-857-2789; http://www.thegoldenbuffalo.com), 407 E. Main Street, Riverton. Take home something uniquely Wyoming with a lovely necklace, ring, bracelet, or earrings designed by The Exclusive Jeweler of the Golden Buffalo, Jerome Hutchison. Each piece of jewelry is handcrafted and backed by a 100-percent satisfaction guarantee.

JB's Wild Wyoming (1-888-945-3996 or 307-332-2065; http://www.jbswildwyoming.com), 628 Main Street, Lander. This Wyoming original specializes in game—antelope, venison, elk, and buffalo. Find it gift boxed and ready to take home with you as a savory souvenir of your travels. JB's also carries Wyoming tourism products, Forest

THE BRONZE CITY

Lander is also known as The Bronze City due to the large number of bronze statues you'll see throughout the city. This is mainly due to the presence of the **Eagle Bronze Foundry** (307-332-5436; http://www.eaglebronze.com), 130 Poppy Street (foundry). This family-run foundry, opened in 1986, "produces world-class art and sculpture for some of the most famous artists and collectors." When in Lander, be sure to stop in at the **Eagle Bronze Gallery of Fine Art** (307-332-3384; http://www.eaglebronzegallery.com), 343 Main Street, to view or consider purchasing not only bronze sculptures, but also, the other fine artwork you'll find here. The gallery also features an artist's studio on the premises (allowing visitors to catch a glimpse of an artist at work) and offers art classes to the public.

A BRONZE STATUE HONORS THE ANNUAL ONE SHOT ANTELOPE HUNT (SEE *SPECIAL EVENTS*)

Circus parody products (which happen to be bestsellers), and more.

See also Wind River Heritage Center in *To See*—Museums; South Pass City Historic Site in *To See*—Historic Landmarks, Places, and Sites; Wild Iris Mountain Sports in *To Do*—Climbing; and Graham's Gluten-Free Foods in *To Do*—Relaxation and Rejuvenation.

✳ Special Events

January to February: **Wild West Winter Carnival** (http://www.wild westwintercarnival.com), Riverton: The multiday celebration of the coldest season of the year includes ice sculptures, casino nights, tethered balloon rides, a wine, scotch, and beer tasting, and more.

❧ *March:* **Wyoming State Winter Fair,** Lander: The fair features livestock show, horse show, trade show, and food vendors.

Memorial Day: **Wyoming's State Championship Old-Time Fiddle Contest,** Shoshoni: This is an annual music competition.

June: **Eastern Shoshone Indian Days,** Fort Washakie: The annual powwow celebration drawing hundreds of dancers and drummers to compete for prizes; also includes concessions, arts and crafts, and more.

June: **Lander Brew Festival,** Lander: This outdoor beer festival in Lander City Park features some 50 different beers on tap from more than 15 brewers.

July: **Annual Ethete Celebration Powwow,** Ethete: One of a number of annual spring and summer powwows held by the Northern Arapaho Tribe, it includes dancing, arts and crafts, and additional festivities.

❧ *July:* **Gold Rush Days,** South Pass City (http://www.southpasscity.com): This yearly celebration features food, drinks, games (including a vintage baseball game), contests, and interpretive programs.

July: **International Climbers' Festival** (http://www.climbersfestival.org), Lander: This annual gathering of rock climbers from around the world, taking place the Thursday through Sunday after the Fourth of July, includes climbing clinics taught by professional climbers, rock climbing, slide shows, movies, food, socializing, fun competitions, and more.

❧ *July:* **1838 Mountain Man Rendezvous** (http://www.1838rendezvous.com), Riverton: An annual celebration featuring historical reenactments of mountain man gatherings, including food, entertainment, dancing, and games.

❧ *July:* **Pioneer Days Parade and Rodeo,** Lander: Lander's annual celebration of the Fourth of July began way back in 1894, and the tradition continues today with a multiday celebration. Activities include a road race, pancake breakfast, parade, rodeo, barbecue, and more.

❧ *July:* **Riverton Rendezvous,** Riverton: The yearly celebration of the city's founding in 1906 includes a hot-air balloon rally, Arts in the Park, a rodeo, street dance, and more.

September: **Annual One Shot Antelope Hunt,** Lander: Taking place for more than 60 years, this yearly hunt allows licensed teams of hunters (drawn by lottery) a single shot each to take down an antelope.

October: **Heart of the West Invitational Art Show and Sale**, Lander: This annual juried art competition and sale includes an art walk, auction, scotch tasting, and a ball.

JACKSON AND DUBOIS

Despite its current reputation, Jackson wasn't always known as a ski town—
in fact, it didn't begin to develop this identity until the establishment of Snow King
Ski Resort in 1939. Before that time and before the time of the first white settlers,
American Indians had inhabited the Jackson Hole area continuously for centuries.
Mountain men constituted the first known travelers of European descent to leave
written accounts of this locale. They passed through this region in the first half of
the 19th century, during the short period of time when beaver fur represented the
pinnacle of high fashion both in America and Europe. These early trappers found
a verdant area rife with wildlife, including those coveted beavers, though they did-
n't really establish any permanent settlements in the valley at that time. Trappers
included such notable and legendary figures of America's past as Jim Bridger, Jedediah Smith, and David Jackson, a founder of the Rocky Mountain Fur Company
for whom the town was named.

By the mid-1840s, the beaver boom had passed, and the valley was pretty much
left to its own devices for the remainder of the century. American Indians still
stayed here, explorers passed through, and a few hale and hardy pioneers dug in
by homesteading the land, attempting to ranch and grow crops in an area not really suited for such endeavors due to its rather harsh climate and short growing season. Soon enough, some of these early settlers turned to the trades that would
become a mainstay of Wyoming's economy—outfitting and guiding—to help bring
in more money when it became evident that ranching and farming would not be
profitable enough to sustain them through the years ahead. The 1872 creation of
Yellowstone National Park just north of Jackson helped the dude ranching business
grow and prosper, as the American public became more familiar with this isolated
area of Wyoming. Nonetheless, the actual population of permanent settlers in the
Jackson Hole area remained small.

As the late 1800s gave way to the 20th century, the town of Jackson sprang up
in response to the growth of the dude ranching and cattle ranching operations in
the valley. Dubbed Jackson in 1894, the town soon had services, and streets and
wooden sidewalks followed in their wake. Tourism continued to sustain the area,
with big game hunting and fishing taking top spots on the itineraries of many visitors to Wyoming's early dude ranches. A desire to preserve and protect the area's
natural resources resulted in the formation of the National Elk Refuge in 1912 and
Grand Teton National Park in 1929, as well as the inclusion of much of the land
surrounding the valley in the Bridger-Teton National Forest. Such moves were not

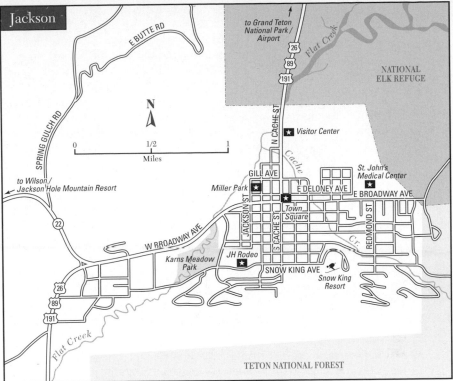

Jackson

to Grand Teton National Park / Airport

NATIONAL ELK REFUGE

N

0   1/2   1
Miles

E BUTTE RD

SPRING GULCH RD

to Wilson / Jackson Hole Mountain Resort

Flat Creek

26
89
191

★ Visitor Center

GILL AVE

Miller Park ★

St. John's Medical Center ★

E DELONEY AVE

E BROADWAY AVE

★

Town Square

N CACHE ST

Cache

JACKSON ST

S CACHE ST

REDMOND ST

22

W BROADWAY AVE

Karns Meadow Park

JH Rodeo ★

SNOW KING AVE

Snow King Resort

26
89
191

Flat Creek

TETON NATIONAL FOREST

© The Countryman Press

without conflict though: In particular, Grand Teton National Park's 1950 expansion to its current size was a controversial move that put some of the valley's ranching families at odds with those responsible for such legislation, as it seriously impacted the amount of land available for cattle grazing.

Nonetheless, the tourism industry that had begun to take off in the early days of Jackson had supplanted cattle ranching and other endeavors as the valley's chief industry, and tourism is the industry that continues to define and shape the area today. With the establishment of Snow King in 1939, Jackson started its journey toward capturing one of the preeminent positions in the psyche of the nation's downhill skiers, who would later be joined by snowboarders as well. Today, Jackson Hole is a thriving ski town, but even the slightest peek under the surface reveals that the area has so much more to offer its visitors, whether they come primarily to ski or whether it's another pursuit that draws them.

In addition to its proximity to Grand Teton National Park and Yellowstone National Park, Jackson Hole and its surrounding environs contain a lifetime's worth of outdoor recreational pursuits, from the endless number of trails to explore by foot, bike, horseback, snowshoe, ski, or snowmobile (among other modes of travel) in the Bridger-Teton National Forest, to the countless streams and lakes that offer top-quality fishing. But that's not all—in the wake of the growth of dude ranches and other services aimed at providing first-rate outdoor adventures, a plethora of complementary services have evolved to support such endeavors. Thus the visitor to Jackson Hole will find plenty of arts and cultural institutions and events, shopping, spas and massage parlors galore, fine dining and casual eateries, and lodging options ranging from basic to luxurious.

On the other side of Togwotee Pass (see *To See*—Scenic Drives) from Jackson, you'll find Dubois, pronounced *due boys*. This much smaller town is situated between the Wind River Mountains to the southwest and the Absaroka Mountains to the northeast. With nearly 1,000 inhabitants today, Dubois traces its history of settlement back to the mid-1800s, when a family from Iowa built a cabin on the banks of the Wind River near the town's present location. For a time, Dubois thrived on the railroad tie hack industry (see Tie Hack Memorial in *To See*—Historic Landmarks, Places, and Sites), but today the mainstays of its economy are the area's livestock ranches and dude ranches, as well as those drawn here by the terrific fishing and big game hunting, as well as other recreational opportunities. The largest known herd of Rocky Mountain bighorn sheep on the planet inhabits the surrounding area, hence the town's National Bighorn Sheep Interpretive Center (see *To See*—Museums), among its other museums.

GUIDANCE Dubois Chamber of Commerce (1-888-518-0502; http://www.duboiswyoming.org), P.O. Box 632Y, Dubois, 82513.

Jackson Hole Central Reservations (1-888-838-6606; http://www.jacksonholewy.com), 140 E. Broadway, Jackson, 83001. This company can book not only lodging at a variety of locations in Jackson and the surrounding area, but also, can hook you up with vacation activities, often wrapped into package deals.

Jackson Hole Chamber of Commerce (307-733-3316; http://www.jacksonhole chamber.com), 990 W. Broadway, P.O. Box 550, Jackson, 83001.

See also Jackson Hole and Greater Yellowstone Visitor Center in *To See*—Museums.

JACKSON

GETTING THERE *By car:* Jackson is accessed from the north via US 26/89/191, from the southwest via US 26/89, from the southeast via US 189/191, and from the west via WY 22. Dubois lies along US 26/287 southeast of Togwotee Pass.

By plane: **Jackson Hole Airport** (307-733-7682; http://www.jacksonhole airport.com) is just north of Jackson.

By shuttle service: **Alltrans, Inc.** (1-800-443-6133 or 307-733-3135; http://www.jacksonholealltrans.com) meets all incoming flights to the Jackson Hole Airport, providing shuttle service not only into Jackson ($16 one way or $31 round trip), but also to a variety of other regional destinations, including lodging establishments in Grand Teton National Park and daily trips to Salt Lake City.

GETTING AROUND Jackson's downtown area is easily explored on foot, but you'll want to get back in your car to explore the rest of Jackson and Jackson Hole. As a much smaller town, Dubois is conducive to walking exploration almost entirely.

In Jackson, one option for footsore explorers is the **START Bus** (307-733-4521; http://www.startbus.com), which runs a free shuttle bus through Jackson regularly. Other destinations include Teton Village, Teton Valley, and Star Valley (see Southwest Wyoming: Evanston and Star Valley), all for very reasonable rates.

MEDICAL EMERGENCY Dial 911.

St. John's Medical Center (307-733-3636; http://www.tetonhospital.org), 625 E. Broadway, Jackson.

✳ To See

TOWNS Alta, the gateway to Grand Targhee Resort (see *To Do*—Snow Sports) is a tiny Wyoming town (population 400) situated just across the border from Driggs, Idaho—and only accessible from Idaho.

Hoback Junction is 14 miles south of Jackson at the junction of US 26/89 and US 189/191. This also happens to be the junction of the Snake River (see *To Do*—Fishing and *To Do*—Paddling/Floating) and the Hoback River.

Kelly is located about 7 miles northeast of US 191/26/89 via Gros Ventre River Road, on the eastern side of Jackson Hole. This small town, situated on the banks of the Gros Ventre River, has about 250 residents. See also Gros Ventre Slide Area in *To See*—Natural Wonders.

Teton Village is located 12 miles northwest of Jackson via WY 390. This full-service resort town serves all of the après-ski needs for those visiting Jackson Hole Mountain Resort (see *To Do*—Snow Sports), as well as being a popular year-round vacation destination.

Wilson is located 6 miles west of Jackson on WY 22, south of Teton Village. It is a popular small town for backcountry skiers to base out of when visiting this region.

See also Moose in Grand Teton National Park.

MUSEUMS 🐾 **Dubois Museum and Wind River Historical Center** (307-455-2284; http://www.duboismuseum .org), 909 W. Ramshorn Street, Dubois. Open daily 9–6 mid-June through mid-September; 10–4 Tuesday through Saturday, mid-September through mid-June; $1 per adult, $.50 per child 6–12,

TETON VILLAGE, AT THE BASE OF JACKSON HOLE MOUNTAIN RESORT

children under 6 free. This extensive museum details the natural and cultural history of the local and regional surroundings, including a main museum building with a variety of historical exhibits, as well as a number of historical structures surrounding the main building. The surrounding historical structures include the **Tie Hack Interpretive Center,** which helps explain the historical significance of the tie hack industry to the area (see also Tie Hack Memorial in Historic Landmarks, Places, and Sites). Exhibits in the main museum include the history of the local mountain Shoshone, or Sheep Eater Indians, legendary hunters of the Rocky Mountain bighorn sheep; displays on the area's pioneers and homesteaders; and natural history exhibits; as well as rotating exhibits that relate to the region's history.

🐾 **Jackson Hole Historical Society and Museum** (307-733-2414 (museum) or 307-733-9605 (historical society); http://www.jacksonholehistory.org), 105 N. Glenwood Street (museum), 105 Mercill Avenue (Historical Society Research Center), Jackson. Museum open 9:30–6 Monday through Saturday, 10–5 Sunday, last Friday in May through Labor Day; free admission on season's opening day, $3 per adult, $2 per senior, $6 per family, $1 per student. Historical Society open 10–5 Tuesday through Friday year-round; free. The Jackson Hole Museum interprets the area's history for you with an impressive collection that includes some 7,000 historic photographs; Indian artifacts including weapons, pottery, and stone tools; artifacts from the fur trade, pioneer days, homesteading, and ranching; and exhibits on Grand Teton and Yellowstone National Parks, among others. The Historical Society, housed in a historic log cabin, includes a small exhibit space with historic photographs, an artifact collection, various archives, and a helpful, knowledgeable staff.

🐾 ♿ **Jackson Hole and Greater Yellowstone Visitor Center** (307-733-3616; http://www.fs.fed.us/jhgyvc/welcome.html), 532 N. Cache Drive, Jackson. Open 8–7 daily, Memorial Day weekend through September 30, 9–5 daily October 1 through Memorial Day weekend, closed Thanksgiving and Christmas; free. Though it's called a visitor center, what you'll find inside—and outside, too—stretches beyond the norm for what you find in a typical visitor center, which is why it's listed under Museums. Operated through interagency cooperation between eight separate local and regional agencies, this center features an overload of free visitor information in the form of brochures, maps, and helpful staff. The center also features wildlife displays and exhibits, a viewing area overlooking the adjacent National Elk Refuge (see Wildlife Refuges and Areas) and beautiful Flat Creek, a bookstore and retail shop, informational films, educational and interpretive programs, a picnic area, a pet exercise area, and much, much more. You can also purchase national park passes and state hunting and fishing licenses here, among other passes and permits available.

START YOUR EXPLORATION OF JACKSON HERE AT THE JACKSON HOLE AND GREATER YELLOWSTONE VISITOR CENTER

🐾 ✒ **National Bighorn Sheep Interpretive Center** (1-888-209-2795 or

307-455-3429; http://www.bighorn
.org), 907 W. Ramshorn Street,
Dubois. Open daily 9–7, Memorial
Day weekend through Labor Day
weekend; 9–5 Monday through Saturday (off-season); $2.50 per adult, $1
per child 12 and under, $6 per family.
Learn more about this majestic and
mysterious mountain-loving creature
with a visit to this marvelous museum,
where a full-size bighorn sheep display
gives you an intimate view of their natural beauty. Start or complete your
journey with a walk along the paved
trail outside the center, which guides
you through some of the hazards faced
by these large mammals as they strug-

THE NATIONAL BIGHORN SHEEP
INTERPRETIVE CENTER IN DUBOIS

gle to survive in a changing world. Nearby, the **Whiskey Mountain Habitat Area**
serves as home to the largest known herd of wintering Rocky Mountain bighorn
sheep in the nation. The museum offers three- to five-hour guided tours of this
area November through March ($25 per person, 24-hour advance reservations
required), providing you with the potential opportunity to view the resident
bighorns up close.

&. ♪ **National Museum of Wildlife Art** (1-800-313-9553 or 307-733-5771;
http://www.wildlifeart.org), 2820 Rungius Road (3 miles north of Town Square on
US 191 across the street from the National Elk Refuge), Jackson. Open 9–5 daily
mid-May through mid-October; 9–5 Monday through Saturday and 1–5 Sunday,
mid-October through mid-May; closed Veterans Day, Columbus Day, Thanksgiving, and Christmas; $10 per adult, $9 per senior 60 and older, $9 per student, $5
per child ages 5–18, children under 5 free, $30 per family (2 adults and 2 children;
additional children are $1 each). If you're both a wildlife lover and an art aficiona-
do, be sure to set aside some time to stroll through the galleries of this unique fine
art museum while you're in Jackson. Children will delight in the hands-on discovery area. You'll likely find yourself captivated by the scope of the museum's collection, which includes 3,000 pieces of artwork by more than 200 artists from around
the world. Exhibits of western wildlife art, including pieces by such notable artists
as Charles M. Russell, Carl Rungius, Albert Bierstadt, and John J. Audubon, are
on permanent display. The museum also features a number of temporary exhibits
at any given time. You can grab a bite for lunch at the **Rising Sage Café** (307-
733-8649; http://www.risingsagecafe.com), which features a wide selection of fine
sandwiches, soups, salads, and more. Inexpensive.

HISTORIC LANDMARKS, PLACES, AND SITES ⚘ **Tie Hack Memorial** is
located 15 miles west of Dubois along US 26/287. This picturesque setting overlooking the beautiful and peaceful Wind River seems somehow suitable for the
simple commemorative structure. The memorial pays tribute to the people, many
of Scandinavian, German, and Eastern European origin, who eked out their livings
by hand-hewing railroad ties from the timber surrounding Dubois. The industry
began in this region with the construction of the Chicago and North Western

railroads in the early 20th century and continued for three decades. The tie hacks became intimately acquainted with the forests north of Dubois, where they lived in temporary camps as they created the railroad ties with their own hands. The ties were then floated down the Wind River to the Riverton tie yards, about 100 miles to the southeast.

See also Dubois Museum and Wind River Historical Center and Jackson Hole Historical Society and Museum in *To See*—Museums; Twin Pines Lodge and Cabins in *Lodging*—Lodges; The Wort Hotel in *Lodging*—Hotels and Motels; Branding Iron Inn in *Lodging*—Other Options; Rustic Pine Steakhouse and Tavern in *Where to Eat*—Eating Out; and The Jackson Hole Playhouse and Saddle Rock Saloon and Teton Theatre in *Entertainment*.

CITY PARKS AND GARDENS ✍ **Dubois Town Park,** located next to the National Bighorn Sheep Interpretive Center (see *To See*—Museums), is a charming little town park (day-use only) that makes for a great place to have a picnic if you're stopped in the area. The park has a paved walkway that gains you access to the Wind River (see *To Do*—Fishing), as well as posted informational material about this natural area. The park also has a playground.

Jackson's Town Square is a centrally located little park with distinctive antler arch entrances at each of its four corners. No trip to Jackson would be complete without a photograph of these unique structures. The Town Square is also a great place to grab a seat and take a break from shopping or sightseeing. See also *Selective Shopping*.

THE TIE HACK MEMORIAL

See also See also Jackson Hole and Greater Yellowstone Visitor Center in *To See*—Museums.

SCENIC DRIVES Wyoming Centennial Scenic Byway is a 155-mile, U-shaped journey that begins (or finishes) in Dubois. Head northwest on US 26/287 to Moran Junction. Go southwest on US 26/89/191 through Jackson Hole to Hoback Junction. Head southeast on US 189/191 to Pinedale. This lengthy journey could be split up into several days of travel. You'll pass by many attractions along the way as well as stunning natural features, such as the impressive Togwotee Pass (9,658 feet) and the beautiful Pinnacle Buttes, encountered on US 26/287 west of Dubois.

NATURAL WONDERS Grand Canyon of the Snake River, along US 26/89 east of Alpine and southwest of Hoback Junction. Scenic pullouts will allow you to stop and take a closer look at this incredible canyon, featuring immense cliffs framing the popular whitewater of the Snake River below. You might even be lucky enough to catch some paddlers in action (or perhaps you'll be one of those paddlers that others are watching from the pull-outs above?). See also Snake River and Snake River Kayak and Canoe in *To Do*—Paddling/Floating.

TOWN SQUARE IN JACKSON

Gros Ventre Slide Geological Area lies in the Gros Ventre Wilderness of the Bridger-Teton National Forest (see *Green Space*—National Lands) off Gros Ventre Road (Forest Road (FR) 30410) near Lower Slide Lake (east of Kelly; see *To See*—Towns). This area changed radically in 1925 when an entire mountainside—some 50 million cubic yards of sandstone—cut loose in a massive landslide, resulting in a huge, naturally formed lake (Lower Slide Lake) in mere minutes. Part of the dam broke two years after the slide, causing huge, but brief, floods, destroying the town of Kelly. Today you can still view the dramatic evidence of the power of natural forces by walking a .25-mile self-guided interpretive trail.

See also Granite Hot Springs in *To Do*—Relaxation and Rejuvenation; and Sleigh Rides on the National Elk Refuge in *To Do*—Unique Adventures.

✳ To Do

BICYCLING ♿ **Jackson Hole Community Pathway System** (307-733-4534; http://www.friendsofpathways.org) is an 8-mile network of trails in Jackson Hole. This system of trails includes **Indian Springs Trail, Melody Ranch Trail, Road Pathway, Russ Garaman Trail, School Trail, Teton Pines/Teton Village,** and the **Wilson Centennial Trail.** The trail system is also open to walking, running, horseback riding, inline skating, and cross-country skiing in winter. If your bike needs a tune up, or you want to rent a bike, stop by **Fitzgerald's Bicycles** (307-734-6886; http://www.fitzgeraldsbicycles.com), 245 W. Hansen Street, Jackson. Open 11–6 Monday through Friday; 10–5 Saturday. The friendly folks there can also recommend great road and mountain bike rides suitable to your ability level.

⌇ **Teton Mountain Bike Tours, LLC** (1-800-733-0788 or 307-733-0712; http://www.tetonmtbike.com), P.O. Box 7027, Jackson. With rides suited to all ability levels, this bicycling outfitter offers half-day, full-day, multiday, and customized tours, with prices varying according to the selected tour ($60 per person for a two- or three-hour adventure gives you an idea of this activity's price tag). You'll be outfitted with a mountain bike, helmet, appropriate gear, a free water bottle (to take with you), a lunch for full-day tours, and an expert, knowledgeable guide who will give you tips on mountain biking as well as filling you in on your surroundings. Families are welcome here—kids ages 8 and up can ride their own bike, while kids 5–7 can ride a nifty Adams Trail-a-Bike, adding their pedaling power to yours.

Children 1–4 can ride along in a child trailer that attaches to your bike. More adventuresome folks should ask about Genuine Jackson combination bike-hike-paddle trips.

See also Cache Creek Trail and Lost Lake Trail in *To Do—Hiking*; Granite Hot Springs in *To Do—Relaxation and Rejuvenation*; Grand Targhee Resort, Jackson Hole Mountain Resort, and Snow King Resort in *To Do—Snow Sports*; and *Green Space*.

BOATING See *To Do—Fishing*; *To Do—Paddling/Floating*; *Green Space*; and *To Do—Boating in Grand Teton National Park*.

CLIMBING ♦ ♞ **Enclosure Indoor Rock Climbing and Fitness Center** (307-734-9590; http://www.enclosureclimbing.com), on US 89, 3.5 miles south of the junction of US 89 and WY 22 in Jackson. Open 11–9 Monday through Friday, 10–8 Saturday through Sunday; $16 per adult, $11 per child 13 and under; equipment rental is $9 per person extra. This state-of-the-art climbing gym and fitness facility offers first-timers one introduction to rock climbing class for free (pre-registration is required). Classes are held on Monday evenings from 6–7. It also offers three-day kids' climbing camps in summer ($129 per child ages 5–14) and a Climb and Dine package, in which you spend the night on the town while your school-aged children enjoy two and one-half hours of supervised climbing and a pizza dinner. This facility also has top-notch exercise equipment, placed in full view of the climbing area—so you can be inspired by the climbers while you work out.

See also Grand Targhee Resort in *To Do—Snow Sports*; *Green Space*; and *To Do—Climbing in Grand Teton National Park*.

FISHING **Gros Ventre River** (307-777-4600; http://gf.state.wy.us/fish/fishing/index.asp), northeast of Jackson, is formed by the confluence of a number of creeks flowing from the Wind River Mountains to the west (including Fish Creek and its forks). It flows west through the Bridger-Teton National Forest (see *Green Space—National Lands*) along Gros Ventre Road (FR 30400), passing through Upper Slide Lake, the Gros Ventre Slide Geological Area (see *To See—Natural Wonders*), and Lower Slide Lake (which has boating access as well), before angling southwest to join the Snake River (see below) near Jackson. The river can be accessed in the forest at various sites along the road, including a number of forest service campgrounds. Game fish species include cutthroat trout, mountain white-fish, and rainbow trout.

Snake River (307-777-4600; http://gf.state.wy.us/fish/fishing/index.asp), originates in the Teton Wilderness of Bridger-Teton National Forest (see *Green Space—National lands*), flows through the southern portion of Yellowstone National Park before entering Jackson Lake in Grand Teton National Park (see Snake River in *To Do—Fishing and Paddling/Floating in Grand Teton National Park*), then flows south out of the lake through the valley of Jackson Hole before curving west to travel alongside US 26/89 just south of Jackson, following this road as it angles southeast through the Grand Canyon of the Snake River (see *To See—Natural Wonders*). This river is popular for fishing and floating—and both together, since access can be tough, particularly the closer you are to Jackson. South of Hoback Junction along US 89, you'll find a number of forest service campgrounds, state access areas, and designated boat launches that provide places for boat launching and fishing. Game fish species include brown and cutthroat trout. See also Snake River in *To Do*—Paddling/Floating.

Wind River (307-332-7723; http://gf.state.wy.us/fish/fishing/index.asp) flows from its origins on Togwotee Pass northwest of Dubois alongside US 26/287, and then roughly parallels US 26 to the Wind River Indian Reservation (see listing in *To Do*—Fishing in Lander and Riverton). Species include brook trout and rainbow trout. Access to the river can be found northwest of Dubois at various points in Shoshone National Forest (see *Green Space*—National Lands), as well as at various signed points off US 26/287 around Dubois. See also Dubois Town Park in *Wilder Places*—Parks.

See also Granite Hot Springs in *To Do*—Relaxation and Rejuvenation; *Green Space*; and Jakey's Fork Homestead in *Lodging*—Bed and Breakfasts.

FITNESS CENTERS ♿ 🐾 **Teton County/Jackson Recreation Center** (307-739-9025; http://www.tetonwyo.org/parks), 155 E. Gill Street. Open 6 AM–9 PM Monday through Friday, noon–9 Saturday, noon–7 Sunday; $6.25 per nonresident adult, $4 per senior 63 and up or child 3–12, $5 per youth 13–17, 2 and under free with paying adult. This community recreation center includes a pool with waterslide (call for open-swim/lap-swim times), exercise equipment, fitness classes, and more.

See Enclosure Indoor Rock Climbing and Fitness Center in *To Do*—Climbing; Grand Targhee Resort in *To Do*—Snow Sports; and Snake River Lodge and Spa and Teton Mountain Lodge and Spa in *Lodging*—Lodges.

FOR FAMILIES See National Bighorn Sheep Interpretive Center and National Museum of Wildlife Art in *To See*—Museums; Dubois Town Park in *To See*—City Parks and Gardens; Enclosure Indoor Rock Climbing and Fitness Center in *To Do*—Climbing; Teton County/Jackson Recreation Center in *To Do*—Fitness Centers; *To Do*—Horseback Riding; Granite Hot Springs in *To Do*—Relaxation and Rejuvenation; Grand Targhee Resort, Jackson Hole Mountain Resort, and Snow King Resort in *To Do*—Snow Sports; Snowshoeing in *To Do*—Snow Sports; Llamaneering with Jackson Hole Llamas, Sleigh Rides on the National Elk Refuge, and Wyoming Balloon Adventures in *To Do*—Unique Adventures; and The Jackson Hole Playhouse and Saddle Rock Saloon in *Entertainment*.

GOLF Antelope Hills Golf Club (307-455-2888; http://www.antelopehillsgolfclub.net), 126 Clubhouse Drive, Dubois, 9 holes.

Jackson Hole Golf and Tennis Club (307-733-3111; http://www.jhgtc.com), 5000 Spring Gulch Road, Jackson, 18 holes.

Teton Pines Resort and Country Club (1-800-238-2223 or 307-733-1005; http://www.tetonpines.com), 3450 N. Clubhouse Drive, Wilson, 18 holes.

HIKING Cache Creek Trail is accessible from the end of Cache Creek Drive on the east side of Jackson. Located in the Bridger-Teton National Forest (see *Green Space*—National Lands), this extremely popular, 6-mile trail features easy access from the town of Jackson, gentle grades, and creek-side access. Opportunities for viewing wildlife abound, and you can choose to walk a portion of the trail or the entire distance—or try it on a mountain bike. Horseback riding is also a possibility on this trail, and in winter, it's popular for cross-country skiing and snowshoeing. The **Tiny Hagen** and **Putt-Putt Trails** are accessible from this area as well.

Lost Lake Trail is accessible by taking US 26/287 east from Moran Junction 26 miles, and then turning left on FR 30200 and taking it to the parking area (where it ends). From here, a short, moderately steep, 1-mile trail leads to Lost Lake. The lake is situated below the Breccia Cliffs, which are home to bighorn sheep that you might spot with a good pair of binoculars. The deeply turquoise-hued lake lies just outside of the Teton Wilderness in the Bridger-Teton National Forest (see Wilder Places—Forests). Fish species include cutthroat trout and mountain whitefish. Horseback riding and mountain biking are also allowed.

See also National Bighorn Sheep Interpretive Center in *To See*—Museums; Gros Ventre Slide Geological Area in *To See*—Natural Wonders; Jackson Hole Community Pathway System in *To Do*—Bicycling; Granite Hot Springs in *To Do*—Relaxation and Rejuvenation; Grand Targhee Resort, Jackson Hole Mountain Resort, and Snow King Resort in *To Do*—Snow Sports; Snowshoeing in *To Do*—Snow Sports; Llamaneering with Jackson Hole Llamas in *To Do*—Unique Adventures; and *Green Space*.

HORSEBACK RIDING ✦ **Hidden Basin Outfitters** (1-866-900-HUNT or 307-733-7980; http://www.hiddenbasin.com), 7895 Cowboy Way, Jackson. In addition to guided hunting trips, this outfitter offers full-day rides (10–4:30) into the Teton range ($125 per person; children must be 10 or older). You can also book a longer horseback riding adventure, as well as a combination trip that also includes whitewater rafting and a rodeo.

✦ **Trail Rides with Jackson Hole Outfitters** (307-654-7008; http://www.jackson holetrailrides.com), 25 US 89 (take US 89 south of Jackson to Alpine) at Greys River Cove RV Park (see *Lodging*—Campgrounds in Southwest Wyoming: Evanston and Star Valley). Enjoy a scenic, daylong trail ride ($140 per person; children 4 and up allowed) in the Bridger-Teton National Forest (see *Green Space*—National Lands).

See also Jackson Hole Community Pathway System in *To Do*—Bicycling; Cache Creek Trail and Lost Lake Trail in *To Do*—Hiking; Granite Hot Springs in *To Do*—Relaxation and Rejuvenation; Grand Targhee Resort and Snow King Resort in *To Do*—Snow Sports; and *Green Space*.

PADDLING/FLOATING **Snake River** (see *To Do*—Fishing) offers something for everyone seeking a little river adventure, from scenic floats through flatter waters to the notorious class III/IV rapids of the Grand Canyon of the Snake River (see *To See*—Natural Wonders). Whether you're floating or paddling, rafting or kayaking, you're probably best off hiring a knowledgeable and experienced guide service to coordinate the details of your trip on this river, as it can be tricky even through the flat sections. Luckily for you, you have a lot of services to choose from, including **Barker-Ewing River Trips** (1-800-448-4202; http://www.barker-ewing .com); **Jackson Hole Whitewater** (1-800-700-RAFT; http://www.jhww.com); and **Snake River Kayak and Canoe** (1-800-KAYAK-01; http://www.snakeriverkayak .com); among others.

See also Teton Mountain Bike Tours, LLC in *To Do*—Bicycling; and *Green Space*.

THE SNAKE RIVER

RELAXATION AND REJUVENATION ☙ **Bear and Doe Massage Works**
(307-732-0863; http://www.bearanddoemassage.com). Open by appointment 10–7
Monday through Friday, 10–5 Saturday through Sunday. Bear and Doe reaches
beyond the normal, routine hour-long massage. Here, your hour ($85) is actually
about 90 minutes from start to finish, including a complimentary hot-paraffin dip
for your hands or feet and heated rice packs on your shoulders, followed by the
massage itself. Après-massage, you get to unwind in the sweat lodge, followed by a
cold plunge. If you're looking for a top-quality sports or deep tissue massage, Bear
and Doe is the place to go.

☙ ✐ **Granite Hot Springs** lie in the Bridger-Teton National Forest (see *Green
Space*—National Lands) and can be accessed by taking US 189/191 southeast of
Hoback Junction for 10 miles, then going north on FR 30500 for about 10 miles.
Open 10–8 daily (summer), 10–6 daily (winter); $6/person. Here you'll find a pool
perfectly engineered to capture the springs' 103–108-degree waters (in winter, in
summer they're only about 93 degrees). There is a **campground** just south of the
hot springs, making it a fun destination for the family (see also Bridger-Teton
National Forest in *Lodging*—Campgrounds). The Granite Falls Hot Springs feature a number of more primitive soaking pools as well, accessed by hiking the 2-
mile trail that begins where Swift Creek meets Granite Creek south of the
developed pool, then follows the east bank of Granite Creek north to the developed pool. Granite Hot Springs are also a popular destination for mountain bikers,
who can bike the distance from the turnoff on US 189 up FR 30500 for a fun,
moderate ride. This road also provides access to **Trail #018** (no bikes allowed),
which follows Granite Creek into the **Gros Ventre Wilderness** and links up with

other trails in the wilderness as well. In winter, the springs are a popular destination for adventuresome snowshoers, cross-country skiers, and snowmobilers. **Jackson Hole Snowmobile Tours** (1-800-633-1733 or 307-733-6850; http://www.jacksonholesnowmobile.com) offers a hot springs adventure (minimum driver age is 13), which includes a day of snowmobile riding, a grilled steak lunch, and of course, soaking in the hot springs ($210).

The Jackson Whole Grocer (307-733-0450; http://www.jacksonwholegrocer.com); 974 W. Broadway, Jackson. Open daily 7 AM–11 PM (deli, coffee bar, juice bar, and meat counter close at 8 PM). Here you'll find a full-scale grocery store dedicated to providing customers with top-notch organic/natural foods, including locally grown produce in season.

Windy Mountain Herbs (307-455-2728); 300 W. Ramshorn, Dubois. Call for current hours/days. Located next to **Kathy's Koffee,** this specialty shop can supply all your supplement/herbal needs, as well as organic chocolate and honey.

See also Grand Targhee Resort in *To Do*—Snow Sports; Sassy Moose Inn in *Lodging*—Bed and Breakfasts; Snake River Lodge and Spa and Teton Mountain Lodge and Spa in *Lodging*—Lodges; and Wild Sage Restaurant in *Where to Eat*—Dining Out.

SNOW SPORTS **Cross-country skiing** opportunities abound in this region on both groomed and ungroomed trails. To get you started, near Jackson, you'll find two groomed trails—Cache Creek Trail (see *To Do*—Hiking) and **Game Creek Trail,** accessible by going south from Jackson for 7 miles on US 89/191, then turning east on FR 30455. For other ideas of where to go in this region, see also Jackson Hole Community Pathway System in *To Do*—Bicycling; Cache Creek Trail in *To Do*—Hiking; Granite Hot Springs in *To Do*—Relaxation and Rejuvenation; and Grand Targhee Ski Resort, Jackson Mountain Ski Resort, and Snowshoeing *To Do*—Snow Sports.

Ice-skating can be found at a number of places in and around Jackson. The Teton County Parks and Recreation Department (307-739-6789; http://www.tetonwyo.org/parks allows public skating at outdoor hockey rinks at Snow King and in Wilson (call for times), as well as at a small rink at 155 E. Gill.

Snowmobiling, like cross-country skiing, is very popular in this region, and the possibilities are virtually endless. For detailed trail reports, call 307-777-6560 or go to http://wyotrails.state.wy.us/snow, the Wyoming Snowmobile Trails Web site, which also provides information about rules, rental agencies, trails around the state, and more. If you're a novice or you want some expert guidance on your adventure, you should hire a guide, such as **Goosewing Ranch** (1-888-733-5251 or 307-733-5251; http://www.goosewingranch.com), **Jackson Hole Snowmobile Tours** (1-800-633-1733 or 307-733-6850; http://www.jacksonholesnowmobile.com), or **High Country Snowmobile Tours** (1-800-524-0130; http://www.hcsnowmobile.com). Such services can help you learn the tools of the trade, while acquainting you with the proper etiquette, rules, and regulations. For more snowmobiling ideas, see Granite Hot Springs in *To Do*—Hot Springs; Jackson Hole Mountain Resort in *To Do*—Snow Sports; Bridger-Teton National Forest in *Green Space*—National Lands; and Togwotee Mountain Lodge in *Lodging*—Lodges.

✎ **Snowshoeing**, like cross-country skiing and snowmobiling, is a great way to see this region in wintertime, with so many places to go that you would need more than a lifetime to explore them all. **The Hole Hiking Experience** (1-866-733-4453 or 307-690-4453; http://www.holehike.com) in Jackson can coordinate a snowshoeing adventure for you, led by a knowledgeable botanist who can help interpret your wintry surroundings (half-day $95 per adult, $75 per child). Hole Hiking also guides cross-country skiing and dog sledding trips, as well as hikes in warmer months. See also Cache Creek Trail in *To Do*—Hiking.

See also Granite Hot Springs in *To Do*—Relaxation and Rejuvenation and *Green Space*.

UNIQUE ADVENTURES ✍ **Llamaneering with Jackson Hole Llamas** (1-800-830-7316 or 307-739-9582; http://www.jhllamas.com), P.O. Box 12500, Jackson. Open May through October. Want to take a day hike with a unique, four-footed companion? Let a llama carry your gear while you hike unencumbered through some of the gorgeous terrain surrounding Jackson, accompanied by an experienced llama handler and guide. Gentle and strong, the llamas will carry along water, a huge lunch (provided by the outfitter), and all of your gear for the day ($125 per person). Children are welcome. Jackson Hole Llamas also offers multiday llamaneering adventures. Call for details and reservations.

& ✍ **Sleigh Rides on the National Elk Refuge** (1-800-772-5386 or 307-733-0277; http://www.fws.gov/nationalelkrefuge/NERSleighRides.htm), rides depart from the Jackson Hole and Greater Yellowstone Visitor Center (see *To See*—Museums). Open mid-December through early April (depending on weather and herd conditions), closed Christmas, rides leave three or four times per hour daily from 10–4; $18 per adult, $14 per child ages 5–12, children 4 and under free; reservations taken for only groups of 20 or more. Bundle up for this exciting, one-hour ride in a horse-drawn sleigh right into the thick of the hundreds to thousands of elk who winter here each year (see also National Elk Refuge in Wilder Places—Wildlife Refuges and Areas).

& **Wild West Jeep Tours** (307-733-9036; http://www.wildwestjeeptours.com/wyomingtours.htm), P.O. Box 7506, Jackson. Open summer months only; $65 per adult, $55 per child ages 12 and under. Let your knowledgeable guide do all of the driving, from the moment he or she picks you up from your lodgings to the moment you're dropped off at your home away from home three hours later. You'll get a real feel for the terrain as you tour through some of the backcountry areas outside of Jackson. The informed, interpretive narration provided by your guide about both the natural and cultural history of the area will provide you with a deeper and more intimate understanding of this incredible locale.

✍ **Wyoming Balloon Adventures** (307-739-0900; http://www.wyomingballoon.com), P.O. Box 2578, Jackson; $295 per adult, $245 per child ages 6–12 (children under 6 not allowed). Imagine yourself floating high above Jackson Hole, with incredible, birds-eye views of the Teton Range and the surrounding natural splendors—sound like a dream? Well, you can make this fairytale image become a reality during your visit to Jackson—and be back in time for breakfast, too! Wyoming Balloon Adventures will pick you up at around 6 AM to get you started on your adventure. You'll spend about an hour in flight in a balloon piloted by an FAA-certified pilot, enjoying the morning sun on the Tetons and the potential to see wildlife, too. Your friendly guides will then have you back by around 9:30 AM.

✎ Jackson Hole Skiing

When you think of Jackson Hole, one thing probably comes to your mind: skiing. The town of Jackson (almost 9,000 people) and the 15-mile by 80-mile valley surrounding it, Jackson Hole, together embody the term ski town, having developed into one of America's premier winter sports destinations during the 20th century. Today Wyoming's three largest ski resorts can be found here—Jackson Mountain Ski Resort, Grand Targhee Ski Resort, and Snow King Ski Resort, Wyoming's oldest ski area. Not only do these resorts offer skiing on some of the best terrain in the country, but also, they offer myriad other activities and services throughout the year.

"♥" ✎ ♿ **Grand Targhee Resort** (1-800-TARGHEE or 307-353-2300; http://www .grandtarghee.com), on FR 025 northeast of Driggs, ID; 3300 E. Ski Hill Road, Alta. High in the Teton Range of the Caribou-Targhee National Forest (see *Green Space*—National Lands) you'll discover this full-service ski resort. Two mountains provide more than 2,500 acres of lift-served skiable terrain, including a terrain park—plus 1,000 more acres served by snowcats—that sees some 500 inches of champagne powder each season. The resort also has cross-country skiing on 9 miles (15 km) of groomed and tracked trails ($10 adult; $6 senior/junior). You'll find information about additional adventures at the resort's Activity Center, located in the main plaza, including dog sledding, snowshoeing, sleigh ride dinners, snow tubing, and more. In summer, the resort offers an array of recreational activities, including hiking, mountain biking, horseback riding, rock climbing, Folf (Frisbee golf), and more. The resort also offers a full-service spa and fitness center, shopping, lodging (expensive to very expensive), and dining (inexpensive to expensive). Lifts: three quads and one double chairlift, and one magic carpet. Trails: 72 trails—10 percent beginner, 70 percent difficult, and 20 percent advanced. Vertical Drop: 2,300 feet. Facilities: Four restaurants and a bar located in base area, as well as three ski-in, ski-out lodges. Ski School: Offers ski and snowboard lessons for all ages and ability levels. For children: Kids' Club (daycare with optional ski lesson) for ages 2 months to 5 years, Little Deer for ages 4–5, Powder Scouts for ages 6–12 (skiing), and Teen Adventures for ages 13–16. Rates: $69 per adult, $39 per senior (ages 65 and up), $39 per junior (ages 6–12), children 5 and under ski free with an adult; half-day and multiday rates also available.

♿ ✎ **Jackson Hole Mountain Resort** (1-888-DEEP-SNO or 307-733-2292; http://www.jacksonhole.com), P.O. Box 290, 3395 Cody Lane, Teton Village. Undoubtedly Wyoming's best-known ski resort, Jackson Hole Mountain Resort's reputation has been gained for good reason. Only 12 miles northwest of the town of Jackson via WY 22 to WY 390, this resort features two mountains that include 2,500 acres of in-bounds skiable terrain and 3,000 more acres of gate-accessed backcountry terrain—but it's the 4,139 feet of vertical drop that might just knock your skis off. Complementing its remarkable downhill skiing and snowboarding (including a terrain park and half pipe), the resort offers a wide range of winter activities, including dog sledding, snowshoeing, dinner sleigh rides, heli-skiing, snowcat skiing, snowmobiling, and more. The resort also has cross-country skiing on 10 miles (17 km) of groomed trails ($14 per person). In summer, visitors can enjoy a sightseeing ride on the resort's aerial tramway, as well as hiking and mountain biking opportunities, among others. Lifts: one aerial tram, one gondola, six quads, two triple, and one double chairlift, and one magic carpet. Trails: 116 trails—10 percent beginner, 40 percent intermediate, and 50 percent expert. Vertical Drop: 4,139 feet. Snowmaking: covering 160 acres. Facilities: Numerous restaurants from cheap eats to fine dining on the mountain, as well as additional eateries and bars in Teton Village. Ski School: Offers a full range of skiing and snowboarding lessons for all ages and ability levels. For children: Kids Ranch offers age-appropriate activities for kids ages 6 months to 17 years, including Wranglers (daycare) for ages 6 months to 2 years, Pioneers for ages 3–4, Rough Riders for ages 3–6, Little Rippers for ages 5–6, Explorers for ages 7–14, and The Fall Line Camp for ages 12–17. Rates: $61 adult (ages 15 and up), $36 per child 14 and under, $38 per senior 65 and up; half-day and multiday rates also available.

"ɪ" ✆ 🦌 **Snow King Resort** (1-800-522-KING or 307-733-5200; http://www.snow king.com), 400 E. Snow King Avenue, Jackson Hole. Just six blocks from downtown Jackson, you'll find Wyoming's first ski area—Snow King, founded in 1939. Every winter season since that time, Snow King has continued to draw skiers from around the world to test their mettle on its worthy terrain. Always changing with the times, the resort welcomes snowboarders to its slopes as well, inviting them to ride in its terrain park, too. Families in particular seem drawn to try out a different sort of snow ride in Snow King's separate area for snow tubing (lift-served); $21 for two hours per adult; $18 for two hours per child 13 and under; must be at least 42 inches tall to ride. In summer, the resort operates an alpine slide, a scenic chairlift, and a miniature golf course, as well as providing opportunities for hiking, mountain biking, and horseback riding, among other activities. Lifts: one triple and two double chairlifts, plus one handle-tow. Trails: 20 trails— 15 percent beginner, 25 percent intermediate, and 60 percent advanced. Vertical Drop: 1,571 feet. Snowmaking: 150 acres. Facilities: base lodge has a cafeteria and indoor ice-skating rink; plus hotels and condos (expensive to very expensive). Ski School: Great American Ski School offers lessons for all ages and ability levels. Rates: $41 adult, $31 junior/senior (13 and under or 65 and older); nighttime, two-hour, half-day, and multiday rates available as well.

See also National Bighorn Sheep Interpretive Center in *To See*—Museums; Teton Mountain Bike Tours, LLC in *To Do*—Bicycling; Jackson Hole Mountain Resort in *To Do*—Snow Sports; and Teton Science Schools Wildlife Expeditions: Grand Teton Expeditions in Grand Teton National Park.

WINERIES AND WINE TASTINGS ✿ **Jackson Hole Wine Company** (307-739-WINE; http://www.jacksonholewinecompany.com); 200 W. Broadway, Jackson. Open 10–10 Monday through Saturday, 12–10 Sunday except Christmas. Free wine tasting 4:30–6:30 every Friday night except in April, May, and November. This treasure trove features not only more than 800 varieties of wine, but also microbrews and spirits, gourmet cheeses, custom-made gift baskets, and even wine delivery. Hungry? Then sit down for dinner (starting at 5:30 nightly) in the chic **Koshu Wine Bar** (307-733-5283; http://www.koshuwinebar.com), which serves delectable pan-Asian cuisine accompanied by JHWC wine by the glass, or a specialty cocktail. Expensive.

See also Dornan's Spur Ranch Cabins in Grand Teton National Park: *Lodging/Dining:* Moose.

✳ Green Space

NATIONAL LANDS Bridger-Teton National Forest (307-739-5500; http://www.fs.fed.us/r4/btnf), P.O. Box 1888, Jackson. Covering more than 3.4 million acres of land, the Bridger-Teton National Forest surrounds most of Jackson Hole. Encompassed within these lands are three pristine, untrammeled wilderness areas—Bridger, Gros Ventre, and Teton, which together comprise 1.2 million acres. The lands of this national forest make up a large portion of the more than 12-million-acre Greater Yellowstone Ecosystem, the lower 48 states' largest remaining intact temperate ecosystem, of which Yellowstone National Park and Grand Teton National Park are the cores. With its numerous mountains, including the Gros Ventre, Salt River, Wind River, and Wyoming Ranges; its abundance of rivers, lakes, and streams; and its 30,000 miles of developed roads and trails, this national forest provides not only abundant wildlife habitat, but also endless recreational opportunities. These include mountain biking, boating, camping, fishing, horseback riding, hot springs, paddling/floating, snow sports, picnicking, hunting, and wildlife watching, among others. See also *Lodging*—Campgrounds.

Caribou-Targhee National Forest (208-524-7500; http://www.fs.fed.us/r4/caribou-targhee), 1405 Hollipark Drive, Idaho Falls, ID. The more than 3 million acres of lands in this forest lie primarily in Idaho. A small portion in northwest Wyoming includes lands below the southwestern border of Yellowstone National Park, south and west of Grand Teton National Park, including the Jedediah Smith Wilderness, a portion of the Teton Range, and a portion of the Snake River Range. Recreational opportunities in this area include camping, fishing, horseback riding, snow sports, and wildlife watching, among others. See also *Lodging*—Campgrounds.

Shoshone National Forest (307-578-1200 or 307-527-6241; http://www.fs.fed.us/r2/shoshone), Wind River Ranger District (307-455-2466), 1403 W. Ramshorn, Dubois. See listing in *Green Space*—National Lands in Cody and Powell, and Lander and Riverton; as well as in *Lodging*—Campgrounds.

http://nationalelkrefuge.fws.gov), 25,000 acres along the west side of US 26/89/191 just north of Jackson. A stop at the Jackson Hole and Greater Yellowstone Visitor Center (see *To See*—Museums) is a great place to start your exploration of the National Elk Refuge, one of the nation's largest ranges for wintering elk. Each season, some 7,500 of these grand animals make this area near Jackson their seasonal abode, and both visitors and residents alike delight in their presence. Of interest to anglers is lovely **Flat Creek,** currently Wyoming's sole fly-fishing-only stream (cutthroat trout), which flows through the refuge. See also Sleigh Rides on the National Elk Refuge in *To Do*—Unique Adventures; and ElkFest in *Special Events*.

See also National Bighorn Sheep Interpretive Center in *To See*—Museums.

✳ Lodging

&. **Jackson Hole Central Reservations** (1-888-838-6606; http://www .jacksonholewy.com), 140 E. Broadway, Jackson. This company can book not only lodging at a variety of locations in Jackson and the surrounding area, but also can hook you up with vacation activities, often wrapped into package deals.

BED AND BREAKFASTS
Dubois
🎣 **Jakey's Fork Homestead** (307-455-2769; http://www.frontierlodging .com), 11 Fish Hatchery Road. On the banks of Jakey's Fork, a trout stream, this rustic homestead welcomes guests to one of two bedrooms that share a bath in the main house. Also available are rooms in the historic Simpson bunkhouse, a three-room cabin (available June through September). The house rests on 22 acres of beautiful Wyoming country, allowing guests access to the lovely landscape surrounding them. Guests enjoy a full breakfast served daily. You can also rent out the entire main house or the entire bunkhouse, if you're interested. Moderate to expensive.

🎣 **The Stone House** (307-455-2555; http://www.duboisbnb.com), 207 S. First Street, P.O. Box 1446. Open May through October. This beautiful, historic stone home invites you to stay in a private, three-room cottage or a two-room suite, both with private baths, or in one of two guest rooms that share a bath. The cottage has two queen-sized beds, a refrigerator, a microwave, and a coffeemaker. The suite has a queen-sized bed, a sofa hide-a-bed, and a fireplace. A full breakfast is included. Moderate to expensive.

Jackson Hole
🦉 **A Teton Treehouse** (307-733-3233; http://www.cruising-america .com/tetontreehouse), P.O. Box 550, 6175 Heck of a Hill Road, Wilson. Open May through September. If you read the contact information closely for this entry, you probably already have a bit of an idea of the lighthearted and playful spirit you'll find infused in every nook and cranny of this lovingly handcrafted B&B. Located on Heck of a Hill Road, the inn itself is a product of the owner/innkeeper's efforts to create a wonderful, whimsical mountainside haven for himself and his family—and you, too! You'll get your exercise in every day as you walk up the 95 steps that lead to the front door—but don't worry, they're not all that steep, just enough to get your heart rate up a little and slow you down a bit from the hurried pace of the outside world. You'll relax in the

comfort of one of six guest rooms, all of which feature private baths, decks, views, and window seats. You can also enjoy an outdoor hot tub, and you'll start each day with a healthy and delicious breakfast. Expensive to very expensive.

  🕎 ⁂ 🐾 **Bentwood Inn** (307-739-1411; http://www.bentwoodinn.com), 4250 Raven Haven Road. Sink into the divinity of your own private hot tub, and then curl up in front of a cozy, private fireplace in any one of the five guest rooms at this award-winning, critically acclaimed bed and breakfast. All rooms also feature cable television, a telephone, a private bath, and a deck or balcony. The elegant, 5,800-square-foot log inn was constructed in 1995 with much of its wood salvaged from the famous Yellowstone National Park fires of 1988. Inside, you'll find a charming blend of fine English antiques and country western furnishings. You'll also enjoy a hearty breakfast in the morning and afternoon refreshments as well, plus the option

GRAND VICTORIAN LODGE

of a bistro dinner twice a week. Very expensive.

  ⁂ **Grand Victorian Lodge** (1-800-584-0532 or 307-584-0532; http://www .grandvictorianlodge.com), 85 Perry Street. You'll know you're staying in style from the moment you pull up in front of this Victorian B&B on the north side of Jackson. The elegant exterior is complemented by the exquisite interior, which features well-matched furnishings throughout. All 11 guest rooms feature cable television and telephones, while some also include private hot tubs, private baths, fireplaces, and canopied, king-sized beds. You'll enjoy a full, gourmet breakfast prepared daily and served either directly to you in your room, or in the dining room—your choice. Afternoon coffee and tea service—with homemade cookies, too—is standard as well. Expensive to very expensive.

  🐾 ⁂ ⁂ 🐾 **Sassy Moose Inn** (1-800-356-1277 or 307-733-1277; http://www .sassymoosejacksonhole.com), 3859 Miles Road. With the Tetons as your backdrop, you can simmer in the serenity of this rustic log inn's outdoor hot tub before you settle into the soothing comfort of your guest room, perhaps reading a story to the children in front of the crackling fireplace before you slip off to slumber. Four of the five guest rooms offer views of Jackson Hole Mountain Resort to tantalize your imagination when you're not actually on the slopes. All rooms feature private baths, views of the Tetons, down comforters, and cathedral ceilings. A full breakfast is included in the rate, and children 11 and under stay for free. This B&B also has an on-site "petit spa" that offers massages and a full range of salon services (extra fee). Moderate to expensive.

  ⁂ ⁂ **Wildflower Inn** (307-733-4710; http://www.jacksonholewildflower.com),

3725 Teton Village Road. This award-winning inn welcomes you in style, whether you're in search of the spot for a perfect romantic getaway or a comfortable, elegant place to relax after a hard day playing on the slopes or in the woods. Situated on 3 acres of land tucked back in the trees, you'll find privacy and solitude aplenty in this log lodging as you rest in the suite, or in one of four guest rooms. All rooms feature down comforters on log-hewn beds, private baths, charming décor, private decks, and televisions. Elegant, country western comfort beckons to you from every corner of the B&B, from the cozy easy chairs to the stone fireplace. Freshly prepared breakfasts with something for everyone, from light appetites to hearty ones, greet you every morning. Very expensive.

LODGES
Dubois
& **The Sawmill Lodge** (1-866-472-9645 or 307-455-2171; http://www.thesawmill.org), 1 Fir Road. Open year-round except April. This gorgeous and remote lodge on Union Pass offers you year-round recreational opportunities right outside your door. Situated on the northeast side of the Wind River Mountain Range, the Sawmill Lodge features a number of different comfortable accommodations to suit your needs. The Sawmill also has an on-premises restaurant, serving lunch and dinner Wednesday through Sunday (expensive), as well as a game room and a full-service bar. Expensive.

¶ **Twin Pines Lodge and Cabins** (1-800-550-6332 or 307-455-2600; http://www.twinpineslodge.com), 218 W. Ramshorn Street. This distinctive lodge and cabins, listed on the National Register of Historic Places, were constructed with incredible craftsmanship and many unique design and architectural features in the early 20th century. Today, you can stay in the very same accommodations that housed earlier travelers to the lodge—with some improvements and modernizations for your comfort and convenience. You can stay in a lodge room or individual cabin, both of which include cable TV/VCR, refrigerators, in-room coffee, and a complimentary continental breakfast. Moderate to expensive.

Jackson Hole
¶ **Buckrail Lodge** (307-733-2079; http://www.buckraillodge.com), 110 E. Karns Avenue. You'll enjoy true country comforts at this 12-room lodge situated among mature trees and grassy lawns at the base of Snow King Resort (see *To Do*—Snow Sports). Within walking distance of downtown Jackson, the lodge itself is a step removed from this scene, offering you a convenient escape into solitude, should you need one. Each room features western red cedar logs in its construction, and cathedral ceilings make for spacious, private accommodations, which also include furniture made from native pine, cable television, and large bathrooms. Guests also enjoy access to a large outdoor hot tub, plus free morning newspapers and coffee/tea served in the lobby. Moderate to expensive.

¶ ✐ **Jackson Hole Lodge** (1-800-604-9404 or 307-733-2992; http://www.jacksonholelodge.com), 420 W. Broadway. A fixture on the Jackson lodging scene since 1942, you can rest assured that your needs will be met at this lovely lodge just a few blocks from the heart of downtown. Lodging options range from your basic, cozy lodge room with hotel-style amenities to two-bedroom condos. Amenities include a 40-foot heated pool, two hot tubs, a sauna, a children's pool, a game room, and free nightly movie rental, among others. Combination deals with activities are often offered; ask for details when you call to make reservations. Moderate to very expensive.

⚑ ♪ ♿ Snake River Lodge & Spa (1-866-975-ROCK or 307-732-6000; http://www.snakeriverlodge.rockresorts.com), 7710 Granite Loop Road, Teton Village. Completely remodeled in 2002, this ski-in, ski-out full-service resort at the base of Jackson Hole Mountain Resort (see *To Do*—Snow Sports) features an array of amenities that can't be surpassed. You can recharge your engine in the heated indoor pool, heated outdoor pool, hot tubs, sauna, on-site fitness club, or at the on-site full-service **Avanyu Spa,** depending on your needs and energy level. A fine dining restaurant, the **gamefish**, means you don't have to go far to fill your belly (open for three meals daily plus 24-hour room service; expensive to very expensive). The lodge often has ski and stay/spa packages, so be sure to check for details when making reservations. Children 14 and under stay free in parents' room. Expensive to very expensive.

♿ ⚑ Teton Mountain Lodge and Spa (1-800-801-6615 or 307-734-7111; http://www.tetonlodge.com), slope side at Jackson Hole Mountain Resort. This new lodge features 129 elegant guest rooms and suites— including a drop-dead gorgeous penthouse suite—with all of the amenities you'd expect from a luxury accommodation. On the premises, you'll also find the 16,000-square-foot **Solitude Spa** (which includes a fitness center), fine dining and cocktails at the **Cascade Grill House and Spirits** (open for three meals daily; expensive to very expensive), and much, much more. Staying at the lodge gives you easy access to Jackson Hole Mountain Resort as well as to Grand Teton National Park. Expensive to very expensive.

☃ ♿ ♪ Togwotee Mountain Lodge (1-866-278-4245; http://www.togwoteelodge.com), about 17 miles past Moran Junction on US 26/287, Moran. A snowmobiler's paradise, Togwotee Mountain Lodge sits in the Bridger-Teton National Forest (see *Green Space*—National Lands), allowing its visitors easy access to the 2.5 million acres of terrain in an area that regularly receives 600 inches of powder in a season. The 35 rooms in the lodge feature basic hotel-style amenities. Cabins include more room to spread out, as well as two televisions, a kitchenette, and full bathrooms. The lodge also has a full-service restaurant, **The Grizzly Steak House,** serving three meals daily (expensive), hot tubs, and a saloon. Ask about package vacations. Expensive to very expensive.

⚑ ♪ 🐾 The Virginian Lodge (1-800-262-4999 or 307-733-2792; http://www.virginianlodge.com), 750 W. Broadway. Founded by a hunter for hunters, this lodge has been serving Jackson Hole's visitors since 1965. Today the large lodge features 170 units designed to meet the needs of any visitor. Rooms range from the basic, motel- or hotel-style room to rooms that include a Jacuzzi or a kitchenette. In summer, guests enjoy an outdoor, heated swimming pool. A saloon with old-fashioned swinging doors, a liquor store, a convention center, a salon, an RV resort, and a restaurant serving three meals daily are all on the premises as well. Moderate to expensive.

See also The Alpenrose and Wild Sage Restaurant in *Where to Eat*— Dining Out.

HOTELS AND MOTELS

Jackson Hole

🐾 ⁙ ♿ ♨ **Antler Inn** (1-800-4TETONS; http://www.townsquareinns.com), 43 W. Pearl Street. Location, location, location. This charming motel gives you a front row seat to all of the action happening in Jackson. A single block separates you from the center of it all—Town Square—and you'll enjoy the ease of your access to all things Jackson. That's not to say that the rooms at the Antler aren't noteworthy—the cozy, cedar log rooms conjure up the feeling of being inside a log cabin, with their deep, earthy tones, and warm lighting. You'll enjoy access to a hot tub, sauna, and fitness equipment. Inexpensive to expensive.

⁙ 🐾 ♨ **The Hostel** (307-733-3415; http://www.thehostel.us), 3315 Village Drive, Teton Village. Inexpensive doesn't mean uncomfortable when it comes to The Hostel. Located conveniently at the base of Jackson Hole Mountain Resort, The Hostel features a game room, beautiful grounds complete with a creek, wireless Internet ($5 extra), and allows pets ($10 extra). Inexpensive to expensive.

♿ ⁙ **The Wort Hotel** (1-800-322-2727 or 307-733-2190; http://www.worthotel.com), Glenwood and Broadway. This historic hotel, listed on the National Register of Historic Places, has graced Jackson's downtown since 1941, embodying the dream of one of the area's original homesteaders, Charles J. Wort. The hotel's restaurant, the **Silver Dollar Bar & Grill,** built in 1950, quickly became a favorite for both travelers and locals, known for its cool bar inlaid with more than 2,000 uncirculated silver dollars from Denver's Federal Reserve (expensive to very expensive). Today travelers can stay in one of 60 modern rooms or

THE HISTORIC WORT HOTEL

three suites, all of which feature country lodgepole pine furnishings, goosedown comforters, western décor, comfy bathrobes, and cute Silver Dollar Sam teddy bears. Very expensive.

See also Grand Targhee Resort and Snow King Resort in *To Do—Snow Sports.*

CAMPGROUNDS ♿ **Bridger-Teton National Forest** (see *Green Space—National Lands*) camping around Jackson is supervised by the forest's Teton Division, which includes the Buffalo Ranger District (307-543-2386) and the Jackson Ranger District (307-739-5400). Together, they have some 20 developed campgrounds, including first-come, first-served **Box Creek Campground,** 46 miles northeast of Jackson via US 26/287 to FR 30500 (Buffalo Valley Road), then left (northeast) to the campground ($10; open mid-May through late September); and first-come, first-served **Granite Campground** (near Granite Hot Springs, see *To Do—Hot Springs;* $15; open mid-May through late September). For more information, visit the Web site or contact the appropriate ranger district. Dispersed camping is also permitted in some areas of the forest. See also Gros Ventre River and Snake River in *To Do—Fishing.*

&. **Caribou-Targhee National Forest** (see *Green Space*—National Lands) camping in this region is managed by the Teton Basin Ranger District (208-354-2312). You'll find six developed campgrounds, including **Teton Canyon Campground,** 9 miles east of Driggs, Idaho on FR 009 ($10–18; open late May through mid-September); and **Trail Creek Campground,** located west of Jackson on WY 22 just before the Idaho border ($10; open mid-May through mid-September). You can reserve sites in advance via http://www.recreation .gov or by calling 1-877-444-6777. Dispersed camping is also permitted. For more information, visit the Web site or contact the ranger district.

&. **Shoshone National Forest** (see *Green Space*—National Lands) camping in this region is managed by the Wind River Ranger District (307-455-2466). The five developed campgrounds ($5–10) in the area of the forest surrounding Dubois include first-come, first-served Horse Creek Campground ($10; open June through September), accessible by going north off US 287 just west of Dubois on Horse Creek Road (FR 285) for 10 miles or so to reach the campground. Dispersed camping is also permitted in much of the forest. For more information, visit the Web site or contact the ranger district.

See also The Virginian Lodge in *Lodging*—Lodges.

OTHER OPTIONS
Dubois
🏕 🐾 ♦ **Branding Iron Inn** (1-888-651-WEST or 307-455-2893; http:// www.brandingironinn.com), 401 W. Ramshorn Street. These handmade Swedish Cope log cabins were constructed in the 1940s. Today they provide you with authentic, rustic vacation lodging accommodations—with all of the modern comforts and amenities you need. The cabins' rich and lustrous wood-paneled interiors almost glow with warmth. Some units include kitchenettes and adjoining rooms as well. Children under 12 stay free in their parents' room; pets are $5 extra. Horse corrals make this a great spot to stop if you're traveling with horses. Plenty of parking accommodates RVs in the summertime and snowmobilers in winter months. Inexpensive to moderate.

Jackson Hole
See Twin Pines Lodge and Cabins in *Lodging*—Lodges.

✳ Where to Eat

EATING OUT
Dubois
Rustic Pine Steakhouse and Tavern (307-455-2430; http://www.rusticpine tavern.com), 119 E. Ramshorn Street. Open 9 AM–2 AM daily. Enjoy classic steakhouse fare in a historic western setting for breakfast, lunch, and dinner. Delicious steaks cooked to perfection are the norm here, accompanied by top-notch, above-average sides. Packed with western memorabilia, the tavern is a veritable museum in and of itself. Moderate to expensive.

See also Windy Mountain Herbs in *To Do*—Relaxation and Rejuvenation.

Jackson Hole
Jedediah's Original House of Sourdough (307-733-5671), 135 E. Broadway. Open 7 AM–2 PM daily. Sourdough is the name of the game at Jedediah's. In the morning, it takes a leading role in the sourjack pancakes, while at lunchtime, it jumps in to hold the sandwiches together. The grilled steaks, chicken, and seafood options come with sourdough biscuits, while the burgers are served on sourdough

buns. You'll even find sourdough in the desserts, with both carrot cake and brownies both made from the divine dough. A hint to breakfast eaters—if you're a granola aficionado, don't pass up the chance to try Jedediah's home-made granola, too! Moderate.

✂ ✎ **Mountain High Pizza Pie** (307-733-3646), 120 W. Broadway. Open daily for lunch and dinner. Reasonably priced and excellent, this is the spot to go when you need something filling and fast. Choose from the creative pizzas topped with ingredients ranging from normal (such as pepperoni, Canadian bacon, and mushrooms) to offbeat (such as corn, broccoli, and spinach), or create your own from the nearly 30 toppings available. You can also choose a calzone, sub, sandwich, or salad, if pizza just isn't your favorite. Dine inside or on the patio in summer, or just call to have a pizza delivered to your door. Moderate.

Shades Café (307-733-2015), 82 S. King Street. Open 7:30–4 Monday through Saturday. This cute little café serves absolutely delicious breakfast fare as well as great coffee and diverse lunch and early dinner options (or grab a sandwich or wrap to go). This favorite local hangout specializes in healthy, freshly made meals. Some mornings, you can catch live music performances here, too. Inexpensive to moderate.

Snake River BrewPub (307-739-2337; http://www.snakeriverbrewing .com/pub.html), 265 S. Millward. Open 11:30 AM–1 AM daily. Stop in for happy hour to sample the award-winning brews of Jackson's own Snake River Brewpub, and grab some cheap appetizers while you're at it. You'll probably wind up staying for dinner. The pub-style fare includes pastas, pizzas, burgers, salads, and sandwiches, all served in a nonsmoking (but usually

loud) environment. Kids are welcome and can choose from their own menu, but it's honestly more of an adult-appropriate hangout spot. During foot-ball season, you can catch up to eight different games playing on the satellite televisions. Moderate to expensive.

✂ **Thai Me Up** (307-733-0003), 75 E. Pearl Street. Open 11:30–2:30 for lunch and 5:30–closing (varies) for dinner daily. If you like Thai food, you're not likely to be disappointed with a meal at this popular restaurant. Reasonable prices, a wide selection of vegetarian and vegan dishes, and a full bar add to the appeal, but it's the delicious, classic Thai entrées and sides (try the spring rolls!) that make this restaurant so good. Choose from two different Pad Thai dishes, an assortment of curries, fried rice, stir-fries, and salads, among other options. The well-decorated restaurant also has a children's menu and welcomes take-out orders. Moderate to expensive.

See also National Museum of Wildlife Art in *To See*—Museums; The Jackson Whole Grocer in *To Do*—Relaxation and Rejuvenation; Grand Targhee Resort and Jackson Hole Mountain Resort in *To Do*—Snow Sports; Togwotee Mountain Lodge and The Virginian Lodge in *Lodging*—Lodges; The Alpenrose in *Where to Eat*—Dining Out; and Mangy Moose Restaurant and Saloon in *Entertainment*.

DINING OUT
Dubois
See The Sawmill Lodge in *Lodging*—Lodges.

Jackson Hole
The Alpenrose (307-733-3242; http://www.alpenhoflodge.com), next to the clock tower in Teton Village. Situated inside the elegant Austrian **Alpenhof Lodge** (expensive to very expensive), the Alpenrose invites you

to sample its delectable German-inspired cuisine. The main menu features specialties such as wiener schnitzel, rabbit loin, elk loin, and duck breast. Fondues are also popular menu selections, both cheese fondues and chocolate fondues. This restaurant is a winner of the prestigious Wine Spectator Award of Excellence. Expensive to very expensive. Also at the Alpenhof Lodge, you'll find the popular après-ski hotspot, the **Alpenhof Bistro,** which offers a more casual dining experience as well as a European-style bar and often, live entertainment (moderate to expensive).

Million Dollar Cowboy Steakhouse (307-733-4790; http://www.cowboy steakhouse.net), 25 N. Cache Drive. Open for dinner 5:30–10 daily. Downstairs from the Million Dollar Cowboy Bar (a Jackson experience unto itself), you can sit down to a full 'n' fancy cowboy dinner in the steakhouse. The full-service bar features an extensive wine list as well as beers and cocktails. The menu includes aged, hand-cut beef prepared in a number of ways to perfection—but that's not all. You can also choose from a wide range of other items, including game (venison, buffalo, duck, and elk) as well as chicken, lamb, pork, pastas, seafood, and more. In the tradition of the Old West, the Million Dollar Cowboy Steakhouse strives to make your dining experience a friendly and delicious one. Very expensive.

Nani's Cucina Italiana (307-733-3888; http://www.nanis.com), 242 N. Glenwood. Open for dinner 5–10 daily. Authentic, acclaimed Italian fine dining awaits you at Nani's—this ain't no pizza 'n' pasta joint! Using the finest and freshest of ingredients available, often from local and regional sources, Nani's always includes a number of favorites from the 20 regions of Italy on its menu. These include handmade ravioli and fettuccine, veal marsala, and frutti del mare, among many others. In addition, each month the menu features specialty dishes from Italy's regions as well, providing repeat customers and newcomers alike with culinary adventures to keep their taste buds intrigued and delighted. The homemade desserts are fantastic, from the tiramisu to the biscotti. Expensive to very expensive.

JACKSON'S FAMOUS MILLION DOLLAR COWBOY BAR

Nikai Asian Grill and Sushi Bar (307-734-6490; http://www.nikaisushi .com), 225 N. Cache. Open for dinner at 6 daily. Despite your rather substantial distance from any ocean, you can be sure that the sushi is always fresh here. Fish is flown in daily from around the globe to meet the needs of Nikai's customers. Start your meal with miso soup and edamame (steamed and salted soybeans—very yummy, if you haven't tried them), then select from the sushi menu. Not a big raw fish fan? Never fear—Nikai also offers a classic Asian grill menu that includes such favorites as chicken teriyaki, vegetable tempura, seared sea scallops, and ahi tuna salad, among other options. A full-service bar offers you whatever drink (sake, anyone?) your heart desires to accompany your meal. Expensive to very expensive.

Ġ Snake River Grill (307-733-0557; http://www.snakerivergrill.com), 84 E. Broadway. Open nightly for dinner at 5:30 in summer; 6:00 in winter. This award-winning, critically acclaimed restaurant has received both the Award of Excellence from Distinguished Restaurants of North America and the Wine Spectator's Award of Excellence. Inspired entrées feature organic produce, fresh fish, and free-range meats, put together in creations designed to please the palate. Dessert choices include made-to-order soufflés, among other house-made options. In addition to the award-winning wine list, the bar also offers a full array of cocktails and beers. Expensive to very expensive.

Wild Sage Restaurant (1-888-739-1749 or 307-733-2000; http://www.rustyparrot.com), 175 N. Jackson Street. Serves breakfast and dinner daily; call for current hours. Situated inside the **Rusty Parrot Lodge and Spa** (very expensive) the Wild Sage Restaurant features an elegant, comfortable atmosphere in which you'll find one of Jackson's premier fine dining experiences. The exhibition-style kitchen allows you to watch as your food is prepared while you relax by the lovely stone fireplace. The seasonal menu includes regional cuisine as well as fish flown in daily, with entrée selections ranging from beef and pork tenderloins to stuffed quail and elk racks. Presentation is an art form at the Wild Sage, and your dinner will be served in a visually appealing and tantalizing fashion—but the delicious blend of creative ingredients is likely to surpass even the artistry of the presentation. A

full wine list is available to complement your meal. Very expensive.

See also Grand Targhee Resort and Jackson Hole Mountain Resort in *To Do*—Snow Sports; Jackson Hole Wine Company in *To Do*—Wineries and Wine Tastings; Snake River Lodge and Spa and Teton Mountain Lodge and Spa in *Lodging*—Lodges; and The Wort Hotel in *Lodging*—Hotels and Motels.

✳ Entertainment

Jackson Hole Twin Cinema (307-733-4939; http://www.jacksonhole cinemas.com), 295 W. Pearl Street, Jackson.

⌀ The Jackson Hole Playhouse and Saddle Rock Saloon (307-733-6994; http://www.jhplayhouse.com), 145 W. Deloney Avenue, Jackson. Call or check Web site for current play. Season runs from early June through late September; tickets are $52 per adult, $47 per youth ages 13–18, $38 per child ages 5–12, under 5 free on parent's lap (dinner theater); or $26 per adult, $22 per youth ages 13–18, $19 per child ages 5–12, under 5 free on parent's lap.

Mangy Moose Restaurant & Saloon (307-733-4913; http://www.mangy moose.net), 1395 Teton Village Road, Teton Village. In addition to its well-known restaurant (expensive) and bar, this popular après-ski hangout also frequently hosts concerts. Call or check the Web site for a current schedule of upcoming shows.

MovieWorks Cinema (307-733-4939; http://www.jacksonholecinemas.com), 860 S. US 89, Jackson.

Off Square Theatre Company (307-733-3900; http://www.offsquare.org), 240 S. Glenwood, Jackson. Contact Wyoming's only year-round professional theatre company for current shows and ticket prices.

Teton Theatre (307-733-4939; http://www.jacksonholecinemas.com), 120 N. Cache, Jackson.

See also Shades Café in *Where to Eat*—Eating Out; The Alpenrose in *Where to Eat*—Dining Out; Grand Teton Music Festival in *Special Events*; Blue Heron Lounge and Pool Snack Bar in *Lodging/Dining:* Jackson Lake Area in Grand Teton National Park; and Pizza Pasta Company in *Lodging/Dining:* Moose in Grand Teton National Park.

✷ Selective Shopping

The area surrounding **Town Square** (see *To See*—City Parks and Gardens) in Jackson has far too many quality shopping establishments to select only a few for inclusion in this book—not to mention the rest of Jackson, or Dubois, for that matter. Suffice it to say that for those who love to shop, Jackson is probably Wyoming's premier shopping destination. Here you'll find everything from fine art galleries to clothing stores, outdoor equipment/gear specialists to fine jewelry, and more. Just take a walk through town, and if you love to shop, you'll probably end up laden with bags bursting with purchases.

See also *To See*—Museums; Grand Targhee Resort in *To Do*—Snow Sports; and Jackson Whole Grocer and Windy Mountain Herbs in *To Do*—Relaxation and Rejuvenation.

✷ Special Events

February: **Cowboy Ski Challenge,** Jackson: Cowboys compete for top honors at roping, riding, and skiing

events to the delight and awe of spectators.

February: **Winterfest,** Dubois: This winter celebration includes sled dog races, skijoring, a soup cook-off, snowman-building contest, and more.

April: **Pole-Pedal-Paddle** (http://www.polepedalpaddle.com), Jackson: Individual athletes and teams (some serious, some silly) compete in a multisport, endurance race that includes skiing, mountain biking, and paddling.

May: **ElkFest** (http://www.elkfest.org), Jackson: A festival centered around the Jackson Hole Boy Scout Elk Antler Auction, the auctioning of antlers shed by wintering elk at the National Elk Refuge.

May: **Old West Days,** Jackson: A celebration of the Old West that includes a mountain man rendezvous, arts and crafts, food, entertainment, and more.

June through mid-August: **Grand Teton Music Festival** (307-733-3050; http://www.gtmf.org), Jackson: Numerous concerts (some free, some not) are held from the end of June through mid-August.

July and August: **Jackson Hole Art Fair** (307-733-8792; http://www.jhartfair.org), Jackson: Two weekends per summer (one in July, one in August), the art fair includes family events, food, vendor booths, artists from around the world, and more.

August: **Buffalo BBQ Weekend,** Dubois: This annual celebration includes a rodeo, a quilt show, chariot races, and—what else?—a buffalo barbecue.

September: **Jackson Hole Fall Arts Festival** (http://www.jacksonhole

galleries.com/festival.html), Jackson: An annual multiday event that celebrates not only visual arts, but also culinary arts, music, and poetry.

September to October: **Jackson Hole Wildlife Film Festival** (http://www .jhfestival.org), Jackson: An annual film competition around the end of September that culminates in two days of winning films being shown at movie theaters in Jackson.

3

Northeast Wyoming

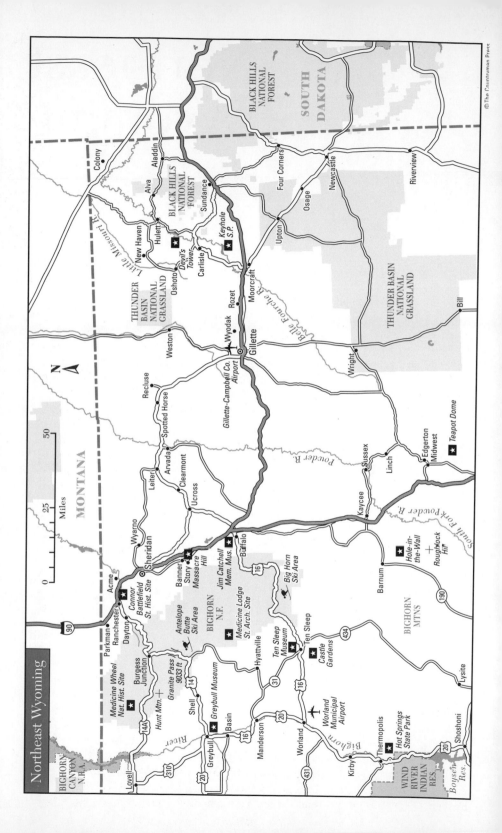

Northeast Wyoming

© The Countryman Press

SHERIDAN AND BUFFALO

With a population of about 16,000 people, Sheridan is a big city by Wyoming standards. Still, it retains a small-town, western feel—after all, in most states, it would be a small town! That being said, Sheridan's relatively large size means that it is home to practically all of the amenities a traveler could want, along with numerous attractions of historical interest. Start your journey into the past at the Sheridan County Museum (see *To See*—Museums), which can provide you with a helpful historical framework in which to fit all of the other historic sites you visit in this region. You can also take a self-guided walking tour or a trolley tour of the historic downtown area thanks to the Downtown Sheridan Association (see Guidance), an organization that is also largely responsible for the sculptures you'll see throughout the city. Also not to miss in Sheridan are the city's incredible parks and pathways (see Whitney Commons in *To See*—City Parks and Gardens and Kendrick Park in *To Do*—For Families), not to mention its fantastic golf courses.

Less than 50 miles south of Sheridan, you'll find the much smaller city of Buffalo (population 4,000), on the eastern flanks of the Big Horn Mountains. Buffalo has its own terrific city park—with a free swimming pool (see *To See*—City Parks and Gardens)—along with an 11-mile pathway system (see Clear Creek Walking Trail in *To Do*—Bicycling) that's perfect for cycling or strolling. Also in Buffalo, you'll find a number of historical attractions, including the Jim Gatchell Memorial Museum and Gift Shop (see *To See*—Museums), among others. For the more adventurous explorer, just east of Buffalo you'll discover the intriguing and isolated Dry Creek Petrified Tree Environmental Education Area (see *Green Space*—Wildlife Refuges and Areas), where you can learn details about a much earlier, pre-human time of this area's past.

Surrounding these two cities is a region rife with recreational and/or historical opportunities as well. Explore the canyons, mountains, and rivers of the Big Horn Mountains on horseback, by foot, or by bike, perhaps as a guest on one of the area's guest ranches. Walk the grounds where battles took place between the encroaching settlers and the American Indians via the area's historic sites (see Fort Phil Kearny State Historic Site and Connor Battlefield State Historic Site in *To See*—Historic Landmarks, Places, and Sites), or wander back to Hole-in-the-Wall, a passage where famous outlaws once herded horses and cattle (see *To Do*—Hiking). Fish and camp at the world-famous Middle Fork of the Powder River Campground/Recreation Area, or toss your line into Lake DeSmet (see *To Do*—Fishing). Don't have much time, or headed to another region of Wyoming (like, perhaps, Yellowstone National Park)? Then consider making the journey through the Big Horn Mountains via one of the region's beautiful scenic drives (see *To See*—Scenic Drives) that are full of natural wonders (see *To See*—Natural Wonders), many of which you can glimpse from the window of your car.

GUIDANCE BIGHORNMOUNTAINS.COM, LLC (http://www.bighorn mountains.com), 20 N. Tisdale Avenue, Buffalo, 82834.

Buffalo, Wyoming Chamber of Commerce (1-800-227-5122 or 307-684-5544; http://www.buffalowyo.com), 55 N. Main Street, Buffalo, 82834.

Downtown Sheridan Association (307-672-8881; http://www.downtownsheridan .org), P.O. Box 13, Sheridan, 82801. This organization provides information on a self-guided, walking tour of historic downtown Sheridan, as well as the Sheridan Trolley (see Getting Around).

Sheridan County Chamber of Commerce (1-800-453-3650 or 307-672-2485; http://www.sheridanwyomingchamber.org), P.O. Box 707, Sheridan, 82801.

✍ **Sheridan Travel and Tourism** (1-888-596-6787 or 307-673-7120; http://www .sheridanwyoming.org), physical location at **State of Wyoming Information Center** (exit 23 off I-90), P.O. Box 7155, Sheridan, 82801. Open 7–7 daily May 15 through October 15, 8–5 Monday through Friday October 16 through May 14. In addition to travel information, here you'll find picnic tables, barbecues, and a playground.

Wyoming Game and Fish Visitor Center (307-672-7418; http://gf.state.wy.us), 700 Valley View Drive, Sheridan, 82801. This visitor center includes a wildlife exhibit.

See also Bighorn Scenic Byway in *To See*—Scenic Drives and Shell Canyon and Falls in *To See*—Natural Wonders.

GETTING THERE *By car:* Sheridan is on I-90 where it intersects with US 14. Buffalo is on I-25 and I-90 where they intersect with US 16.

By plane: **Sheridan County Airport** (307-674-4222; http://www.sheridancounty airport.com) is about 2 miles southwest of downtown Sheridan.

GETTING AROUND Both Buffalo and Sheridan have small enough downtown areas to make exploration on foot feasible and fun. In Sheridan, you can grab a ride (and get a tour of historical sites) on the **Sheridan Trolley** from Memorial Day through Labor Day ($1). To explore outlying attractions in this region, you'll need to get back in your car.

MEDICAL EMERGENCY Dial 911.

Johnson County Healthcare Center (307-684-5521; http://www.buffalohealth care.vcn.com), 497 W. Lott, Buffalo.

Sheridan Memorial Hospital (307-672-1000; http://www.sheridanhospital.org), 1401 W. Fifth Street, Sheridan.

✳ To See

TOWNS Dayton and Ranchester are located northwest of Sheridan via I-90 to US 14. Both towns have populations hovering around 700 people. Nestled in the foothills of the northern Big Horn Mountains, both towns serve as gateways to the recreational opportunities therein as well as peaceful getaways from the bustle of city life (see also *Lodging*).

Kaycee is 45 miles south of Buffalo, just off I-25. Kaycee—population 250—is situated on the banks of the Powder River (see *To See*—Fishing). Strongly rooted in the traditions of the Old West, Kaycee takes pride in being one of the smallest towns in the nation to host a professional rodeo, the PRCA-sanctioned Deke Latham Memorial Rodeo (see *Special Events*). For more information: **Kaycee, Wyoming Chamber of Commerce** (307-738-2444; http://www.kayceewyoming .org), P.O. Box 147, Kaycee, 82639.

Story is a short way east of I-90 via exit 44 between Buffalo and Sheridan, in the foothills of the Big Horn Mountains. Proximity to historic sites (see also *To See*— Historic Landmarks, Places, and Sites), a thriving little art community, gorgeous ponderosa pine forests, and tons of recreational opportunities make Story a desirable place to visit and seek accommodations (see *Lodging*).

MUSEUMS & **Jim Gatchell Memorial Museum and Gift Shop** (307-684-9331; http://www.jimgatchell.com), 100 Fort Street, Buffalo. Open 9–4 May through mid-October; $5 per adult, $3 per child ages 6–16, children under 6 free, family rate $12 per family. Here you'll find Buffalo's frontier history kept alive and illustrated via a fine collection of roughly 7,000 artifacts, most of which came from the private collection of Jim Gatchell. Gatchell moved to Buffalo and opened up a drugstore just as the one of the most tumultuous eras of Wyoming's frontier history was dying down. Avidly interested in local history, during the more than 50 years that he spent in Buffalo Gatchell befriended and was trusted by local Indian tribes, who bestowed upon him many invaluable gifts from the frontier days. Following Gatchell's death in 1954, his family donated his collection to the people of Johnson County, and this collection largely comprises the museum's exhibits to this day.

& **Sheridan County Museum** (307-673-0644; http://www.sheridancountyhistory .org), 850 Sibley Circle, Sheridan. Open 1–5 daily May and September through mid-December, 10–6 daily June through August; $4 per adult, $2 per student, $3 per senior (61-plus), children 12 and under free. This relatively new (2006) museum aims to tell the story of the inhabitants of Sheridan County, past and present. Extensive collections of artifacts and photographs cover the lives of the American Indians, pioneers, ranchers, artists, miners, and others who have called this area home over the years.

& ❦ **Trail End State Historic Site** (307-674-4589; http://www.trailend.org), 400 Clarendon Avenue, Sheridan. Open 9–6 daily June- through August, hours vary seasonally in other months, closed to the public December 15 through February 28; $2 per adult (resident), $4 per adult (nonresident), children 17 and under free, use of grounds is free. This nearly 14,000-square-foot mansion—now a historic house museum—was built in the Flemish Revival style in 1913, serving as the home for Texas-born Wyoming politician John B. Kendrick and his family. Situated on almost 4 landscaped acres, the mansion today houses an interesting collection of permanent exhibits focused on depicting everyday life for its residents during the period from 1913–1933, as well as temporary exhibits. See also Kendrick Park in *To Do*—For Families.

See also Historic Occidental Hotel in *Lodging*—Hotels and Motels.

TRAIL END STATE HISTORIC SITE

HISTORIC LANDMARKS, PLACES, AND SITES ✍ **Connor Battlefield State Historic Site** (307-684-7629; http://wyoparks.state.wy.us/Site/SiteInfo.asp?siteID=13), south of US 14 in Ranchester. Open year-round for day use ($2 resident, $4 nonresident); May 1 through September 30 for camping ($10 resident, $17 nonresident). You'd never guess from its current incarnation as a placid camping and picnic area that this was once the scene of the 1865 Battle of Tongue River, which took place between troops headed by General Patrick E. Connor and Black Bear's Arapaho village. Aggressively attacked by Connor's troops, the Indians managed to make the soldiers withdraw and actually pursued them as they marched in retreat. Situated in an oxbow of the Tongue River, the park features shaded camping, a playground, fishing, and two restrooms.

& **Fort Phil Kearny State Historic Site** (307-684-7629; http://wyoparks.state.wy.us/Site/SiteInfo.asp?siteID=17), 20 miles south of Sheridan at exit 44 off I-90. Grounds open 8–6 (summer), noon–4 (winter); visitor center closed to the public December through March; $2 per resident, $4 per nonresident. Tour this historic fort, one of three constructed in 1866 to help protect travelers along the Bozeman Trail and to draw Indian attention away from the construction of the Union Pacific Railroad to the south, as well as to stave off warfare between Native American tribes. In this vicinity the Cheyenne, Sioux, and Arapaho fought to maintain control of some of their only remaining great buffalo hunting grounds. A visitor center provides exhibits and interpretive materials, and you can take a self-guided, interpretive tour. Within 5 miles lie two historic battlefields from the era—the sites of the **Fetterman Fight** and the **Wagon Box Fight,** both of which have interpretive trails that provide both American Indian and white perspectives on the events that took place. Fort Phil Kearny also hosts the Bozeman Trail Days (see *Special Events*).

FORT PHIL KEARNY STATE HISTORIC SITE

🏛 & **Medicine Wheel National Historic Landmark** (307-674-2600; http://wyoshpo.state.wy.us/aamonth/1997.asp), located east of Lovell just off US 14 Alternate atop Medicine Mountain in the Bighorn National Forest (see *Green Space*—National Lands). Open 8–5 daily; free. This site has long mystified archaeologists, who are unable to fully explain the original function and construction of this enor-

mous medicine wheel. Measuring 75 to 80 feet in diameter and made up of stones that radiate out from a central cairn in 28 spokes, the medicine wheel is believed to have been of religious significance to American Indians (as it still is today)—but estimates on when or exactly why it was constructed vary widely. The site includes an interpretive center and bathrooms. Visitors must walk 1.5 miles to view the medicine wheel.

See also Downtown Sheridan Association in Guidance; Trail End State Historic Site in *To See*—Museums; Lake DeSmet in *To Do*—Fishing; The Historic Bozeman Crossing in *To Do*—For Families; Hole-in-the-Wall Trail in *To Do*—Hiking; Mansion House Inn in *Lodging*—Bed and Breakfasts; Historic Occidental Hotel and Mill Inn in *Lodging*—Hotels and Motels; and 1893 Grille & Spirits in *Where to Eat*—Dining Out.

CITY PARKS AND GARDENS ♿ 🐾 🏞 **Buffalo City Park** (see Buffalo Chamber of Commerce in Guidance) in Buffalo can be reached by turning east onto E. Fetterman Street off Main Street in Buffalo. Open daily; free. This terrific city park includes a free outdoor swimming pool, a playground, tennis courts, trails, and a picnic area, among other attractions.

♿ 🐾 🏞 **Whitney Commons** (307-674-7303; http://www.whitneybenefits.org), 326 Alger, Sheridan. Open 7 AM–10 PM daily; free. This sparkling addition to Sheridan's park system features a playground (including an interactive water feature), a fountain, a botanical reflection garden, bicycle/pedestrian paths, and a meditation labyrinth. It also has an amphitheatre. Whitney Commons hosts many community events and celebrations, in addition to serving as home to the **Sheridan Farmers' Market** (5 PM–7 PM every Thursday from late July through mid-September), which features not only fresh local fare but also arts and crafts as well as entertainment and children's activities. Whitney Commons is linked to other parks, including **Thorne-Rider Park** (tennis, volleyball, skateboarding, BMX) and Kendrick Park (see *To Do*—For Families) in Sheridan, by 7 miles of paved pathways. A map is available online at http://www.city-sheridan-wy.com/info/pathways.php.

See also Sheridan Travel and Tourism in Guidance; and Kendrick Park in *To Do*—For Families.

SCENIC DRIVES Bighorn Scenic Byway runs for about 50 miles on US 14, starting west of Dayton (see *To See*—Towns) at the edge of the Bighorn National Forest (see *Green Space*—National Lands) and ending in the tiny town of Shell (see *To See*—Towns in Thermopolis and Worland). This incredible drive takes you high into the Bighorn Mountains as you wind past Fallen City (see *To See*—Natural Wonders), Steamboat Rock, and numerous additional picturesque rock outcroppings before surmounting Granite Pass and beginning your grad-

MEDICINE WHEEL NATIONAL HISTORIC LANDMARK

BUFFALO CITY PARK

ual descent down through Shell Canyon (see *To See*—Natural Wonders). The plentiful recreational opportunities along this drive include fishing, picnicking, hiking, and skiing. Stop on your drive at the **Burgess Junction Visitor Center,** .5 mile east of Burgess Junction on US 14, open daily 8–5:30 in summer (free) for information, exhibits, maps, and a self-guided trail.

Crazy Woman Canyon is accessed by taking exit 291 off I-25 south of Buffalo. Go south on WY 196 and west on CR 14/FR 33 (or via US 16 west from Buffalo, then east on FR 33 to go down the canyon). Not for RVs or trailers, this narrow, rutted, dirt road joins US 16 (Cloud Peak Skyway Scenic Byway, see *To See*—Scenic Drives in Thermopolis and Worland) before Powder River Pass. Travel is slow going through Crazy Woman Canyon, but you won't mind—the incredible, sheer canyon cliffs and the gorgeous Crazy Woman Creek will likely have you jumping out of your car to take a closer look. Just be sure to watch for traffic coming the other way. Primitive camping is available in many spots throughout the canyon. Crazy Woman Canyon is home to some established rock climbs, as are some of the limestone buttes visible off US 16 east of Powder River Pass.

Medicine Wheel Passage Scenic Byway runs for 27 miles along US 14 Alternate from the border of Bighorn National Forest (see *Green Space*—National Lands) east of Lovell to the junction with US 14 at Burgess Junction (along the Bighorn Scenic Byway, see *To See*—Scenic Drives). This lovely drive takes you by the Medicine Wheel National Historic Landmark (see *To See*—Historic Landmarks, Places, and Sites), and then up out of the Big Horn Basin into higher elevations, where ponderosa pines, Engelmann spruce, lodgepole pines, and Douglas firs are interspersed with fields of wildflowers such as lupine and balsamroot (in the spring and summer), along with fantastic views of the Big Horn Mountains, the Absarokas, and the Bighorn Basin. Recreational opportunities include wildlife viewing, fishing, hiking, picnicking, and camping, among others.

See also Cloud Peak Skyway Scenic Byway in *To See*—Scenic Drives in Thermopolis and Worland.

NATURAL WONDERS Fallen City and Steamboat Rock, off US 14 between Dayton and Burgess Junction. Viewable from the road, to the south you'll see the jumbled collection of boulders and precipices known as Fallen City, prompting the imagination to conjure up images of the sorts of creatures who might have once dwelt within its walls. Farther to the west, you'll be overwhelmed by the enormity of the dolomite formation appropriately deemed Steamboat Rock, which juts up just at a turning point in the road, commanding all who pass this way to be staggered by its monolithic presence.

🐚 **Shell Canyon and Falls** are on US 14 east of the small town of Shell, along the Bighorn Scenic Byway (see also *To See*—Scenic Drives) in the Bighorn National Forest (see *Green Space*—National Lands). Shell Canyon's amazing walls of sandstone, limestone, and granite will impress you—but you'll be even more impressed when you stop midway up the canyon at Shell Falls, a100-foot waterfall cut through the granite by Shell Creek, flowing at a rate of 3,588 gallons per second. The **Shell Falls Interpretive Center** (open 8–5:30 in summer; free) has restrooms, information, a coffee shop, and a gift shop. A self-guided trail takes you to view the falls and provides you with information about them.

Tongue River Cave, in the Bighorn National Forest (see *Green Space*—National Lands), is accessed via US 14 to west on CR 92 (River Road to Tongue Canyon Road) just west of Dayton; the road ends in the parking lot where the trailhead departs. Take the trail from the west end of the parking lot, and then drop down to cross the footbridge over the river, and you're on your way. About 1 mile of switchbacks takes you up the slope of the canyon to the cave's entrance, a small opening in a limestone outcrop. Prepare yourself well for a journey inside this 9-mile labyrinth, or simply enjoy the hike to the entrance and shine a light inside if that's as far as you want go, since a true exploration of the cave requires responsible planning and preparation as well as you being comfortable with uneven footing and narrow passages. Spelunkers will find rain rooms, bats, tiny passageways to worm through, wind tunnels, and more. Practice safe caving—be sure to bring food, water, a headlamp with extra batteries, a helmet with a chinstrap, warm clothes, hat, gloves, and a partner, and tell someone that you're going and when you expect to be back. If you don't cross the footbridge, you can continue strolling up the lovely canyon (which is home to some established rock climbs) for a mellow, gradually ascending hike, turning back whenever you are ready to (see also Tongue River in *To Do*—Fishing).

See also *To See*—Scenic Drives.

✳ To Do

BICYCLING ♿ ♂ **Clear Creek Walking Trail** in Buffalo is a paved trail running for more than 11 miles along Clear Creek in Buffalo, making it perfect for a leisurely bike ride to explore your surroundings and take in some fresh air. Wildlife viewing and scenic views abound. You'll find the trail easily—it's right along Main Street in Buffalo. Call the Buffalo Chamber of Commerce (see Guidance) for information about current providers of bicycle rentals.

See also Whitney Commons in *To See*—City Parks and Gardens; Bucking

FALLEN CITY

Mule Falls National Recreation Trail and Penrose Trail in *To Do*—Hiking; Cross-country skiing and snowshoeing in *To Do*—Snow Sports; *Green Space*; and Sheridan/Big Horn Mountains KOA in *Lodging*—Campgrounds.

BOATING See *To Do*—Fishing.

CLIMBING See Crazy Woman Canyon in *To See*—Scenic Drives; and Tongue River Cave in *To See*—Natural Wonders.

FISHING **Lake DeSmet** (307-672-7418; http://gf.state.wy.us/fish/fishing/index.asp), north of Buffalo via exits 44, 47, 51, 53, and 56a off I-90. This lake takes its name from a Belgian priest, Father DeSmet, who came to Wyoming in 1840 as a missionary to the Flathead Indians. The Indians believed Lake DeSmet to be bottomless, and thus it served as the origin of many of their religious and superstitious beliefs. A monument memorializing Father DeSmet stands near the shores of the lake today. Anglers know Lake DeSmet better as a prime year-round fishing destination (ice fishing is popular in winter), with species including brown trout, rainbow trout, rock bass, crappies, and yellow perch. This lake is also popular for water sports, including boating. See also Lake DeSmet Fishing Derby in *Special Events*.

Middle Fork of the Powder River Recreation Area, accessible by taking WY 190 southwest from Kaycee for about 15 miles, and then going south on the BLM Bar C road for roughly 5 miles to the recreation area. A pristine blue-ribbon trout stream (with numerous additional surrounding trout streams) is the standout attraction of this BLM-managed area, which draws fishermen by the hundreds annually (see also *Green Space*—National Lands). Situated at 7,500 feet, the nearby **Outlaw Cave Campground** features restrooms, drinking water, and campfire rings (open May through September; free).

Powder River (307-672-7418; http://gf.state.wy.us/fish), flows along WY 192 west of Kaycee and along Upper Powder River Road into Montana. The Powder River and its many creeks, streams, and forks offer tremendous trout fishing opportunities. Species include brown trout and rainbow trout. See also Middle Fork of the Powder River Recreation Area, above.

Tongue River (307-672-7418; http://gf.state.wy.us/fish/fishing/index.asp), in the Bighorn National Forest (see *Green Space*—National Lands), is accessed via US 14 to west on CR 92 (River Road to Tongue Canyon Road) just west of Dayton; the road ends in the parking lot where the trailhead departs. Take the trail from the west end of the parking lot to gain access to the river, which flows from high in the Big Horn Mountains northeast into Montana, eventually joining the Yellowstone River. The Tongue River and its many side streams and creeks present fabulous fishing prospects, with species including brook trout, brown trout, and rainbow trout. See also Connor Battlefield State Historic Site in *To See*—Historic Landmarks, Places, and Sites; and Tongue River Cave in *To See*—Natural Wonders.

See also *To See*—Scenic Drives.

FITNESS CENTERS **Sheridan Recreation Center Facility** (307-674-6421; http://www.sheridanrecreation.com), Sheridan. This new, 25,000-square-foot recreation center was in the construction process at the time of publication. Call or check the Web site for details.

Sheridan Snap Fitness Center (307-673-0115; http://www.snapfitness.com/sheridan), 2240 Coffeen Avenue, Sheridan. Open to members 24/7.

See also Mill Inn in *Lodging*—Hotels and Motels.

FOR FAMILIES ✍ **The Historic Bozeman Crossing** (307-684-2531, http://www.bozemancrossing.com), 655 Hart Street, Buffalo. Once the location where the Bozeman Trail crossed the Powder River's Clear Fork at its low point, providing the military and emigrants with the easiest way across, you'll find here today an attraction of a different sort. From an ice cream parlor and a restaurant (see Bozeman Trail Steakhouse in *Where to Eat*—Eating Out) to a miniature golf course, restored 1920s carousel, and Ferris wheel, a stop at this collection of attractions is sure to bring a smile to the kids' faces (and maybe to yours, too).

✍ **Kendrick Park** (307-674-6483, ext. 250), located adjacent to Trail End State Historic Site (see *To See*—Museums), Sheridan. A playground, a municipal pool with a water slide, an ice cream vendor with lots of flavors, seasonal concerts, and acres of grass make this park a guaranteed kid pleaser. Kendrick Park is also home to a buffalo and elk refuge. This is a perfect place for a picnic lunch alongside Goose Creek in the shade of the cottonwood trees. See also Whitney Commons in *To See*—City Parks and Gardens.

See also Sheridan Travel and Tourism in Guidance; Connor Battlefield State Historic Site and Medicine Wheel National Historic Landmark in *To See*—Historic Landmarks, Places, and Sites; Clear Creek Walking Trail in *To Do*—Bicycling; Buffalo City Park and Whitney Commons in *To See*—City Parks and Gardens; Trails West Outfitters in *To Do*—Horseback Riding; and Lake DeSmet Fishing Derby and Buffalo Bill Days Wild West Show in *Special Events*.

GOLF Buffalo Golf Club (307-684-5266; http://www.buffalowygolf.com), 500 W. Hart, Buffalo, 18 holes.

Horseshoe Mountain Golf Club (307-655-9525), US 14, Dayton, 9 holes.

Kendrick Municipal Golf Course (307-674-8148; http://www.city-sheridan-wy.com/info/kgc), 65 Golf Course Road, Sheridan, 18 holes.

Powder Horn Ranch and Golf Club (307-672-5323; http://www.thepowderhorn.com), 161 WY 335, Sheridan, 27 holes.

Sheridan Country Club (307-674-8135; http://www.sheridancountryclub.com), 1992 W. Fifth Street, Sheridan, 18 holes.

HIKING Bucking Mule Falls National Recreation Trail (#53), in the Bighorn National Forest (*Green Space*—National Lands), can be accessed via US 14 Alternate east of Lovell (Medicine Wheel Passage Scenic Byway, see also *To See*—Scenic Drives). Take Forest Highway (FH) 11 north 3.5 miles to FR14. Go west on FR 14 for 7 miles to parking lot at the end of the gravel road. Best to hike in July and August due to its high elevation, this 3-mile, moderate, out-and-back trail takes you to view the tumbling 550-foot Bucking Mule Falls. Folks who are more adventurous can plan to explore more of the trail, which totals about 12 miles in length. Horseback riding and mountain biking are also allowed on this trail.

Hole-in-the-Wall Trail, on BLM-managed lands (see *Green Space*—National Lands), is accessible by taking exit 249 (TTT) off I-25 south of Kaycee, and then proceeding about 14 miles south on TTT Road to FR 111 (Willow Creek). Take this road about 18 miles west to a junction with CR 105 (Buffalo Creek), a rough, two-track road heading north, suitable for high-clearance vehicles during dry conditions only. This road dead-ends at the trailhead (be sure to close livestock gates behind you as necessary). If you're a western history buff in decent physical shape, this long drive in to the trailhead is probably worth your while. Hike to one of the most-beloved hangouts of some of the most famous outlaws of the Old West— Butch Cassidy and the Wild Bunch Gang. Back in the 1800s, local lore has it that the Wild Bunch Gang clandestinely moved horses and cattle through a notch in the Red Wall—the hole that you will see after a rugged, 2.5-mile hike. No services are available, so come prepared with food, water, and proper attire. Please stay on the trail, as the land surrounding it is private.

Penrose Trail, in the Bighorn National Forest (see *Green Space*—National Lands), is accessed from the town of Story, which lies on WY 193 north of exit 44 off I-25. In Story, take Fish Hatchery Road to the parking area on Penrose Lane. This trail leads you up into the foothills and then the mountains behind Story, ultimately depositing the serious hiker at the boundary of Cloud Peak Wilderness. You'll wind your way up through the wildflowers in the foothills into more forested terrain, where ponderosa pines give way to Douglas firs and lodgepole pines, followed by alpine meadows with granite outcrops. Stunning, sweeping views of the badlands stretch away as far as the eye can see from various vantage points on the way. This is a multi-use trail, so don't be surprised if an ATV comes barreling by.

See also Fort Phil Kearny State Historic Site in *To See*—Historic Landmarks, Places, and Sites; Whitney Commons in *To See*—City Parks and Gardens; *To See*—Scenic Drives; Shell Canyon and Falls in *To See*—Natural Wonders; Tongue River Cave in *To See*—Natural Wonders; Clear Creek Walking Trail in *To Do*— Bicycling; Dry Creek Petrified Tree Environmental Education Area in *Green Space*—Wildlife Refuges and Areas; and Deer Park RV Park and Campground in *Lodging*—Campgrounds.

HORSEBACK RIDING Little Piney Ranch (307-683-BOOT; http://www.littlepineyranch.com), 430 Wagon Box Road, Banner (near Story). This ranch has both an indoor arena and access to numerous outdoor trails, offering horseback riding lessons ($40/hour; private) to novices as well as experienced riders. You can also choose to book a two-hour trail ride ($50 per person) or a half-day trail ride ($80 per person), as well as longer rides. This ranch also has two cabins available for rent (expensive to very expensive).

South Fork Mountain Lodge & Outfitters (307-267-2609; http://www.southfork-lodge.com), US 16, Buffalo. Mountain trail rides depart from the lodge, situated next to Clear Creek in the Big Horn Mountains above Buffalo. Choose from two-hour ($55 per person), half-day ($90 per person, includes lunch), or full-day ($150 per person, includes lunch) trail rides led by experienced guides. Overnight pack trips and fishing trips are also offered by this full-service outfitter. The lodge's dining room serves three meals a day. You can purchase activities and meals a la carte, or just rent a rustic cabin on the ranch grounds (expensive).

✿ **Trails West Outfitters** (1-888-283-9793; http://www.trailswestoutfitters.com), Buffalo. Family pack trips are one of the specialties offered by this outfitter. Each family member rides a gentle horse along trails through the Big Horn Mountains, enjoying fantastic scenery and wildlife viewing opportunities while learning about the ins and outs of trail riding in the process ($250 per person per day; advance reservations required).

See also Bucking Mule Falls National Recreation Trail in *To Do*—Hiking; and Double Rafter Cattle Drives in *To Do*—Unique Adventures.

PADDLING/FLOATING See Lake DeSmet in *To Do*—Fishing.

RELAXATION AND REJUVENATION Holistic Health Center (307-684-7474; http://www.poisoninthepantry.com), 90 S. Main Street, Buffalo. Make an appointment here in advance for all of your whole-health needs. Services include acupuncture, massage, allergy elimination, nutritional counseling, Reiki, emotional clearing, detoxification, chakra balancing, micro-current body and face sculpting, and more. After your treatment, head next door for lunch or dinner to relax on the outdoor patio with a brew and some BBQ at **Up in Smoke** (under the same ownership), new in late 2009. Moderate.

Simply Beautiful (307-752-5260 or 307-752-3786; http://www.simplybeautiful .net), 45 E. Loucks, Suite 18, Sheridan. Call for an appointment. Simply Beautiful offers a full range of salon treatments including facials, waxing, body treatments, and massages.

SNOW SPORTS Antelope Butte Ski Area in the Bighorn National Forest (see *Green Space*—National Lands), was currently closed as of publication (2010). Check the forest service Web site for updates.

Cross-country skiing and snowshoeing opportunities are abundant in this region, especially in the Bighorn National Forest (see *Green Space*—National Lands). If you need to rent skis or snowshoes (or a mountain bike in summer), try **Backcountry Bike and Mountain Works** (307-672-2453), 330 Main Street, Sheridan. For more ideas of where to go, see *To Do*—Hiking.

Ice fishing is possible on many of this region's frozen lakes and ponds come wintertime, including Lake DeSmet (see *To Do*—Fishing).

Ice-skating can be found in Sheridan at the **Sheridan Community Rink** (307-674-9423; http://www.sheridanice.org), 475 E. Brundage Street. Call for current rates, hours, and season.

Snowmobiling: see Snowmobiling in *To Do*—Snow Sports in Northwest Wyoming: Thermopolis and Worland.

UNIQUE ADVENTURES Bob King's Cowboy School (307-736-2236 or 520-686-3776; http://www.cowboyschool.net), Arvada (on US 14/16 between Buffalo and Gillette), reservations required. So you want to learn to be a cowboy—really? Then saddle up for a five-day adventure packed with learning the ropes, customized to your preferences. You'll ride a horse chosen according to your ability level and enjoy days of hands-on instruction. Meals and comfortable accommodations are included ($1,750 per five-day course, or $5,900 for a month-long course).

Double Rafter Cattle Drives (1-800-704-9268 or 307-655-9539; http://www .doublerafter.com), Ranchester. June through September, about $2,000 per person; reservations required. For a real western living experience, sign up for a six-day

191

SHERIDAN AND BUFFALO

adventure at the historic Double Rafter Ranch, the first ranch known to bring cattle to graze in the Bighorn National Forest (see *Green Space*—National Lands). Since 1895, the Double Rafter has been raising cattle for beef, and since 1989, it has been inviting vacationers in pursuit of a down 'n' dirty western adventure to join in on its six-day, six-night cattle drives. Don't expect this to be a relaxing, dude-ranch experience, though—you'll be working hard to earn your chuck wagon meals every day.

✳ Green Space

STATE PARKS See Connor Battlefield State Historic Site in *To See*—Historic Landmarks, Places, and Sites.

NATIONAL FORESTS Bighorn National Forest (307-548-6541; http://www .fs.fed.us/r2), Forest Headquarters/Tongue District, 203 Eastside Second Street, Sheridan; and Powder River District (307-684-7806), 1415 Fort Street, Buffalo. See *Lodging*—Campgrounds; and listing in *Green Space*—National Lands in Northwest Wyoming: Thermopolis and Worland.

Bureau of Land Management (BLM) (307-684-1100; http://www.blm.gov/wy/ st/en/field_offices/Buffalo.html), Buffalo Field Office, 1425 Fort Street, Buffalo. The BLM in this region manages almost 800,000 acres of public lands and almost 5 million acres of mineral estate. Much of the land administered by the BLM is open to recreational pursuits, including bicycling, boating, camping (see Middle Fork of the Powder River Recreation Area in *To Do*—Fishing), fishing, hiking, horseback riding, paddling, rock climbing, wildlife viewing and snow sports, including snowmobiling and cross-country skiing. BLM lands tend to be the most unregulated of public lands, meaning that most typical outdoor recreational pursuits are allowed on most BLM lands, guided by the dictates of Leave No Trace (1-800-332-4100 or 303-442-8222; http://www.lnt.org) outdoor ethics. To find out additional information about the BLM lands in this region, including maps, developed campgrounds, and other recreational pursuits, contact the field office.

RECREATION AREAS See Middle Fork of the Powder River Recreation Area in *To Do*—Fishing.

WILDLIFE REFUGES AND AREAS Dry Creek Petrified Tree Environmental Education Area, located 13 miles southeast of Buffalo via I-90 to exit 65 (Red Hills Road), and then north on Tipperary Road about 6 miles to the Petrified Tree access road (all-weather gravel). Explore Wyoming's petrified past at this remote and intriguing natural area located in the middle of the badlands, managed by the BLM (see *Green Space*—National Lands). A .8-mile interpretive loop trail fills you in on the formative processes of the petrified trees and the way this land used to look some 60 million years ago when these very same trees—the giant Metasequoias—covered the landscape.

Story Fish Hatchery (307-683-2234; http://gf.state.wy.us/fish/culture/story .asp), 311R Fish Hatchery Road, Story. Call for current hours. Tucked away in beautiful Story (see *To See*—Towns), this hatchery gives you an opportunity to learn about how the state of Wyoming raises fish. It is one of 11 hatcheries in the state's system.

See also Kendrick Park in *To Do*—For Families.

✻ Lodging

BED AND BREAKFASTS

Buffalo

"¶" ♿ **Historic Mansion House Inn** (1-888-455-9202 or 307-684-2218; http://www.mansionhouseinn.com), 313 N. Main Street. Built in 1903, this historic Victorian house offers guests lodging in seven well-appointed rooms, all with private baths (expensive). Also available are 11 motel rooms (moderate) in the annex. Continental breakfast is served every morning.

Sheridan

Spahn's Big Horn Mountain Bed & Breakfast (307-674-8150; http://www.bighorn-wyoming.com), 70 Upper Hideaway, Big Horn (15 miles from Sheridan). Built by its owners, this lovely, solar-powered log home and its surrounding cabins bring with them incredible, 100-mile views of the Big Horn Mountains. Whether you stay in the main home or in a cabin, you'll have a private bath and a queen-sized bed, as well as a full breakfast every morning. For $39 per person, you can enjoy this B&B's Evening Wildlife Safari, which includes a full steak dinner and a four-wheel-drive wildlife viewing tour. Expensive.

Story

Hitchin' Post Lodge (719-646-0977 or 719-233-0642; http://www.storybnb.com), 12 Ridgecrest Drive. Enjoy creek-side accommodations and beautiful grounds at this B&B in Story, where you can choose from renting the entire three-bedroom guest house (your home away from home), complete with kitchen, dining room, and living room (very expensive); or simply renting a room, with or without a private bath, depending on your needs (expensive).

DRY CREEK PETRIFIED TREE
ENVIRONMENTAL EDUCATION AREA

LODGES

Buffalo

See South Fork Mountain Lodge and Outfitters in *To Do*—Horseback Riding.

HOTELS AND MOTELS

Buffalo

♿ 🐾 **Arrowhead Motel** (1-877-277-6948 or 307-684-9453; http://www.arrowheadmotel.com), 749 Fort Street. A family-owned and -operated establishment, the Arrowhead Motel offers travelers on a budget a clean, friendly place to stay near all of Buffalo's attractions. Moderate.

🐾 "¶" 🐾 **Blue Gables Motel and Coffee Bar** (1-800-684-2574 or 307-684-2574; http://www.bluegables.com), 662 N. Main Street, Buffalo. Guests stay in one of 17 modern log cabins at this privately run motel. Enjoy the outdoor heated swimming pool and barbecues, or sit back and sip a coffee in the lounge area (or grab one to go at the drive-through window). Moderate.

& ᵗ₁ᵗ 🐾 **Historic Occidental Hotel** (307-684-0451; http://www.occidental wyoming.com), 10 N. Main Street. Step back in time at this 128-year-old hotel where the likes of Buffalo Bill, Butch Cassidy, and Calamity Jane all stayed. The hotel's Grand Lobby houses the free Occidental Hotel Museum, bringing you a little bit closer to the Old West with its photographs and other memorabilia from days gone by. Fully restored (2007) with modern amenities, the Occidental Hotel today nonetheless retains much of its original décor, including the original embossed ceilings in the lobby and bar, and antique period furniture in each individually decorated room or suite. All accommodations include a private bathroom, king or queen-sized bed, and a complimentary continental breakfast. Inexpensive to very expensive. See also The Virginian Restaurant at the Historic Occidental Hotel in *Where to Eat*—Dining Out and Thursday Night Jam Sessions in *Entertainment*.

Sheridan
🐾 ᵗ₁ᵗ & **Mill Inn** (1-888-FLR-MILL or 307-672-6401; http://www.sheridan

HISTORIC OCCIDENTAL HOTEL IN BUFFALO

millinn.com), 2161 Coffeen Avenue. Listed on the National Register of Historic Places, this former flour mill has been converted into a modern, 45-unit hotel. Learn all about the inn's history while you enjoy a stay in one of the rooms, which come with a complimentary continental breakfast and access to a fitness center on-site. Expensive.

See also Historic Mansion House Inn in *Lodging*—Bed and Breakfasts.

CAMPGROUNDS & **Bighorn National Forest:** see *Green Space*—National Lands and listing in *Lodging*—Campgrounds in Northwestern Wyoming: Thermopolis and Worland.

ᵗ₁ᵗ **Deer Park RV Park and Campground** (1-800-222-9960 or 307-684-5722; http://www.deerparkrv.com); 146 US 16 East, Buffalo. Open May 1 through September 30. Here you'll find RV sites, tent sites, and camping cabins, along with a swimming pool and hot tub, as well as a private 1-mile walking path. Deer Park hosts a nightly ice cream social Memorial Day through Labor Day. Very inexpensive to inexpensive.

ᵗ₁ᵗ **Indian Campground and RV Park** (1-866-808-9601 or 307-684-9601; http://www.indiancampground.com), 660 E. Hart Street, Buffalo. Open April 15 through October 15. This campground features RV sites, tent sites, and camping cabin rentals, along with a swimming pool and a gift shop. Very inexpensive to inexpensive.

✐ ᵗ₁ᵗ **Sheridan/Big Horn Mountains KOA** (1-800-562-7621 or 307-674-8766; http://www.koa.com), 63 Decker Road, Sheridan. Open year-round. This full-service KOA is independently owned and operated, offering RV and tent sites as well as cabin rentals. Amenities include creekside camping, playground, swimming pool (seasonal), mountain views, mini golf, bike rentals, fishing, and more. Very inexpensive to inexpensive.

See also Middle Fork of the Powder River Recreation Area in *To Do*— Fishing.

OTHER OPTIONS

Banner

See Little Piney Ranch in *To Do*— Horseback Riding.

Sheridan

⁰ᴛ⁰ **Melissa's Cottages** (307-673-4425; http://www.melissascottages .com), Sheridan. Rent one of three full-size, fully furnished 1900s cottages within walking distance of Sheridan's downtown, and enjoy all of the comforts of home while you're on vacation. Cottages rent by the week. Expensive to very expensive.

⁰ᴛ⁰ **Sheridan Cottages** (307-751-0793; http://www.sheridancottages .com), 1185 Sugarview Drive. One of these five new and distinctive, fully furnished vacation homes can serve as your vacation headquarters, providing a relaxing retreat after a day spent exploring Sheridan. Cottages rent by the week. Moderate to expensive.

See also Spahn's Big Horn Mountain Bed and Breakfast in *Lodging*—Bed and Breakfasts.

Story

See also Wagon Box Inn Restaurant and Cabins in *Where to Eat*—Dining Out.

✳ Where to Eat

EATING OUT

Buffalo

Bozeman Trail Steakhouse (307-684-5555, http://www.bozemantrail steakhouse.com), 675 Hart Street, Buffalo. Open 11–9 daily. This large, family-oriented restaurant serves as the centerpiece for a veritable village of

entertainment options (see Historic Bozeman Crossing in *To See*—For Families). The restaurant offers a large menu with options for all types of eaters, including terrific specialty salads and burgers done a number of ways, as well as steaks, prime rib, and buffalo. Expensive.

Sagewood Gifts & Café (307-684-7670; http://www.sagewoodcafe.com), 15 N. Main Street. Open for lunch 11–3 Monday through Saturday; inexpensive. This café bakes its own bread (as well as great dessert goodies) and makes soups daily. Sit down for a creative specialty sandwich or satisfy your sweet tooth either before or after you browse through the eclectic gift shop (open 9–5:30 Monday through Friday, 10–5 Saturday). You'll find an extensive and interesting collection of somewhat random items for the kitchen, kids, and kinfolk.

See also Holistic Health Center in *To Do*—Relaxation and Rejuvenation.

Sheridan

✍ **Ole's Pizza and Spaghetti House** (307-672-3636); 927 Coffeen Avenue Open 11–10 Monday through Saturday (summer), 11–9 Monday through Saturday (winter), noon–9 Sunday. Serving up top-notch homemade pizza since 1972, Ole's is a fixture on the Sheridan eating scene. You'll also find a salad bar, BBQ ribs, pastas, appetizers, and sandwiches on the menu. A lunch buffet is served Monday through Saturday. Moderate to expensive.

✍ **Sanford's Grub and Pub** (307-674-1722), 1 E. Alger Street. Open daily for lunch and dinner. Though it's not for everyone, most kids will probably dig the Wyoming/South Dakota restaurant chain known as Sanford's, with its junkyard décor (remember the television show?) and its plethora of televisions tuned to all different channels. Beer aficionados will appreciate the enormous beer list. If you're really hungry, perhaps you won't be overwhelmed by the super-sized pub entrées, served with plentiful sides on oversized platters to be eaten with oversized silverware. The huge menu includes salads, burgers, sandwiches, and all sorts of entrée selections—you'll have to see it to believe how large and extensive it is. Moderate to expensive.

See also Kendrick Park in *To Do*—For Families; Blue Gables Motel and Coffee Bar in *Lodging*—Hotels and Motels; High Mountain Mercantile in *Selective Shopping*; and Wyoming Rib and Chop House in *Where to Eat*—Dining Out in Northwest Wyoming: Cody and Powell.

DINING OUT
Buffalo
The Virginian Restaurant at the Historic Occidental Hotel (307-684-0451; http://www.occidentalwyoming.com), 10 N. Main Street. Open for lunch and dinner; call for current hours/days. Buffalo steaks are the house specialty, along with steaks, seafood, and prime rib at this beautifully restored restaurant located within the Historic Occidental Hotel (see *Lodging*—Other Options). This elegant dining experience is complemented by exceptional service and impeccable décor. Expensive to very expensive.

Sheridan
1893 Grille & Spirits (307-673-2777; http://www.1893grille.com), at the historic Sheridan Inn, 856 N. Broadway. Open for lunch and dinner; call for current hours/days. If you want a true dose of good old western fun, check out this restaurant, which happens to be located in one of Buffalo Bill Cody's old hangouts. Every lunch menu item ends in ".93," and many items have interesting western trivia incorporated into their descriptions. For all of this fun, you'll also enjoy a truly wonderful meal, with dinner options ranging from elk stew and filet mignon to entrée salads. Vegetarian options are available. Expensive.

Story
Wagon Box Inn Restaurant and Cabins (1-800-301-3120 or 307-683-2444; http://www.wagonbox.com), 108 N. Piney Creek. Call for current hours and days. Known for its fabulous fare by both locals and visitors, this fantastic restaurant offers western dining at its finest. Specialties are seafood and steaks, with a variety of combinations including both, available. Other options include chicken, pastas, and burgers. Entrées come with a ton of sides. Kids' and seniors' menus are offered. Larger cuts of meat than those listed on the menu are available if you so desire. Patio dining in summer yields potential for viewing whitetail deer that often graze on the grounds at dusk. Expensive. Cabins are also available (expensive).

✳ Entertainment
The Buffalo Theatre (307-684-9950; http://www.thebuffalotheater.com), 235 S. Main Street, Buffalo.

Centennial Theaters (307-672-5797), 36 E. Alger Street, Sheridan.

Skyline Drive-In Theatre (307-674-4532), 1739 E. Brundage Lane, Sheridan.

❧ Thursday Night Jam Sessions at the Occidental Saloon (see Occidental Hotel in *Lodging*—Hotels and Motels) are free, impromptu gatherings of local bluegrass, western, and folk musicians. Sessions start at 6:30 and go until whenever they stop. Grab a chair and get in on some truly amazing entertainment.

WYO Theater (307-672-9084; http://www.wyotheater.com), 42 N. Main Street, Sheridan. This theater offers live entertainment and performing arts events September through May.

See also Whitney Commons in *To See*—City Parks and Gardens; Kendrick Park in *To Do*—For Families; and Deer Park RV Park and Campground in *Lodging*—Campgrounds.

✳ Selective Shopping

Bozeman Trail Gallery (307-672-3928; http://www.bozemantrailgallery.com), 190 N. Main Street, Sheridan. Call for current hours. This fine art gallery offers exquisite works by master western artists from both the 19th and 20th centuries. It also carries American Indian artwork, including Navajo blankets.

Crazy Woman Trading Co. (307-672-3939; http://www.crazywomantrading.com), 120 N. Main Street, Sheridan. Call for current hours. Everyone loves the local name Crazy Woman that's attached to both a creek and a canyon, among other features. This store lets you take it home with its wide range of cool Crazy Woman clothing. What else? It also carries other fun souvenir items such as Wyoming Road Kill seasonings and Crazy Woman Chili.

High Mountain Mercantile (1-866-445-5614; http://www.highmountainmercantile.net), 130 N. Main Street, Sheridan. Open 10–5:30 Monday through Thursday, 10–5 Friday through Saturday. High-class western wear here includes rhinestone studded belts, turquoise jewelry, authentic cowboy hats, and more. They also carry children's western wear and toys, and western books. The Cowboy Coffee Bar in the back of the store provides pick-me-ups in the form of coffee, doughnuts, hot dogs, and more.

Margo's Pottery and Fine Crafts (307-684-9406; http://www.margospottery.com), 1 N. Main Street, Buffalo. Open 10–5:30 Monday through Saturday, noon–5 Sunday. You can browse through and/or purchase interesting and unique locally made pottery as well as other arts and crafts (including jewelry, glasswork, and woodwork) in this cool historic building in the heart of Buffalo.

See also Jim Gatchell Memorial Museum and Gift Shop in *To See*—Museums; Whitney Commons in *To See*—City Parks and Gardens; Indian Campground and RV Park in *Lodging*—Campgrounds; Sagewood Gifts and Café in *Where to Eat*—Eating Out; and Buffalo Bill Days Wild West Show in *Special Events*.

✳ Special Events

May: **Rocky Mountain Leather Trade Show,** Sheridan: An annual gathering of leatherworkers to display their wares, it includes workshops and contests.

May: **Lake DeSmet Fishing Derby** (1-800-227-5122 or 307-684-5544), Buffalo: Held Memorial Day weekend, anglers of all ages can compete for prizes at this community-oriented event. See also Lake DeSmet in *To Do*—Fishing.

June: **Celebrate the Arts,** Sheridan: A three-day festival in which local artists display their works in downtown Sheridan, it includes crafts, live music, poetry readings, and book signings.

June: **Bozeman Trail Days** (http://www.bozemantrail.org/bozemantraildays.html), Fort Phil Kearny State Historic Site, Story: This is a three-day event with living history, symposiums, and tours of historic battlefields.

June: **Bighorn Wild and Scenic Trail Runs** (307-673-7500; http://www.big horntrailrun.com), Sheridan: Runners from all over the world converge to compete for top honors in races of 30K, 50K, 50 miles, and 100 miles.

♂ June: **Buffalo Bill Days Wild West Show** (http://www.buffalobilldays.org), Sheridan: A crowd-pleasing favorite annual event with three days of celebration, activities include a grand ball, a pony express ride, live music, chil-dren's events, a trade show, a parade, the actual wild west show, and more.

August: **Johnson County Fair and Rodeo** (307-684-7357; http://www.big hornmountains.com/jcf&r.htm), Johnson County Fairgrounds, Buffalo: This is a traditional county fair and rodeo.

September: **Deke Latham Memorial PRCA Rodeo** (307-738-2444; http://www.dekelathamrodeo.com), Kaycee: This is a four-day PRCA rodeo.

GILLETTE AND THE DEVILS TOWER AREA

A mashed-potato sculpture in *Close Encounters of the Third Kind* (1977) provided the first and most lasting image of Devils Tower National Monument for me, as it probably did for many people of my generation (I was three years old when the movie came out, and I must have seen it at a relatively young age). This association still sticks, but little did I know then that this unique natural feature, our nation's first national monument (established in 1906), would come to have a different sort of significance to me later in life—nor did I realize the significance it already had for many tribes of American Indians.

This 1,267-foot monolith was called Bears Lodge (along with a number of similar variations) by the more than 20 tribes of American Indians who viewed it as a sacred site long before its Hollywood theatrical debut. They referred to it as a landmark in many of their tribal tales, among other cultural and historic connections with the tower. It continues to hold a sacred place in their culture and rituals to this day.

As for Devils Tower's personal significance to me (an avid rock climber), that comes from its reputation as a rock climbing destination of international renown. This unique feature draws climbers from around the globe every season to test their crack-climbing skills on this unusual formation of phonolite-porphyry (a type of rock formed by cooling magma).

These two user groups—the American Indians and rock climbers—share a love and respect of Devils Tower, for entirely different reasons. Their different perspectives on the monument's appropriate usage led to conflicts, which were ultimately at least somewhat resolved in 1995 with the implementation of a voluntary climbing closure on the tower every year during the month of June out of respect for the American Indian ties to the monument. Most rock climbers choose to adhere to this closure, understanding that both user groups should have a say in how this astounding natural resource is impacted by human activities.

Surrounding Devils Tower National Monument, you'll find a number of towns offering an array of visitor services, starting with the Sundance Information Center (see *To See*—Towns). Other attractions include golf courses (see *To Do*—Golf) and lodging options (see *Lodging*), along with numerous additional recreational activities (see various listings in *To See* and *To Do*) and an abundance of public lands to explore (see *Green Space*).

If you prefer a more urban setting, about 50 miles west, you'll find the big city

BARGAINS AWAIT YOU IN NORTHEAST WYOMING

Travelers on a budget should note the abundance of free and low-cost attractions in this region. Free attractions include three museums, a historic site, Gillette's 26 city parks, the Gillette City Swimming Pool, the CCSD Planetarium and Science Center, a coal mine tour, and a community art center, in addition to all of the sorts of attractions that are typically free, such as hiking, scenic drives, bicycling, and so forth. You'll also find that many of the attractions—even Devils Tower National Monument, in fact—have lower-than-average admission prices than you might expect to find at similar attractions situated elsewhere.

of Gillette, with a population of about 25,000. A major coal-mining city, Gillette is poised to become an even greater player on the nation's energy scene, with its mines producing an abundance of clean-burning, low-sulfur coal—coal that is compliant with the Clean Air Act. While in Gillette, you can sign up for a free tour of a coal mine (see *To Do*—Unique Adventures), perhaps see a show or rodeo at the CAM-PLEX Multi-Event Facilities (see *Entertainment*), enjoy a great workout (see *To Do*—Fitness Centers), and play golf at one of three courses (see *To Do*—Golf), among other possibilities.

GUIDANCE **Campbell County Chamber of Commerce** (307-682-3673; http://www.gillettechamber.com), 314 S. Gillette Avenue, Gillette, 82716. The chamber has free brochures detailing **wildlife loop tours** and **historic walking tours** of downtown Gillette.

A STREET SCENE IN GILLETTE

City of Gillette (307-686-5200; http://www.ci.gillette.wy.us), 201 E. Fifth Street, P.O. Box 3003, Gillette, 82717.

Devils Tower National Monument (307-467-5283; http://www.nps.gov/deto), P.O. Box 10, Devils Tower, 82714.

See also *To See*—Towns.

GETTING THERE *By car:* Gillette is accessible from exits 124-128 on I-90 in northeast Wyoming. It can also be accessed from the north via US 14/16 or WY 59 and from the south via WY 50 or 59. Devils Tower National Monument is north of I-90 via US 14 at exit 154 or exit 185. Either way, it's about 20 miles to WY 24, and then 6 miles north to the monument. This US 14 loop off I-90 makes for a nice **scenic drive** as well.

By plane: **Gillette-Campbell County Airport** (307-686-1042; http://www.iflygillette.com) is just north of Gillette.

GETTING AROUND You'll want to be out of the car walking around at Devils Tower. Most of the small towns around the tower (Hulett, Sundance, and Newcastle included) are easily explored on foot. In Gillette, you'll find that you can walk between some attractions, but you'll need to drive to others. Outlying attractions throughout the region will require driving.

MEDICAL EMERGENCY Dial 911.

Campbell County Memorial Hospital (307-688-1000; http://www.ccmh.net), 501 S. Burma Avenue, Gillette.

Weston County Health Services, (307-746-4491), 1124 Washington Boulevard, Newcastle.

✷ To See

TOWNS **Hulett,** 9 miles north of Devils Tower National Monument on WY 24, is home to the Hulett Rodeo (see *Special Events*), as well as an annual biker rally. For more information: **Hulett Chamber of Commerce** (307-467-5747; http://www.hulett-wyoming.com), 146 Main Street, Hulett, 82720.

Newcastle can be reached from the east and northwest via US 16, from the north and south via US 85, and from the west via WY 450. A recreational haven situated on the edge of Black Hills National Forest and Thunder Basin National Grassland (see *Green Space*—National Lands), Newcastle was actually named after Newcastle upon Tyne, its sister city in England. For more information: **Newcastle Area Chamber of Commerce** (307-746-2739; http://www.newcastlewyo.com), 1323 Washington Boulevard, Newcastle, 82701.

Sundance can be accessed from exits 187 and 189 off I-90. Be sure to stop in at the **Sundance Information Center** at exit 189 off I-90 to gather information about the local area (as well as to use the restroom, if need be!). For more information: **Sundance Area Chamber of Commerce** (1-800-477-9340 or 307-283-1000; http://www.sundancewyoming.com), P.O. Box 1004, Sundance, 82729.

MUSEUMS **Anna Miller Museum** (307-746-4188; http://www.artcom.com/Museums/nv/af/82701.htm), 401 Delaware Avenue, Newcastle. Open 9–5 Monday through Friday or by appointment; free. This western history museum includes a one-room schoolhouse and the oldest structure still standing from the Black Hills Gold Rush—the Jenney Stockade Cabin—as well as numerous items of historic significance from frontier times and earlier. See also Beaver Creek Loop Tour in *To See*—Scenic Drives.

Campbell County Rockpile Museum (307-682-5723; http://www.ccgov.net/departments/museum), 900 W. Second Street, Gillette. Open 9–5 Monday through Saturday; free. Learn about the local history of Campbell County portrayed through the museum's collection of western artifacts. The collection includes Native American items such as projectile points and scrapers, as well as items from frontier days such as saddles, rifles, newspapers, and more. A fun children's dress-up area allows kids one of many opportunities for hands-on play. The museum also

AN EXHIBIT AT THE CAMPBELL COUNTY
ROCKPILE MUSEUM

has a gift shop and hosts performances and educational events. See also Annual Native American Artifact Show in *Special Events*.

❧ **Crook County Museum** (307-283-3666; http://www.crookcountymuseum.com), 309 E. Cleveland Street, Sundance. Open 8–5 March through December; free. Focused on the history of Crook County, museum collections include Indian artifacts, furniture from the 1888 courthouse where the Sundance Kid was put on trial, pioneer relics, dioramas, and historic photographs. The museum also has a bookstore.

HISTORIC LANDMARKS, PLACES, AND SITES ❧ **Vore Buffalo Jump** (307-283-1192; http://www.s201264329.onlinehome.us), between exits 199 and 205 off I-90. Open for tours in summer; free at time of publication (donations gladly accepted). Discovered during the 1970s construction of I-90, this is the site of an American Indian buffalo jump, or a place where, from about 1500–1800, Indians drove buffalo en masse to their deaths in a natural sinkhole. Much of this incredible archaeological site still remains to be excavated (only about 5 percent has been unearthed thus far). The Vore Buffalo Jump Foundation plans to add an incredible visitor center and a top-notch research facility to the site.

See also Campbell County Chamber of Commerce in *To Do*—Guidance; Beaver Creek Loop Tour in *To See*—Scenic Drives; and Flying V Cambria Inn in *Lodging*—Bed and Breakfasts.

CITY PARKS AND GARDENS ❧ 🐾 ♿ **Gillette City Parks** (307-686-5275; http://www.ci.gillette.wy.us/pubw/PK/CityParks.html) include 26 parks totaling about 430 acres. Open 5 AM–11 PM (unless otherwise posted); free. You'll find playgrounds and fishing access, picnic areas and barbecues, horseshoes and Frisbee golf, and more, at many of Gillette's parks, including **Dalbey Memorial Park**, 900 Edwards Street, which has a fishing lake. For a park map and a complete list of facilities, visit the Web site, where you can also find a map of the city's established bike paths.

DALBEY MEMORIAL PARK

SCENIC DRIVES Beaver Creek Loop Tour is a 50-mile loop tour around Newcastle. Stop at the Anna Miller Museum (see *To See*—Museums) to get a map that will send you on your way to exploring 26 marked sites around Newcastle. Featuring both scenic and historic destinations, highlights of this drive include old stage stops, ghost towns, a pioneer cemetery, and scenic overlooks.

A NATURAL WONDER

♿ Devils Tower National Monument (307-467-5283; http://www.nps.gov/deto), I-90 to exit 154 or 185, then north on US 14 to WY 24. Grounds always open, visitor center open 8–7 in summer (hours vary the rest of the year); $10 per vehicle for a seven-day pass, $12 per night for overnight camping (first-come, first-served; late April through late October). One of the most recognizable features of Wyoming's landscape, this 1,267-foot geological wonder towers over the Belle Fourche River (see *To Do—Fishing*). Devils Tower is a vertical monument of sacred and historic significance to American Indians and a longtime favored destination of rock climbers (see chapter introduction and *To Do—Climbing*). President Teddy Roosevelt declared Devils Tower the nation's first national monument in 1906, and it continues to attract and amaze visitors today. Recreational opportunities include hiking, wildlife viewing, bird-watching, fishing, rock climbing, and camping. For the average visitor to Devils Tower, a hike around the Tower Trail (see *To Do—Hiking*) and a visit to the visitor center will probably complete the experience. However, those who want a more exciting experience can consider hiring a rock climbing guide (see *To Do—Climbing*) and scaling the tower. For the not-quite-so-adventurous, Devils Tower also offers a number of ranger-led interpretive activities in the summer season, as well as 8 miles of hiking trails.

See also Tower Trail in *To Do—Hiking*.

DEVILS TOWER NATIONAL MONUMENT

See also Getting There; Campbell County Chamber of Commerce in *To Do—Guidance*; and Thunder Basin National Grassland in *Green Space—National Lands.*

✷ To Do

BICYCLING **Bearlodge Trail** is situated near Sundance, with access via Cook Lake Recreation Area (see *To Do—Hiking*). More than 50 miles of this multi-use trail (#90) in the Black Hills National Forest (see *Green Space—National Lands*) await the avid mountain biker, taking you through some of the rugged terrain and gorgeous scenery of this national forest. This is one of many multi-use trails that you'll find in the Black Hills National Forest.

See also Gillette City Parks in *To See—City* Parks and Gardens; Cook Lake Trail in *To Do—*Hiking; Cross-country skiing and snowshoeing in *To Do—*Snow Sports; *Green Space*; and Devils Tower KOA in *Lodging—*Campgrounds.

BOATING See Cook Lake Trail in *To Do—*Hiking; and Keyhole State Park in *Green Space—*State Parks.

CLIMBING **Above Ouray Ice & Tower Rock Guides** (1-888-345-9061 or 307-290-1641; http://www.towerguides.com), 157 WY 24; Devils Tower, 82714. Rock climbing courses offered year-round; $45–250 per person per day, depending on course selection. Beginners are welcome at this well-regarded, AMGA-certified climbing guide service at Devils Tower.

Devils Tower Climbing (1-888-314-JAMS or 307-467-JAMS; http://www.devils towerclimbing.com), c/o Devils Tower Lodge, P.O. Box 66, Devils Tower, 82714. Available year-round; $250–350 per person per day, depending on course selection. Also available are climb-n-stay package deals that include lodging at the **Devils Tower Lodge** (http://www.devilstowerlodge), a bed and breakfast with views of Devils Tower, a hot tub, and an indoor climbing gym on the premises, and massages by appointment. Expensive.

Exum Mountain Guides (307-733-2297; http://www.exumguides.com), South Jenny Lake, P.O. Box 56, Grand Teton National Park, Moose, 83012. Available May and July through September; $395 per person (one person) or $300 per person (two people), plus a $150 travel expense fee. Call Exum for details on routes and reservations.

See also Devils Tower National Monument in *To See—*A Natural Wonder and Campbell County Recreation Center in *To Do—*Climbing.

FISHING **Belle Fourche River** (307-672-7418; http://gf.state.wy.us/fish/fishing/index.asp), flows from south of Gillette near WY 59 north to Keyhole Reservoir, along WY 24 between Moorcroft and Hulett, and then northeast to US 212 before arcing southeast into South Dakota. This river and its many creeks and streams offer the opportunity to catch black bullhead, channel catfish, smallmouth bass, and sunfish. The river can be easily accessed by anglers from within Devils Tower National Monument (see *To See—*A Natural Wonder) and just above Keyhole Reservoir (see *Green Space—*State Parks), among other access points.

See also Gillette City Parks in *To See—*City Parks and Gardens; Cook Lake Trail in *To Do—*Hiking; *Green Space*; Devils Tower KOA in *Lodging—*Campgrounds.

FITNESS CENTERS *✿* ✿ ᐸ **Campbell County Recreation Center** (307-682-7406; http://www.ccprd.com), 250 Shoshone Ave., Gillette. Open 5 AM–10 PM Monday–Friday, 8 AM.–6 PM Sat., and 1–5 Sun.; free for seniors 60+, $4 per adult/college student, $3 per youth, $2 per elementary-aged child and under, $10.25 per family. This new (spring 2010) 189,000-square-foot facility features three full-sized basketball courts, an aerobics room, a huge state-of-the-art weightlifting room, massive cardio area, racquetball, and a four-lane walking track. It also has a junior Olympic swimming pool and diving well, a kiddie pool (with zero level entrance and a lazy river), plus an adjacent field house with a 200-meter Olympic-quality track. And then, there's the climbing structure: A 42-foot pinnacle (approximately 3,000 square feet of climbing surface created by Eldorado Walls), with 12 top rope anchors and one auto-belay station, plus leading capabilities. To add to the fun, half of the structure replicates Devils Tower.

✿ **Wright Recreation Center** (307-464-0198; http://www.ccprd.com), 225 Wright Boulevard, Wright. Open 6 AM–9 PM Monday through Friday, 1–5 Saturday and Sunday; free for seniors 60-plus, $4 per adult/college student, $3 per youth, $2 per elementary-aged child and under, $10.25 per family. This recreation center includes a swimming pool, weight room, and cardio equipment.

FOR FAMILIES *✿* **Campbell County Pool** (307-682-5470; http://www.ccprd .com), W. Warlow Drive, Gillette. Open year-round, hours vary; free for seniors 60-plus, $4 per adult/college student, $3 per youth, $2 per elementary-aged child and under, $10.25 per family. A waterslide is open Memorial Day through Labor Day.

✿ ✿ **Campbell County School District (CCSD) Planetarium** (307-682-4307; http://www.ccsd.k12.wy.us/schools/SV/planetarium/planetarium/Welcome.html), Sage Valley Jr. High School, 1000 W. Lakeway Road, Gillette. Open twice a month for free public shows, including a Family Show designed to entertain younger attendees. The planetarium also occasionally hosts laser shows; call or check online for a current schedule.

✿ ✿ **CCSD Science Center** (307-686-3821; http://web.ccsd.k12.wy.us/ Adventuarium/index.htm), 525 W. Lakeway Road, Suite 101, Gillette. Open 10–noon and 1–3 Tuesday through Thursday (summer), 10–3 Monday through Thursday and 10–noon Friday (school year); free. Inside the Lakeway Learning Center, kids will find more than 60 hands-on exhibits that invite them to learn more about the fascinating world around them.

✿ ✿ **Gillette City Swimming Pool** (307-682-1962; http://www.ci.gillette.wy .us/pubw/PK/pool.html), 909 S. Gillette Avenue, Gillette. Open daily in summer, hours vary; free. This outdoor pool complex also has playground equipment, climbing structures, concessions, a wading pool, and more.

See Campbell County Rockpile Museum in *To See*—Museums; Gillette City Parks in *To See*—City Parks and Gardens; *To Do*—Fitness Centers; and Keyhole State Park in *Green Space*—State Parks.

GOLF Bell Nob Golf Course (307-686-7069; http://www.ccprd.com/html/ bell_nob_golf.html), 4600 Overdale Drive, Gillette, 18 holes.

Gillette Golf Club (307-682-4774), 1800 Country Club Road, Gillette, 9 holes.

Haycreek Golf Club (307-464-0747), 1229 E. Elkhorn Drive, Wright, 9 holes.

The Golf Club at Devils Tower (307-467-5773; http://www.devilstowergolf .com), 75 Tower View Drive, Hulett, 18 holes.

Keyhole Country Club (307-756-3775), 230 Pine Haven Road, Pine Haven, 9 holes.

Newcastle Country Club (307-746-2639), 2302 W. Main Street, Newcastle, 9 holes.

Sundance Golf Club (307-283-1191), 1632 Cleveland Street, Sundance, 9 holes.

HIKING Cook Lake Trail, in the Black Hills National Forest (see *Green Space*—National Lands), is accessible by taking exit 185 off I-90, and then going west about a mile before turning north (right) onto FR 838 (Warren Peak Road). Proceed north for about 7 miles before turning east (right) on FR 843 for about 1.7 miles, continuing on it for another 3 miles or so after it turns left. Make a left onto FR 842 and proceed 1 mile to find the trailhead at the campground. Day use fee of $3 charged from May through September. This easy, 1-mile trail takes you around the **Cook Lake Recreation Area,** a lovely, serene place great for fishing (handicapped-accessible pier), wildlife viewing, paddling, mountain biking, and camping (open seasonally, $14–17 per night, some sites can be reserved).

Tower Trail, located at Devils Tower National Monument (see *To See*—A Natural Wonder), offers a 1.3-mile paved excursion that takes you up closer to the tower for better views, enabling you to watch rock climbers should they happen to be present. With numerous interpretive signs along the way, this trail takes you through variable environments including stands of ponderosa pine, the edges of fields, and jumbles of boulders. Benches along the way provide areas to stop and take a breather or to simply soak in some of the magic of this one-of-a-kind natural feature.

See also Gillette City Parks in *To See*—City Parks and Gardens; Bearlodge Trail in *To Do*—Bicycling; Cross-country skiing and snowshoeing in *To Do*—Snow Sports; and *Green Space*.

HORSEBACK RIDING See Bearlodge Trail in *To Do*—Bicycling; Cross-country skiing and snowshoeing in *To Do*—Snow Sports; *Green Space*; and Devils Tower KOA in *Lodging*—Campgrounds.

PADDLING/FLOATING See Cook Lake Trail in *To Do*—Hiking.

RELAXATION AND REJUVENATION General Nutrition Center (GNC) (307-686-7043; http://www.gnc.com), 2610 Douglas Highway, Gillette. Call for current store hours. Anyone who is into health and nutrition probably already knows what to expect from a GNC!

Wyoming Yoga Studio (307-680-7762; http://www.wyoga.net), 810 Madison Street, Gillette. Call or check online for current schedule; $8 per class. This studio offers a wide variety of classes for both beginners and for experienced yogis.

See also Devils Tower Climbing in *To Do*—Climbing.

SNOW SPORTS Cross-country skiing and snowshoeing opportunities can be found throughout this region in wintertime. In addition to many miles of ungroomed trails, you'll find a number of groomed and marked trails. These include **Carson Draw Trails**, located in the Black Hills National Forest (see *Green Space*—National Lands) on FR 838, 3 miles north of US 14 outside of Sundance. This 6.8-mile trail system is a great cross-country skiing destination, as the system is groomed weekly as snow permits from December 15 through March 30. The rest of the year it makes for great hiking, mountain biking, and horseback riding. Also explore the nearby **Sundance Trails**, which include 47.3 miles of trails accessible 3.5 miles north of Sundance via CR 123 (Government Valley Road). A downloadable brochure with trail maps is available at the forest service Web site.

Ice-skating can be found at two locations in Gillette: **Campbell County Ice Arena** (307-682-2927; http://www.ccprd.com) and **Spirit Hall Ice Arena** (307-687-1555; http://www.ccprd.com; see also CAM-PLEX in *Entertainment*). Call or check online for the current season's hours for public skating. Cost is $5 per adult, $4.50 per child 12 and under, $3 for additional skate rental.

Snowmobiling options in this region include the **Sundance Snowmobile Trail**, accessible from Reuter Campground in the Black Hills National Forest (see *Green Space*—National Lands). Take I-90 to exit 185, go north 1 mile on US 14, then north on FR 838 for 2 miles to the campground. You'll find 62 miles of groomed trails (weekly grooming as snow permits) open for snowmobiling December 15 through March 30. For detailed trail reports, call 307-777-6560 or go to http://wyo trails.state.wy.us/snow, the Wyoming Snowmobile Trails Web site, which also provides information about rules, rental agencies, trails around the state, and more. See also Keyhole State Park in *Green Space*—State Parks.

UNIQUE ADVENTURES ❧ **Coal Mine Tour**, Gillette. Available June through August; free. Sign up through the Chamber of Commerce's visitor center (located just off I-90 at exit 126 in the Flying J parking lot), and then go on a mind-blowing tour of a local coal mine. When you get up close to the massive equipment used to literally move the earth in order to make the coal accessible, you might be surprised to realize just how big this machinery has to be. This is a must-see attraction for anyone who wants to educate themselves about how energy gets from underground to us.

WINERIES AND WINE TASTINGS See Prime Rib Restaurant and Blue Martini Wine Bar in *Where to Eat— Dining Out*; and Rotary Wine and Microbrew Festival in Special Events.

✳ **Green Space**

STATE PARKS ✐ ♿ **Keyhole State Park** (307-756-3596; http://wyoparks .state.wy.us/Site/SiteInfo.asp?siteID =10), 22 Marina Road, Moorcroft, north of I-90 via exit 165. Open year-round for day use ($4 resident/$6 non-

SIGN UP HERE TO TAKE A COAL MINE TOUR IN GILLETTE

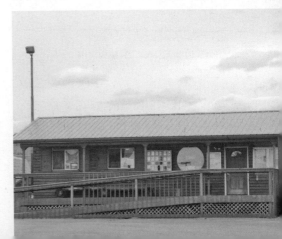

resident), and camping ($10 resident/$17 nonresident). Keyhole Reservoir's nearly 15,000 acres of surface area makes this park a popular destination for boating, with its three boat ramps, as well as a privately run marina and motel (307-756-9529). Fishing is also popular, with species including catfish, northern pike, smallmouth bass, and walleye. At Keyhole you'll also find a playground, swimming beaches, hiking trails, and bird-watching opportunities, as well as snowmobiling trails in wintertime.

NATIONAL LANDS **Black Hills National Forest** (307-283-1361; http://www .fs.fed.us/r2/blackhills), Bearlodge Ranger District, 121 S. 21st Street, Sundance. Though most of the Black Hills National Forest lies within South Dakota, a portion of this forest lies in Wyoming. You can access the Wyoming portions near Sundance off I-90 and near Newcastle off US 85. Recreational opportunities include camping (see *Lodging*—Camping), fishing, hiking, horseback riding, bicycling, snowmobiling, wildlife viewing, and more.

Bureau of Land Management (BLM): See listing in *Green Space*—National Lands in Sheridan and Buffalo.

Thunder Basin National Grassland (307-358-4690; http://www.fs.fed.us/r2/mbr) is located mostly south of I-90 and north of I-25 between Gillette and Douglas and accessible via WY 59 and WY 450. Stretching between the Big Horn National Forest and the Black Hills National Forest in northeastern Wyoming, and south almost to Douglas, this grassland encompasses much of the Powder River Basin. Managed by the Douglas Ranger District of the Medicine Bow and Routt National Forests, the grassland provides numerous recreational opportunities, including hiking, fishing, mountain biking, camping (undeveloped), and wildlife viewing. A **scenic drive** along WY 59 or WY 450 will take you through some relatively untrammeled country, giving you ample opportunities for wildlife viewing. Visit the forest service Web site for more information.

RECREATION AREAS **Weston Hills Recreation Area**, 25 miles north of Gillette via WY 59, is a jointly managed (BLM and National Forest Service) recreation area offering free, primitive camping opportunities as well as 7 miles of multi-use roads and trails.

See also Cook Lake Trail in *To Do*—Hiking.

✳ Lodging

BED AND BREAKFASTS

Devils Tower
See Devils Tower Climbing in *To Do*—Climbing.

Gillette
᥊ᵀᣴ **A White House Inn Bed & Breakfast** (307-687-1240; http://www .awhitehouseinn.com), 2708 Ridgecrest Drive. This charming, two-story B&B with its white-columned front porch and sky-blue shutters offers you fine

hospitality with its lovely, well-kept gardens and delicious, full breakfasts prepared every morning and served in its cozy dining room. Choose from a suite with a private bath or an individual room. Expensive.

Newcastle
Flying V Cambria Inn (307-746-2096; http://www.flyingvcambriainn

.com), 23726 N. US 85, Newcastle. Stay at this historic castle of a B&B, where you can enjoy not just bed and breakfast, but also easy access to fishing, hiking, and horseshoes. Or, stay instead in the campground (RV or tent). Either way, you can enjoy a home-style dinner every night (if you want) from the inn's restaurant. Moderate.

Sundance

Sundance Mt. HideAway Bed and Breakfast (1-877-838-0063 or 307-283-3766; http://www.sundancemoun tainhideaway.com), WY 585 via exit 187 off I-90. Open April through November. Three log cabins (all with private baths)—the Getaway Cabin, the Wildlife Cabin, and the Romantic Getaway—offer you a choice of luxurious amenities, including private decks, TV/VCRs, a Jacuzzi, and more. A gourmet, mouthwatering, full breakfast is included in the rate. Moderate to expensive.

HOTELS AND MOTELS

Hulett

🦌 🎖 ⁗₁⁗ **Hulett Motel** (307-467-5220; http://www.hulettmotel.com), 202 Main Street, Hulett. Clean, comfortable, and modern motel rooms or a whole cabin rental (new in 2009) are your options at this above-average lodging facility located a mere 10 minutes' drive from Devils Tower National Monument (see To See—A Natural Wonder). There is also a gift shop on the premises. Moderate to expensive.

Gillette

Gillette's accommodations feature mainly hotels or motels that are part of a national chain, such as **Country Inn and Suites** (307-682-0505; okay, they do have an **indoor water park,** and that *is* unique), **Holiday Inn Express** (307-686-9576), and **Motel 6** (307-686-8600). As these tend to be pre-

dictable, I'll let you pick your favorite one instead of wasting precious book space to tell you what you already know.

Newcastle

🦌 ⁗₁⁗ 🎖 **Sage Motel** (307-746-2724; http://www.sagemotel.vcn.com), 1227 S. Summit Avenue, Newcastle. Enjoy clean, budget accommodations, complete with in-room refrigerators, at this friendly motel in Newcastle. Moderate.

Sundance

🦌 ⁗₁⁗ **Bear Lodge Motel** (307-283-1611; http://www.bearlodgemotel .com), 218 Cleveland Street, Sundance. This clean, well-kept motel offers both single and double rooms. In addition, a collection of free DVDs (including child-appropriate movies) ensures that the whole family can stay entertained. Moderate to expensive.

CAMPGROUNDS Black Hills National Forest (see Green Space—National Lands) has four developed campgrounds in this region open from late spring to early fall. These include **Bearlodge Campground** ($6), **Cook Lake Campground** (see Cook Lake Trail in To Do—Hiking) **Sundance Campground** ($16), and **Reuter Campground** ($11). All four campgrounds are located north of Sundance. Reservations (1-877-444-6777; http://www.recreation.gov) are accepted at Sundance, Cook Lake, and Reuter in season. Sundance is closed in winter. See also Snowmobiling in To Do—Snow Sports.

& ⁗₁⁗ ✿ **Devils Tower KOA** (1-800-562-5785 or 307-467-5395; http://www .devilstowerkoa), 60 WY 110, Devils Tower. Open year-round; make advance reservations. This full-service KOA offers RV sites, tent sites, and cabins. Additional amenities include a (seasonal) heated swimming pool, evening hayrides, bicycle rentals, horseback riding, fishing, an extensive gift shop, and an on-premises **restaurant** (moderate) serving three meals a day. Inexpensive to expensive.

ሌ **High Plains Campground** (307-687-7339), 1600 S. Garner Lake Road, Gillette. Open year-round; make reservations in advance. Take exit 129 off I-90. This full-service campground in Gillette offers daily, weekly, and monthly rates, providing a budget alternative to other Gillette-area lodging options. Very inexpensive to inexpensive.

ቀ **Mountain View Campground** (1-800-792-8439; http://www.mtnview campground.com), exit 189 off I-90, Sundance. Open April 1 through November 1. This full-service campground offers RV sites, tent sites, and cabins. Amenities include a seasonal heated pool and a general store. Very inexpensive to moderate.

See also Keyhole State Park in *Green Space*—State Parks; Weston Hill Recreation Area in *Green Space*—Recreation Areas; and CAM-PLEX in *Entertainment*.

✳ Where to Eat

EATING OUT
Gillette
Breanna's Bakery (307-686-0570), 208 S. Gillette Avenue. Open 5 AM–4 PM Tuesday through Saturday. Serving up homemade pastries, breads, bagels, sandwiches, and other baked goods, Breanna's is a locals' favorite. Stop in for a tasty treat for breakfast or lunch. Inexpensive.

Las Margaritas (307-682-6545), 2107 S. Douglas Highway. Open 11–9 daily. If you're not in the mood for fast food or steaks tonight (both of which Gillette has plenty), then try for a relatively authentic Mexican experience—right in the heart of Wyoming. Las Margaritas features all of your

favorites, taking you south of the border with both its festive decorations and its menu. Moderate.

Hulett
Ponderosa Café and Bar (307-467-5335; http://www.theponderosacafe .com), 115 Main Street, Hulett. Open for three meals; call for current hours/days. Under new management since 2006, this restaurant near Devils Tower National Monument has already earned its spot as a favorite eatery for travelers and locals alike. You'll find classic American food served here (burgers, sandwiches, and steaks), as well as creative daily specials. Moderate to expensive.

Newcastle
✒ **The Hop** (307-746-2585), 1114 W. Main Street. Open 7 AM–9 PM Tuesday through Saturday, 7–2 Sunday. Remember the 1950s? Well, even if you don't, you'll get to dine like you're living in a bygone era at The Hop. In addition to breakfast, lunch, and dinner served daily, you can also cool off with a fabulous malt or milkshake, or eat a hand-dipped ice cream cone. Try the house specialty—a 10-ounce, hand-battered, chicken fried steak, and top it off with a slice of homemade pie. Inexpensive to moderate.

Isabella's Italian Restaurant (307-746-3500), 12 S. Sumner. Open 11–8 Monday through Thursday, 11–9 Friday through Saturday, noon–2 Sunday. Italian food lovers, rejoice—you will have a wide selection of all your favorites to choose from at this eatery. Options range from pastas of all shapes and types topped with a variety of sauces to strombolis, pizzas, Italian subs, salads, and more. Moderate.

Sundance
Aro Restaurant (307-283-2000), 203 E. Cleveland Street. Open daily 6 AM–10 PM (summer), 6 AM–9 PM (win-

ter). This restaurant serves up stomach-busting-sized entrées three meals a day. You'll find all kinds of hearty American favorites on this menu, including homemade pancakes at breakfast and giant steaks (as well as pizza and Mexican options) at dinnertime. Diet-conscious eaters, be forewarned: you'll be hard pressed to stick to it when confronted with all that Aro has to offer. Moderate.

DINING OUT
Gillette
The Chop House Restaurant (307-682-6805; http://www.gillettechophouse.com), 113 S. Gillette Avenue. Open for lunch 11–3 Monday through Friday and dinner 5–10 Monday through Saturday. Aged, hand-cut, black angus steaks are the house's pride at this fine-dining establishment in Gillette. You'll also find seafood, salads, pasta, and more on the extensive menu. Expensive.

Prime Rib Restaurant and Blue Martini Wine Bar (307-682-2944), 1205 S. Douglas Highway, Gillette. Open for lunch 11–4 Monday through Friday and dinner 4–10 daily. This recently remodeled and expanded (2009) award-winning restaurant is one of Gillette's finest dining spots. Step into the darkened interior and instantly escape from the bustle outdoors. The menu includes an impressive wine list to complement the acclaimed cuisine, which includes steak, seafood, pasta, prime rib, and more. Expensive.

✷ Entertainment
CAM-PLEX Multi-Event Facilities (1-877-4CAMPLEX or 307-682-0552; http://www.cam-plex.com). This huge facility hosts events year-round, including rodeos, concerts, trade shows, and more—there is literally something happening every day. It also includes

numerous camping facilities on-site for use during special events.

Dogie Theatre (307-746-2187), 111 W. Main Street, Newcastle.

Foothills Theater (307-682-6766; http://www.gillettetheatres.com), 650 N. US 14-16, Gillette.

Powder River Symphony (307-660-0919; http://www.prs.vcn.com), P.O. Box 3964, Gillette. Season runs October through April; call or check online for a current schedule.

Sky Hi Cinema (307-686-7144; http://www.gillettetheatres.com), 2201 S. Douglas Highway, Gillette.

See also Campbell County Rockpile Museum in *To See*—Museums.

✷ Selective Shopping
🏵 **AVA Community Art Center** (307-682-9133; http://www.avacenter.org), 509 W. Second Street, Gillette. Gift shop open 10–5 Monday through Friday. Select a piece of original artwork by a local artist to take home with you from the gift shop here. You'll find pottery, paintings, jewelry, music, children's clothing, and more. A portion of the proceeds supports the art center, which also holds art classes and exhibitions.

THE ADVOCACY FOR VISUAL ARTS COMMUNITY ART CENTER

Western Heritage (307-682-1347), 1301 Rawhide Drive, Gillette. Wondering where you can get an elk-antler chandelier? Right here, along with additional western décor and original fine art. Call for a brochure and more information.

See also Campbell County Rockpile Museum and Crook County Museum in *To See*—Museums; Devils Tower KOA in *Lodging*—Campgrounds; and Cambria Coal Mine Days, Newcastle Fall Festival in the Park, and Ride a Horse, Feed a Cowboy in *Special Events*.

✳ Special Events

March: **Rotary Wine and Microbrew Festival**, Gillette: Enjoy an evening of sipping fine wines and tasting great brews.

June: **Hulett Rodeo and Parade,** Hulett Rodeo Grounds, Hulett: This is a traditional rodeo and associated festivities.

✍ *June:* **Cambria Coal Mine Days**, Newcastle: This celebration includes street vendors, food, a parade, a walk/run, and an off-road vehicle and jeep show.

July: **Concerts in the Park**, Gillette: Concerts are held Thursday evenings at City Park.

July to August: **Crook County Fair and Rodeo** (http://www.crookcofair .com), Sundance: This traditional rodeo and county fair runs from end of July to beginning of August.

August: **Ride a Horse, Feed a Cowboy** (http://www.rideahorsefeedacow boy.com), Hulett: This is an annual benefit for cowboys that includes a cowboy and Indian trade and art show, live bands, cowboy poetry, barbecue, and horseback riding.

✍ *September:* **Newcastle Fall Festival in the Park,** Newcastle: This event includes a kids' parade, carnival, vendors, and 1950s–60s music.

November: **Annual Native American Artifact Show**, Gillette: Enjoy an annual weeklong showing of artifacts at the Campbell County Rockpile Museum (see *To See*—Museums).

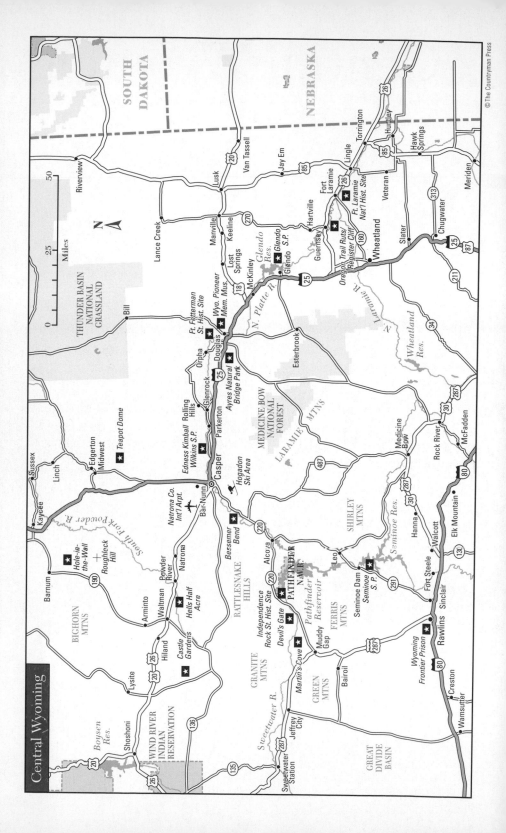

Central Wyoming

© The Countryman Press

CASPER AND DOUGLAS

The enormous North Platte River flows through this part of Wyoming, running right through the center of the region's big city—Casper. With about 53,000 residents, Casper is Wyoming's second largest city, smaller than Cheyenne by roughly 3,000 people. In addition to providing the familiar array of hotels and eateries one would expect to find in a large urban area (large by Wyoming standards, anyhow), Casper is also home to a number of distinctive cultural and historical attractions of interest, including the Nicolaysen Art Museum and Discovery Center (see *To See*—Museums) and the Fort Caspar Museum and Historic Site (see *To See*—Museums). In addition, Casper is home to the lovely Platte River Parkway (see *To Do*—Bicycling) and the Casper Whitewater Park (see *To Do*—Paddling), providing visitors and residents with a number of ways to easily enjoy the proximity of the North Platte River. Families, too, will find plenty of fun places to explore here, from the Casper Planetarium (see *To See*—For Families) to Edness K. Wilkins State Park (see *Green Space*—State Parks), among others.

By heading east from Casper on I-25, you'll reach the smaller city of Douglas. Douglas is home to the distinctive jackalope, a hybrid cross between a jackrabbit and a pronghorn (don't be fooled—of course it's not real!). Nonetheless, here you'll find statues aplenty of jackalopes that can't be missed if you're visiting Douglas for any period of time . . . just keep your eyes peeled. Douglas also has ample in-town recreational opportunities—in addition to Riverside Park (see *To Do*—Camping), you'll find a paved pathway alongside the North Platte River, great for walking, jogging, and biking (see *To See*—City Parks and Gardens). For those interested in history, along with the Wyoming Pioneer Memorial Museum (see *To See*—Museums), the town has a self-guided walking tour of historic sites, starting at the Douglas Railroad Interpretive Center (see *To See*—Museums). If you're hungry, you'll find a number of restaurant options, including nationwide chains and some local hangouts, just off I-25.

From its plentitude of parks to its planetarium, from its prehistoric population to its pioneer paths and its presidential scandal, this area will undoubtedly provide you with plenty of places to pique your interest while you pick your own path through the region's attractions, many of which are either free or very inexpensive.

GUIDANCE Casper Area Convention and Visitors Bureau (1-800-852-1889 or 307-234-5362; http://www.casperwyoming.info), 992 N. Poplar Street, Casper, 82601.

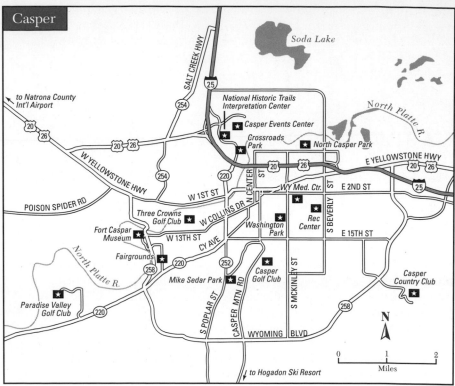

Casper

to Natrona County Int'l Airport

Soda Lake

North Platte R.

National Historic Trails Interpretation Center

Casper Events Center

Crossroads Park

North Casper Park

W YELLOWSTONE HWY

E YELLOWSTONE HWY

POISON SPIDER RD

W 1ST ST

WY Med. Ctr.

E 2ND ST

Three Crowns Golf Club

W COLLINS DR

N CENTER ST

Washington Park

Rec Center

S BEVERLY ST

E 15TH ST

Fort Caspar Museum

W 13TH ST

CY AVE

North Platte R.

Fairgrounds

Mike Sedar Park

Casper Golf Club

S MCKINLEY ST

Casper Country Club

Paradise Valley Golf Club

S POPLAR ST

CASPER MTN RD

WYOMING BLVD

N

to Hogadon Ski Resort

0 1 2
Miles

©The Countryman Press

Casper Chamber of Commerce (1-866-234-5311or 307-234-5311; http://www
.casperwyoming.org), 500 N. Center, Casper, 82601.

Converse County Tourism and Promotional Board (http://www.converse
countytourism.com), P.O. Box 1212, Douglas, 82633.

Douglas Wyoming Chamber of Commerce (1-877-937-4996 or 307-358-2950;
http://www.jackalope.org), 121 Brownfield Road, Douglas, 82633. See also Douglas
Railroad Interpretive Center in *To See*—Museums.

Natrona County (307-235-9200; http://www.natrona.net), 200 N. Center Street,
Casper, 82601.

GETTING THERE *By car:* I-25 runs through Casper and Douglas where it jogs
east west. US 287 to WY 220 reaches Casper from the southwest. US 20/26 runs
through Casper east west. WY59 reaches Douglas from the north.

By plane: **Natrona County International Airport** (NCIA) (307-472-6688;
http://www.iflycasper.com) is just 12 miles west of Casper on US 20/26.

GETTING AROUND You can walk around Casper's downtown area, but you'll
need to drive to get to a number of attractions both within the city and outside.

The Bus (307-265-1313; http://www.casperareatransportation.com/thebus.html) provides inexpensive transportation around Casper ($1.00 per adult, $.75 per student, $.50 per senior/disabled, children under 5 free). You can obtain a printable map online of bus routes. Douglas is small enough to walk to most attractions. You'll have to get in the car to drive to the region's outlying attractions.

MEDICAL EMERGENCY Dial 911.

Glenrock Health Center (307-436-9206), 925 W. Birch Street, Glenrock.

Memorial Hospital of Converse County (307-358-2122; http://www.converse hospital.com), 111 S. Fifth Street, Douglas.

Wyoming Medical Center (1-800-822-7201 or 307-577-7201; http://www.wmc net.org), 1233 E. Second Street, Casper.

✳ To See

TOWNS Glenrock, east of Casper and west of Douglas on I-25, is home to roughly 2,500 people. Glenrock's attractions include the Glenrock Paleontological Museum (see *To See*—Museums), a number of parks, a recreation center, and a golf course (see *To Do*—Golf), among others. For more information: **Glenrock Chamber of Commerce** (307-436-5652; http://www.glenrockchamber.com), 506 W. Birch Street, Glenrock, 82637.

MUSEUMS 🍴 ✏ **Douglas Railroad Interpretive Center** (1-877-937-4996 or 307-358-2950), 121 Brownfield Road, open 8–8 Monday through Friday, 10–5 Saturday (summer), call for hours in winter; free. If your child (or your inner child) loves to play with model trains, here's the perfect opportunity to introduce them to the real thing. You'll find a 19th-century passenger depot plus a locomotive and its cars, all of which can be explored, outside and in. This is also home to the Douglas Area Chamber of Commerce and Visitor Bureau (see Guidance), so you can grab area information while you're there . . . and catch sight of a jackalope.

🍴 ♿ **Fort Caspar Museum and Historic Site** (307-235-8462; http://www.fort casparwyoming.com), 4001 Fort Caspar Road, Casper. Open 8 AM–7 PM daily June through August, 8–5 daily May and September, 8–5 Tuesday through Saturday October through April; $3 per adult, $2 per child ages 13, children 12 and under free. At this city-run museum and historic site, you can explore a piece of Wyoming's military and pioneer past. The authentically furnished fort buildings—listed on the National Register of Historic Places—are reconstructions of the actual buildings, built in 1865, which sat on this site and served as a trading outpost established by the U.S. Army. The strategically placed outpost lay along the path of many of the pioneer trails passing

RECONSTRUCTIONS OF FORT BUILDINGS AT FORT CASPAR MUSEUM AND HISTORIC SITE

THE OREGON TRAIL

During the middle of the 19th century, experts estimate that more than 500,000 people traveled along the 2,000-mile Oregon Trail, nearly 500 miles of which is found in Wyoming. In addition, from 1846 through 1869, some 300,000 Mormons traveled west through Wyoming on the Mormon Trail (following a similar route as the Oregon Trail), seeking a new home far from the religious persecutions and general hostility they had endured during their tenure in the more civilized areas of the United States. This historic movement of such massive numbers of people through its lands has ensured Wyoming a place of significance in the history books and in the collective memory of the nation as a whole.

What began as a journey undertaken by a few venturesome souls in the middle of the 1830s became a full-scale river of emigration in less than a decade, with the first large wagon train of 1,000 wagons undertaking the Oregon Trail journey in 1843. The news spread quickly—moving west offered the prospect of abundant, open lands and the potential to leave the past behind and reinvent oneself. The discovery of gold in California in 1848 only increased the traffic, as gold seekers began rushing in hordes to California the following year, starting a boom 'n' bust cycle that would characterize selected areas of the west throughout the 19th century, as more gold was discovered elsewhere.

Approximately 10 percent of the emigrants on the Oregon Trail died on the journey westward, succumbing to sickness, exhaustion, hunger, thirst, accidents, or the occasional skirmish with American Indians (which accounted for fewer deaths than you might think). For about 25 years the emigration by wagon train continued at a somewhat steady clip, until it was brought to a trickle by the completion of the transcontinental railroad in 1869, finally drying up entirely by the early 20th century. But the pioneers had left their mark on the terrain for future generations, both in the now-fading physical remains of their passage—such as names carved in rocks and ruts left by the wheels of thousands of wagons—and in the legacy of the unstoppable tide of humanity that permanently displaced the American Indian population, disrupting their traditional ways of living forever and introducing new ways of living to the land.

Should you wish to learn more about the emigrants' lives and journeys, you'll find numerous museums throughout Wyoming housing artifacts and exhibits that help interpret and explain the various hardships and realities of life as an emigrant. First and foremost among these is Casper's National Historic Trails Interpretive Center (see *To See*—Museums), which is dedicated to bringing this vital piece of the nation's history to life for today's visitors.

through this region, including the Mormon Trail, Oregon Trail, and Pony Express Trail. In 1847, Mormon leader Brigham Young and his followers crossed the North Platte River via a ferry near here, setting a precedent followed by future wagon trains until the establishment of toll bridges provided a more suitable alternative. A replica of the ferry—two dugout canoes joined by planks—can be found on the grounds, as can the remains of one of the toll bridges—the Guinard Bridge. In addition to the ferry, bridge, and fort buildings, the Fort Caspar Museum features exhibits covering aspects of central Wyoming history, including the history of the area's American Indian residents and the history of oil development in the region. The grounds also include a **city park,** which is a great place for a picnic. See also Fort Caspar Campground in *Lodging*—Campgrounds; and Fort Caspar Chautauqua in *Special Events*.

🦕 𝄞 **Glenrock Paleontological Museum** (1-888-461-5015 or 307-436-2667; http://www.paleon.org), 506 W. Birch Street, Glenrock. Open 9–5 Tuesday through Friday; free (donations gladly accepted). If your children love dinosaurs (or you do), plan a stop at the Glenrock Paleontological Museum. Here you can not only view specimens of some of the world's most notorious dinos, such as a triceratops discovered near the town of Glenrock in 1994, but also you can watch scientists actually prepare the specimens in the lab for preservation and presentation. For a more in-depth prehistoric experience, inquire about the daylong or weeklong **Dig School** dinosaur digging excursions that the museum offers. The museum also has a gift shop.

♿ 𝄞 **National Historic Trails Interpretive Center** (307-261-7700; http://www .blm.gov/wy/st/en/NHTIC.html), 1501 N. Poplar Street, Casper. (I-25 at Exit 189). Open 8–7 late April through mid-October, 9–4:30 mid-October through late April; $6 per adult, $5 per senior age 60 and older, $4 per student 16 and up with valid ID, children 15 and under free. If you're interested in the historic pioneer trails that crisscrossed Wyoming in the 1800s, you should certainly plan a visit to this museum. Interactive exhibits bring you along on the journeys taken by pioneers and others on the Bozeman, Bridger, California, Mormon, Oregon, and Pony Express Trails. The uniquely constructed center also incorporated its actual construction materials into the exhibits themselves, thus drawing you even closer to the people who passed this way in the past. These include tiles engraved with entries from pioneer diaries as well as illustrations of the various hardships and obstacles faced by travelers along the trails. American Indian history, particularly in relation to the trails, is incorporated as well. See also Pony Express Re-Ride in *Special Events*.

THE NATIONAL HISTORIC TRAILS INTERPRETIVE CENTER

🎨 𝄞 **Nicolaysen Art Museum and Discovery Center** (307-235-5247; http://www.thenic.org), 400 E. Collins Drive, Casper. Open 10–5 Tuesday through Saturday, noon–4 Sunday, closed Monday; $5 per adult, $3 per child (5–17)/student (with ID); on Sundays families get in free. An art

museum that won't bore the kids to tears? You bet—the Nicolaysen Art Museum will keep their little hands and minds busy with its cool and fun hands-on Children's Discovery Center. There they'll learn all about the various forms of media used by artists in creating their masterpieces (and perhaps they'll even create some masterpieces of their own!). The art museum's exhibits feature not only pieces by Wyoming and regional artists, but also national and international artists of note, which are displayed in its eight galleries. Exhibits change frequently, so repeat customers are likely to find something new to engage them with each visit. The museum also has a gift shop. See also Nic Fest in *Special Events.*

&. ✦ ✿ **Tate Geological Museum** (307-268-2447; http://www.caspercollege.edu/tate), 125 College Drive (at Casper College), Casper. Open 9–5 Monday through Friday, 10–4 Saturday; free. Children are particularly welcome at Tate, where the mineral exhibits include a visually stimulating black room, showcasing minerals that glow in the dark. Additional displays include meteorites, Indian artifacts, dinosaur fossils and other fossils (the majority of which are from Wyoming), and crystals. Children (and adults, too) can touch all they want at the museum's touch tables, where mineral specimens are set out to help further their knowledge of the world of minerals through direct interaction. The museum also has a gift shop.

✿ &. **Wyoming Pioneer Memorial Museum** (307-358-9288; http://www.wypioneermuseum.com), 400 W. Center Street, Douglas. Open 8–5 Monday through Friday year-round, 1–5 Saturday; free (donations gladly accepted). This extensive pioneer museum, situated on the state fairgrounds, features an enormous collection of relics and artifacts from the early days of the country's westward expansion. Of course, the focus of the museum is centered on Wyoming's early pioneer families and homesteaders. You'll also enjoy viewing the museum's collection of Western artwork. The museum houses a research library that includes relevant historical documents as well as genealogies, photographs, and books. See also Douglas Invitational Art Show and Sale in *Special Events.*

HISTORIC LANDMARKS, PLACES, AND SITES &. **Fort Fetterman State Historic Site** (307-358-9288; http://wyoparks.state.wy.us/Site/SiteInfo.asp?siteID=15), 752 WY 93, Douglas (exit 140 off I-25). Open 9–5 (Visitor Center and Ordnance Building), sunrise to sunset (grounds), Memorial Day through Labor Day, closed in winter; for day use ($4/resident; $6/nonresident), and camping ($10 resident/$17 nonresident; call 307-358-2864 for reservations). Located at the intersection of the Bozeman Trail and the Oregon Trail, this once critical military supply site preserves and interprets a crucial slice of Wyoming's frontier history. Established by the U.S. military in 1867, after the close of the Civil War, the outpost served as a military base of operations for supplies, and as a starting point for actions taken against the Indians, who were struggling to keep their cultures and lands intact during this time. It also became known as a relatively safe haven for the pioneers passing through on the road to westward expansion. You'll tour through two of the fort's original buildings, which house exhibits on historic Fort Fetterman City, local American Indians and their history, and the military's role in the development of the frontier. A 1-mile interpretive trail guides you to a number of significant points of interest, and picnic tables provide a great place for stopping to eat while reflecting on the past.

🐾 ♿ **Independence Rock State Historic Site** (307-577-5150; http://wyoparks .state.wy.us/Site/SiteInfo.asp?siteID=19), located northeast of Muddy Gap and southwest of Casper on WY 220. Open year-round in daylight hours (no overnight camping allowed); free. Also known as The Register of the Desert, a name given to this huge granite outcropping by Father Peter J. DeSmet way back in 1840, Independence Rock served as an iconic landmark for nearly all of those traveling on the Oregon Trail and other historic trails—as well as a place to leave a mark of their passage for some. Here, though erosion has worn many inscriptions away, you'll still find some of the names and dates inscribed by a number of the more than half-million or so pioneers who passed by this very spot on their journeys to points westward. Christened Independence Rock by William Sublette on the Fourth of July in 1830, the 6,208-foot hunk of stone serves as a silent witness to the veritable flood of pioneers who once traveled through this stark landscape in pursuit of the already legendary and elusive American dream. You are welcome to walk around the rock (it's more than a mile around the base) or even on top of it, but please leave the rock itself as you find it, so that future generations can enjoy this piece of history just as much as you do. See also Devil's Gate in *To See*—Natural Wonders.

See also Douglas Railroad Interpretive Center and Fort Caspar Museum and Historic Site in *To See*—Museums; South Big Horn/Red Wall Scenic Backway in *To See*—Scenic Drives; Teapot Dome in *To See*—Natural Wonders; and Morton Mansion Bed and Breakfast and Hotel Higgins in *Lodging*—Bed and Breakfasts.

CITY PARKS AND GARDENS ♂ ♿ 🐾 **Casper** (307-235-8403; http://www .casperwy.gov) has 45 developed city parks, which include more than 1,200 acres of land. Here you'll find ample opportunities for all sorts of recreational activities, from playgrounds to fishing access, picnic areas to athletic fields, hiking trails to fitness courses, swimming pools to band shells, and more. Print out a free, downloadable parks map and parks brochure from the Web site. See also Fort Caspar Museum and Historic Site in *To See*—Museums; Platte River Parkway in *To Do*—Bicycling; and Casper Whitewater Park in *To Do*—Paddling/Floating.

INDEPENDENCE ROCK STATE HISTORIC SITE

🐾 ♿ 🐕 **Douglas** (http://www.cityof douglas.com) has almost 180 acres of parks and paths to explore, including **Jackalope Square** (Third and Center; picnicking facilities), **Heritage Trail** (4 miles of pedestrian/bicycle paths), and **Washington Park** (Sixth and Oak; playground, pavilions, and picnicking facilities). See also Douglas Municipal Water Park in *To Do*—For Families and Riverside Park in *Lodging*—Campgrounds.

♿ 🐾 🐕 **Glenrock Parks System** (http://www.glenrock.org) has a number of parks and facilities, including **Glenrock Town Park** (east of Deer Creek off Birch Street.), which has a great playground as well as a skateboard park and access to **Al's Way**, a paved, 2.5-mile walking path.

See also Ayres Natural Bridge Park in *To See*—Natural Wonders; and Douglas Municipal Water Park in *To Do*—For Families.

JACKALOPE SQUARE IN DOUGLAS

SCENIC DRIVES **South Big Horn/Red Wall Scenic Backway** takes you on a 100-mile journey, beginning about 15 miles west of Casper via US 20/26 to CR 125 (Bucknam Road). The trek winds northwest on 33-Mile Road (CR 110) to CR 109 (Bighorn Mountain Road) to CR 105 (Buffalo Creek Road) to CR 104 (Arminto/Waltman Road), depositing you back onto US 20/26 at Waltman, west of your starting point. This mostly graveled backcountry drive should be undertaken only in good weather conditions and in a suitable vehicle (meaning that if you're in an RV, you might want to consider spending the day elsewhere). You'll drive through country used historically by some of the first ranchers to inhabit this area, who drove both sheep and cattle to the pastures on the higher ground of the Big Horn Mountains. Along the way, among other wildlife you may see pronghorn antelope, as they make their homes on windswept prairies such as those found here. You'll pass by **Roughlock Hill,** a place where emigrants along the Oregon Trail locked their wagon wheels and simply slid down the steep slope to the valley below, rather than trying to negotiate the hill with rotating wheels—certainly a more dangerous prospect. You can also access the Hole-in-the-Wall Trail (see *To Do*—Hiking in Northeast Wyoming: Sheridan and Buffalo) from this drive by taking Buffalo Creek Road (CR 105) north instead of south.

See also Seminoe to Alcova Scenic Backway in Southeast Wyoming: Rawlins and Laramie.

NATURAL WONDERS 🐾 ♿ **Ayres Natural Bridge Park** (307-358-3532), 208 Natural Bridge Road, 12 miles west and 5 miles south of I-25 at exit 151 (near

AYRES NATURAL BRIDGE

Douglas). Open April through October, dawn through dusk (some overnight camp-ing); free. The lovely red rocks of this park surround the parking area, but it's the top-heavy natural arch of stone over La Prele Creek that gives the park its name. Easily accessed for viewing, the arch is made up of 150 acres of stone, and is pur-portedly one of the few known natural bridges that still have water flowing beneath them. Early pioneers along the Oregon Trail visited the arch during their journeys west, marveling at its solidity, enormity, and beauty. Today the park sur-rounding the arch offers opportunities for picnicking, hiking, camping, and wildlife viewing—but pets are absolutely prohibited, and if you get caught with Fido or Fluffy inside the grounds, you're in for a sizable fine.

Devil's Gate, situated southwest of Casper on WY 220 just southwest of Inde-pendence Rock (see *To See*—Historic Landmarks, Places, and Sites), features a dramatic canyon cut by the Sweetwater River. Here, where the river turns, it has worked through a granite wall, leaving a 330-foot deep canyon that spans 400 feet at its rim, narrowing to a mere 30 feet across where the river flows through it. You'll find a convenient scenic turnout offering you views of this natural phenomenon, which appears much the same as it did to the emigrants who passed this way on the Oregon, Mormon, and Pony Express Trails. This was one of many distinctive natural landmarks that lay along the journey westward through Wyoming. Also, you can stop at the **Mormon Handcart Visitors' Center** (307-328-2953; http://www.lds.org/placestovisit/location/0,10634,1787-1-1-1,00.html), open 8–7 daily (summer), 9–4 daily

DEVILS GATE

(winter); free; situated just up the road at **Sun Ranch/Martin's Cove.** On the National Register of Historic Places, this is where the members of a Mormon pioneer group got trapped for five days while journeying to Salt Lake City in 1856.

Hell's Half Acre can be found 45 miles west of Casper just south of US 20/26 before Waltman. More like 320 acres, this pocket of dramatic, multi-hued badlands-esque terrain earned its name from some of the adventurers who passed this way in the 1830s. These travelers noted not only the area's odd appearance, but also the even odder phenomenon of the sulfuric smoke rising from the ground— the result of the smoldering coal fires that lay beneath the surface, unbeknownst to them at the time. If this terrain seems strangely familiar to you during your visit, then perhaps you actually have seen it before—this was the site where the 1996 film *Starship Troopers* was shot. After all, it does look like the perfect sort of place where we'd imagine aliens would feel right at home, doesn't it? American Indians also used this area as a place to hunt and trap buffalo.

Teapot Dome, situated in the Salt Creek Oil Fields about 25 miles north of Casper via I-25 to WY 259, is the very formation that gave the notorious Teapot Dome Scandal of the early 1920s its name. This distinctively shaped butte would receive national attention not merely for being shaped like a teapot, but also due to its being the defining feature of the richly endowed oil fields surrounding it— fields that would lie at the very heart of the scandal. The Teapot Dome area came under controversy and great scrutiny in its connection with the administration of President Warren G. Harding. The president himself was unaware of the shady goings-on, which involved the illegal conveyance of the oil rights to these and other fields by one of his appointees, Secretary of the Interior Albert Fall, to the oil magnate Harry F. Sinclair. Though the spout and the handle of the teapot were destroyed by a storm in the 1960s, the butte still stands today, not only as a unique natural feature, but also as a symbolic reminder of the scandal that rocked the country in 1923.

HELL'S HALF ACRE

✳ To Do

BICYCLING ♿ **Platte River Parkway** (307-577-1206; http://www.platte riverparkway.org), a paved trail open to non-motorized traffic only, runs for about 10 miles along the North Platte River in Casper, from the **North Casper Soccer Complex** (at K Street. and Beverly Street.) to **Paradise Valley Park** (at the end of Paradise Drive, where it turns into Riverbend Road). In addition, numerous side trails connect the main trail to a variety of recreational areas and parks through the city. These parks include **Casper Park, Crossroads Park,** and **North Platte Park.** Mountain bikers and hikers will find an abundance of trails shooting off the main trail in the section between the North Casper Soccer Complex and the **Historic Trails Overlook Shelter** to the west. Fishing access, several boat ramps, and the Casper Whitewater Park (see *To Do*—Paddling) can be found along the trail as well. See also Casper in City Parks and Gardens and North Platte River in *To Do*—Fishing.

See also *To See*—City Parks and Gardens; Laramie Peak Trail and Muddy Mountain Environmental Education Area Interpretive Nature Trail in *To Do*—Hiking; and *Green Space*.

BOATING 🐟 ♿ **Pathfinder Reservoir and Alcova Reservoir** lie on lands cooperatively managed by Natrona County and the BLM (see *Green Space*—National Lands), and are accessible by taking WY 220 about 30 miles southwest of Casper. For Alcova Reservoir, go south on CR 407 or 406. For Pathfinder Reservoir, go south on CR 408 or 410. Open year-round (visitor center only in summer); free. The larger of the two water bodies, Pathfinder Reservoir, is partially situated in the Pathfinder National Wildlife Refuge (see *Green Space*—Wildlife Refuges and Areas in Southeast Wyoming: Rawlins and Laramie). Three boat ramps gain you access to the enormous reservoir. In addition to boating, recreational opportunities include fishing (brown trout, cutthroat trout, ohrid trout, rainbow trout, and walleye), camping (three campgrounds), a 1.7-mile interpretive hiking trail, and an interpretive center. Alcova Reservoir, though smaller, also features numerous recreational opportunities, including boating (marina, boat ramps, and rental boats). Sailboating and windsurfing are popular here as well as swimming, fishing, and ice fishing (brown trout, cutthroat trout, rainbow trout, and walleye). The reservoir also has a short, interpretive dinosaur trail, camping areas, and picnicking facilities.

See also Casper in *To See*—City Parks and Gardens; Platte River Parkway in *To Do*—Bicycling; North Platte River in *To Do*—Fishing; Edness K. Wilkins State Park in *Green Space*—State Parks; and Goldeneye Wildlife and Recreation Area in *Green Space*—Recreation Areas.

CLIMBING **Fremont Canyon** (http://www.fremontcanyon.com) is situated south of Casper via WY 220 to CR 407 to CR 408 (Fremont Canyon Road). This beautiful rock climbing area features several hundred granite rock climbs ranging from 5.6 to 5.13 in difficulty. Routes ascend above the North Platte River that flows through the canyon, making it imperative that only experienced and well-trained rock climbers challenge themselves on this terrain.

✐ **The Peak Rock Climbing Gym** (307-472-4084; http://www.rockhardkore .com/thepeak.shtml), 410 N. Beverly, Casper. Open Monday through Saturday 9–7; $5 (bouldering) or $8 (toproping), gear rental is extra. Families are welcome. The Peak is run by **Rock Hard Fitness Club** (307-266-1635; http://www.rockhardkore .com), 3037 CY Avenue, Casper. Open Monday through Saturday 9–7; $8. This full-service fitness club includes cardio equipment, tanning beds, fitness equipment, and an easy-chair massage room.

See also *Green Space*; and Seminoe to Alcova Scenic Backway in *To See*—Scenic Drives in Southeast Wyoming: Rawlins and Laramie.

FISHING **North Platte River** (307-473-3400; http://gf.state.wy.us/fish/fishing/ index.asp), originates in northern Colorado, flowing north over the Wyoming border along WY 230 and WY 130 before reaching Seminoe Reservoir, then Kortes Reservoir, then Pathfinder Reservoir, and then Alcova Reservoir. The 5.5-mile stretch between Kortes and Pathfinder is known as the Miracle Mile of the North Platte River (see *To See*—Natural Wonders in Southeast Wyoming: Rawlins and Laramie) due to its abundance of trout, making it one of Wyoming's most renowned blue-ribbon fishing streams. From Alcova Reservoir, the river arcs east, flowing alongside WY 220 to Casper, through Casper, and then roughly along I-25 to Glendo Reservoir and Guernsey Reservoir, making a slow turn toward the south to flow southeast along US 26 past Torrington before crossing the border into Nebraska. In addition to access at the reservoirs and the Miracle Mile section, numerous additional state-run access points can be found along the river's course, some with boat ramps and camping facilities. Species vary depending where you fish the river, but can include brown trout, catfish, cutthroat trout, rainbow trout, and walleye. The river is also popular for floating, float fishing, and whitewater paddling, with a number of access points suitable for these endeavors as well. See also Platte River Parkway in *To Do*—Bicycling; Pathfinder Reservoir and Alcova Reservoir in *To Do*—Boating; Casper Whitewater Park in *To Do*—Paddling/Floating; and Edness K. Wilkins State Park in *Green Space*—State Parks.

Sweetwater River (307-332-7723; http://gf.state.wy.us/fish/fishing/index.asp) flows south from its origins in the Wind River Mountains southwest of Lander before turning east and flowing by South Pass (see *To See*—Historic Landmarks, Places, and Sites in Northwest Wyoming: Lander and Riverton) northeast to Sweetwater Station (along US 287/WY 789 southeast of Lander), and then making its way east past **Split Rock** (a distinctive natural feature recognized as a landmark by emigrants on the Oregon Trail and other historic trails), Devil's Gate (see *To See*—Natural Wonders), and Independence Rock (see *To See*—Historic Landmarks, Places, and Sites), before emptying into Pathfinder Reservoir (see *To Do*—Boating). Species include brook trout, brown trout, cutthroat trout, and rainbow trout. Much of the river flows through private land, making access somewhat difficult, though the state game and fish department has leased some land for access from ranchers and other landowners. You'll find a couple of these points around South Pass, as well as five access points near Sweetwater Station, including two accessed by taking CR 233 (Graham Road) northwest of US 287/WY 789 just west of Sweetwater Station.

See also Casper in *To See*—City Parks and Gardens; *To Do*—Boating; Casper Whitewater Park in *To Do*—Paddling/Floating; and *Green Space*.

FITNESS CENTERS & **Casper Recreation Center** (307-235-8383; http://www.casperwy.gov), 1801 E. Fourth Street, Casper. Open 5 AM–8 PM Monday through Friday, 8–6

THE NORTH PLATTE RIVER

Saturday, 1–6 Sunday (summer; call for hours in other seasons); $3.25 per person. This full-service fitness center has weight rooms and exercise equipment, among other services. Classes, including yoga, are also available. The Rec Center is adjacent to the Casper Ice Arena (see Ice-skating in *To Do—Snow Sports*) and the Casper Family Aquatic Center (see *To Do—For Families*).

See also Glenrock in *To See—Towns*; Casper in *To See—City Parks and Gardens*; and The Peak Rock Climbing Gym in *To Do—Climbing*.

FOR FAMILIES &. ✨ **Casper Family Aquatic Center** (307-235-8383; http://www.casperwy.gov), 1801 E. Fourth Street, Casper. Call or check the Web site for current schedule; $5.50 per person, children under 5 free. In addition to this indoor municipal swimming pool, Casper has five seasonal outdoor swimming pools as well. See also Casper in City Parks and Gardens.

✨ **Casper Planetarium** (307-577-0310; http://www.natronaschools.org/school .php?id-112), 904 N. Poplar Street, Casper. Call for current schedule of shows; $2.50 per person, not recommended for children under 6. Topics covered range from today's hottest astronomical developments to historic and prehistoric themes, including dinosaurs. The planetarium also gives laser light shows set to contemporary popular music.

✨ **Douglas Municipal Water Park** (307-358-4488; http://www.douglaswaterpark .com) 701 E Center, Douglas. Open 11–5 Memorial Day through Labor Day (depending on weather), plus evenings in mid-summer; $3 per person, $2 per child ages 3–7, children under 3 free. Kids will love cooling off at this fun water park, situated in Washington Park (see Douglas in *To See—City Parks and Gardens*).

See also Douglas Railroad Interpretive Center, Glenrock Paleontological Museum, National Historic Trails Interpretive Center, Nicolaysen Art Museum and Discovery Center, and Tate Geological Museum in *To See—Museums*; *To See—City Parks and Gardens*; Casper Whitewater Park in *To Do—Paddling/Floating*; Hogadon Ski Area and Ice-skating in *To Do—Snow Sports*; Adventures West Tours in *To Do—Unique Adventures*; Edness K. Wilkins State Park in *Green Space—State Parks*; and Deer Forks Ranch in *Lodging—Other Options*.

GOLF Casper Country Club (307-265-0767), 4149 E. Country Club Road, Casper, 18 holes.

Casper Golf Club (307-234-2405; http://www.casperwy.gov), 2120 Allendale Boulevard, Casper, 27 holes.

Douglas Community Club & Golf Course (307-358-5099; http://www.douglas golfclub.com), 64 Golf Course Road, Douglas, 18 holes.

Glenrock Golf Course (307-436-5560; http://www.glenrock.org), 933 W. Grove Street, Glenrock, 9 holes.

Paradise Valley Country Club (307-237-3673; http://www.paradisevalleyccwyo .com), 70 Magnolia Street, Casper, 18 holes.

Salt Creek Country Club (307-437-6207), WY 387, Midwest, 9 holes.

Three Crowns Golf Club (307-472-7696; http://www.threecrownsgolfclub.com), 1601 King Boulevard, Casper, 18 holes.

HIKING Laramie Peak Trail, Trail #602, in the Medicine Bow National Forest (see *Green Space*—National Lands), is accessible from Friend Park Campground (see Medicine Bow National Forest in *Lodging*—Camping). You must pay a $2 per vehicle parking fee to use the trail, which involves a steep, somewhat arduous 10-mile round trip to reap the reward—panoramic views from atop 10,772-foot Laramie Peak, the tallest mountain for miles around. Not only will you enjoy the fantastic scenery of this Rocky Mountain peak, but you should also know that for emigrants heading west on the Oregon Trail and other historic trails, this very peak served as a significant landmark indicating their arrival at the Rocky Mountains. For many of these pioneers, this was also the first real mountain they had seen in their lives. So when you hike Laramie, you're not only getting a great workout and taking in fabulous views, but also, you're hiking to the summit of a piece of American history. If that seems too far, just turn around at the beautiful waterfalls about 2 miles up the trail. The trail is also open to use by mountain bikers, horseback riders, and ATVs.

Lee McCune Braille Trail is in Casper Mountain Park (see *Green Space*—Other Wild Places), accessible by taking WY 251 (Casper Mountain Road) 6 miles south of Casper and parking in the Skunk Hollow area. This unique, .3-mile interpretive nature trail includes 36 signs, all of which are written in Braille as well as standard print. The trail also includes guide ropes lining the pathway to help ensure the safety of its visually impaired visitors. Sighted visitors will enjoy the short interpretive walk as well. See also Casper Mountain Campgrounds in *Lodging*—Camping.

& **Muddy Mountain Environmental Education Area Interpretive Nature Trail** is accessible by taking WY 251 9 miles south of Casper to the top of Casper Mountain, and then heading south on CR 505 for roughly 6 miles (3 paved, 3 graveled). Turn east on Circle Drive and proceed another 4 miles to access the area and the trail. Day use is $3. This is an easy, 2-mile interpretive trail open to foot traffic only, situated in the 1,260-acre Muddy Mountain Environmental Education Area (EEA), managed by the BLM (see *Green Space*—National Lands). The trail connects the two (handicapped-accessible) campgrounds in the area (Rim and Lodgepole; $5/night), offering great views of the valley below, as well as potential for viewing wildlife such as antelope and mule deer. Though this trail is limited to foot traffic, the EEA features numerous additional trails, some of which are limited to foot traffic, mountain bikes, and horseback riders, and some of which permit off-road motorized vehicles, including snowmobiles in wintertime. See also BLM Campgrounds in *Lodging*—Campgrounds.

See also Fort Fetterman State Historic Site and Independence Rock State Historic Site in *To See*—Historic Landmarks, Places, and Sites; *To See*—City Parks and Gardens; Ayres Natural Bridge Park in *To See*—Natural Wonders; Platte River Parkway in *To Do*—Bicycling; Pathfinder Reservoir and Alcova Reservoir in *To Do*—Boating; and *Green Space*.

HORSEBACK RIDING See Laramie Peak Trail; Muddy Mountain Environmental Education Area Interpretive Nature Trail in *To Do*—Hiking; *Green Space*; and Deer Forks Ranch in *Lodging*—Other Options.

PADDLING/FLOATING 🏞 🛶 **Casper Whitewater Park** (307-577-1206; http:// www.platteriverparkway.org/whitewater.aspx) is a free, city-owned and operated park for whitewater enthusiasts that runs for a distance of .5 mile on the North Platte River (see also *To Do*—Fishing). The park parallels First Street from Wyoming Boulevard to just east of Poplar Street. The park features four manmade rock structures in the river, designed with beginner and intermediate-level boaters in mind. If you want to experience the excitement of this whitewater park on the North Platte River under the watchful eye of an experienced guide, **Platte River Raft n' Reel** (307-267-0170; http://www.raftnreel.com) runs daily, 40-minute float trips through the park in summertime ($22 per adult, $20 per child ages 12 and under; make reservations in advance). This guide service also offers longer scenic and whitewater rafting trips on the North Platte as well as guided fishing trips; call for details and reservations. See also Platte River Parkway in *To Do*—Bicycling.

See also Pathfinder Reservoir and Alcova Reservoir in *To Do*—Boating; North Platter River in *To Do*—Fishing; and *Green Space*.

RELAXATION AND REJUVENATION **Alpenglow of Wyoming Natural Foods** (307-234-4196; http://www.alpenglownaturalfoods.com), 109 E. Second Street, Casper. Open 9:30–6 Monday through Friday, 9:30–5 Saturday. This family-owned and -operated establishment has been a Casper mainstay since 1967. The store's huge selection includes supplements, vitamins, bulk foods, organic foods, gluten-free foods, beauty products, incense, gifts, and more.

🏞 **Bamboo Spa & Salon** (307-234-9033; http://www.bamboospasaloncasper.com), 214 S. Wolcott, Casper. Call to make an appointment in advance. This luxurious Aveda spa and salon offers a full range of hair- and body-care services. Pamper yourself on your vacation with the Ultimate Gift, an intensive spa experience that includes a massage, an exfoliation, a facial, a pedicure, and a delicious spa lunch ($210).

The Purple Potato (307-358-0132; http://www.thepurplepotato.com), 117 N. Second Street, Douglas. Open 10–5 Monday through Friday. This small, family-owned health food store is just off Douglas' main drag. Step inside to fill up on all of your fresh, organic grocery needs. Weekly lists of what's in stock are posted on the Web site. They also sell gluten-free products.

Rising Lotus Wellness Center/Rising Lotus Allergy Center, LLC (307-577-6333; http://www.risinglotus.net), 132 W. Collins Drive, Casper. Call to make an appointment in advance. Rising Lotus offers acupuncture and a variety of massage modalities, along with

BAMBOO SPA & SALON

Chinese medicine, allergy treatment, detoxification, weight loss programs, smoking cessation programs, and much more.

See also The Peak Rock Climbing Gym in *To Do*—Climbing and Casper Recreation Center in *To Do*—Fitness Centers.

SNOW SPORTS **Cross-country skiing** opportunities are virtually limitless in this region, with miles and miles of trails for both the fit and seasoned skier as well as the novice to explore. A good place to start is the **Casper Nordic Center** (307-235-4772; http://www.caspernordic.com), located in Casper Mountain Park (see *Green Space*—Other Wild Places), accessible by driving south on WY 251 (Casper Mountain Road) for 8 miles. The center features 25 miles (42 km) of trails groomed for skate skiing, cross-country skiing, and snowshoeing, including a 0.7 mile (1.2 km) lighted loop trail for night skiing ($5 per person for access to all trails). You can purchase a ski pass, rent skis, and get more information on area trails from **Mountain Sports** (307-266-1136), 543 S. Center Street.

✍ **Hogadon Ski Area** (307-235-8499; http://www.casperwy.gov/Content/Leisure/ hogadon/hogadon.asp), Casper Mountain Park, 11 miles south of Casper via WY 251 (physical address); 1800 E. K Street, (mailing address), Casper. Owned and managed by the city of Casper, this small, family-oriented ski area features easy access from the city, and terrain suitable for all ability levels. The area welcomes snowboarders as well as skiers. Daily ski rentals are available from Mountain Sports (see above). Lifts: Two double chairlifts and one Poma lift. Trails: 15 trails—20 percent beginner, 40 percent intermediate, and 40 percent expert. Vertical Drop: 600 feet. Snowmaking: 50 percent. Facilities: Full-service restaurant and snack bar. Ski School: Offers lessons for all ages and ability levels. For children: Age-specific lessons are available; on-premises childcare is not available. Rates: $37 adult (19 and older), $31 student (13–18), $21 child (5–12), $14 for Poma lift only; half-day rates available as well.

Ice fishing opportunities can be found in this region at a number of its lakes and reservoirs. Throw your line in at Pathfinder Reservoir and Alcova Reservoir (see *To Do*—Boating), among other popular spots.

🐾 ✍ **Ice-skating** is available at the **Casper Ice Arena** (307-235-8484; http:// www.casperwy.gov/Content/Leisure/cia/ice.asp), 1801 E. Fourth Street. Call for current public skating hours; $3 per person, $2 extra for skate rental, children 4 and under free with paid admission.

Snowmobiling opportunities in this region are incredible, including 46 miles of signed, groomed trails located just south of Casper in Casper Mountain Park (see *Green Space*—Other Wild Places). For detailed trail reports, call 307-777-6560 or go to http://wyotrails.state.wy.us/snow, the Wyoming Snowmobile Trails Web site, which also provides information about rules, rental agencies, trails around the state, and more. See also Muddy Mountain Environmental Education Area Interpretive Nature Trail in *To Do*—Hiking.

Snowshoeing is a great way to explore this region's abundance of developed trails in wintertime. You'll find plenty of trails to keep you busy and warm in the Medicine Bow National Forest (see *Green Space*—National Lands) and Casper Mountain Park (see *Green Space*—Other Wild Places).

UNIQUE ADVENTURES 🛷 **Adventures West Tours** (1-877-TOUR-WYO or 307-577-1226; http://www.usatouring.com), 4486 Moonbeam Road, Casper. Let Adventures West be your guide to all things western! This tour company can provide you with a number of unique and interactive western adventures. You can take a six-hour Wagons Ho wagon train journey on the historic Oregon Trail, learning about the pioneers who passed this way from your costumed guide while you ride ($100 per adult; $40 per child 2–12, under 2 free). You'll also enjoy a meal cooked the old-fashioned way—in a Dutch oven, on the campfire. This package also includes admission to the Fort Caspar Museum and Historic Site (see *To See*—Historic Landmarks, Places, and Sites) and National Historic Trails Interpretive Center (see *To Do*—Museums). Adventure Tours also does multiday wagon train rides, among its other western adventures.

See also Glenrock Paleontological Museum in *To See*—Museums.

WINERIES AND WINE TASTINGS See Lockwood Vineyards Wine Tasting in *Special Events*.

✳ Green Space

STATE PARKS ♿ 🛷 **Edness K. Wilkins State Park** (307-577-5150; http://wyo parks.state.wy.us/Site/SiteInfo.asp?siteID=5), 6 miles east of Casper on US 20/26/87. Open 7 AM–10 PM daily; $4 (resident), $6 (nonresident). This 315-acre park is a popular place for family outings in summertime—for good reason. Three playgrounds, a pond with a sandy beach, numerous picnic areas, and 2.8 miles of paved, handicapped-accessible trails are just some of the park's attractions. The park also features a boat ramp perfect for launching canoes and rafts, bird-watching opportunities aplenty, and fishing in the North Platte River (see *To Do*— Fishing).

NATIONAL LANDS **Medicine Bow National Forest** (307-745-2300; http:// www.fs.fed.us/r2/mbr), 2468 Jackson Street, Laramie. Though the forest lies mostly south (see listing in Southeast Wyoming: Rawlins and Laramie), this region is home to the land managed by the Douglas Ranger District (307-358-4690), 2250 E. Richards Street, Douglas. The central feature of this district is the **Laramie Mountains**, which run from just southeast of Casper on a southeastern slant to just northwest of Wheatland, with I-25 arcing around them. In and around the Laramie Mountains, you'll find numerous recreational opportunities, including fishing (LaBonte Creek is a popular spot), hiking (see Laramie Peak Trail in *To Do*—Hiking), mountain biking, camping, picnicking, rock climbing (LaBonte Canyon has technical routes), off-road vehicle travel (ATVs and snowmobiles), horseback riding, snow sports, hunting, wildlife viewing, and more. The Douglas Ranger District also manages the Thunder Basin National Grassland, situated northeast of Casper (see listing in Northeast Wyoming: Gillette and the Devils Tower Area). See also *Lodging*—Campgrounds.

Bureau of Land Management (BLM) (307-261-7600; http://www.blm.gov/wy/ st/en/field_offices/Casper.html), Casper Field Office, 2987 Prospector Drive, Casper. This BLM field office manages more than 32,500 square miles of public lands and has administrative responsibility for more than 17,000. Much of the land administered by the BLM is open to recreational pursuits, including bicycling, boating, camping (see *Lodging*—Campgrounds), fishing, hiking, horseback riding, paddling, rock climbing, wildlife viewing (including wild horses) and snow sports, including snowmobiling and cross-country skiing. BLM lands tend to be the most unregulated of public lands, meaning that most typical outdoor recreational pursuits are allowed on most BLM lands, guided by the dictates of Leave No Trace (1-800-332-4100 or 303-442-8222; http://www.lnt.org) outdoor ethics. To find out general information about the BLM lands in this region, including maps, developed campgrounds, and other recreational pursuits, contact the field office.

RECREATION AREAS ⚘ **Goldeneye Wildlife and Recreation Area,** partially managed by the BLM (see *Green Space*—National Lands), is 29 miles northwest of Casper just off US 20/26. It offers boating, fishing, and wildlife viewing opportunities.

WILDLIFE REFUGES AND AREAS ⚘ **Pathfinder National Wildlife Refuge** (970-723-8202; http://refuges.fws.gov/profiles/index.cfm?id=65523), accessible by taking WY 220 southwest of Alcova for 20 miles to CR 410 (Buzzard Road), or turning off earlier at CR 409 (Pathfinder Road). Open dawn to dusk; free. This unstaffed national refuge was set aside by an executive order in 1928. Actually made up of four separate tracts of land, the refuge totals 16,807 acres, established mainly to protect and provide habitat for migratory waterfowl. Wyoming Audubon assists with the management of this refuge, and helped to create the interpretive signs and overlook for visitors. Additional wildlife viewing opportunities include small mammals such as cottontail rabbits, as well as mule deer and pronghorn antelope, among others. Fishing and hunting are also popular activities. See also Pathfinder Reservoir and Alcova Reservoir in *To Do*—Boating.

OTHER WILD PLACES Casper Mountain Park (307-235-9311; http://www .natrona.net), located just south of Casper via WY 251, along with the adjacent **Beartrap Meadow Park,** is a 3,000-acre area managed by the Natrona County Roads, Bridges, and Parks Department. The area features recreational opportunities for all sorts of outdoor enthusiasts, including bicycling (mountain biking trails), camping (see Casper Mountain Campgrounds in *Lodging*—Campgrounds), hiking, off-road vehicle use, snow sports, and more.

See also Ayres Natural Bridge Park in *To See*—Natural Wonders.

✳ Lodging

BED AND BREAKFASTS

Casper

ᵗᵀᵗ ✎ ⚘ **Casper Mountain Bed and Breakfast** (307-237-6712; http://www .caspermountainbnb.com), 4471 S. Center Street. You'll feel right at home at this unpretentious B&B, situated in a peaceful residential neighborhood in Casper. Stay in one of two clean, comfortable guest rooms that share a bath-

room. Enjoy access to the lovely deck and the yard with mountain views. Every morning you'll be treated to a delicious, homemade breakfast. Inexpensive to moderate.

ᵗᵀᵗ ♿ **Ivy House Inn Bed and Breakfast** (307-265-0974; http://www .ivyhouseinn.com), 815 S. Ash Street. A

BnBfinder.com Property of Distinction, this historic, Cape Cod-style house accommodates travelers in one of five well-appointed, uniquely themed guest rooms or suites. From the masculine Fir Tree Lodge to the whimsical island feel of the Palm Tree Court, both of the suites include private bathrooms, kitchenettes, and private entrances. The three guest rooms on the main floor share a guest kitchen and two bathrooms in the hall. Additional amenities include a hot tub and Internet access in each room. A full breakfast is served daily. Moderate to expensive.

🍴 🐾 **Red Butte Ranch Privacy Lodging** (307-472-3784; http://www .redbutteranchlodging.com), 8550 S. Bessemer Bend. Privacy, solitude, and the grandeur of nature will define your stay at Red Butte Ranch. Your private cottage (sleeping up to six people) rests on the shores of the North Platte River, with the splendor of Bessemer Mountain's red rock formations as your backdrop. Furnished with rustic log furniture, the cottage has a full kitchen and a full bath (expensive). Access to the river is a few short steps out your door. Or, if you prefer, you can take a room in the main house (inexpensive). Outdoor pets are welcome. Either way, breakfast is included.

♿ 🍴 **Sunburst Lodge Bed and Breakfast** (307-235-9086; http://www .sunburst-lodge.com), 2700 Micro Road, Casper. Situated on Casper Mountain, this relatively new (2006–7) B&B is close enough to town to be convenient, yet far enough from the bustle to serve as your peaceful retreat. Hiking trails, scenic vistas, and delicious food await you, along with luxurious accommodations. Expensive.

Douglas

🍴 **Morton Mansion Bed and Breakfast** (307-358-2129; http://www

.mortonmansion.com), 425 E. Center Street. Listed on the National Register of Historic Places, this 1903 Queen Anne Victorian mansion features an elegant formal parlor and dining room, a wraparound porch, and beautiful antiques throughout. The mansion is situated in close proximity to local attractions including the Wyoming Pioneer Memorial Museum (see *To See—Museums*). A full breakfast is served each morning. Moderate to expensive.

Glenrock

🍴 ♿ 🐾 **Hotel Higgins** (1-800-458-0144 or 307-436-9212; http://www .higginshotel.com), 416 W. Birch Street, P.O. Box 741. Constructed in the early 20th century, Hotel Higgins has been restored to its former grandeur, and it is listed on the National Register of Historic Places. Guests stay in one of six rooms, all with private baths. The house's décor includes antique period pieces, including brass beds, iron beds, and oak and walnut dressers, which fit in nicely with the deep mahogany and stained oak woodwork of the interior. Guests enjoy a full-service breakfast served

HOTEL HIGGINS

daily. Moderate to expensive. Also on the premises is the acclaimed fine-dining establishment, **The Paisley Shawl,** serving gourmet American food for lunch and dinner (expensive), as well as the full-service **Highlander Bar and Lounge**.

HOTELS AND MOTELS
Casper
🦐 **Ranch House Motel** (307-266-4044), 1130 E. F Street, Casper. This simple, little, older motel offers you an alternative to paying a high price for accommodations. It may not be fancy, but you can shower and sleep for cheap here. Inexpensive.

Douglas
¶¹ 🦐 🐾 ♪ ♿ **The Plains Motel** (307-358-4484; http://www.douglasplains.com), 628 E. Richards Street, Douglas. This family-owned and -operated establishment is perfect for travelers on a budget. You'll also find an on-premises restaurant (inexpensive to moderate), coffee shop (open 24/7), an old-fashioned ice cream store, and a gift shop. Inexpensive to moderate.

CAMPGROUNDS
♿ **BLM Campgrounds** (see Bureau of Land Management in *Green Space*—National Lands) in this area include the two developed campgrounds (managed by the Casper Field Office) inside the Muddy Mountain Environmental Education Area (see Muddy Mountain Environmental Education Area Interpretive Nature Trail in *To Do*—Hiking).

Casper Mountain Campgrounds (307-235-9311) include **Beartrap Meadow Campground** (7 miles south of town on Casper Mountain Road (WY 251), **Casper Mountain Campground** (8 miles south of town on Casper Mountain Road (WY 251), **Gray Reef Reservoir Campground**

(26 miles west of town on WY 220), and **Ponderosa Park Campground** (10 miles south on WY 1301). Very inexpensive. See also Casper Mountain Park in *Green Space*—Other Wild Places.

¶¹ ♪ **Casper KOA Campground** (1-888-562-4704 or 307-577-1664; http://www.casperkoa.com), 1101 Prairie Lane, Bar Nunn. You'll find a playground, a covered pool and hot tub, and a miniature golf course here in addition to the usual KOA accommodations, including RV sites, tent sites, and cabins. Inexpensive.

¶¹ ♪ **Douglas KOA Campground** (1-800-562-2469 or 307-358-2164; http://www.douglaskoa.com), 168 Cold Springs Road, Douglas. This KOA has a miniature golf course, heated swimming pool, and cabin rentals, plus all the usual amenities, including both RV and tent camping areas. Very inexpensive.

¶¹ ♪ **Fort Caspar Campground** (1-888-243-7709 or 307-234-3260; http://www.ftcasparcamp.org), 4205 Fort Caspar Road, Casper. This full-service RV park includes playgrounds, nature trails, fishing access, and a game room as well as all of the usual amenities. Very inexpensive to inexpensive. See also Fort Caspar Museum and Historic Site in *To See*—Historic Landmarks, Places, and Sites.

Medicine Bow National Forest (see *Green Space*—National Lands) has four, first-come, first-served developed campgrounds in this region as well as plentiful opportunities for dispersed camping (free). All of the developed campgrounds provide access to trails suitable for both hiking and mountain biking, while some also have opportunities for fishing, horseback riding, rock climbing, and off-road vehicle use as well. **Campbell Creek Campground** ($5; open June 1 through

October 15) is accessible by taking WY 91 (Cold Springs Road) for about 20 miles southwest of Douglas, and then going 13 miles southwest on CR 24. **Curtis Gulch Campground** ($10; open June 15 through October 15) is accessible by taking WY 91 for 20 miles southwest of Douglas, going south for 14 miles on CR 16, and then east for 4 miles on FR 658. **Esterbrook Campground** ($10; open May 15 through October 15) is accessible by taking WY 94 for 17 miles south of Douglas, going 11 miles south on CR 5, and then 3 miles east on FR 633. **Friend Park Campground** ($10; open June 1 through October 15) is accessible by taking WY 94 south 17 miles south of Douglas, going 11 miles south on CR 5, going 15 miles southwest on FR 653, and then 3.5 miles southeast on FR 671, turning left at the sign for the campground and proceeding another 1 mile to reach it. This campground is also the access point for the Laramie Peak Trail (see *To Do*—Hiking). The district also rents out the **LaPrele Guard Station,** a two-bedroom CCC-built log cabin 40 miles from Douglas, to overnight visitors ($80; call 1-877-444-6777 for reservations or make them at http://www.recreation.gov).

🐟 **Riverside Park** (307-358-9750), 420 W. Grant. This park is run by the City of Douglas (see *To See*—City Parks and Gardens). Campers are allowed to stay for a maximum of 48 hours (free). The park has 20 campsites, water, showers, restrooms, and picnic tables.

See also Fort Fetterman State Historic Site in *To See*—Historic Landmarks, Places, and Sites; Ayres Natural Bridge Park in *To See*—Natural Wonders; Pathfinder Reservoir and Alcova Reservoir in *To Do*—Boating; and North Platte River in *To Do*—Fishing;

OTHER OPTIONS
Casper
See Red Butte Ranch Privacy Lodging in Bed and Breakfasts.

Douglas
✦ **Deer Forks Ranch** (307-358-2033; http://www.guestranches.com/deer forks), 1200 Poison Lake Road. Deer Forks offers guests lodging in one of two well-appointed, log guest houses. The houses both include fully equipped, modern kitchens, two bedrooms (one with queen-sized bed), private bathrooms, and a living room. Another option is to take the guest room in the main house, or to go big and rent a six-bedroom, three-bathroom house. Linens are provided, so guests just need to bring food. Guests can also request to partake in family-style breakfasts and dinners in advance (extra fee), or to join in on horseback rides (extra fee). Children under 16 are half price on accommodations and meals. Moderate to expensive.

See also Medicine Bow National Forest in Campgrounds.

✳ Where to Eat
EATING OUT
Casper
Metro Coffee Company (307-472-5042; http://www.metrocoffeeco.com), 241 S. David. Open 6:30 AM–11 AM Monday through Friday, 8–noon Saturday, 3 PM–midnight Tuesday through Saturday. Spacious and inviting, the dark hues of the Metro Coffee House's interior evoke the sense of a European coffeehouse. Step up to the counter and select from an array of coffee specialty drinks, or just have a cup of the house brew—or a smoothie, if you prefer. Choose a delicacy or light snack to accompany your beverage, with options including pastries, muffins, bagels, ice cream, and desserts. Then

you can saunter back to find the perfect seat to enjoy your treat—maybe a couch, or an overstuffed chair? You never know . . . even though you are in the middle of Wyoming, you might end up caught in the middle of an intellectual debate as the sensations of the continent infuse your soul. The Metro hosts live entertainment and other events as well. Inexpensive.

🍴 **Poor Boys Steak House** (307-237-8325; http://www.poorboyssteakhouse.com), 739 N. Center Street. Open 11–2 (lunch) and 5–closing (dinner) daily. Want a big ole steak? Love huge portion sizes? Then head on over to Poor Boys, where they guarantee that you won't ever leave the table hungry. You can dine in the regular restaurant, or choose to have your meal in the Pump Room, a western bar with an array of microbrews on tap that serves the full dinner menu. Along with steaks in more than a dozen varieties (and up to 20 ounces in size), you can also choose from an assortment of salads, chicken dishes, pork, pastas, ribs, seafood, burgers, and sandwiches. Desserts are rich, varied, and extravagant. A children's menu is available. Expensive.

🍴 **Sidelines Sports Bar** (307-234-9444; http://www.sidelines.us), 1121 Wilkins Circle. Open 11–2 (lunch) and 5–9 (dinner) Monday through Friday, 11–9 Saturday and Sunday. If you're looking to catch a sporting event during your travels and to grab some food and fun with it, this is the place. The 12,000-square-foot facility has more than 30 televisions, including 5 big screen TVs, plus a game room with pool tables and darts. At night, the sports bar transforms into a hopping nightclub, with a deejay and dancing until 2 AM. If you're hungry for a meal, the extensive menu features an array of sandwiches, burgers, pub-style appetizers, salads, soups, sandwiches, and full

entrées with all of the fixings. If you love meat, you can even treat yourself to a multi-meat plate (you'll see what I mean). A children's menu is available. Moderate to expensive.

See also La Costa Mexican Restaurant (below); Blue Heron Books and Espresso in *Selective Shopping*; and The Jazz Spot in *Entertainment*.

Douglas

La Costa Mexican Restaurant (307-358-2449), 1213 Teton Way. Open 11–9 Sunday through Thursday, 11–10 Friday through Saturday. In the mood for some south of the border fare? Step into La Costa, and you're there! Nacho lovers will rejoice when they read the seven different nacho options on the menu—if you're like me, you're always happy to substitute this substantial appetizer for an entrée. If you're not such a cheese fiend, you'll certainly find another Mexican dish on the extensive menu (try the José Special if you're really hungry) that suits your desire for spicy food, whether you prefer a burrito, fajitas, taco salad, enchiladas, or a combination plate. Generous sides accompany each main dish. Moderate to expensive. La Costa also has a Casper location (307-235-6599), 1600 E. Second Street.

See also The Plains Motel in *Lodging*—Hotels and Motels.

DINING OUT

Casper

Dsasumo (307-237-7874; http://www.dsasumo.com), 320 W. First Street, Casper. Open 11–2:30 (lunch) and 4:30–9 (dinner) Monday through Thursday, 11–2:30 and 4:30–10:30 Friday, 11–10 Saturday. Whether you're in search of sumptuous sushi or Thai/Asian fusion food, you'll find it here at this locally acclaimed restaurant. Settle into the meticulously decorated restaurant, order a cocktail, and await your delicious eating experience. Expensive.

303, Inc. (307-233-4303), 303 S. Wolcott, Casper. Open 11–2 (lunch) Monday through Friday, 5:30–10 (dinner) Monday through Saturday. Housed in the historic Prairie Publishing Company Building, 303 sports an elegant atmosphere, world-influenced cuisine, and an incredible selection of wines handpicked from around the globe. The menu features a wide selection of inspired and creative items—including a number of intriguing vegetarian options. Even the most basic of entrées here has a special, unique twist, such as an espresso-crusted filet mignon or mac 'n' cheese prepared with Gouda and lobster. Expensive to very expensive.

Glenrock
See Hotel Higgins in *Lodging*—Bed and Breakfasts.

✳ Entertainment

America Stadium Theatre (307-472-4747, http://www.wyomovies.com), 119 S. Center Street, Casper.

🚻 **Casper Events Center** (1-800-442-2256 or 307-577-3030; http://www.casperwy.gov), 1 Events Drive, Casper. This events center hosts rodeos and other sporting events as well as trade shows, concerts, and other performing arts events. Call or check online for a current schedule.

🎦 **Eastridge Movie 4 $ Saver** (307-472-7469; http://www.wyomovies.com), 601 S.E. Wyoming Boulevard, Casper.

Fox III Theatre (307-472-4747, http://www.wyomovies.com), 150 W. Second Street, Casper.

Iris Stadium 8 (307-472-4747, http://www.wyomovies.com), 230 W. Yellowstone Highway, Casper.

🎵 🎶 **The Jazz Spot** (307-235-JAZZ; http://www.thejazzspot.net), 128 E.

Second Street, Casper. Open for breakfast 8–2 Saturday and Sunday, lunch 11–3 Monday through Sunday, dinner 5–10 Wednesday through Saturday. The whole family is welcome to eat and catch some tunes here, whether you're on stage yourself (for karaoke night), or there's a genuine musical act in town. Expensive.

Mesa Theatre (307-358-6209), 104 N. Third Street, Douglas.

Rialto Theatre (307-472-4747, http://www.wyomovies.com), 100 E. Second Street, Casper.

Studio City Stadium 10 (307-472-4747, http://www.wyomovies.com), 5020 E. Second Street, Casper (under construction at publication time).

Wyoming Symphony Orchestra (307-266-1478; http://wso.ramshorn.us), 130 W. Second Street, Casper.

See also Metro Coffee Company and Sidelines Sports Bar in *Where to Eat*—Eating Out.

✳ Selective Shopping

Blackberry Mountain Gift Shoppe (307-234-6605; http://www.bbmgs.com), 251 S. Center Street, Casper. Open 10–5 Tuesday through Friday, 10–2 Saturday. At this charming gift shop you'll find one-of-a-kind hand-stitched art pieces available for purchase, along with a full array of candles, gift cards, home décor items, jewelry, and more.

Blue Heron Books & Espresso (307-265-3774; http://www.blueheronwyoming.com), Atrium Plaza, Casper. Open 9–5 Monday through Saturday. Independent bookstore lovers, rejoice! Situated in the Atrium Plaza in historic downtown Casper, this establishment in Casper is still doing well, making for a great place to stop in, grab a coffee treat, and browse through its eclectic collection of books—or just hang out with friends in a cool setting. The Atrium also houses **Donells Candies and Homemade Ice Cream** (1-877-461-2009 or 307-234-6283; http://www.donellschocolates.com), open 10–6 Monday through Thursday, 10–8 Friday through Saturday; and **Country Charm Gift and Gourmet** (307-265-4438), open 9:30–5:30 Monday through Friday, 9:30–5 Saturday.

Casper Artists' Guild/West Wind Art Gallery (307-265-2655; http://www.casperbusiness.com/ArtistsGuild), 1040 W. 15th Street. Open noon–4 Tuesday through Saturday. Support local artists by stopping in, browsing through the gift shop, and picking out a piece of artwork to take home with you.

See also Glenrock Paleontological Museum, Nicolaysen Art Museum and Discovery Center, and Tate Geological Museum in *To See*—Museums; Alpenglow of Wyoming Natural Foods and The Purple Potato in *To Do*—Relaxation and Rejuvenation; and The Plains Motel in *Lodging*—Hotels and Motels.

✷ Special Events

May: **Lockwood Vineyards Wine Tasting** (307-577-5000), Casper: An annual fine wine tasting event along with hors d'oeuvres takes place at the Holiday Inn.

June: **Pony Express Re-Ride** (http://www.xphomestation.com), Atlantic City, Casper, Douglas, and Torrington: This annual reenactment of the entire Pony Express ride from Missouri to California is performed by the National Pony Express Association. Contact the National Historic Trails Interpretive Center (see *To See*—Museums) for details.

↗ *June:* **Nic Fest** (http://www.nicfest.org), Casper: An annual art show that includes exhibitions, entertainment, kids' activities, and more.

↗ *July:* **Fort Caspar Chautauqua,** Fort Caspar Museum and Historic Site (see *To See*—Museums): An annual historical celebration featuring reenactments, period dress, food booths, children's activities, and music.

July: **Douglas Railroad Days,** Douglas: This celebration of railroads includes a train-related photography and art exhibition and a model train show.

July: **Beartrap Summer Festival** (307-266-5252; http://www.beartrapsummerfestival.com), Casper: The annual music festival includes vendor booths, plenty of live music, and more.

↗ *August:* **Wyoming State Fair** (307-358-2398; http://www.wystatefair.com), Douglas: A traditional state fair featuring food vendors, booths, livestock, entertainment, and more.

August: **Douglas Invitational Art Show and Sale,** Douglas: This annual benefit for the Wyoming Pioneer Memorial Museum (see *To See*—Museums) includes a silent auction, artist demonstrations, and an art sale.

WHEATLAND AND TORRINGTON

W heatland, about 70 miles north of Cheyenne on I-25, is the county seat of Platte County, with about 3,500 inhabitants. An agricultural town, Wheatland is also home to a good-sized industrial power plant, the Laramie River Station (tours by appointment only; see Ruts to Reservoir in *To See*—Scenic Drives). In Wheatland, you'll find an array of visitor services (including parks, a swimming pool, and a bowling alley) as well as easy access to the surrounding recreational opportunities, including the Laramie Mountains in the Medicine Bow National Forest (see *Green Space*—National Lands). History buffs and architecture aficionados should be sure to drive past the **Platte County Courthouse,** built in 1911, as well as to visit the Laramie Peak Museum (see *To See*—Museums), among other historical attractions within the city.

Torrington is east of Wheatland near the Nebraska border. Back in pioneer times, Torrington was on or near the path of many of the area's historic trails, including the Oregon Trail and the Mormon Trail, and you'll find evidence of early travelers and former settlements both in and around the town. Today, this town of almost 6,000 people welcomes visitors to explore its historic downtown district with a self-guided walking tour that will gain you a greater understanding of this area's past. You can also stop for a picnic lunch in Torrington—in addition to Pioneer Park (see *To Do*—Camping), the city has five other parks, including a skate park. Joggers and cyclists will enjoy the 10-block paved **Grassroots Trails** that go through residential areas of town. Dining options in Torrington include a number of restaurants along US 26 and Main Street, mainly serving traditional American food, as well as Mexican and Chinese options. North of Torrington on US 85 about halfway to Lusk (see *To See*—Towns), you'll find the **Jay Em Historic District,** listed on the National Register of Historic Places, which affords you another chance to explore the pioneer history of this region.

PLATTE COUNTY COURTHOUSE

Beyond these two cities, this region features a number of notable towns (see *To See*—Towns), each with their own distinctive amenities and character. You'll also discover an impressive amount of Green Space to explore. What else? Don't forget Fort Laramie National Historic Site (see *To See*—Historic Landmarks, Places, and Sites), or to stop for a free taste of chili from the Chugwater Chili Corporation (see *Selective Shopping*). And perhaps best of all (at least for the traveler on a budget), you'll discover that this area has many free and very inexpensive attractions.

GUIDANCE Goshen County Chamber of Commerce (307-532-3879; http://www.goshencountychamber.com), 350 W. 21st Avenue, Torrington, 82240.

Platte County Chamber of Commerce (307-322-2322; http://www.plattechamber.com), 65 16th Street, Wheatland, 82201.

GETTING THERE *By car:* Torrington is located at the junction of US 26 and US 85 in southeastern Wyoming. Wheatland is on I-25 about 70 miles north of Cheyenne.

By plane: **Cheyenne Regional Airport** (307-634-7071; http://www.cheyenneairport.com) is about 70 miles south of Wheatland.

GETTING AROUND You'll do fine walking around the downtown areas of both Wheatland and Torrington, but you'll need to get in your car to explore the rest of the region's towns and outlying attractions.

MEDICAL EMERGENCY Dial 911.

Community Hospital (307-532-4181), 2000 Campbell Drive, Torrington.

Niobrara Health and Life Center (307-334-4000; http://www.niobrarahospital.com), 921 Ballancee Avenue, Lusk.

Platte County Memorial Hospital (307-322-3636), 201 14th Street, Wheatland.

✳ To See

TOWNS Chugwater, located at exit 54 off I-25, might just be best known for the Chugwater Chili Cook-off (see *Special Events*). The town has a population of about 250, but it's probably at least three times that during the cook-off. For more information: **Chugwater, Wyoming** (http://www.chugwater.com). See also Chugwater Chili Corporation in *Selective Shopping*.

Glendo is a town of about 230 residents located 100 miles north of Cheyenne on I-25 near Glendo State Park (see *Green Space*—State Parks). It is also home to the **Glendo Historical Museum** (307-735-4314); 204 S. Yellowstone. For more information: **Town of Glendo** (http://www.glendowy.com).

Guernsey is northeast of Wheatland and east of I-25 on US 26. This town of about 1,200 lies 1 mile south of Guernsey State Park (see *Green Space*—State Parks). Named for a New Yorker who came to the area in the late 19th century to become a legislator, rancher, and author, Guernsey is directly on the Oregon Trail and is surrounded by a number of related historical attractions. Stop at the **Guernsey Visitor Center and Museum** (307-836-2715), 90 S. Wyoming Avenue—open 9–7 Monday through Saturday, noon–4 Sunday, Memorial Day through Labor Day—to get your bearings. Guernsey also has the **North Platte**

River Walk, a 2.5-mile trail circling the city, and the **City of Guernsey Swimming Pool** (307-836-2923), 58 S. Wyoming Avenue. For more information: **Town of Guernsey** (http://www.townofguernseywy.us).

Lingle is 10 miles west of Torrington at the junction of US 85 N and US 26. About 500 people call Lingle home. The seasonal **Lingle Municipal Pool** at **Whipple Park** (307-837-2794) offers families a chance to cool off and perhaps catch a performance in the patriotically painted band shell. For more information: **Town of Lingle** (http://www.townoflingle.org).

LINGLE'S PATRIOTICALLY PAINTED BAND SHELL

Lusk is at the junction of US 20 and US 85. This town of 1,500 puts on the annual Legend of Rawhide (see *Special Events*). It is also home to the Stagecoach Museum (see *To See—Museums*). For more information: **Niobrara Chamber of Commerce** (1-800-223-5875 or 307-334-2950; http://www.luskwyoming.com), 224 S. Main Street, Lusk, 82225.

MUSEUMS ♿ ⚘ **Homesteaders Museum** (307-532-5612; http://www.city-of -torrington.org/museum.htm), 495 Main Street, Torrington. Open 9:30–4 Monday through Wednesday, 9:30–7 Thursday through Friday, noon–6 Saturday, June 1 through August 28; 9:30–4 Monday through Friday (off-season); free (donations gladly accepted). Situated in the historic Union Pacific railroad depot, this local history museum features relics and artifacts detailing the area's past, all of which were donated by the people of Goshen County. Included are exhibits on the history of the local Indians, the pioneers, ranching, military service, and more. Of particular interest is a shack, constructed by Ben Trout in 1910, which viscerally illustrates some aspects of the difficulties of eking out a living in this area in the early 20th century.

♿ ⚘ **Laramie Peak Museum** (307-322-2052), 1601 16th Street, Wheatland. Open 10–5 Monday through Friday, 10–3 Saturday, May through September; free (donations gladly accepted). This local history museum features collections and exhibits illustrating the history of the Wheatland area.

♿ **Stagecoach Museum** (307-334-3444), 322 S. Main Street, Lusk. Open 10–5 Monday through Saturday; $2 per adult, children under 10 free. Along with one of the last remaining stagecoaches from the Cheyenne-Black Hills Stage Line, this museum also has a number of other old buggies, a storefront, and additional artifacts and exhibits detailing the local area's history.

See also Glendo in *To See—Towns*, and Guernsey State Park in *Green Space—State Parks*.

HISTORIC LANDMARKS, PLACES, AND SITES ⚘ **Register Cliff and Oregon Trail Ruts** (307-864-2176; http://wyoparks.state.wy.us/Site/SiteInfo .asp?siteID=33), 2 miles south of Guernsey (via exit 92 off I-25), follow well-

FORT LARAMIE

🏕 ♿ ✎ **Fort Laramie National Historic Site** (307-837-2221; http://www.nps.gov/fola), 965 Gray Rocks Road, Fort Laramie. Visitor center and museum open daily 8–7 June through August (shorter hours in winter); grounds open daily dawn to dusk; $3 per person ages 16 and up (seven-day permit), under 16 free. This is the site of one of the earlier outposts established in Wyoming, dating back to 1834, when it was built as a trading and supply post for fur traders. At that time, the Cheyenne and Arapaho frequented the post and interactions were, for the most part, friendly. In 1849, when the trickle of emigrant traffic had become a sweeping wave of pioneers flooding the Oregon Trail in hopes of striking it rich out west, the post became a military fort. In that capacity, it served not only as a crucial place to stop for supplies, but also as a base of operations for planning military actions against American Indians. During this time, the Indians had grown increasingly violent and resistive to being forced onto reservations due not only to the encroachment of the increasing numbers of pioneers, but also by the repeated making and breaking of treaties and the refusal to allow them to remain on their ancestral homelands, among other factors. The fort closed in 1890 after all was said and done, having served its purpose—the removal of the Indians, making way for permanent pioneer settlements and future westward expansion. The fort remains today as a testament to the struggle for the west, a struggle that ultimately and permanently displaced the many tribes who had long made these lands their homes, disrupting their traditional ways of living forever. Visitors can tour through some 50 restored rooms of the fort, furnished with authentic period pieces; watch a video presentation; tour the fort with an audio tour; and attend interpretive programs. Children can participate in a Junior Ranger program and receive a Junior Ranger badge.

FORT LARAMIE NATIONAL HISTORIC SITE

signed roads guiding you to the sites. Open sunrise to sunset daily; free. Listed on the National Register of Historic Places, the 100-foot high Register Cliff provided pioneers on the Oregon Trail with a ready-made place to leave behind evidence of their travels. This rock precipice, made up of soft stone, towered over the popular camping spot that was one day's journey beyond Fort Laramie (see above). As pioneers rested and rejuvenated for another day on the trail, many of them found time to carve their names, the date, from whence they came, and/or their

OREGON TRAIL RUTS

hoped-for destinations. An interpretive kiosk provides some information about the site, and a walkway allows you to stroll along the cliff. Please do your part in protecting this historical place, which has already been the site of vandalism. You can see the tracks of the Oregon Trail passing by this way. Just .5 mile south of Guernsey off US 26 lie some of the more prominent remaining trail ruts that lie scattered throughout this region, evidence of the passage of thousands of wagons in trains as they made their way westward more than a century ago. See also Ruts to Reservoir in *To See*—Scenic Drives.

See also *To See*—Scenic Drives; Glendo State Park and Guernsey State Park in *Green Space*—State Parks; and The Sager House Bed and Breakfast in *Lodging*—Bed and Breakfasts.

CITY PARKS AND GARDENS NPVCD Botanical Garden lies just off US 85 on the south side of Torrington. This meticulously cared for garden provides a short walking trail through its beautifully landscaped grounds.

See Lingle in *To See*—Towns; Dale Jones Municipal Swimming Pool and Water Slide in *To Do*—For Families; and Pioneer Park and Wheatland City Park-Lewis Park in *Lodging*—Campgrounds.

SCENIC DRIVES Goshen County Chamber of Commerce (see Guidance) provides free maps of several self-guided historical loop driving tours in the region.

Ruts to Reservoir is a roughly 30-mile scenic journey that begins as you head south on S. Guernsey Road after visiting the Oregon Trail Ruts and Register Cliff (see *To See*—Historic Landmarks, Places, and Sites), allowing you to bypass the interstate on your way to Wheatland. When the pavement ends, hang a right onto the

NORTH PLATTE VALLEY CONSERVATION DISTRICT BOTANICAL GARDEN IN TORRINGTON

paved Grayrocks/Power Plant Road, winding past the gorgeous Grayrocks Wildlife Habitat Management Area and Grayrocks Reservoir (see *Green Space—*Wildlife Refuges and Areas). Soon after this, you'll pass the impressive Laramie Power Station on the outskirts of Wheatland, and then proceed into Wheatland by going south on WY 320 shortly thereafter.

See also Pine Bluffs to Torrington in *To See—*Scenic Drives in Southeast Wyoming: Cheyenne.

NATURAL WONDERS ♦ **Paleo Park** (307-334-2270; http://www.paleopark .com), 25 miles off US 85 north of Lusk. Call or email for reservations in advance. This unique park takes visitors along on dinosaur dig tours in an area rife with bones and fossils. Tours range from two hours ($20 per adult, $10 per child 7–13, 6 and under free) to overnight or weeklong stays. Guests participate in every step of the fossil recovery process on longer adventures, as well as enjoying ranch-style food (extra fee per meal) and lodging accommodations. The park even has a three-hole golf course.

✳ To Do

BICYCLING See Grassroots Trail in the Introduction and *Green Space*.

BOATING See Glendo State Park and Guernsey State Park in *Green Space—*State Parks; Hawk Springs State Recreation Area in *Green Space—*Recreation Areas; and Grayrocks Wildlife Habitat Management Area in *Green Space—*Wildlife Refuges and Areas.

FISHING See Glendo State Park and Guernsey State Park in *Green Space—*State Parks; Hawk Springs State Recreation Area in *Green Space—*Recreation Areas; Grayrocks Wildlife Habitat Management Area in *Green Space—*Wildlife Refuges and Areas; North Platte River in *To Do—*Fishing in Casper and Douglas; and Laramie River in *To Do—*Fishing in Rawlins and Laramie.

FITNESS CENTERS **North Platte Physical Therapy** (307-322-1878; http:// web.mac.com/nppts/North_Platte_Physical_Therapy/Wheatland.html), 953 Walnut Street, Wheatland. Call for current rates and hours. The on-premises fitness center is open to the general public. You can find additional locations in Torrington (307-532-5355) and Lusk (307-334-2272).

FOR FAMILIES ♣ ♦ **Dale Jones Municipal Swimming Pool and Water Slide** (307-532-7798; http://www.city-of-torrington.org/parks.htm#Pool), by Jirdon Park, 25th Avenue and E. G. Street, Torrington. Open daily in summer, call for current hours; $2 per adult, $1.50 per child 6th–12th grade, $1 per child K–5th grade, free for preschool; $1 per person extra for water slide.

♣ ♦ **Wheatland City Pool** (307-322-1946; http://www.plattecountyrecreation .com/City-Pool.html), Wheatland. Open daily in summer, call for current hours; $1 per person, children 5 and under free with paid admission. The pool is close to Wheatland City Park-Lewis Park (see *Lodging—*Campgrounds).

See also Guernsey and Lingle in *To See—*Towns; Fort Laramie National Historic Site in *To See—*Historic Landmarks, Places, and Sites; Paleo Park in *To See—*Natural Wonders; Glendo State Park and Guernsey State Park in *Green Space*—State Parks; and Hawk Springs State Recreation Area in *Green Space*—Recreation Areas.

GOLF City of Torrington Municipal Golf Course (307-532-3868; http://www .city-of-torrington.org/golf_course.htm), W. 15th Street and Golf Course Road, Torrington, 18 holes.

Cottonwood Country Club (307-532-4347; http://www.cottonwoodcountryclub .net), 2101 Golf Course Road, Torrington, 18 holes.

Niobrara Country Club (307-334-2438; http://www.luskwyoming.com/ncc.html), 34 WY 273, Lusk, 9 holes.

Trail Ruts Golf Club (307-836-2255; http://www.golfandcamp.com), 100 S. Guernsey Road, Guernsey, 9 holes. See also Larson Park Campground in *To Do*—Camping.

Wheatland Golf Club (307-322-3675), 1253 E. Cole, Wheatland, 9 holes.

See also Paleo Park in *To See*—Natural Wonders.

HIKING See Guernsey in *To See*—Towns; Register Cliff and Oregon Trail Ruts in *To See*—Historic Landmarks, Places, and Sites; NPVCD Botanical Garden in *To See*—City Parks and Gardens; Glendo State Park and Guernsey State Park in *Green Space*—State Parks; and Grayrocks Wildlife Habitat Management Area in *Green Space*—Wildlife Refuges and Areas.

PADDLING/FLOATING See Glendo State Park and Guernsey State Park in *Green Space*—State Parks; Hawk Springs State Recreation Area in *Green Space*—Recreation Areas; Grayrocks Wildlife Habitat Management Area in *Green Space*—Wildlife Refuges and Areas; and North Platte River in *To Do*—Fishing in Casper and Douglas.

RELAXATION AND REJUVENATION 🐾 **Community Hospital** (307-534-7204; see also Medical Emergency) in Torrington offers massage therapy by appointment 8–7 Monday through Friday; $45 per hour. Choose from a variety of different massage techniques (Swedish, deep tissue, and sports, among others). An array of complementary services, including herbal therapy and ear candling, is also available.

Goshen County Farmers' Market, Torrington (location varies; check with Goshen County Chamber of Commerce—see Guidance). Open 3:30–6:30 PM Thursday and 7:30 AM–11 AM Saturday, July through October. Stock up on your fruits and veggies with a visit to this farmers' market, which features fresh, in-season produce grown locally along with other locally made products.

SNOW SPORTS See Hawk Springs State Recreation Area in *Green Space*—Recreation Areas.

UNIQUE ADVENTURES See Paleo Park in *To See*—Natural Wonders.

WINERIES AND WINE TASTINGS 🐾 **Table Mountain Vineyards** (307-459-0233; http://www.tablemountainvineyards.com), P.O. Box 24, Huntley. Tasting

MAKE AN APPOINTMENT TO TASTE WINE
AT TABLE MOUNTAIN VINEYARDS

room open by appointment; free. Call for directions. True Wyoming wine can be found at this out-of-the-way vineyard close to the Nebraska border, made from 100 percent Wyoming-grown grapes along with other fruits blended in (raspberries, cherries, and apples) from suppliers around the state. They also make mead from Wyoming honey. This rapidly growing family-owned and -operated winery started in 2001, processed 500 pounds of grapes in 2004, and 25 tons of grapes in 2008. Table Mountain Vineyards now has numerous additional Wyoming grape growers supplying grapes for the wine as well. The grape varieties aren't the usual, but rather are known as cold, hardy hybrids, which are able to survive through typical Wyoming winter temperatures (from minus 15 to minus 60 degrees Fahrenheit). Make an appointment in advance, and then settle in for an informative wine tasting experience in the new (2010) tasting room. You'll find their products available for purchase at a number of liquor stores throughout the state if you can't make the journey to the vineyard itself. See also Goshen County 2 Shot Goose Hunt Annual Sportsmen's Invitational in *Special Events*.

See also Chugwater Chili Cook-off in *Special Events*.

✳ Green Space

STATE PARKS & ♂ **Glendo State Park** (307-735-4433; http://wyoparks.state.wy.us/Site/SiteInfo.asp?siteID=6), 397 Glendo Park Road, off I-25 at Glendo. Open year-round for both day use $4 (resident), $6 (nonresident); and camping $10 (resident), $17 (nonresident). For water lovers, Glendo State Park is a popular destination. Boaters will find a marina and boat ramps, along with ample room on the 14-mile-long reservoir for water skiing and top-notch fishing. A sandy beach invites swimmers to test the waters as well, and windsurfers enjoy the reservoir frequently. A great place for families, Glendo also has a plethora of campsites, a playground, 500 picnicking sites, and 4 miles of handicapped-accessible trails near the reservoir. History buffs will find that though the 1957 completion of the earthen dam forming the reservoir covered up some of the tracks of the historic trails that passed this way, including the Oregon Trail, the area still shows evidence of earlier human activities. Not only have indications of pioneer passage been found here, but also evidence of American Indian inhabitation, including tipi rings, can still be found in and around the park.

♂ & **Guernsey State Park** (307-836-2334; http://wyoparks.state.wy.us/Site/SiteInfo.asp?siteID=7), 15 miles east of I-25 on US 26 to CR 317, then 1.5 miles north to the park entrance. Open year-round (museum closed October 1 through April 30) for both day use $4 (resident), $6 (nonresident); and camping $10 (resident), $17 (nonresident). A National Historic Landmark that is listed on the National Register of Historic Places, Guernsey State Park showcases the work of the Civilian Conservation Corps (CCC) that was performed here throughout the

1930s. Here you'll find structures, including the park's museum, the castle, and a number of other picnic shelters, all of which were constructed through the hard work of the CCC and illustrate the architectural and planning abilities of those involved in this extensive project. Additionally, the CCC put in much of this gorgeous park's network of trails (17 miles). Camping is available in seven campgrounds, five of which are on the lakeshore. Ponderosa pines and scenic cliffs line the shores of the lake. Boating is also a major focus at this park, with its nearly 2,400 surface acres of water and three boat ramps to provide easy access. Other popular water sports include swimming and fishing. The park has playgrounds as well.

NATIONAL LANDS Medicine Bow National Forest: See listing in Casper and Douglas.

RECREATION AREAS & ✿ **Hawk Springs State Recreation Area** (307-836-2334; http://wyoparks.state.wy.us/Site/SiteInfo.asp?siteID=8), 3 miles east of US 85 via CR 186, about 39 miles south of Torrington. Open year-round for both day use $4 (resident), $6 (nonresident); and camping $10 (resident), $17 (nonresident). This remote destination in the southeastern corner of the state features great opportunities for boating and fishing alike. Boaters will enjoy the opportunity to explore more remote areas of the reservoir not accessible by land (as only a relatively small portion of the shore is publicly accessible). In particular, the south end of the reservoir affords the potential for viewing blue herons, among other birds in the area. Fish species include black crappie, channel catfish, largemouth bass, walleye, and yellow perch. Additional recreational opportunities include camping, playground equipment, and picnicking.

WILDLIFE REFUGES AND AREAS ✿ **Grayrocks Wildlife Habitat Management Area** (307-777-4600; http://gf.state.wy.us/accessto/access/grayrocks.asp),

GUERNSEY STATE PARK

about 10 miles northeast of Wheatland via Grayrocks Road. Open year-round; free. This WHMA includes the breathtaking 3500-acre Grayrocks Reservoir, a popular fishing, boating, and swimming destination. Bird-watching (have you ever seen wild pelicans? You can here!) and wildlife-watching opportunities abound, as do campgrounds. This area also provides access to **Cottonwood Draw Wildlife Habitat Management Area,** home to hiking, wildlife watching, and an archaeological site. See also Ruts to Reservoir in *To See*—Scenic Drives.

✳ Lodging

BED AND BREAKFASTS

Lusk

The Sager House Bed and Breakfast (1-800-435-2468 or 307-334-2423; http://www.sagerhouse.com), 310 S. Main Street. Luxury and elegance await you at the turn-of-the-century Sager House, an inn of distinction. This well-appointed B&B features six guest rooms, all with private, tiled bathrooms. Guests enjoy special touches including down comforters, robes, slippers, fresh flowers, and ironed sheets, as well as the inn's common areas, including a library, living room, dining room, exercise room, and game room. Lovely antiques make up much of the house's interior décor. Expensive.

Torrington

♨ ♿ **Tea Kettle Bed and Breakfast** (307-532-5375; http://www.wyoming bnb-ranchrec.com/teakettle.html), 9634 Van Tassell Road. You'll find this charming bed and breakfast 13 miles north of Torrington on a plateau overlooking its scenic surroundings. New in 2001, the house includes four guest bedrooms that share baths, as well as a pool table, ping-pong table, and three decks. They also offer a Steak 'n' Stay package, which includes a steak dinner in addition to the breakfast (extra fee). Moderate.

HOTELS AND MOTELS

Lusk

🐾 ⁱⁱⁱ ♨ **Townhouse Motel** (307-334-2376 or 1-866-550-2376; http://www .lusktownhouse.com), 525 S. Main

Street. This friendly motel will not disappoint. Single, double, and triple rooms are available for the traveler on a budget to kick back and relax without breaking the bank. Kids 12 and under are free; pets are $5 extra. Inexpensive to moderate.

Torrington

ⁱⁱⁱ ♨ 🐾 **Grandma's Inn** (307-532-4064), 4577 US 26/85. Pets are welcome at this small, privately run motel. You can unwind on the large grassy area or throw something on the barbecue (great for families on a budget who can't afford eating out). Three rooms also have kitchenettes. Inexpensive.

Wheatland

♨ ⁱⁱⁱ **Wyoming Motel** (1-800-839-5383 or 307-322-5383; http://www .wyomingmotel.com), 1101 Ninth Street. Recently renovated and very clean, this motel might have discount prices, but you won't feel short-changed when you relax in your basic, quiet room for the night or get checked in by the friendly owners. Inexpensive.

See also Vimbo's Dusty Boots Restaurant in *Where to Eat*—Eating Out.

CAMPGROUNDS ♿ ⁱⁱⁱ **BJ's Campground** (307-334-2314), 902 S. Maple, Lusk. Open year-round. This campground has long pull-throughs, covered picnic tables, and all the regular amenities. Very inexpensive.

Larson Park Campground/RV Park
(307-836-2255; http://www.golfand
camp.com), 100 S. Guernsey Road,
Guernsey. Open seasonally. This
municipal park, adjacent to the city's
Trail Ruts Golf Club (see *To Do—
Golf*), has campsites for both tent
campers and RVs. Facilities include
drinking water, hot showers, and
hookups. The city offers a special golf
and camp rate; call for details. Very
inexpensive.

❀ **Pioneer Park** (307-532-5666), W.
15th Avenue, Torrington. This free
municipal park includes a dump station, restrooms, and picnic tables. You
can also camp nearby at the **Goshen
County Fairgrounds** (307-532-2525),
7078 Fairgrounds Road, which
includes hot showers, restrooms, a
dump station, and horse boarding facilities. Very inexpensive.

❀ **Wheatland City Park-Lewis Park**
(307-322-2962), 600 Ninth Street. This
free city park offers overnight camping, including a dump station, electri-
cal hookups, showers at the adjacent
municipal pool ($1, see Wheatland
City Pool in *To Do—For Families*),
restrooms, drinking water, picnic
tables, and grills. The park may be
loud at times, but you can't beat the
price.

See also Glendo State Park and
Guernsey State Park in *Green Space—
State Parks*; Hawk Springs State
Recreation Area in *Green Space—
Recreation Areas*; and Grayrocks
Wildlife Habitat Management Area in
*Green Space—Wildlife Refuges and
Areas*.

OTHER OPTIONS
Lusk
See Paleo Park in *To See—Natural
Wonders*.

✷ Where to Eat

Chugwater
Stampede Steakhouse (307-422-
FEED; http://www.stampedesteak
house.com), 417 First Street. Open
11–9 Wednesday through Saturday,
11–2 PM Sunday; bar open until 2 AM.
Grab your dancing shoes and head to
this western-style eatery that also features a hardwood dance floor and
some toe-tapping acts. The extensive
menu includes everything from salads
and fish to steaks and *cowzones* (calzones). You will not leave hungry.
Moderate.

See also Chugwater Chili Corporation
in *Selective Shopping*.

Lusk
The Coffee Shoppe (307-334-3434),
216 S. Main Street, Lusk. Call for current hours/days. If you're looking for a
latte in Lusk, you can find your fix
here. In addition to basic and gourmet
coffee selections, they also serve
smoothies. While you're sipping, you
can pick out a local gift basket to bring
home with you. Inexpensive.

Torrington
❀ **Canton Dragon** (307-532-3888),
2126 Main Street. Open 11–8 Sunday
through Friday. In a town where most
restaurants are closed on Sundays,
Canton Dragon provides a place to eat
on everyone else's day off. Specializing
in Cantonese, Mandarin, and Szechuan
cuisine, Canton Dragon offers a daily
lunch buffet (11–2) and dinner buffet
(Friday 5–7). Family dinner specials
($10.50 per person) include soup,
appetizer, and a choice of entrées for
each person, making for a great option
for hungry budgeters. Inexpensive to
moderate.

Deacon's Restaurant (307-532-
4766), 1558 Main Street. Open 6 AM–8

PM Monday through Saturday. A local favorite, Deacon's bustles with activity almost any time of day. The menu includes salads, burgers, sandwiches, seafood, and red meat (steaks, prime ribs, and roast beef), as well as pies and cheesecake for dessert. Deacon's also has a coffee bar serving a full menu of coffees and specialty drinks. With its homey, diner feel and friendly staff, Deacon's will leave everyone satisfied, and the large portions will likely result in one or more doggie bags going with you when you leave. Moderate to expensive.

Grampa Chuy's Authentic Mexican Restaurant (307-532-2982), 1915 Main Street. Open 11–8 Monday through Thursday, 11–9 Friday through Saturday. In a place with several good Mexican restaurants to choose from, this one comes recommended by the locals as the place to go for south-of-the-border flavor. Enjoy hearty Mexican fare on Torrington's Main Street in a diner-like setting. Inexpensive to moderate.

The Java Jar (307-532-8541), 1940 Main Street. Open 6:30 AM–4 PM Monday through Friday, 7:30–11 AM Saturday. Just like people everywhere in this country, Wyomingites have grown to like good coffee. That's just what you'll find here at The Java Jar, as well as plenty of indoor seating. Inexpensive.

Wheatland

🐾 ♿ 🏵 ✐ **Vimbo's Dusty Boots Restaurant** (1-800-577-3842 or 307-322-3725; http://www.vimbos.com), 203 16th Street. Open 6 AM–9 PM Sunday through Thursday, 6 AM–10 PM Friday through Saturday. This restaurant, adjacent to the motel (inexpensive to moderate) and lounge of the same name, is a family-owned operation that serves breakfast, lunch, and dinner. You'll find traditional American food here. Breakfasts include a number of omelet selections, freshly baked goods, and hearty combinations. Lunches include a weekday buffet and sack lunches to go as well as sandwiches and salads. Dinnertime brings with it steak done in a number of cuts and styles, as well as seafood, daily specials, burgers, sandwiches, and more. A long list of desserts, including pies, pies, and more pies, among other options, means you should certainly leave room for a slice (or two!). A children's/seniors' menu is available as well. Vimbo's also has a gift shop. Inexpensive to moderate.

🏵 **Wheatland Inn** (307-322-9302), 86 16th Street. Open 5:30 AM–9 PM Monday through Saturday, 6 AM–9 PM Sunday. The friendly mom-and-pop/old diner atmosphere of the Wheatland Inn makes you comfortable right away, but the kind and helpful service might be what makes you want to come back again. They serve breakfast and dinner whenever you feel like it, delivered quickly and perfectly prepared, with that particular level of service that somehow manages to not be invasive, yet be perfectly attentive to all of your needs. The menu features a great diversity of breakfast offerings, such as eggs and pork chops, or Belgian waffles. Lunch and dinner offerings are extensive as well, ranging from burgers and sandwiches to seafood and steaks. Inexpensive to moderate.

✷ Entertainment

Cinema West Theatre (307-322-9032), 609 10th Street, Wheatland.

Wyoming Theater II (307-532-2226), 126 E. 20th Avenue, Torrington.

See also Lingle in *To See*—Towns and Stampede Steakhouse in *Where to Eat*—Eating Out.

✳ Selective Shopping

Chugwater Chili Corporation (1-800-97-CHILI or 307-422-3345; http://www.chugwaterchili.com), 210 First Street, Chugwater. Call for current hours. Even if you can't make it to the Chugwater Chili Cook-off in June (see *Special Events*), you can still share in some of the fun of this town's namesake event by stopping in at the store that started it all for a free taste. The Chili Corporation offers unique gifts including not only chili products, books, and gift sets, but also quilted items and other gift ideas.

Downtown Torrington has a great Main Street. shopping district, with stores such as **The Glitz Boutique** (open 10–5 Wednesday through Saturday), **Heartland Embroidery** (open 9–5 Monday through Friday and 9–1 Saturday), and **Western Mall** (open 10–5 Monday through Friday and 10–3 Saturday), among many others.

See also Table Mountain Vineyards in *To See*—Wineries and Wine Tastings; and The Coffee Shoppe and Vimbo's Dusty Boots Restaurant in *Where to Eat*.

✳ Special Events

♪ *June:* **Chugwater Chili Cook-off** (307-422-3345; http://www.chugwaterchilicookoff.com), Chugwater: This annual Wyoming State Championship competition draws top chili chefs from around the country; it also includes a wine tasting, art show, live music, games, and children's activities. See also Chugwater Chili Corporation in *Selective Shopping*.

July: **Legend of Rawhide** (307-334-2950; http://www.legendofrawhide.com), Lusk: An annual community performance depicting life on a wagon train and in the Sioux Indian Nation during pioneer times.

July: **Summer Fun Fest and Antique Tractor Pull,** Wheatland: This is a celebration of summer that includes a street dance in Lewis Park.

July: **Niobrara County Fair,** Lusk: This is your traditional county fair.

August: **Platte County Fair and Rodeo,** Wheatland: Enjoy a traditional county fair and rodeo.

See also Pony Express Re-Ride in *Special Events* in Casper and Douglas.

September: **Classic Cars in the Park,** Torrington: An annual showing of classic cars from all over the country, it includes games, prizes, a picnic, and more.

December: **Goshen County 2 Shot Goose Hunt Annual Sportsmen's Invitational** (http://www.2shotgoose.com), Torrington: This annual goose hunt draws hunters from around the nation; Table Mountain Vineyards (see *To See*—Wineries and Wine Tastings) produces specialty wines for the event.

Southwest Wyoming

5

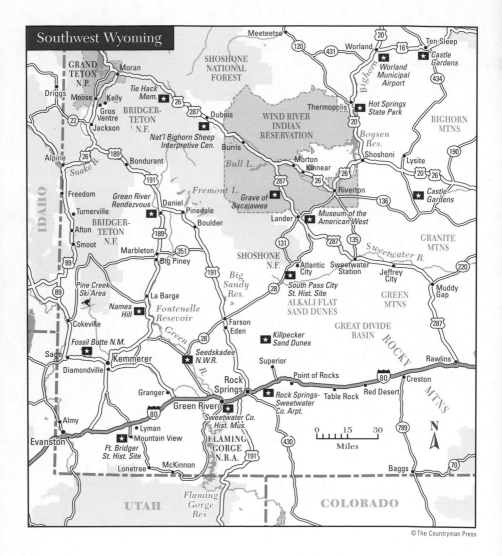

Southwest Wyoming

GRAND TETON N.P.
Driggs
Moran
Tie Hack Mem.
Moose
Kelly
Gros Ventre
Jackson
BRIDGER-TETON N.F.
Dubois
Nat'l Bighorn Sheep Interpretive Cen.
Burris
Alpine
Bondurant
Snake R.
Freedom
Turnerville
Green River Rendezvous
Daniel
Pinedale
Boulder
IDAHO
Afton
BRIDGER-TETON N.F.
Smoot
Marbleton
Big Piney
Pine Creek Ski Area
La Barge
Names Hill
Fontenelle Resevoir
Green R.
Cokeville
Fossil Butte N.M.
Sage
Kemmerer
Seedskadee N.W.R.
Diamondville
Granger
Rock Springs
Superior
Almy
Lyman
Mountain View
Sweetwater Co. Hist. Mus.
Ft. Bridger St. Hist. Site
Evanston
McKinnon
FLAMING GORGE N.R.A.
Lonetree

Meeteetse
120
431
Worland
20
Ten-Sleep
16
Castle Gardens
434
SHOSHONE NATIONAL FOREST
Worland Municipal Airport
Bighorn
Thermopolis
Hot Springs State Park
20
BIGHORN MTNS
WIND RIVER INDIAN RESERVATION
Boysen Res.
287
Bull L.
Morton
Kinnear
Shoshoni
Lysite
190
Fremont L.
26
26
20
26
Grave of Sacajawea
287
Riverton
136
Lander
Museum of the American West
Castle Gardens
131
287
135
GRANITE MTNS
Sweetwater R.
SHOSHONE N.F.
Atlantic City
Sweetwater Station
Jeffrey City
220
Big Sandy Res.
28
South Pass City St. Hist. Site
GREEN MTNS
Muddy Gap
191
ALKALI FLAT SAND DUNES
287
Farson
Eden
Killpecker Sand Dunes
GREAT DIVIDE BASIN
ROCKY MTNS
Rawlins
28
Point of Rocks
80
Creston
Rock Springs-Sweetwater Co. Arpt.
Table Rock
Red Desert
Green River
430
789
789
UTAH
Flaming Gorge Res.
191
Baggs
70
COLORADO

0   15   30
Miles

N

© The Countryman Press

EVANSTON AND STAR VALLEY

Like practically every other town or city located along Wyoming's I-80 corridor, Evanston's ties to the railroad defined its past and continue to define it in the present-day as well. Begin your stay here with a stop at the Bear River Travel Information Center (see Guidance), where you can view captive herds of bison and elk, take a walk along Bear River, and gather some information about the area (especially worthwhile if you're starting your journey in Wyoming here and heading east). Explore Evanston's history at Historic Depot Square (see *To See*—Historic Landmarks, Places, and Sites), including the history of the Chinese emigrants who came here to work on the railroad and to mine the coal needed to fuel the trains. Also, more than 15 city parks lie scattered throughout Evanston, many of which can be accessed from both Historic Depot Square and Bear River State Park (see *Green Space*—State Parks) via the Bear River Greenway (see *To Do*—Bicycling).

North of Evanston (and south of Jackson Hole), you'll discover even more opportunities for outdoor adventures—minus the crowds. The small town of Pinedale, nestled on the western side of Wyoming's highest mountain range, the Wind Rivers, offers you a full array of recreational pursuits for all seasons. There you'll find White Pine Ski Area and Resort (see *To Do*—Snow Sports), Fremont Lake and its neighboring lakes (see *To Do*—Boating), the Green River and the New Fork River (see *To Do*—Fishing), and a huge amount of land included in the Bridger-Teton National Forest, with more public lands managed by the BLM (see *Green Space*—National Lands). This is an area where the mountain men held one of their famed rendezvous trading events annually for several years during the 1830s—happenings that are commemorated at Pinedale's Green River Rendezvous Days each July, among other such events (see *Special Events*).

To the west, from Alpine and Star Valley in the north to Kemmerer in the south (see *To See*—Towns), you'll find even more remote and less-traveled terrain ripe for exploring, from the local Pine Creek Ski Area by Cokeville (see *To Do*—Snow Sports), to the fishing, hiking, biking, and riding opportunities in both the national forest and on BLM lands. Here, too, you can learn about the area's prehistoric times with a visit to Fossil Butte National Monument, showcasing an incredible concentration of quality fossils (see *To See*—Natural Wonders). You can visit off-beat attractions like the Tri-State Monument and Names Hill (see *To See*—Historic Landmarks, Places, and Sites). You can walk or ride in the footsteps of the early pioneers who passed this way on historic trails, including the Overland Trail, the Oregon Trail, and the Mormon Trail. You can fish the Greys River and the Salt River or their tributaries, or float or paddle portions of them (see *To Do*—Fishing). You can camp at numerous spots, many of them free of charge, and enjoy the opportunity to get away from it all in this remote portion of the state that beckons with its mystical charm to the adventurer within.

GUIDANCE &. **Bear River Travel Information Center** (307-789-6540), Exit 6 off I-80 in Evanston, open daily. See also Bear River State Park in *Green Space*— State Parks.

City of Evanston (307-783-6300; http://www.evanstonwy.org), 1200 Main Street, Evanston, 82930.

Evanston Chamber of Commerce (1-800-328-9708 or 307-783-0370; http://www.etownchamber.com), 1020 Front Street, P.O. Box 365, Evanston, 82931.

Greater Bridger Valley Chamber of Commerce (307-787-6738; http://www.bridgervalleychamber.com), P.O. Box 1080, Lyman, 82937.

Lincoln County (307-877-9056; http://www.lcwy.org), 925 Sage Avenue, Kemmerer, 83101.

Star Valley Chamber of Commerce (1-800-426-8833 or 307-883-2759; http://www.starvalleychamber.com), 606 N. Main Street, P.O. Box 1171, Thayne, 83127.

Star Valley Online Marketplace (1-888-249-6963 ext. 0 or 307-654-7827; http://www.starvalley.com).

Sublette County Chamber of Commerce (1-888-285-7282 or 307-367-2242; http://www.sublettechamber.com or http://www.mountainmancountry.com), 19 E. Pine Street, (at the **Sublette County Visitor Center**), Pinedale, 82941.

Uinta County (307-783-0301; http://www.uintacounty.com), 225 Ninth Street, Evanston, 82930.

See also *To See*—Towns.

GETTING THERE *By car:* Evanston is in the southwest corner of Wyoming near the Utah border at the junction of I-80 and WY 150 and WY 89. Star Valley is near the central-western border of Wyoming on US 89 south of Jackson Hole and north of Evanston.

THE SUBLETTE COUNTY CHAMBER OF COMMERCE

By plane: **Jackson Hole Airport** (307-733-7682; http://www.jacksonhole airport.com) is north of Star Valley in Jackson Hole. See Getting Around in Northwest Wyoming: Jackson and Dubois for information on shuttle service to Star Valley. **Rock Springs–Sweetwater County Airport** (307-352-6880; http://www.rock springsairport.com) is east of Evanston about 100 miles via I-80.

GETTING AROUND You can explore Evanston's downtown area on foot easily. Each town in Star Valley is conducive to foot traffic, but to explore the whole valley you'll need to use your car. Outlying attractions throughout this region will require a car for exploration.

MEDICAL EMERGENCY Dial 911.

Evanston Regional Hospital (307-789-3636; http://www.evanstonregional hospital.com), 190 Arrowhead Drive, Evanston.

Pinedale Medical Clinic (307-367-4133), 619 E. Hennick, Pinedale.

South Lincoln Medical Center (307-877-4401; http://www.southlincolnmedical .com), 711 Onyx Street, Kemmerer.

Star Valley Medical Center (307-885-5800; http://www.svmcwy.org), 901 Adams Street, Afton.

❋ To See

TOWNS Afton is located along US 89 just east of Wyoming's border with Idaho, in Star Valley. At close to 2,000 inhabitants, it is the largest of Wyoming's towns in the Star Valley area. Other towns (south to north) include **Smoot, Osmond, Fairview, Auburn, Grover, Turnerville, Bedford, Thayne, Star Valley Ranch, Freedom, Etna,** and **Alpine**. All of these towns are part of Lincoln County, which is rife with year-round outdoor recreational pursuits for those seeking an out-of-the-way destination. Afton is home to the annual **Lincoln County Fair**, held in early August, but its real claim to fame is the **World's Largest Elkhorn Arch**, an 18-foot structure containing more than 3,000 elk antlers. See also Jonathan the Bear Man in *Selective Shopping*.

Big Piney, with about 450 people, is north of Kemmerer and south of Pinedale on US 189, just south of Marbleton (see below). For more information: **Town of Big Piney** (307-276-3554; http://www.bigpiney.com), P.O. Box 70, Big Piney, 83113.

Cokeville is on US 30 in southern Lincoln County near Wyoming's border with Idaho. Cokeville has a visitor center and a nice city park located at Park and Main Streets, with a playground and a picnic area. You can access the Tri-State Monument (see *To See*—Historic Landmarks, Places, and Sites) from Cokeville, as well as the Pine Creek Ski Resort (see *To Do*—Snow Sports). For more information: **Cokeville Chamber of Commerce** (307-279-3200; http://www.cokevillewy.com), 110 N. US 30, P.O. Box 358, Cokeville, 83114.

La Barge is north of Kemmerer on US 189 at the northern end of Fontenelle Reservoir (see *To Do*—Boating). For more information: **La Barge Chamber of Commerce** (307-386-2676), P.O. Box 331, La Barge, 83123.

Kemmerer lies at the intersection of WY 233, US 30, and US 189. This

THE WORLD'S LARGEST ELKHORN ARCH IN AFTON

town serves as a gateway to Fossil Butte National Monument (see *To See*—Natural Wonders), one of Wyoming's two national monuments (the other being Devils Tower). The town's nickname, The Fossil Fish Capital of America, echoes this role, as do several commercial dig sites on the way to the monument, which allow you to try your hand at uncovering fossils (for a fee). Kemmerer, with a population of about 3,000, is also home to the original J. C. Penney (bet you didn't know that it all started in Wyoming) and the Fossil Country Frontier Museum (see listings in *To See*). The town has a tent camping area on WY 233 near City Hall. For more information: **Kemmerer-Diamondville Chamber of Commerce** (1-888-300-3413 or 307-877-9761; http://www.kemmererchamber.com), 800 Pine Avenue Kemmerer, 83101.

Marbleton, with a population nearing 1,000, is north of Kemmerer and south of Pinedale on US 189, just north of Big Piney (see above). For more information: **Marbleton Town Hall** (307-276-3815; http://www.marbleton.com), 10700 US 189, Marbleton, 83113.

Pinedale lies on US 191, 10 miles east of Daniel and the junction of US 189/191. Situated at the western entrance to the Wind River Mountains, the town of 1,400 is surrounded by incredible mountain scenery, providing opportunities for year-round recreation, including rock climbing and bouldering. The **Pinedale Town Park** (on Franklin, just off Pine Street) has a kids' fishing pond, playground, and picnic areas, and the town has many paved walking trails, plus a recreation center. Pinedale is also home to the Museum of the Mountain Man (see *To See*—Museums), and it hosts the annual Green River Rendezvous Days (see *Special Events*), commemorating the 1830s mountain man rendezvous that occurred in this area. The **Upper Green River Rendezvous-Trapper's Point National Historic Site** lies 6 miles west of Pinedale on US 191 at the Cora Junction, commemorating these events as well. For more information: **Pinedale Online!** (307-360-7689; http://www.pinedaleonline.com), 43 S. Sublette, Pinedale, 82941.

MUSEUMS ♿ ♞ **Chinese Joss House Museum** (307-783-6320), 920 Front Street (in Historic Depot Square; see Historic Landmarks, Places, and Sites), Evanston. Open 9–5 Monday through Friday, (summer), call for winter hours; free (donations gladly accepted). You might not know about the history of southwestern Wyoming's Chinese immigrants and their descendents, but you'll learn about it with a visit here. This unique museum is housed in a replica of the Joss House, a Chinese temple that stood in Evanston from 1874 until it burned down in 1922. Exhibits include collections of artifacts unearthed in Chinatown, photographs, decorations, and more.

PINEDALE TOWN PARK

♿ ♞ **Fossil Country Frontier Museum** (307-877-6551; http://www.hams fork.net/~museum), 400 Pine Avenue, Kemmerer. Open 9–5 Monday through

Saturday late May through early September, 10–4 Monday through Friday early September through late May; free (donations gladly accepted). This museum's exhibits capture the local history and interpret it for visitors. You'll see a prehistoric dinosaur footprint, an exhibit on the area's coal mining heritage, bootlegging equipment from prohibition, and even (gulp!) a two-bodied lamb. The museum hosts many community, cultural, and concert events throughout the year. The museum also has a gift shop.

🐾 **Green River Valley Museum** (307-276-5343; http://www.grvm.com), 206 N. Front Street, Big Piney. Open noon–4 June15 through October 15, Tuesday through Saturday; free (donations gladly accepted). Featured exhibits cover the area's history, including American Indians, ranching, mining (coal, oil, and gas), and pioneers and homesteads, including a restored homesteader's cabin. The museum's building was constructed after another building—the old jailhouse—burned to the ground in 1948, with the exception of the metal jail cell, which continued to be used for a while to house prisoners—this despite the lack of a surrounding building. The new building was built around the old cell, and today, you can take a peek inside and imagine what it might have been like to be imprisoned in the cell.

Museum of the Mountain Man (1-877-686-6266; http://www.museumofthe mountainman.com), 700 E. Hennick, Pinedale. Open 9–5 daily May 1 through September 30, 9–4 Monday through Friday in October, closed November through April; $5 per adult, $4 per senior, $3 per child ages 6–12. Learn all about the history and times of the notorious mountain men who made their livings in the fur trade during the early 1800s. The museum also includes numerous additional exhibits detailing other aspects of the area's past, including American Indian artifacts and clothing, and information about Pinedale's formative years.

See also Fort Bridger State Historic Site and Historic Depot Square in *To See—Historic Landmarks, Places, and Sites*.

HISTORIC LANDMARKS, PLACES, AND SITES ♿ Fort

Bridger State Historic Site (307-782-3842; http://wyoparks.state.wy .us/Site/SiteInfo.asp?siteID=14), 3 miles off I-80 via Exit 34 between Evanston and Green River. Grounds open 8 AM to sunset daily year-round; museum/visitor center open 9–5:30 daily June through August, 9–4:30 Saturday and Sunday, April and October; closed November 1 through April 30; $2 per resident, $4 per nonresident. Established in 1843 by two of the most famed mountain men of the 19th century, Jim Bridger and Louis Vasquez, Fort Bridger's original incarnation was to serve those traveling on the Oregon Trail as a place to purchase more sup-

THE FOSSIL COUNTRY FRONTIER MUSEUM

FORT BRIDGER STATE HISTORIC SITE

plies. After changing hands, becoming first the property of the Mormons, and then the U.S. Military in 1858, by 1890, the fort had been abandoned. Nearly half a century later, efforts were made to restore the historic fort, and in 1933, it was declared a Wyoming Historical Landmark. Today, you can tour through the beautifully restored fort grounds and buildings. In some structures, you'll even find friendly guides clad in period dress, ready to tell you all about the building's purpose. You can even trade with the traders at the Bridger/Vasquez Trading Post (a gift shop), and view the related historical artifacts on display at the museum located at the site. For the full-scale mountain man experience, plan to attend the Mountain Man Rendezvous (see *Special Events*). Much of the site includes Braille signs as well.

✦ 🐾 **Historic Depot Square** (307-783-0370; http://www.etownchamber.com), 36 Front Street, Evanston. Anchoring **Historic Downtown Evanston** (a National Historic District), the Historic Depot Square is home to a number of historical attractions, all set in a beautifully landscaped and organized setting. Here you'll find the **Uinta County Museum** (307-789-8248), 1020 Front Street, open 9–5 daily, Memorial Day through Labor Day, 9–5 Monday through Friday, 10–4 Saturday, Labor Day through Memorial Day; free. The museum, situated in Evanston's historic **Carnegie library building,** strives to preserve the county's history with exhibits on the railroad, ranching, American Indians, Chinese immigrants, pioneers, and more; the building also houses the chamber of commerce. Depot Square is also home to the Chinese Joss House Museum (see *To See*—Museums), and a restored **Union Pacific passenger railroad depot,** as well as a children's play area and sand volleyball courts. See also Bear River Greenway in *To Do*—Bicycling; and Pine Gables Inn Bed and Breakfast in *Lodging*—Bed and Breakfasts.

& **J. C. Penney Homestead and Historical Foundation** (307-877-3164; http://www.kemmerer.org/jcpenney.php), 722 J. C. Penney Drive, Kemmerer. Homestead is open 9–6 Monday through Saturday, 1–6 Sunday, Memorial Day through Labor Day; free. Most of the customers who walk through the doors of one of the many J. C. Penney stores around the nation probably don't realize that the original Mother Store was—and still is—in the small western town of Kemmerer, Wyoming. Opened in 1902 under the name Golden Rule Store by James Cash Penney, the store enjoyed a virtual overnight success. A decade later, more than 30 Golden Rule Stores were in operation, and in 1913, the decision was made to change the stores' names to J. C. Penney. Today, visitors can stroll through the original J. C. Penney homestead, a six-room cottage decorated with authentic period pieces that is a National Historic Landmark. Kemmerer's Mother Store is still open for business as well for those wanting to shop where it all started.

Names Hill is 6 miles south of La Barge, just west of US 189. At this location, you'll find inscriptions in the sandstone cliffs of two sorts: American Indian petroglyphs from long ago; and more recent inscriptions made by some 2,000 pioneers who passed this way traveling west on the Overland Trail via the Sublette Cutoff. The pioneers' inscriptions date back to 1827, and included among them is the signature of the famed mountain man James "Jim" Bridger.

Tri-State Monument is accessible by driving 8.5 miles south of Cokeville on WY 207, and then turning west onto WY 208. Continue 4 or so miles on a rough, isolated dirt road to reach the monument. No, it's not the Four Corners Monument . . . but rather, it's Wyoming's less-traveled version of a place to stand in multiple states at once. After a short walk, you'll arrive at a spot where you can stand in three states—Idaho, Utah, and Wyoming—at one time. This is one of those attractions for the true explorer of this area of the country to visit. After all, do you know anyone who's visited the Tri-State Monument? I didn't think so.

See also Pinedale in *To See*—Towns; Fossil Butte National Monument in *To See*—Natural Wonders; and The Log Cabin Motel in *Lodging*—Hotels and Motels.

CITY PARKS AND GARDENS See Cokeville and Pinedale in *To See*—Towns; Historic Depot Square in *To See*—Historic Landmarks, Places, and Sites; Periodic Geyser in *To See*—Natural Wonders; Bear River Greenway in *To Do*—Bicycling; Sulphur Creek Reservoir in *To Do*—Boating; Kemmerer Community Recreation Center in *To Do*—Fitness Centers, Ice-skating in *To Do*—Snow Sports; and Bear River State Park in *Green Space*—State Parks.

SCENIC DRIVES Big Springs Scenic Backway is a 68-mile journey on partially paved, partially graveled and dirt roads, starting in Kemmerer. Go north on WY 233 (Hams Fork Road), which changes to oiled gravel just north of Lake Viva Naughton, and then to just plain gravel when you enter the Bridger-Teton National Forest (FR 10062). Follow FR 10062 as its winds around to its junction with WY 232, and then follow this road south to Cokeville and the official terminus of the backway. To avoid becoming lost, it's helpful to get a map from the Kemmerer Ranger Station (307-877-4415), 308 US 189, Kemmerer. This winding, scenic backway could be driven in about two hours—but what would be the point? You'll be better off scheduling a day (or more) to explore all of the scenic, historic, and recreational highlights you'll encounter on this drive that passes through the path of the historic Oregon Trail. You'll pass by Viva Naughton Reservoir (see *To Do*—Boating), numerous old homesteaders' cabins, **Mayfield and Nugent Park Winter Sports Area,** (popular with Nordic skiers and snowmobilers), numerous creeks, and several developed campgrounds in the Bridger-Teton National Forest (see *Lodging*—Campgrounds), among other attractions.

Mirror Lake Scenic Byway, or WY 150/UT 150, is about an 80-mile drive

THE J.C. PENNEY MOTHER STORE IN KEMMERER

that is mostly in Utah, though it has a brief span of about 20 miles in Wyoming. Begin by exiting I-80 at exit 5 in Evanston, heading south toward Utah on WY 150. This portion of the journey takes you over Bear River and passes by Sulphur Creek Reservoir (see *To Do*—Boating). Upon entering Utah, simply stay on UT 150 as it continues south, and then heads west, through the beautiful Wasatch-Cache National Forest. The byway officially terminates in Kamas, Utah, and it is closed seasonally.

See also Fossil Butte National Monument in *To See*—Natural Wonders.

NATURAL WONDERS ✐ ⚒ 🐾 **Fossil Butte National Monument** (307-877-4455; http://www.nps.gov/fobu), roughly 15 miles west of Kemmerer on WY 30. Open 8–7 Memorial Day through Labor Day, 8–4:30 Labor Day through Memorial Day, closed on winter holidays; free. While you've undoubtedly heard of Wyoming's other national monument (Devils Tower), this one should be included in your travel plans, too, if you happen to be in the area. Not only is it free (yes, free!), but also, Fossil Butte is home to one of the world's most extensive collection of freshwater fossils. Here some 50 million years ago there existed a huge lake, as the plentiful fossils discovered here show. The visitor center allows you the opportunity to view more than 80 of these specimens up close, providing you with educational and interpretive information about them as well. If you have some time to spare, you can watch a film to learn even more about the fossils, or attend a ranger-led talk. During summer from 11–4 on Friday and Saturday, the whole family can go with a paleontologist to dig for fossils at the monument's active quarrying area. Remote and beautiful, the monument's cold, high desert environment sustains an abundance of wildlife as well, which you might view if you walk one of the two interpretive trails—the 2.5-mile **Historic Quarry Trail,** or the 1.5-mile **Fossil Lake Trail.** A 7.5-mile (partially paved) scenic drive is also an option. Children ages 5–15 can participate in a Junior Ranger Program (free) to earn a Junior Ranger badge, among other hands-on activities. Overnight camping is not allowed.

FOSSIL BUTTE NATIONAL MONUMENT

Cross-country skiing is popular here in winter. Bikes are allowed in paved areas of the monument, but not on the trails.

Grand Canyon of the Snake River is along US 26/89 east of Alpine and southwest of Hoback Junction. See listing in Northwest Wyoming: Jackson and Dubois.

Periodic Geyser, also known as Intermittent Spring, lies in the Salt River Range of the Bridger-Teton National Forest, just east of Afton. Take FR 10211 east of Afton to the trailhead for Periodic Spring Trail, passing by **Canyon View Park** at Second and Monroe on your way. A short, .8-mile hike (one-way) takes you to the spring, North America's only known cold-water geyser, and one of only three such phenomenon known to exist in the world. The spring's cycle of starting and stopping is most pronounced in late summer and early fall, but the reasons behind why it does this are unknown. Mountain bikes are allowed on this trail. Trail #35 leaves from the parking area as well, and it links up with other trails should you wish to explore the surrounding terrain a bit more.

See also Clear Creek Trail in *To Do*—Hiking.

✳ To Do

BICYCLING ♿ ❀ **Bear River Greenway** (307-789-1770; http://www.bear rivergreenway.org), along Bear River Drive, Evanston. Open 5 AM–11 PM; free. This 2.3-mile system of paved trails connects up with the trail system at Bear River State Park (see *Green Space*—State Parks). The "Bear" stands for Better Environment And River Project. Winding along the pathway of the Bear River, this trail is popular not only for bicycling, but also for running, strolling, skating, and in wintertime, cross-country skiing. Situated along the pathway, you'll also find two ice-skating ponds (seasonal); fishing, floating, paddling, and boating access; a whitewater park; an interpretive center; and easy access to many of Evanston's parks and attractions, including Historic Depot Square (see *To See*—Historic Landmarks, Places, and Sites).

See also Fossil Butte National Monument and Periodic Geyser in *To See*—Natural Wonders; Fremont Lake in *To Do*—Boating; Lake Alice Trail and Lake Barstow Trail in *To Do*—Hiking; White Pine Ski Area and Resort in *To Do*—Snow Sports; and *Green Space*.

BOATING ⚓ ♿ **Fontenelle Reservoir** is 15 miles south of La Barge, located on US 189 and managed by the BLM (see *Green Space*—National Lands). This reservoir, with 8,000 acres of surface area, offers opportunities not only for boating (boat launch), but also for swimming, fishing (species include brown trout, cutthroat trout, rainbow trout, and smallmouth bass), and camping ($5). It also has a playground.

❀ **Sulphur Creek Reservoir** (307-789-1770), 12 miles south of Evanston

BEAR RIVER GREENWAY

FONTENELLE RESERVOIR

on WY 150. Open year-round for day use only; free. Sulphur Creek Reservoir is a popular destination for boaters and anglers alike. The area has a boat dock as well as developed picnic facilities, including a grill. Restrooms are available, but no running water. Windsurfing is popular here as well.

Viva Naughton Reservoir lies on WY 233 about 14.5 miles north of Kemmerer and is managed by the BLM (see *Green Space*—National Lands). This reservoir offers opportunities not only for boating (boat launch), but also for fishing (species include brown trout, cutthroat trout, rainbow trout, splake, and whitefish). Just south of this reservoir is **Kemmerer Reservoir,** which also permits fishing (species include brown trout, cutthroat trout, rainbow trout, and whitefish).

See also Bear River Greenway in *To Do*—Bicycling and *Green Space*.

CLIMBING Exum Mountain Guides (307-733-2297; http://www.exumguides .com), South Jenny Lake, P.O. Box 56, Grand Teton National Park, Moose, WY 83012. Trips run June through September; $1,320–2,400+, call for details and reservations. Prior experience with Exum required for most trips. Exum offers guided, multiday rock climbing trips in the Wind River Mountain Range east of Pinedale in the Bridger-Teton National Forest (see *Green Space*—National Lands). Trips include summiting Gannett Peak, Wyoming's highest mountain.

Jackson Hole Mountain Guides (1-800-239-7642 or 307-733-4979; http:// www.jhmg.com), P.O. Box 7477, 165 N. Glenwood Street, Jackson, WY 83002. Trips run June through September; $1,000–3,000+; call for details and reservations. JHMG offers guided, multiday rock climbing trips in the Wind River Mountain Range east of Pinedale in the Bridger-Teton National Forest (see *Green Space*—National Lands). Trips include summiting Gannett Peak, Wyoming's highest mountain.

See also Pinedale in *To See*—Towns and *Green Space*.

FISHING Green River: See listing in Green River and Rock Springs.

Greys River (307-777-4600; http://gf.state.wy.us/fish/fishing) flows right alongside FR 10138 southeast of Alpine in the Bridger-Teton National Forest (see *Green Space*—National Lands). Game fish species include cutthroat trout. Numerous streams in this area provide great fishing opportunities as well. Five first-come, first-served forest service campgrounds lie along FR 10138, providing easy access to the river ($12). Kayakers enjoy paddling portions of this river in springtime's higher waters, often putting in at an area 4 miles from Alpine along FR 10138.

Hams Fork River (307-777-4600; http://gf.state.wy.us/fish/fishing) has a state fishing access site on WY 233 north of Kemmerer (follow signs). Game fish species

WYOMING'S LAND OF MANY LAKES

& **Fremont Lake** is the largest of a number of lakes situated around Pinedale, and the second largest natural lake in Wyoming. Fremont Lake is
accessible by taking Fremont Lake Road 3.2 miles northwest of Pinedale.
This glacially formed lake—the largest (11 miles long) and deepest (up to
600 feet deep) of its kind in the Green River Basin—lies partially in the
Bridger-Teton National Forest (see *Green Space*— National Lands). For
boaters, the lake has boat launches, a marina, and several providers of boat
rentals. The lake is famed for its mackinaw trout fishing, with other game
fish species including brown and rainbow trout. Additional nearby lakes
with both boating access and fishing in this area include (north to south)
New Fork Lakes, Willow Lake, Half Moon Lake, and **Boulder Lake.** Fishing
is available at numerous additional nearby lakes, including **Long Lake, Soda
Lake, Fayette Lake,** and **Burnt Lake.** Overnight camping is available at several developed campgrounds (see BLM Campgrounds and Bridger-Teton
National Forest in *Lodging*—Campgrounds), and hiking trails abound in the
area. On the way to Fremont Lake, you'll also find a number of CCC ponds
with handicapped-accessible trails around them for fishing access as well
as strolling and biking. Several fishing derbies are held annually on these
lakes, which are also popular for ice fishing in winter. See also Lakeside
Lodge in *Lodging*—Lodges.

FREMONT LAKE

include brook trout, brown trout, cutthroat trout, rainbow trout, and whitefish.

New Fork River (307-367-4353; http://gf.state.wy.us/fish/fishing) originates in the New Fork Lakes (see Fremont Lake in *To Do*—Boating) 24 miles north of Pinedale. The river then flows south to join the Green River (see above) just south of WY 351. This river is popular for both fishing and floating. Game fish species include brook trout, brown trout, mountain whitefish, and rainbow trout. The New Fork has a number of signed and unsigned public access sites along US 191, starting in Pinedale, where the river becomes large enough to float. The most popular of these is the **Boulder Bridge** access point (signed) just off US 191 in Boulder. Another popular access site is at the BLM-managed **Piney Cutoff** area on WY 351, right where the river crosses the road.

Salt River (307-367-4353; http://gf.state.wy.us/fish/fishing) flows north along US 89 through Star Valley to the Palisades Reservoir (which is mostly in Idaho with a small portion in Wyoming). The river is popular for both fishing and floating—and especially the two combined—with flat water and tremendous scenery making it great for scenic floats and paddles as well. Easy access is a bonus for users of this river as well, with numerous signed state access points along US 89. Game fish species include brook trout, brown trout, cutthroat trout, mountain whitefish, and rainbow trout.

See also Bear River Greenway in *To Do*—Bicycling; *To Do*—Boating; Green River Outfitters in *To Do*—Horseback Riding; and *Green Space*.

FITNESS CENTERS **Evanston Recreation and Fitness Center** (307-789-1770; http://www.evanstonwy.org), 275 Saddle Ridge Road, Evanston. Call or check online for current rates, classes, and hours. This full-service, modern recreation facility offers a swimming pool and fitness classes, including yoga.

✒ **Kemmerer Community Recreation Center** (307-828-2365; http://www.kemmerer.org/rec_center.php), 1776 Del Rio Drive, Kemmerer. Call for current hours; $4 per adult, $2 per senior (60-plus) and child 6–18, children 5 and under free, $6 per family. An indoor track, exercise equipment, hot tub, sauna, and steam room are some of the offerings at this recreation facility. Kemmerer also has an indoor pool (307-877-6256), 1525 3rd West Avenue; and an outdoor pool at **Archie Neil Park** (307-877-9641) open in summer months and appropriate for children.

See also Pinedale in *To See*—Towns.

FOR FAMILIES See Historic Depot Square in *To See*—Historic Landmarks, Places, and Sites; Fossil Butte National Monument in *To See*—Natural Wonders; Fontenelle Reservoir in *To Do*—Boating; Kemmerer Community Recreation Center in *To Do*—Fitness Centers; Wind River Yoga and Body Works in *To Do*—Relaxation and Rejuvenation; and Bear River State Park in *Green Space*—State Parks.

GOLF **Aspen Hills Golf Course** (307-883-2899; http://www.svrawy.com/main/page_aspen_hills_.html), 781 Vista W. Drive, Thayne, 9 holes.

Cedar Creek Golf Course (307-883-2230; http://www.svrawy.com/main/page_cedar_creek__cedar_creek_1.html), Star Valley Ranch, 1800 Cedar Creek Drive, Thayne, 18 holes.

Fossil Island Golf Club (307-877-6954; http://www.kemmerer.org/golf.php), 105 WY 189, Kemmerer, 9 holes.

Purple Sage Golf Course (307-789-2383; http://www.purplesagegolf.com), 401 Kindler Drive, Evanston, 18 holes. Also home to **Nordic Center Winter Cross-country Skiing.**

Rendezvous Meadows Golf Club (307-367-4252; http://www.pinedaleonline .com/Golf.HTM), 55 Clubhouse Drive, Pinedale, 9 holes.

Valli Vu Golf Club (307-885-3338; http://www.vallivu.com), 83492 US 89, Afton, 18 holes.

HIKING **Clear Creek Trail** (#184), in the Bridger-Teton National Forest, is accessible via WY 352 to FR 10091, 52 miles northwest of Pinedale to the Green River Lakes. The 8-mile round-trip Clear Creek Trail takes you along the western shore of the northern Green River Lake (species include cutthroat and rainbow trout) before turning east into the Bridger Wilderness. The trail then takes you to a natural wonder—a natural bridge formed where Clear Creek wore a passageway through stone, an impressive demonstration of the persistent, erosive power of water. You can continue on for another 2 miles to Clear Lake if you wish, though this trail is not well maintained. This is one of several popular trails accessible from the Green River Lakes area, including Trail #144, which skirts the western shore of Upper Green Lake, and Trail #094, which takes you along the eastern shore of Lower Green Lake. Horseback riding is also popular here.

Lake Alice Trail, (#025), departs from Hobble Creek Campground (see Bridger-Teton National Forest in *Lodging*—Campgrounds). A moderate, 1.5-mile hike takes you to the south shore of Lake Alice, a lovely, unspoiled lake with fishing opportunities. The trail continues along the lakeshore, should you wish to explore further. There are a number of primitive, hike-in, tent-only, free campsites at Lake Alice. Formed by a landslide that dumped a mile of debris into Poker Creek, 3-mile long Lake Alice reaches depths up to 200 feet. As the lake's outlet flows beneath the natural dam, the lake's cutthroat trout population was effectively trapped and isolated by the landslide, and this is the only species you'll find in the lake. Horseback riding and mountain biking are also popular here.

Lake Barstow Trail, (#088), is accessible by taking FR 10138 southeast from Alpine, then going west on FR 10043 to the trailhead. This easy, 3-mile round-trip in the Bridger-Teton National Forest (see *Green Space*—National Lands) takes you along Three Forks Creek to Lake Barstow in the Salt River Range. Off-road motorized vehicles are allowed on this trail as well as foot traffic, horseback riders, and mountain bikes.

See also Pinedale in *To See*—Towns; Fossil Butte National Monument and Periodic Geyser in *To See*—Natural Wonders; Bear River Greenway in *To Do*—Bicycling; *To Do*—Boating; White Pine Ski Area and Resort in *To Do*—Snow Sports; and *Green Space.*

HORSEBACK RIDING **Green River Outfitters** (307-733-1044; http://www .greenriveroutfitters.com), P.O. Box 727, Pinedale. Ride a full day ($225 per person) in the Gros Ventre Mountains 35 miles south of Jackson. You'll enjoy the peaceful solitude of your surroundings, far from the normal tourist beat of the

Jackson Hole area. Longer trips are available as well, including an overnight bed & breakfast trail ride. Guided fishing and snowmobiling trips are available as well.

See also *To Do*—Hiking; White Pine Ski Area and Resort in *To Do*—Snow Sports; *Green Space*; Pole Creek Ranch Bed and Breakfast in *Lodging*—Bed and Breakfasts; and Big Sandy Lodge LLC, Boulder Lake Lodge, and Box Y Lodge and Guest Ranch in *Lodging*—Lodges.

PADDLING/FLOATING See Bear River Greenway in *To Do*—Bicycling; Fremont Lake in *To Do*—Boating; Greys River, New Fork River, and Salt River in *To Do*—Fishing; and *Green Space*.

RELAXATION AND REJUVENATION Blue Planet Foods (307-367-3833), 432 Pine Street, Pinedale. Call for current hours/days. At Blue Planet, you'll find natural and organic food options as well as other environmentally conscious products.

Cattle Kate's Salon and Spa (307-367-7669), 1175 W. Pine Street, Pinedale. Call to make an appointment in advance. Your aromatherapy treatment starts before you even walk through the door at Cattle Kate's, where soothing scents waft out the door to greet visitors. You can choose from a wide range of western-themed spa services including tanning, hairstyling, manicures, pedicures, wraps, massages, and a sauna, among others. Packages are also available.

Health Gone Wild Organic Foods (307-367-7625), 20 W. Pine Street, Pinedale. Call for current hours/days. Stop in at Your Trail to Good Health to stock up on all of your natural and organic food needs while in Pinedale.

Mountain Star Wellness Center (307-883-7433), 781 Vista E. Drive, Lower Level, Star Valley Ranch. Call for an appointment in advance. You can enjoy a soothing massage here at Star Valley Ranch. Choose from hot stone, Swedish, deep tissue, and more.

Spa 551 (307-367-7724), 551 S. Pine Street, Pinedale. Call for an appointment in advance. This full-service day spa offers a wide range of treatments, including massage, reflexology, aromatherapy, facials, pedicures, manicures, body wraps, and more.

✔ **Wind River Yoga & Body Works** (307-367-3156; http://www.windriveryoga .com), 220 S. Cole Avenue, Pinedale. Call or check online for a current schedule of classes; $10 per class. This studio offers kids' classes as well.

See also *To Do*—Fitness Centers.

SNOW SPORTS Cross-country skiing opportunities abound in this region on both groomed and ungroomed trails. For ideas of where to go, see Big Springs Scenic Backway in *To See*—Scenic Drives; Fossil Butte National Monument in *To See*—Natural Wonders; Bear River Greenway in *To Do*—Bicycling; Purple Sage Golf Course in *To Do*—Golf; White Pine Ski Area and Resort *To Do*—Snow Sports; and Bear River State Park in *Green Space*—State Parks.

Ice fishing opportunities can be found in the many lakes and reservoirs in this region, including Fremont Lake (see *To Do*—Boating).

✔ **Ice-skating** can be found in this region in a number of towns. Try the **Sublette County Ice Arena** (307-367-3613; http://www.sublette.com/hockey), 1219 W.

Washington Street, Pinedale; call for current rates and skate times. Evanston has a number of outdoor ponds that freeze hard enough for ice-skating (see Bear River Greenway in *To Do*—Bicycling). You can also ice skate farther south in this region at the **Cokeville Ice-skating Rink** (outdoors in **Cokeville Town Park** on Main Street), among other places.

Pine Creek Ski Resort (307-279-3201; http://www.pinecreekskiresort.com), 4061 Pine Creek Road/CR 204, Cokeville. Situated in the Tunp Mountain Range 7 miles east of Cokeville, this little ski area might be off the beaten path, but its terrain packs a punch without leaving you broke. The area has a terrain park and a half pipe, too. Lifts: one quad chairlift. Trails: 30—30 percent beginner, 35 percent intermediate, 35 percent advanced. Vertical Drop: 1,400 feet. Rates: $35 adult, $30 child.

Snowmobiling, like cross-country skiing, is very popular in this region. One key place to check out is the Wyoming Range Trail (http://www.sledwyoming.com), north of Kemmerer. For detailed trail reports, call 307-777-6560 or go to http://wyotrails.state.wy.us/snow, the Wyoming Snowmobile Trails Web site, which also provides information about rules, rental agencies, trails around the state, and more. For more snowmobiling ideas, see Big Springs Scenic Backway in *To See*—Scenic Drives; Green River Outfitters in *To Do*—Horseback Riding; Bridger-Teton National Forest and Bureau of Land Management in *Green Space*—National Lands; and Triple Peak Guest Ranch and Lodge in *Lodging*—Lodges.

Snowshoeing opportunities can be found on many of the region's public lands and trails. See *To Do*—Hiking and *Green Space* for ideas.

✎ **White Pine Ski Area and Resort** (307-367-6606; http://www.whitepineski .com), P.O. Box 1420, 10 miles northeast of Pinedale via Fremont Lake Road in the Bridger-Teton National Forest (see *Green Space*—National Lands). This resort, nestled just above the lovely small town of Pinedale (see *To Do*—Towns), includes many of the elegant amenities you might expect from a larger ski area—without all of the crowds and the hefty price tag. Cross-country skiers can access 21 miles (35+ km) of trails (free) from the resort's parking area, 5 miles (9 km) of which are groomed with both classic and skating lanes (additionally, the surrounding area has some 36 miles (60 km) of marked, groomed trails). In summer, the resort's activities include scenic chairlift rides, mountain biking, hiking, and horseback riding. Lifts: two triple chairlifts. Trails: 25+ trails—25 percent beginner, 45 percent intermediate, and 30 percent advanced. Vertical Drop: 1,100 feet. Facilities: three-story base lodge includes family-style dining at **White Pine Grill** (moderate to expensive) and more upscale dining at **The Grubsteak Restaurant** (reservations recommended; expensive) as well as a ski and rental shop; plus (new in 2004–5) duplex cabins available for rent near the lodge. Ski School: Offers ski and snowboard lessons for all ages and abilities. For children: Mountain Explorer and Junior Racer for ages 6–12. Rates: $40 per person; half-day rates available as well.

See also *Green Space*; Pole Creek Ranch Bed and Breakfast in *Lodging*—Bed and Breakfasts; and Green River Valley Winter Carnival in *Special Events*.

UNIQUE ADVENTURES See Fossil Butte National Monument in *To See*—Natural Wonders.

✳ **Green Space**

STATE PARKS ♿ 🏛 🐾 **Bear River State Park** (307-789-6547; http://wyoparks
.state.wy.us/Site/SiteInfo.asp?siteID=1), 601 Bear River Drive, Evanston (via Exit 6
off I-80). Park open 8 AM–10 PM daily; free (donations gladly accepted). If you're
looking for a quick place to stop, stretch your legs, and learn a little bit about
Wyoming—or you're in search of a longer recreational outing, perhaps involving
some wildlife viewing, picnicking, bicycling, cross-country skiing, or fishing (cutthroat trout), Bear River State Park has what you seek. Easily accessed from I-80,
the park features two protected, captive herds of Wyoming native mammals—bison
and elk, as well as a helpful travel information center (see Guidance). Nearly 3 miles
of trails (1.2-miles paved) afford hiking, biking, and cross-country skiing opportunities, linking into the Evanston Parks and Recreation Department's Bear River
Greenway system of trails (see *To Do*—Bicycling). Children will enjoy playing on the
playground equipment as well. See also Bear River Rendezvous in *Special Events*.

NATIONAL LANDS Bridger-Teton National Forest (307-739-5500; http://
www.fs.fed.us/btnf), P.O. Box 1888, Jackson, 83001. See listing in Northwest
Wyoming: Jackson and Dubois, as well as listing in *Lodging*—Campgrounds.

Bureau of Land Management (BLM) has two offices in this region—the Pinedale
Field Office (307-367-5300; http://www.blm.gov/wy/st/en/field_offices/
Pinedale.html), 1625 W. Pine Street, Pinedale, managing 912,000 acres of federal
surface land and mineral estate and almost 300,000 acres of private surface land and
mineral estate; and the Kemmerer Field Office (307-828-4500; http://www
.blm.gov/wy/st/en/field_offices/Kemmerer.html), 312 US 189 North, Kemmerer,
managing 1.4 million acres of surface lands and 1.6 million acres of mineral estate.
Much of this land is open to recreational pursuits, including bicycling, boating,
camping (see *Lodging*—Campgrounds), fishing, hiking, horseback riding, paddling,
and snow sports, including snowmobiling and cross-country skiing. BLM lands tend
to be the most unregulated of public lands, meaning that most typical outdoor recreational pursuits are allowed on most BLM lands, guided by the dictates of Leave No
Trace (1-800-332-4100 or 303-442-8222; http://www.lnt.org) outdoor ethics.

RECREATION AREAS See *To Do*—Boating.

✳ **Lodging**

BED AND BREAKFASTS
Pinedale
🍴 🐾 ♿ **The Chambers House Bed
and Breakfast** (1-800-567-2168 or
307-367-2168; http://www.chambers
house.com), 111 W. Magnolia Street.
Built in 1933 by one of Pinedale's pioneers, this historic, renovated log
structure combines the flavor of the
past with the comforts of modernity to
weave you an exquisite lodging experience. Throughout the inn and in the

five guest rooms, décor features family
antiques and handmade quilts. Some
guest rooms have private baths, and
two have private fireplaces as well. A
homemade breakfast is served daily.
The kids are welcome here. Moderate
to expensive.

🏛 🐾 🍴 🐾 ♿ **Pole Creek Ranch Bed
and Breakfast** (307-367-4433; http://
www.bbonline.com/wy/polecreek), 244

Fayette Pole Creek Road Rustic, ranch-style accommodations and adventures can be found year-round at Pole Creek Ranch. Choose to stay in one of three rooms, one with a private bath and two with a shared bath, or go for the out-of-the-ordinary and book a night or two in the ranch's tipi. You and the kids ($10 extra apiece) will find plenty of activities to keep you occupied, from horseback riding to buggy rides or horse-drawn sleigh rides in wintertime—and if you're traveling with a horse, boarding is also available. Soaking in the hot tub can help relax the most tired of muscles after day of play. You'll enjoy a full ranch breakfast served each morning. Moderate.

Star Valley

🌿 🍴 ♿ **Cabin Creek Inn** (307-883-3262; http://www.cabincreekinn.com), 211 S. Main, Thayne. Open April through November. Stay in one of 19 differently themed cabins—all of which are beautiful—at this inn. Clean and comfortable spacious accommodations will please even the most discerning of travelers—as will the reasonable rates. A swimming pool is on the property as well. Breakfast is served in the morning in the lobby. This is a great alternative if you want to visit the Jackson area but stay out of town. Moderate to expensive.

LODGES

Big Piney

🌿 **Triple Peak Guest Ranch and Lodge** (1-866-302-7753 or 307-276-3408; http://www.triplepeak.com), HCR 3000. Remote and rustic, you can have it all at this guest ranch and lodge (reservations required). Whether you are just looking for a place to rest your weary head, or you want a coordinated ranch-style vacation, Triple Peak can help you out. Eight guest bedrooms with private baths are available

by the night—and you can add in three home-cooked meals a day for not much more. It's also a great place for snowmobiling in winter. Moderate.

Pinedale

🌿 **Big Sandy Lodge LLC** (307-382-6513; http://www.big-sandy-lodge .com), 44 miles southeast of Boulder at 1050 Big Sandy Opening Road (ask for directions when you make reservations). Open late May through early October. Situated at the Big Sandy entrance to the Wind River Mountains, this remote mountain lodge sits at 9,100 feet and offers you a great jumping-off point for your mountain adventures. In operation since 1929, the rustic lodge has been providing guests with a place to dine on family-style meals and relax in front of a massive stone fireplace. You'll sleep in 1 of 10 rustic, one-room log cabins with wood-burning stoves, kerosene lamps, and no electricity or phone lines—but never fear, modern bathroom facilities are just a short walk out of your door, as are tremendous fishing opportunities. The lodge also offers package deals, horseback riding, pack trips, and gear drops. Moderate.

🍴 🌿 **Boulder Lake Lodge** (1-800-788-5401 or 307-537-5400; http://www.boulderlake.com), 48 Bridger Drive, Boulder (south of Pinedale). Located in the Bridger-Teton National Forest (see *Green Space*—National Lands), this lovely lodge features the pristine scenery most people only dream of seeing, let alone spending time in. You'll enjoy the modern comfort of your lodge room and private bath, while also spending some time in the lodge's central area, where three delicious meals are served family-style every day. Lodge activities include guided horseback riding, fishing trips, hunting, and float trips on the Green River and/or the New River. Ask about inclusive package deals. See also Fremont Lake in *To Do*—Boating. Moderate to expensive.

" 🐾 ♿ Lakeside Lodge, Resort, and Marina (1-877-755-LAKE or 307-367-2221; http://www.lakeside lodge.com), 99 FR 111, Fremont Lake. Stay in a basic, rustic cabin or a luxury cabin at this resort on the shores of Fremont Lake (see *To Do*—Boating)—or if you want, just pull up in your RV and camp at one of the resort's campsites (very inexpensive), enjoying the same access to the bathhouse as those staying in the rustic cabins. The lodge also features a dining room, marina, and access to the abundance of recreational opportunities in the surrounding environs. Moderate to expensive.

Star Valley

✎ Box Y Lodge and Guest Ranch (307-654-7564; http://www.boxylodge .com), P.O. Box 3051, Alpine. Situated between the majestic Wyoming and Salt River Ranges, this ranch gladly provides you with overnight lodging, should that be all you desire. Guests stay in one of eight private cabins (sleeping two to six people) that include full baths. The main lodge has satellite television, a large common area, and a casual dining room where the home-cooked meals are served. Summer activities include horseback riding, fishing, hiking, mountain biking, and more. Snowmobiling is popular in winter. Very expensive.

🐟 ✎ Silver Stream Lodge (307-883-2440; http://www.silverstreamlodge .com), 95329 US 89, Afton. Families and groups are welcomed to this lodge, where you'll stay in individual, modern cabins tucked in the woods next to a trout stream. The cozy and comfy cabins all have private baths, but no phone, televisions, or Internet connections, making them truly places to

escape from the constant distractions of the outside world. RV pads are also available. Moderate.

HOTELS AND MOTELS

Evanston

🐟 ♿ " 🐾 Prairie Inn Motel (307-789-2920), 264 Bear River Drive. Clean and comfortable, this no-frills accommodation gives you close access to Bear River State Park (see *Green Space*—State Parks). Yes, it may look a bit dated, but if you can get past that, you'll find little to complain about—especially not the price. Inexpensive to moderate.

Kemmerer

🐟 " 🐾 ♿ ✎ Fossil Butte Hotel (307-877-3996; http://www.fossilbutte motel.com), 1424 Central Avenue, Kemmerer. Kemmerer may not have much in the way of fancy accommodations, but if you're looking for somewhere tidy and modern to call home for a night, this little motel should do nicely. Moderate.

Pinedale

✎ 🐾 " ♿ The Log Cabin Motel (307-367-4579; http://www.thelogcabin motel.com), 49 E. Magnolia. Listed on the National Register of Historic Places, this 1929 motel offers you the privacy of your own historic cabin right in the classic mountain town of Pinedale. These cabins are the real deal—the original cabins constructed by local shop owner and businessman Walter Scott to provide travelers with overnight accommodations. Through the years since they have served additional purposes, including housing CCC workers, and they have changed names several times. Nonetheless, they also have been renovated several times and today stand restored and beautifully cared for, offering travelers comfortable, homey accommodations. Moderate to expensive.

See also Half Moon Lake Resort in *Where to Eat*—Dining Out.

Star Valley
See Brenthoven's Restaurant and Bull Moose Restaurant and Saloon in *Where to Eat*.

CAMPGROUNDS 🏕 ♿ **BLM Campgrounds** (see *Green Space*—National Lands) in the area include four developed facilities near Fontenelle Reservoir (see *To Do*—Boating) that are managed by the Kemmerer Field Office: **Fontenelle Creek Campground** (see *To Do*—Boating); **Slate Creek Campground,** 4 miles south of the reservoir (free); **Tail Race Campground**, .25 mile south of the reservoir (free); and **Weeping Rock Campground,** 1 mile south of the reservoir (free); among others. The Pinedale Field Office manages a number of free campgrounds as well, including **North Boulder Lake Campground,** from US 191 by Boulder, go 7 miles northeast on BLM 5106; **Upper Green River Campground,** 30 miles north of Pinedale along WY 352; **New Fork River Campground,** on WY 351 12 miles west of junction with US 191; **Scab Creek Campground,** about 15 miles northeast of Boulder via WY 353 to BLM 5423; and **Stokes Crossing Campground,** about 5 miles north of Boulder via Boulder N. Road. **Warren Bridge Campground** ($10) is 20 miles northwest of Pinedale on US 191. You should also know that in general, access to campgrounds is limited to the summer season, and that primitive camping is permitted on most BLM lands unless otherwise marked. For a complete list of BLM campgrounds in the area, call or stop by one of the field offices. See also Green River in *To Do*—Fishing.

♿ **Bridger-Teton National Forest** (see *Green Space*—National Lands) has a number of developed campgrounds in this regions. Big Piney Ranger District (307-276-5835) has two developed campgrounds, both of which lie west of Big Piney via WY 350/Middle Piney Road (Road 111/FR 10024): **Middle Piney Lake Campground** (early July through late September; free); and **Sacajawea Campground** (mid-June through late September; $7). The ranger district also has **two guard stations** available for rent ($30 per night; http://www.recreation.gov). Greys River Ranger District (307-886-5300) has seven developed campgrounds, five of which lie along FR 10138 on the Greys River (see *To Do*—Fishing), and two on the Star Valley Front, including **Swift Creek Campground,** just east of Afton off US 89 on Second Avenue to CR 138 to FR 10211 (mid-May through mid-October; $12). Kemmerer Ranger District (307-877-4415) has three developed campgrounds: **Allred Flat Campground,** 20 miles south of Afton on US 89 (late May through late October; $5; handicapped accessible); **Hobble Creek Campground** (see also Lake Alice Trail in *To Do*—Hiking), located on FR 10070, 34 miles northeast of Cokeville; follow WY 232 northeast 12 miles to a Y where the pavement ends; then go right, continuing 20 miles on graveled FR 10062, 10066, and 10193 to 10070 (early June through late October; $12); and **Hams Fork Campground,** 38 miles north of Kemmerer on Hams Fork Road (late May through late October; $12). The ranger district also has three **rental cabins** ($30 per night) available. The Pinedale Ranger District (307-367-4326) has nine developed campgrounds (some free), five of which are in the area around Fremont Lake (see *To Do*—Boating), including **Fremont Lake Campground** (mid-May through mid-September; $12), at which you can reserve sites in advance (http://www.recreation.gov). For more information, contact the appropriate ranger district.

⊕↑⊕ **Greys River Cove RV Park and Campground** (307-880-2267; http://www.greysrivercove.com), 25 US 89, Alpine. This RV park allows tent camping as well—or you can just pay for a shower if you need one. See also Trail Rides with Jackson Hole Outfitters in *To Do*—Horseback Riding in Northwest Wyoming: Jackson and Dubois. Very inexpensive.

⊕↑⊕ **Phillips RV Trailer Park** (1-800-349-3805 or 307-789-3805; http://www.phillipsrvpark.com), 225 Bear River Drive, Evanston. Tent sites are available as well at this full-service RV park close to Bear River State Park (see *Green Space*—State Parks). Very inexpensive.

See also Kemmerer in *To See*—Towns; Fremont Lake in *To Do*—Boating; and Lakeside Lodge, Resort, and Marina and Silver Stream Lodge in *Lodging*—Lodges.

OTHER OPTIONS

Pinedale

🖋 **Cow Cabins** (307-367-2428 or 307-276-3748; http://www.cowcabins.com), 45 miles from Jackson and 30 miles from Pinedale off US 191. Stay in one of two modern log cabins on a private ranch property of more than 2,000 acres. Breathtaking views of the surrounding mountains and secluded privacy make these cabins a destination in and of themselves—not to mention their central location between two charming Wyoming towns. At the Cow Cabins, you'll enjoy immediate access to all of the outstanding recreational opportunities afforded by your surroundings. Expensive to very expensive.

Star Valley

Old Mill Cabins (307-886-0520; http://www.oldmillcabins.com), 3497 Dry Creek Road, Afton. For spacious, private cabin accommodations in Star Valley, Old Mill Cabins can't be beat! Choose one of four log cabins to suit your needs. The Aspen, Cottonwood, and Lodgepole cabins all feature two queen-sized beds, private baths, private porches, access to the hot tub, gas fireplaces, cable television, and mini fridges. The larger Willow farmhouse features three bedrooms, sleeping up to eight people, as well as a full kitchen, washer/dryer, private porch, private picnic area, cable television, private bathroom, and access to the hot tub. Expensive to very expensive.

See also Bridger-Teton National Forest in *Lodging*—Campgrounds.

✳ Where to Eat

Evanston

Bon Rico Supper Club (307-789-1753); 925 Front Street. Call for current hours/days; reservations recommended. One of the best places to get a steak in Wyoming, Bon Rico has earned the respect of travelers and locals alike. You'll find other options on the menu (shrimp scampi, for example), but why bother? People come to Bon Rico to eat great steaks, with great service. Moderate to expensive. Bon Rico also has locations in Lyman (307-782-2667) and Kemmerer (307-877-4503).

TC's Steakhouse (307-789-3957; http://www.tcs-steakhouse.com), 1945 Harrison Drive. Open 4 PM–9 PM Monday through Saturday. This relatively new (2006) Evanston establishment promises to fill up your belly (and your family's, too) without breaking your budget. Situated in a remodeled fast-food restaurant, the ambiance is decent nonetheless. Choose from steak, seafood (fried shrimp is a specialty), and pasta, and help yourself to the salad bar. The full bar serves up a variety of specialty drinks. Moderate.

Kemmerer

♣ **Lola Z's Diner** (307-877-4350), 315 US 189. Open 11–8 Tuesday through Friday, 11–5 Saturday. Step back into your favorites 50s diner at Lola Z's, where you'll find portraits of such icons as James Dean, Betty Boop, and Marilyn Monroe on the walls along with tons of other fun signs from yesteryear. The menu includes at least 15 different styles of hamburgers, along with salads, sandwiches, steaks, chicken, shrimp, and even vegetarian options. An old-fashioned soda fountain offers you malts, shakes, and flavored sodas. Perhaps most impressive of all, Lola Z's has mastered the art of serving up a big, juicy burger with lots of toppings on a bun hefty enough to handle the load without disintegrating into a sloppy mess—and yet, it's still manageable enough for the diner to take reasonably sized bites. Inexpensive.

See also Bon Rico Supper Club, above.

La Barge

♪ **Historic Moondance Diner** (307-386-2103; http://www.historicmoon dancediner.com), 584 Main Street. Open 5:30 AM–9:30 PM Monday through Saturday. You won't miss the Moondance if you drive through La Barge. A huge glittery sign welcomes you back in time to the days of diners past. Inside, you'll discover that the food is out of this world. This cool hangout offers generous helpings of American favorites for breakfast, lunch, and dinner, often with a heavenly theme (think Man in the Moon and Stellar Steak). A children's menu is available. Moderate to expensive.

Lyman

See Bon Rico Supper Club, above.

Pinedale

♪ **Café on Pine** (307-367-3111), 807 W. Pine. Open 11–4:30 Monday through Friday (lunch), 5–9 Monday through Friday and Saturday in summer (dinner). Whether you're craving American or Italian fare, you can enjoy a delicious meal here in either department. Freshly prepared pastas, seafood, and steaks are the dinner menu's mainstays. Lunchtime brings lighter fare, including wraps, salads, sandwiches, and soups. You can even find fresh Alaskan salmon here. The kids can choose from their own menu. Everyone should leave room to at least share a homemade dessert creation by the chef. Patio seating is available in season. Moderate.

Pitchfork Fondue (307-367-3607; http://www.pitchforkfondue.com), at the Pinedale Rodeo Grounds, 9888 US 191; P.O. Box 894. Open for dinner Thursday through Saturday 5:30–8:30 mid-June through September. Watch as experienced chefs prong choice steaks on the tines of a pitchfork, and then cook them to perfection in mere minutes. That's the experience you'll find when you reserve your place for Pitchfork Fondue. To accompany your cauldron-sizzled steak, you'll choose from a number of sauces, as well as enjoying salad, rolls, and dessert. Seating is on covered pine picnic tables for up to 240 diners. Moderate.

& ⁽ᵀ⁾ **Rock Rabbit Coffee Shop** (307-367-2485; http://www.rockrabbit .com), 432 Pine Street. Call for current hours/days. This funky, hippie hangout is not just a place to fill up on your favorite brew, but also a place to browse through the assortment of trend-setting apparel. They also serve ice cream. The Rock Rabbit hosts numerous events, including concerts and parties. Call for details or check the online calendar. Inexpensive.

See also White Pine Ski Area and Resort in *To Do*—Snow Sports; and Lakeside Lodge, Resort, and Marina in *Lodging*—Lodges.

Star Valley

&. ⁹₁⁹ **Brenthoven's Restaurant** (307-654-7556; http://www.brent hovens.com), 1 mile east of the junction of US 89 and US 26 in Alpine. Open 8–11:30 (breakfast), 11:30–1:30 (lunch), 6:30–10 (dinner) Memorial Day through September; reservations recommended. Whether you're in the mood for a salad or a full Thanksgiving-style turkey dinner, you'll find something to please you on the menu here. Seafood, chicken, and steak are also featured on the dinner menu. You can also grab a room at the **Nordic Inn** (moderate to expensive). Moderate to expensive.

Bull Moose Restaurant and Saloon (1-877-498-7993 or 307-654-7593; http://www.bullmoosesaloon.com), 91 US 89, Alpine. Saloon open 8 AM–2 AM daily; restaurant has shorter hours. Stop in for a smoked prime rib, steak, or salmon, or go for some less-expensive, pub-style fare, including an assortment of burgers and sandwiches. You can also just choose a couple of appetizers and nosh for a quick pick-me-up during your travels. Step into the saloon to experience more true western flair, with its moose and elk chandeliers, wood paneled walls, and animal mounts. You can also grab a room at the new (2007) **Bull Moose Lodge** (moderate to expensive). The Bull Moose also has a liquor store, gift shop, and sometimes, live music. Moderate to expensive.

Star Valley Grille at the Cheese Factory (307-883-2510), 290 S. Main Street, Thayne. Call for current hours/days. While the cheese factory itself closed its doors in 2005 after half a century of being the place in Star Valley where dairy farmers brought their milk for processing, the restaurant (serving American fare) is still in operation. Even better, you might find that this historic cheese factory itself is back up and running, producing great local cheese once again.

✳ Entertainment

Evanston Valley Cinema (307-789-0522), 45 Aspen Grove Drive E., Evanston.

Ford Theater (307-886-5684), 443 Washington Street, Afton.

Pinedale Entertainment Center (307-367-6688), 153 S. Entertainment Lane, Pinedale.

Pinedale Fine Arts Council (307-367-7322; http://www.pinedalefinearts .com), P.O. Box 1586, Pinedale. PFAC organizes numerous concerts and performances throughout the year.

Victory Theatre (307-877-6684), 720 JC Penney Drive, Kemmerer.

Wyoming Downs (307-789-0512; http://www.wyomingdowns.com), 10180 US 89 N, Evanston. Open 11:30 (first post time at 1:05 PM) Saturday and Sunday late June and July.

See also Fossil Country Frontier Museum in *To See*—Museums; and Rock Rabbit Coffee Shop and Bull Moose Restaurant and Saloon in *Where to Eat*.

✳ Selective Shopping

Cowboy Shop (1-877-56-RODEO or 307-367-4300; http://www.cowboy shop.com), 120 W. Pine, Pinedale. Call for current hours/days. Feeling a little underdressed—for a cowboy or cowgirl? If you want to really get into the role while you're visiting Wyoming, the Cowboy Shop can help you out. For more than 60 years, this shop has been outfitting cowboys and cowgirls (and cow-kids, too) from all over the world.

John Dickie Custom Iron Work (307-276-3247; http://www.johndickie .com), P.O. Box 693, Big Piney. Absolutely gorgeous pieces of welded art range from silhouetted wildlife on lampshades to coat racks, historic pistol replicas to iron work for entrance gates, and more. Visit the Web site or contact the artist directly for more information or to purchase/commission a piece.

Jonathan the Bear Man (307-866-9862; http://www.jonathanbearman .com), P.O. Box 1329, Afton. Wondering who created Afton's elk-antler arch (see *To See*—Towns)? Jonathan the Bear Man did, and you can take a piece of his artwork home with you as a permanent reminder of your trip to Wyoming, if you so desire. Call or visit the Web site for a list of current pieces or to arrange for a custom-made work.

Star Valley Artisans (http://www.star valleyartisans.com) is an online marketplace that features the works of artists, musicians, and craftsmen from Star Valley. These include **Wyoming Wild Woods** (307-885-5707), featuring carved bears and lifelike wildflowers, among other notable contributors. Consider commemorating your Wyoming visit by supporting local artisans.

See also Fossil Country Frontier Museum in *To See*—Museums; Fort Bridger State Historic Site and J. C. Penney Homestead and Historical Foundation in *To See*—Historic Landmarks, Places, and Sites; and Bull Moose Saloon and Restaurant in *Where to Eat*.

✳ Special Events

✍ *March:* **Green River Valley Winter Carnival,** Pinedale: This winter festival includes children's games, arm wrestling competitions, ice-water swimming challenge, and more frozen fun.

April: **Aniel Daniel Chili Cook-Off,** Daniel: This cooking competition pits chili wizards against one another in a tasting extravaganza.

✍ *May:* **B.E.A.RiverFest,** Evanston: This celebration centered on the Bear River includes kayak/boat races, live music, vendors, a gear swap, a raffle, and children's activities. See also Bear River Greenway in *To Do*—Bicycling.

✍ *June:* **Alpine Mountain Days,** Alpine: An annual celebration of western and mountain heritage held over Father's Day weekend, events include Dutch-oven cook-offs, music, black powder shoots, and children's activities, among others.

✍ *July:* **Green River Rendezvous Days** (http://www.meetmeonthe green.com), Pinedale: The annual mountain man celebration includes a pageant reenacting the 1830s rendezvous that happened annually in this area, as well as camping, children's activities, lectures, and more.

July: **Shakespeare in the Park** (307-332-2905; http://www.wyomingshake speare.com), Pinedale: A statewide touring theater group performs Shakespeare in American Legion Park (other performances given in parks around the state as well).

🦪 *July, August:* **Oyster Ridge Music Festival** (http://www.oysterridgemusic festival.com), Kemmerer: An annual free music festival featuring local and regional artists.

August: **Bear River Mountain Man Rendezvous,** Evanston: This celebration the weekend before Labor Day at Bear River State Park (see *Green Space*—State Parks) includes reenactments of traditional 19th-century mountain man rendezvous events, with costumed competitors engaging in black powder shoots and other competitions.

September: **Fort Bridger Rendezvous** (http://www.fortbridgerrendezvous .net), Fort Bridger State Historic Site (see *To See*—Historic Landmarks, Places, and Site): This annual Labor Day weekend event with costumed actors recreating historical rendezvous activities includes games, entertainment, food, and more.

See also Afton in *To See*—Towns; and Fremont Lake in *To Do*—Boating.

GREEN RIVER AND ROCK SPRINGS

On the western side of the Great Divide Basin (see *To See*—Natural Wonders), you'll find Rock Springs and Green River, both historic railroad towns. Stop first, perhaps, at the Rock Springs Historical Museum or the Sweetwater County Historical Museum (see *To See*—Museums) for background information on the area's historical ties to both mining and the railroad. From here, you can also access the one-of-a-kind Flaming Gorge National Recreation Area (see *Green Space*—Recreation Areas), taking a scenic loop driving tour on the Flaming Gorge-Green River Basin Scenic Byway (see *To See*—Scenic Drives). If you're shorter on time, you can also potentially see wild horses (see *To See*—Scenic Drives) north of the city, or go for a jaunt to the Killpecker Sand Dunes, one of the largest active dune systems in the country (see *To See*—Natural Wonders). In Green River, you'll find a unique in-town recreational opportunity at the Green River Whitewater Park (see *To Do*—Paddling/Floating), one of 26 parks found in the city.

GUIDANCE City of Green River
(307-872-0500;
http://www.cityofgreenriver
.org), 50 E. Second N. Street, Green
River, 82935.

City of Rock Springs (307-352-1500;
http://www.rswy.net), 212 D Street,
Rock Springs, 82901.

Green River Chamber of Commerce (1-800-FL-GORGE or 307-875-5711; http://www.grchamber.com),
1155 W. Flaming Gorge Way, Green
River, 82935.

Rock Springs Chamber of Commerce (1-800-46-DUNES or 307-362-3771; http://www.rockspringswyoming
.net), 1897 Dewar Drive, P.O. Box
398, Rock Springs, 82902-0398.

SWEETWATER COUNTY HISTORICAL
MUSEUM

BE WARY OF WINTRY DRIVING IN SOUTHERN WYOMING

I would be remiss to leave you to your travels through these cities along I-80 (as well as the others, including Evanston, Rawlins, Laramie, and Cheyenne) without mentioning that though I-80 is an interstate highway, and though it is one of the country's major east-west transportation routes, traveling on I-80 during inclement weather conditions can be a hair-raising and even life-threatening event. High winds blow semis off the roadway at times (I've seen this), and I've driven for miles upon miles holding the steering wheel sideways and thinking that my car's alignment must be off, only to realize that I've been compensating for the winds all along. And if it snows, well, you'd better be good at dealing with slick, slippery surfaces and blinding, blowing snow—not to mention semis screaming by you at 70 or 80 miles per hour, seemingly impervious to the horrendous conditions of the roadway.

Don't be too scared, though—just be prepared, use good judgment, respect all road closures, and postpone your travels if need be. If you do encounter bad weather, perhaps you'll even feel a little bit of kinship with the American Indians and pioneer emigrants who braved this harsh and unforgiving environment with drastically fewer resources than we have today—after all, they couldn't just call it quits and grab a hotel room for the night!

Sweetwater County (307-872-3732 or 307-922-5208; http://www.co.sweet .wy.us), 80 W. Flaming Gorge Way, Green River, 82935.

Sweetwater County Joint Travel and Tourism Board (307-382-2538; http://www.tourwyoming.com), 404 N. Fourth Street, P.O. Box 38, Rock Springs, 82902.

YOU CAN ENJOY A SELF-GUIDED WALKING TOUR OF HISTORIC DOWNTOWN ROCK SPRINGS

GETTING THERE *By car*· Rock Springs (Exit 104) and Green River (Exit 91) are just off I-80 in southwest Wyoming. Rock Springs can also be reached by US 191 from the north and WY 430 from the south. Green River can also be reached by WY 372 from the north and WY 530 from the south.

By plane: **Rock Springs–Sweetwater County Airport** (307-352-6880; http://www.rockspringsairport.com) is a few miles east of downtown Rock Springs.

GETTING AROUND You can walk around the downtown areas of both Green River and Rock Springs, but some attractions in both cities will be easier to reach by car. Likewise, you'll need to use your car to explore this region's outlying attractions.

MEDICAL EMERGENCY Dial 911.
Memorial Hospital of Sweetwater County (307-362-3711; http://www.sweetwatermedicalcenter.com), 1200 College Drive, Rock Springs.

✱ To See

MUSEUMS ♿ ❦ **Community Fine Arts Center** (307-362-6212; http://www.cfac4art.com), 400 C Street, Rock Springs. Open 10–6 Monday through Thursday, noon–5 Friday through Saturday; free. View exhibits featuring works by some of the finest Western

COMMUNITY FINE ARTS CENTER

artists of the 20th century, including Grandma Moses and Norman Rockwell, among other notable figures. The center also features works by local and regional contemporary artists of note, as well as hosting an array of rotating exhibits and arts-related community events throughout the year.

❦ **Rock Springs Historical Museum** (307-362-3138; http://www.rswy.net/Museum/Intro.htm), 201 B Street, Rock Springs. Open 10–5 Monday through Saturday; free. The museum's exhibits are centered around the history of the Rock Springs area, particularly focused on the time period beginning with the coming of the transcontinental railroad (1868) onward. Learn about not only the impact of the railroad, but also the area's ties to the coal mining industry. The first stop on the Historic Downtown Walking Tour, the museum itself is housed in the old city hall, which features beautiful architecture, including a gorgeous clock tower.

THE STRIKING ROCK SPRINGS HISTORICAL MUSEUM, IN THE OLD CITY HALL BUILDING

♿ ❦ **Sweetwater County Historical Museum** (307-872-6435 or 307-352-6715; http://www.sweetwatermuseum.org), 3 E. Flaming Gorge Way, Green River. Open 10–6 Monday through Saturday; free. Dedicated to the preservation and presentation of the local and regional area's history, this county museum features exhibits on prehistoric inhabitants of the area, the American Indians, early explorers, mountain men and fur trading, the historic trails that passed this way (including the Oregon Trail and the Overland

282

Stagecoach Trail), the transcontinental railroad, coal mining, and more. Situated in a historic building itself—a restored 1931 U.S. Post Office building—the museum's collection also includes a remarkable number of historical photographs.

HISTORIC LANDMARKS, PLACES, AND SITES ✿ ♿ **Reliance Tipple** (307-872-6435 or 307-352-6715; http://www.sweetwatermuseum.org/reliance _tipple.htm), 5 miles north of Rock Springs via WY 191 to Reliance Road (CR 42); open dawn to dusk daily; free. View one of the few such structures that remain intact. Used to sort and grade coal, and then to load it into railroad cars for transport, the tipple today stands as a testament to this area's strong historical ties to both the railroad and the mining industries. A self-guided interpretive tour is available, allowing you to learn more about the tipple during your visit.

See also Rock Springs Historical Museum and Sweetwater County Historical Museum in *To See*—Museums.

CITY PARKS AND GARDENS ♿ ✿ **The City of Green River** (see Guidance) has 26 parks and eight pathways throughout the city. Park features include playground equipment, water features, picnic areas, athletic fields, natural areas, a skate park, and more. You can download a map of the parks from the city's Web site. See also Green River in *To Do*—Fishing and Green River Whitewater Park in *To Do*—Paddling/Floating.

♿ ✿ **The City of Rock Springs** (see Guidance) has 24 parks and walkways situated throughout the city. Park features include playground equipment, waterslides, paved pathways, historical displays, picnic areas, and more. For a complete list of the parks and a map, visit the city's Web site.

SCENIC DRIVES **Flaming Gorge-Green River Basin Scenic Byway** is a journey that can be taken as a 160-mile loop from US 191 to WY 530 with a brief passage through Utah on UT 44, or as a one-way, 70–90-mile journey entering or exiting Wyoming via US 191 or WY 530. Begin the loop by exiting at exit 99 off I-80 just west of Rock Springs and head south on US 191 for about 70 miles to Dutch John, passing over the Flaming Gorge Dam shortly thereafter. Watch for signs for UT 44, and head west then northwest for about 40 miles to Manila, UT, which is right on the border. From there, head north on WY 530, a journey of about 50 miles. If you choose to do the entire loop, you'll get a remarkably complete overview of the beautiful Flaming Gorge National Recreation Area (see *Green Space*—Recreation Areas). Just don't expect your drive to be a quick one, as some of the roads are winding and slow—plus, the dramatic scenery will likely make you want to make more than one stop. Another caveat—like many

RELIANCE TIPPLE

Wyoming roads, this route can be dangerous, even if it's not officially closed due to inclement weather, so use good judgment.

Wild Horse Tours make for a fun adventure in this region, as you search to see some of Wyoming's bona fide wild horses while traversing windswept prairies and open terrain on back roads. One designated loop tour through the area with the largest population of wild horses in Wyoming—the BLM's **White Mountain Herd Management Area**—departs from just north of Rock Springs (see *Green Space*—National Lands). Take US 191 north for 14 miles to CR 14, and then go west, following signs for the tour. Head south on CR 53 (White Mountain Road) as it arcs around the base of **Pilot Butte,** a defining natural landmark, depositing you in Green River. Please respect the wild horses (it's illegal to chase them), and be sure you are prepared—this means having a spare tire, plenty of water, and paying attention to the weather, since back roads can quickly become quagmires in poor driving conditions.

NATURAL WONDERS

See also Wild Horse Tours in *To See*—Scenic Drives; and Flaming Gorge National Recreation Area in *Green Space*—Recreation Areas.

✶ To Do

BICYCLING See *To See*—City Parks and Gardens and *Green Space*.

BOATING ⚓ **Big Sandy Reservoir**, managed by the Bureau of Reclamation (801-379-1000; http://www.recreation.gov/detail.cfm?ID=1229), is located just off US 191, 9.5 miles north of Farson, then east on CR 28. Big Sandy Reservoir, with 2,500 acres of surface area, offers opportunities not only for boating (boat launch), but also for wildlife viewing, swimming, hunting, camping (free), and fishing (species include brown trout, channel catfish, cutthroat trout, and rainbow trout). South of Big Sandy Reservoir is **Eden Reservoir,** accessed by taking WY 28, 4 miles east of Farson, and then going north on Farson Second E. Road (Eden Reservoir Road) for 7 miles. This reservoir also permits fishing (species include cutthroat trout and rainbow trout).

See also *Green Space*.

CLIMBING See Rock Springs Family Recreation Center in *To Do*—Fitness Centers.

FISHING Green River (307-875-3223; http://gf.state.wy.us/fish/fishing/index.asp), originates from the Green River Lakes in the Bridger Wilderness of the Wind River Range, in the Bridger-Teton National Forest (see *Green Space*—National Lands in Evanston and Star Valley). The river arcs south and continues for 730 miles, eventually emptying into the Colorado River in Utah. In this lower portion of the Green River, before it enters Flaming Gorge Reservoir, it flows through the town of Green River, where you'll find easy access from numerous parks along the river's banks, including Evers Park, Expedition Island Park, the Greenbelt Pathway, and Scotts Bottom Nature Area. The nature areas also include unpaved trails with interpretive signs. Fish species include brown trout, catfish, cutthroat trout, kokanee salmon, and rainbow trout. See also City of Green River

UNIQUELY WYOMING: THE GREAT DIVIDE BASIN
AND THE RED DESERT

The Great Divide Basin, roughly bordered by US 287 to the northeast, by WY 28 to the northwest, by US 191 and by Rock Springs to the west, from near Rock Springs to Rawlins along I-80 to the south, and jutting out near Seminoe Reservoir to the east, is a topographic feature that is truly unique to the state of Wyoming. Here, the 3,100-mile Continental Divide splits in two, encircling the basin. And the water that falls here? It stays right here, in this 90-mile-wide, 2.5-million-acre basin, which has no river outlet, meaning that water can't escape to the east or the west. Not that much precipitation falls here anyhow—this area forms a rather large portion of Wyoming's incredible Red Desert (see below). Managed by the BLM (see *Green Space— National Lands*), you'll pass through part of the basin if you drive from Rock Springs to Rawlins. For a closer look at the incredible vast and stark terrain of the basin, which includes a prolific amount of animal life, see Wild Horse Tours in *To See*—Scenic Drives. See also Continental Divide National Scenic Trail in *To Do*—Hiking.

Killpecker Sand Dunes are part of the Red Desert (see below). They lie on the southwestern side of the Great Divide Basin (see above) on the other side of the Continental Divide. Accessed by driving north from Rock Springs on WY 191 for about 10 miles, and then heading northeast on CR 17 (Chilton Road, a decent dirt road) for about 20 miles, these dunes are one of the largest active dune systems in North America. Towering up to 150 feet in height, the dunes constantly shift in shape and size due to the winds blowing them eastward. They measure 75 miles in length and are 3 miles wide. A particularly intriguing feature of these dunes is the phenomenon known as eolian ice cells, in which layers of sand blow over banks of snow on the dunes in colder months, keeping them frozen until summer's heat begins to melt them. As they melt, they form pools of water at the bases of the dunes, creating true oases in this desert environment. Part of this area is designated by the BLM as the **Killpecker Sand Dunes Open Play Area,** open to motorized off-road vehicles (see http://www.blm.gov/wy/st/en/field _offices/Rock_Springs/rec/dunes.html for details). Use care whether you're exploring by foot, horseback, or on an off-road vehicle to keep track of where you are, since the similarity of the terrain can lead to confusion and disorientation (a compass is recommended).

Red Desert encompasses an enormous, 8-million acre tract of BLM-managed lands in southern Wyoming, including the Great Divide Basin and

Killpecker Sand Dunes (see above). This desert, with its brilliantly hued red sands (hence the name), is one of the country's few remaining relatively undisturbed high desert ecosystems. Home to the largest migratory herd of pronghorn antelope in the lower 48 states (50,000 animals), the Red Desert sustains numerous additional species of animals, including the largest herd of desert elk, rare birds, and more—350 species of animals, all told. The desert is home to the unique natural features mentioned above, along with other distinctive natural features including the **Oregon Buttes**. Historical features include portions of the Oregon Trail, Overland Trail, Mormon Trail, and Pony Express Trail, as well as American Indian cultural sites. The future of the desert as an intact ecosystem has been threatened in recent years by oil and gas mining interests. For more information about this issue, as well as detailed background information on the Red Desert, contact the Wyoming Outdoor Council (307-332-7031; http://www.wyomingoutdoorcouncil.org).

KILLPECKER SAND DUNES OPEN PLAY AREA

in *To See*—City Parks and Gardens; Green River Whitewater Park in *To Do*—Paddling/Floating; and Flaming Gorge National Recreation Area in *Green Space*—Recreation Areas.

See also Big Sandy Reservoir in *To Do*—Boating; *Green Space*; and Sweetwater River in *To Do*—Fishing in Central Wyoming: Casper and Douglas.

FITNESS CENTERS ✔ **Green River Recreation Center** (307-872-0511; http://www.cityofgreenriver.org), 200 E. Railroad Avenue, Green River. Open 5 AM–9 PM Monday through Friday, 10–7 Saturday, noon–7 Sunday (summer); call for winter and pool hours; $4.25 per adult, $2.50 per senior 60-plus, $2.25 per child 8–18, under 7 free with paid admission, $11.50 per family. This full-service recreation center includes a pool with a diving board and kiddie structure, fitness equipment, racquetball courts, a nursery, and more.

✔ **Rock Springs Family Recreation Center** (307-352-1440; http://www.rswy .net/departments/FRC_Main.htm), 3900 Sweetwater Drive, Rock Springs. Open 4:30 AM–8 PM Monday through Friday, 7–5 Saturday and Sunday (summer); call for winter and pool hours; $6 per nonresident adult, $5 per resident adult, $1.50 per senior 62+, $3.75 per nonresident youth/student 7–18/ under 24 with ID, $2.75 per resident youth/student, 6 and under free. This 129,000-square-foot recreation center offers a full-range of fitness opportunities, along with Rock Springs' smaller **Civic Center** (307-352-1420; http://www.rswy.net/departments/ CC_Main.htm), 410 N. Street. Open 5 AM–9 PM Monday through Friday, 7–5 Saturday and Sunday (summer); call for winter and pool hours; same fees as Rec Center. Facilities include a rock climbing wall (Civic Center only; $1.25 extra for shoe/harness rental), swimming pool, exercise equipment, gymnasiums, an indoor track, batting cage, and an array of fitness classes, including yoga.

FOR FAMILIES See *To See*—City Parks and Gardens; Green River Recreation Center and Rock Springs Family Recreation Center in *To Do*—Fitness Centers; and Flaming Gorge National Recreation Area in *Green Space*—Recreation Areas.

FAMILIES WITH CHILDREN CAN ENJOY GREEN RIVER'S PARK WATER FEATURES, SUCH AS THIS ONE NEAR EXPEDITION ISLAND

GOLF Rolling Green Country Club (307-875-6200), 1050 Elk Mountain, 3 miles west of Green River, 9 holes.

White Mountain Golf Course (307-352-1415; http://www.rswy.net/ Departments/golf_course.htm), 1501 Clubhouse Drive, Rock Springs, 18 holes.

HIKING See *To See*—City Parks and Gardens; *Green Space*; and Three Patches Recreation Area in *Lodging*—Campgrounds.

HORSEBACK RIDING See *Green Space*.

PADDLERS ENJOYING THE GREEN RIVER WHITEWATER PARK

PADDLING/FLOATING Green River Whitewater Park, on the Green River in Green River (see Guidance), features several manmade drops designed by Coloradoan Gary Lacy. With exciting names like The Electrocutioner, Powell's Plunge, and Castle Falls, these U-drop features are fun for the whitewater enthusiast, whether you're a kayaker or a canoeist. Access is easy, particularly from Evers Park and Expedition Island Park (off Second Street.). See also Green River in *To Do—Fishing.*

See also Big Sandy Reservoir in *To Do*—Boating and *Green Space.*

RELAXATION AND REJUVENATION Escape Day Spa (307-362-5005; http://www.escapedayspa.us), 617 Broadway Suite C, Rock Springs. Open 9–7 Monday through Friday, 9–9 Wednesday, 9–6 Saturday; call for an appointment. Prepare yourself for a true spa experience right here in southwest Wyoming. Services offered include massage ($65/hour), hair care, hair removal, facials, spa treatments, makeup, permanent makeup, manicures, and pedicures. Spa packages are available. You'll also find a boutique with an array of beauty/health products for sale, so you can continue your pampering while you travel or at home.

See Rock Springs Family Recreation Center in *To Do*—Fitness Centers.

SNOW SPORTS Ice fishing is possible at Big Sandy Reservoir (see *To Do—* Boating).

✆ **Ice-skating** can be found in Rock Springs at the Rock Springs Family Recreation Center Ice Arena (307-352-1445; http://www.rswy.net/Departments/FRC_IceArena.htm), 3900 Sweetwater Drive, Rock Springs. Call for current hours/rates.

See also *Green Space.*

UNIQUE ADVENTURES See Wild Horse Tours in *To See*—Scenic Drives.

❋ Green Space

NATIONAL LANDS Bureau of Land Management (307-352-0256; http://www.blm.gov/wy/st/en/field_offices/Rock_Springs.html), Rock Springs Field Office, 280 US 191 North, Rock Springs. The Rock Springs Field Office is responsible for managing more than 3.6 million acres of public lands and more than 3.5 million acres of federal mineral estate. On BLM lands in this region, you'll find a number of natural wonders, including the Great Divide Basin, Killpecker Sand Dunes, Red Desert (see *To See*—Natural Wonders), and wild horses (see Wild Horse Tours in *To See*—Scenic Drives). Much of the land administered by the BLM is open to recreational pursuits, including bicycling, boating, camping (see *Lodging*—Campgrounds), fishing, hiking, horseback riding, paddling, rock climbing, wildlife viewing, and snow sports, including snowmobiling and cross-country skiing. BLM lands tend to be the most unregulated of public lands, meaning that most typical outdoor recreational pursuits are allowed on most BLM lands, guided by the dictates of Leave No Trace (1-800-332-4100 or 303-442-8222; http://www.lnt.org) outdoor ethics.

WILDLIFE REFUGES AND AREAS ❧ Seedskadee National Wildlife Refuge (307-875-2187; http://seedskadee.fws.gov), accessible by taking WY 372 northwest from Green River for 27 miles, is a tremendous place for wildlife viewing and solitude. Situated on a 36-mile stretch of the Green River, this 27,230-acre wildlife refuge is home to pronghorn antelope, moose, and mule deer, as well as hundreds of bird species, including trumpeter swans, golden eagles, and sage grouse. You might also stumble upon the ruins of a pioneer cabin or two, as this area was briefly inhabited by pioneers in the late 1800s.

See also Wild Horse Tours in *To See*—Scenic Drives; Big Sandy Reservoir in *To Do*—Boating; and Three Patches Recreation Area in *Lodging*—Campgrounds.

❋ Lodging

BED AND BREAKFASTS
Rock Springs
🍴 **Miner's Repose Bed and Breakfast** (307-362-7880; http://www.minersrepose.com), 716 B Street, Rock Springs. Housed in a home constructed in 1940 for a local physician, this B&B is within walking distance of many of Rocks Springs' attractions. Two beautifully furnished rooms (adults only, please) both have private baths, mini-fridges, and access to an outdoor hot tub. Expensive.

HOTELS AND MOTELS Green River and **Rock Springs** feature mainly mainstream, national-brand hotel and motel chains, of which both

cities have plenty. In Green River, suitable options include **Super 8** (307-875-9330; http://www.super8.com) and **Hampton Inn** (307-875-5300; http://www.hamptoninn.com), among others. In Rock Springs, decent choices include **Super 8** (307-362-3800), **America's Best Value Inn and Suites** (307-362-9600; http://www.americasbestvalueinn.com), and **Hampton Inn** (307-382-9222). Call for reservations or book online.

CAMPGROUNDS 🍴 🐾 ♿ **Rock Springs KOA** (1-800-562-8699 or 307-362-3063; http://www.rockspringskoa

RECREATION AREAS

FLAMING GORGE

🔱 ♿ **Flaming Gorge National Recreation Area** (435-784-3445; http://www
.fs.fed.us/r4/ashley/recreation/flaming_gorge/index.shtml) is along WY 530
south of Green River. Open year-round; day use is $5 per vehicle per day in
managed areas; see information about camping below. Green River **Flaming
Gorge Visitor Center** (307-875-2871; southwest on WY 530) is open Monday
through Saturday, hours vary seasonally. Managed by Ashley National Forest (which is mostly in Utah), the Flaming Gorge National Recreation Area
offers a number of recreational opportunities in an area of land that strad-
dles the Wyoming and Utah border, with the majority of developed services
in Utah. The chief feature of this area is the enormous Flaming Gorge Reservoir, with its 42,000-acre surface area, 300 miles of shoreline, and its length
of 91 miles, which was created in the early 1960s by the construction of the
Flaming Gorge Dam, damming the Green River. Flaming Gorge itself received
its name from the famed explorer John Wesley Powell, who deemed it thus
upon viewing the brilliantly hued sandstone walls of the canyon during his
1869 exploration of the area. Popular activities include fishing (brown trout,
channel catfish, cutthroat trout, kokanee salmon, mackinaw trout, rainbow
trout, and smallmouth bass); boating (in Wyoming, numerous access sites
for launching located at the end of dirt roads off WY 530, including **Buckboard Marina**, 25 miles southwest of Green River off WY 530, which also
rents boats); and seasonal camping (go to http://www.recreation.gov to
reserve some sites). Campgrounds include **Buckboard Campground** ($14),
located 23 miles southwest of Green River via WY 530 to FR 009, then 1.5
miles southeast to the campground; and **Firehole Campground** ($14), located
23 miles south of Rock Springs on WY 191. Hiking, bicycling/mountain biking,
horseback riding, picnicking, and snow sports are also permitted in the
area. For more information, contact **Lucerne Valley Marina** (435-784-
3483;http://www.flaminggorge.com), which also offers cabin and houseboat
rentals (expensive to very expensive). See also Green River in *To Do*—Fishing; and Flaming Gorge Days in *Special Events*.

.com), 86 Foothill Boulevard, Rock
Springs. This full-service KOA
includes a swimming pool, hot tub
(adults only), playground, espresso bar,
game room, and more. Cabins and tent
camping are available as well. Very
inexpensive to inexpensive.

🦫 **Three Patches Recreation Area**
is a popular spot for picnicking that
also allows primitive camping (free),
accessible by taking WY 430 southeast
out of Rock Springs to Aspen Mountain Road (CR 27), and following this
south for about 10 miles to reach the

area, which is managed by the BLM (see *Green Space*—National Lands). See also Big Sandy Reservoir in *To Do*—Boating.

OTHER OPTIONS See Flaming Gorge National Recreation Area in *Green Space*—Recreation Areas and Rock Springs KOA in Campgrounds.

✳ Where to Eat

EATING OUT

Green River

China Garden Restaurant (307-875-3259), 190 N. Fifth E. Open 11–9 Monday through Saturday, 11–8 Sunday. For a good selection of classic Chinese entrées, all at reasonable prices, this restaurant fits the bill. Mongolian beef, sesame chicken, egg foo young— you'll find all of your favorites here, plus a number of less-mainstream options. You can even please those in your party who are not interested in ethnic food, as the restaurant also serves some American fare for less adventurous diners. If you want to catch that important sporting event, this is a likely place to watch it, as the restaurant has a sports bar as well. Moderate.

✿ **Krazy Moose Restaurant** (307-875-5124), 211 E. Flaming Gorge Way (in the Red Feather Bar). Open for three meals a day. The entire family is welcome to sit down and enjoy a hearty, delicious meal at this Green River establishment. The restaurant features traditional American fare served just the way you like it, from hearty burgers and sandwiches to steaks (8-ounce to 24-ounce), seafood, and chicken entrées. Top off your meal with a delectable homemade dessert. A children's menu is available. Moderate.

Rock Springs

✿ **Bitter Creek Brewing** (307-362-4782; http://www.bittercreekbrewing

.com), 604 Broadway. Open 11:30–10 daily. Above-average pub fare in a comfortable, welcoming atmosphere is what you'll find at this local establishment, which serves up an array of microbrews crafted in the brewery on the premises, including Red Desert Ale and Mustang Pale Ale, among others. The kids can even sample a microbrew, too—a root beer, that is! The extensive menu includes something for everyone, including burgers and sandwiches, steaks, pastas, and pizzas, plus salads and appetizers. Unique creations include Thai chicken nachos, and chicken and portabella mushroom linguini, among others. Vegetarians will find a few choices to suit their dietary restrictions. Be sure to save room for dessert—the microbrew root beer float shouldn't be missed. Moderate.

Hooligan's Espresso (307-382-3220; http://www.hooligansespresso.com), 1481 Dewar Drive. Open 5:30 AM–6 PM Monday through Friday, 7–4 Saturday, 8–2 Sunday. Hopefully there's still one in every town—an independently owned coffee establishment serving up all those delicious favorites with a unique twist. A drive-through coffee hut, Hooligan's special Grandma B's Favorite Pink Cookie goes down well with a freshly brewed latté, though it might not be the healthiest of breakfast choices. You can always choose a fresh-fruit smoothie instead! Inexpensive.

✿ **Sands Chinese and American Restaurant** (307-362-5633; http://www.sandschinese.com), 1549 Ninth Street. Open 10–10 daily; breakfast served all day. Withstanding the toughest test of all—the test of time—this restaurant has served up its fine Chinese and American food for more than half a century, establishing itself as a mainstay and local favorite in southwestern Wyoming. Here you'll find a complete array of all of your favorite Chinese entrées, including cashew chicken, moo shu pork, kung pao shrimp, and lo mein, among many others. You'll also find a delicious selection of traditional American favorites, also expertly prepared, including pastas, steaks, seafood, burgers, and sandwiches. Portion sizes are generous, while prices are reasonable. Sands has a senior menu for more mature patrons, plus an extensive dessert menu featuring an incredible *death by chocolate* chocolate cake. Moderate.

DINING OUT
Rock Springs
Coyote Creek Steakhouse and Saloon (307-382-4100; http://www .coyotecreekrs.com), 404 N Street. Open 11–10 Monday through Friday, 4–10 Saturday. If you're in the mood for an unbelievable dining experience in Wyoming, you just might find it here at this new (2007) Rock Springs fine-dining establishment. Hand-cut steaks are prepared perfectly, as are other menu options, including sesame encrusted ahi tuna, orange chicken, king crab legs, and a variety of salads and pastas. Whichever entrée you select, you'll find that it comes with an attention to detail and gorgeous presentation. Start your meal with a specialty drink from the full bar, and then round out your meal with a homemade dessert. Expensive to very expensive.

✳ Entertainment
Star Stadium 10 (307-362-2101), 618 Broadway Street, Rock Springs.
Star Twin (307-875-4702), 699 Uinta Drive, Green River. Movie theater.
&. **Sweetwater Events Complex** (307-352-6789 or 307-872-6348; http:// www.sweetwaterevents.com), 3320 Yellowstone Road, Rock Springs. In addition to hosting Wyoming's Big Show

(see *Special Events*), this facility hosts numerous other events throughout the year, including BMX racing, stock car racing, horse events, 4-H events, and more. Call or check online for what's happening now.

See also Community Fine Arts Center in *To See*—Museums; and China Garden Restaurant in *Where to Eat*—Eating Out.

✳ Selective Shopping
TLC Accents for Living (307-382-6776; http://www.tlcaccents.com), located in the **White Mountain Mall,** 2441 Foothill Boulevard, Rock Springs. Open 10–9 Monday through Friday, 10–7 Saturday, noon–6 Sunday. This gift shop has a wide selection of Wyoming-related items, including wildlife art, as well as general gift items and home décor.

West of Center Studios and Gifts (1-866-655-2423; http://www.westof center.com), 204 Center Street, Rock Springs. Open 1–5 and 7 PM–9 PM Tuesday through Saturday (generally; call for seasonal hours). You can pick up a piece of original artwork or craftsmanship here, made by one of more than 40 contributing local artists/ craftsmen.

See also Escape Day Spa in *To Do*—Relaxation and Rejuvenation; and Wild Horse and Western Art Show and Sale in *Special Events*.

✳ Special Events
♂ *June:* **Flaming Gorge Days** (307-875-5711; http://www.flaminggorge days.com), Green River: This annual four-day event includes a rodeo, children's entertainment, parade, concerts, and more.

June: **Rod and Rails Car Show** (307-352-1434), Rock Springs: The annual benefit for urban improvements to

Rock Springs includes a car (and other vehicles) show, music, food, and more.

July: **Wild Horse and Western Art Show and Sale** (307-382-7129; http://www.rockspringsartshow.com), Rock Springs: This annual art show includes cash prizes for artists and original artwork for sale.

July: **Wyoming Senior Olympics** (307-352-1420; http://www.wysenior olympics.com): An annual competition for individuals 50-plus includes events such as swimming, horseshoes, triathlon, tennis, disc golf, golf, and many, many more.

✍ *July to August:* **Wyoming's Big Show,** at the Sweetwater Events Complex (see *Entertainment*), Rock Springs: Southwestern Wyoming's summer festival includes carnival rides,

livestock shows, a rodeo, entertainment, an art show, and more.

✍ *August:* **River Festival,** Green River: This event includes food, music, kids' games, a brew fest, a dog show, and Art on the Green, along with the Run with the Horses Marathon (see below).

August: **Art on the Green** (307-872-0580; http://www.artonthegreen.net), Green River: Artists compete to loan their works to the City of Green River to be publicly displayed for a year.

August: **Run with the Horses Marathon** (307-297-0062; http://www.grchamber.com/run_with_the_horses_marathon.htm), Green River: This event includes a half-marathon and a 10K along with the full marathon, plus a shrimp boil the night before the races.

Southeast Wyoming

6

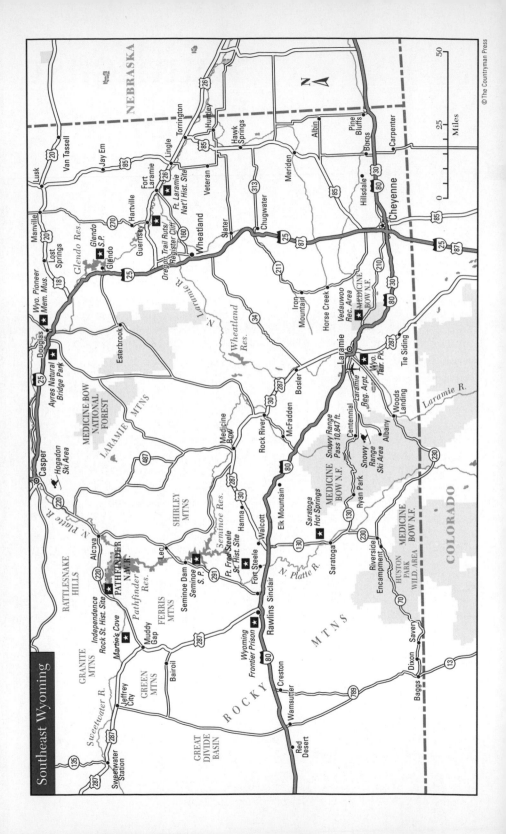

Southeast Wyoming

© The Countryman Press

RAWLINS AND LARAMIE

L aramie, Wyoming's third largest city (a whopping 27,000 people), is home to the University of Wyoming, which has several free museums (see University of Wyoming Art and Geological Museums, and the American Heritage Center in *To See*—Museums). More than a dozen city parks lie within city limits, providing ample opportunities for urban recreation ranging from the Laramie River Greenbelt (see *To Do*—Bicycling) to LaBonte Park, home to the Wyoming Children's Museum and Nature Center (see *To See*—For Families). Shoppers will delight in Historic Downtown Laramie (see *Selective Shopping*), with its eclectic and intriguing array of stores and restaurants. If you're arriving in Laramie from the east, consider taking Happy Jack Road (see *To See*—Scenic Drives) for a slower, more scenic journey. Just east of Laramie, you can visit the Lincoln Monument at the Summit Information Center (see Guidance), accessible via Exit 323 off I-80.

You can stay on I-80 to go west from Laramie, but why not mix it up a bit? West of Laramie off WY 130 (Snowy Range Scenic Byway; see *To See*—Scenic Drives) and southwest off WY 230, you'll find the concentrated recreational opportunities of the Medicine Bow Mountains and the Sierra Madre Mountains in the Medicine Bow National Forest (see *Green Space*—National Lands). A number of charming, small towns lie in this area, including Centennial, Encampment/Riverside, and Saratoga (see *To See*—Towns), all providing an array of visitor services, including great lodging choices. Another option is to head northwest from Laramie on US 30/287 to see the historic attractions found in the town of Medicine Bow (see *To See*—Towns).

Either way you go, you'll rejoin I-80 near Sinclair (see *To See*—Towns) and Fort Fred Steele State Historic Site (see *To See*—Historic Landmarks, Places, and Sites). Your journey continues to Rawlins, another historic railroad town with a population of about 9,000. Rawlins got its name from General John A. Rawlins, a surveyor for the Union Pacific Railroad. Seeking to quench his thirst during a surveying trip to this area, he discovered a spring and declared it to be the finest water he'd ever tasted. The county seat of Carbon County, Rawlins, situated on the eastern edge of the Great Divide Basin (see *To See*—Natural Wonders) has a number of historic and natural attractions. These include the Wyoming Frontier Prison (see *To See*—Historic Landmarks, Places, and Sites) and wild horses (see *To See*—Scenic Drives).

GUIDANCE Albany County Tourism Board (1-800-445-5303; http://www .laramie-tourism.org), 210 Custer Street, Laramie, 82070.

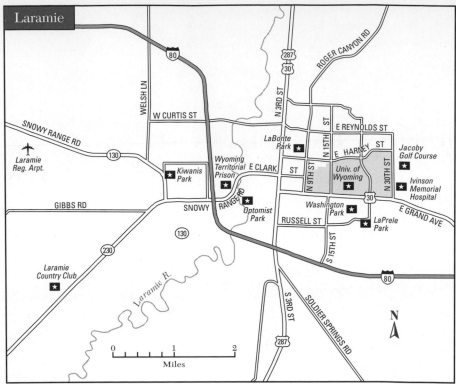

Laramie

© The Countryman Press

Carbon County Visitors Council (1-800-228-3547; http://www.wyoming carboncounty.com), 816 W. Spruce Street, P.O. Box 1017, Rawlins, 82301.

City of Laramie (307-721-5200; http://www.ci.laramie.wy.us), 406 Ivinson Street, Laramie, 82073.

City of Rawlins (307-328-4500; http://www.rawlins-wyoming.com), 521 W. Cedar Street, Rawlins.

Laramie Chamber of Commerce (1-866-876-1012 or 307-745-7339; http://www .laramie.org), 800 S. Third Street, Laramie, 82070.

Rawlins-Carbon County Chamber of Commerce (307-324-4111; http:// www.rawlinschamberofcommerce.org), 519 W. Cedar Street, P.O. Box 1331, Rawlins, 82301.

Summit Information Center (307-721-9254), Exit 323 off I-80 south of Laramie at Happy Jack, open mid-May through mid-October.

University of Wyoming (307-766-1121 or 307-766-5000 (calendar line); http:// www.uwyo.edu), 1000 E. University Avenue, Laramie.

See also *To See*—Towns.

GETTING THERE *By car:* Laramie is just off I-80 at exits 310–316 in southeast Wyoming. It can also be accessed from the north and south via US 287. Rawlins is about 100 miles west of Laramie just off I-80 at exits 211–215. Rawlins can also be accessed from the north via US 287 and from the south via WY 71.

By plane: **Laramie Regional Airport** (307-742-4164; http://www.laramieairport .com) is in Laramie.

GETTING AROUND Laramie has a nice downtown area great for strolling and shopping, and many of the city's attractions can be easily reached on foot, though if you're feeling tired, you might end up back in your car. Rawlins is also fairly easy to explore on foot. Both cities and their outlying attractions will require some use of a car.

MEDICAL EMERGENCY Dial 911.

Ivinson Memorial Hospital (307-742-2141; http://www.ivinsonhospital.org), 255 N. 30th Street, Laramie, 82072.

Memorial Hospital of Carbon County (1-800-967-1817 or 307-324-2221; http://www.imhcc.com), 2221 Elm Street, Rawlins.

✳ To See

TOWNS Centennial (population about 200) is 35 miles west of Laramie on WY 130. The town came about as a result of the construction of the transcontinental railroad, serving as a hub for the tie hack industry—the cutting of railroad ties. Less than a decade later, in 1875 Centennial was also home to a gold strike, bringing gold-hungry hopefuls to the area. Named in honor of the United States' 100th birthday, Centennial provides an array of services for outdoor recreation lovers, as well as being home to the Nici Self Museum (see *To See*—Museums). For more information: **Carbon County Visitors Council** (see Guidance).

Encampment (population 440) and **Riverside** (population 60) lie less than a mile apart on the other side of the Snowy Range from Centennial, about 90 miles west of Laramie via WY 130 to WY 230. They can also be reached by taking Exit 235 off I-80 at Walcott Junction, and then heading south past Saratoga on WY 130. This area was known to mid-1800s fur trappers as the Grand Encampment, a location historically used by numerous Indian tribes as a gathering spot to hunt buffalo and other game animals. Today, you'll find river access points (see Encampment River in *To Do*—Fishing), parks, lodging, and restaurants, aimed particularly at those adventuring into the nearby Medicine Bow National Forest (see *Green Space*—National Lands). For more information: **Carbon County Visitors Council** (see Guidance).

Medicine Bow, population 300 or so, is accessed by taking US 30/287 northwest out of Laramie, or by taking exit 235 northeast off I-80 at Walcott Junction. The name Medicine Bow comes from the Cheyenne and Arapaho, who found that this area of Wyoming had particularly good medicine, or top-quality resources, for the making of bows. Medicine Bow also provided author Owen Wister with much of the inspiration for the famous novel, *The Virginian,* published in 1902 (see *Lodging*—Hotels and Motels). About 10 miles east of town is Como Bluff, a (currently closed to the public) National Natural Landmark, where in 1877, railroad employees happened upon a place that would yield thousands of nearly perfectly pre-served dinosaur bones. For more information: **Medicine Bow** (307-379-2225; http://www.medicinebow.org), 319 Pine Street, P.O. Box 225, Medicine Bow, 82329-0156.

Saratoga (population 2,000), accessed by going south on WY 130 off I-80 at exit 235 at Walcott Junction, is perhaps best known for its free, 24/7 hot mineral pool—the Hobo Pool (see Saratoga Hobo Hot Pool in *To Do*—Relaxation and Rejuvenation). The town took its name from New York's renowned Saratoga Springs. Saratoga has numerous attractions, including **Saratoga Lake**, about a mile north of town. Managed by the town, Saratoga Lake features boating (boat dock), all-season fishing (rainbow trout; see also Ice Fishing Derby in *Special Events*), and camping (small fee). The town has an array of visitor attractions and services, including gift shops, eateries, and lodging accommodations. For more information: **Saratoga/Platte Valley Chamber** (307-326-8855; http://www.saratogachamber.info), P.O. Box 1095, Saratoga, 82331.

Sinclair, just east of Rawlins off I-80 at exit 221, has a population of about 500. Its defining landmark is the enormous **Sinclair Refinery**, which can be seen from I-80, often spitting an eerie flame from one of its stacks. For more information: **Town of Sinclair** (307-324-3058; http://www.townofsinclair.com), 300 Lincoln Avenue, Sinclair, 82334.

MUSEUMS ✿ ⓑ **Carbon County Museum** (307-328-2740; http://www.carbon countymuseum.org), Ninth and Walnut, Rawlins. Open 10–6 Tuesday through Friday, 1–6 Saturday, June through September; 1–5 Tuesday through Saturday, October through May; free. This county museum strives to preserve the history of the surrounding region, with unique exhibits including a 1920 fire truck and shoes made from the skin of a notorious criminal named "Big Nose George" Parrott. These shoes were worn by Wyoming's governor, Dr. John Osborne, to his 1893 inaugural ball. You'll also find an array of artifacts and documents explaining and interpreting the roles of various peoples and industries in shaping this region, including American Indians, pioneers, mining, ranching, the railroad, and more. A new museum is planned, but not yet constructed, as of this book's publication (2010).

✿ **Grand Encampment Museum** (307-327-5308), 817 Barnett Avenue, Encampment. Open 10–5 Monday through Saturday, 1–5 Sunday, late May through early September; noon–4 Thursday through Sunday, late September; closed October through May; free (donations gladly accepted). The Official National Repository of the United States Forest Service Memorabilia, this replica town includes historic structures from Forest Service days gone by, as well as numerous additional historic structures, creating a reproduction of a pioneer town. Exhibits detail the local area's history, including its ties to the mining, timber, and agriculture industries. Tucked away to one side, you'll also find a replica two-story outhouse (guess you'll have to visit to find out just how that works), constructed in 1976.

The Laramie Plains Museum at the Historic Ivinson Mansion (307-742-4448; http://www.laramiemuseum.org), 603 E. Ivinson Avenue, Laramie. Open year-round Tuesday through Saturday, call for hours (vary by season and events); $10 per adult, $7 per senior, $5 per student, children under 6 are free, $25 per family. This exquisitely restored 1892 Victorian mansion, once the home of prominent Laramie banker, Edward Ivinson, and his wife, Jane, is listed on the National Register of Historic Places. On your guided tour through the mansion, you'll see numerous artifacts and items of historical significance, including period furnishings, historical photographs, and many relevant pieces that help illustrate Laramie's past.

THE HISTORIC IVINSON MANSION

☎ Nici Self Museum (307-742-7763), 2740 WY 130, Centennial. Open noon–4 Thursday through Monday, June through September; free. Hearkening to this region's railroad roots, a portion of this museum is situated in a restored 1907 Hahn railroad depot, giving you a sense of history through its very structural composition, in addition to its contents. Another train exhibit features a Union Pacific caboose that dates to 1944. The museum's focus is on the history of the settlement of the Centennial Valley environs, with exhibits detailing the impacts of the mining, ranching, farming, railroad, and lumber industries on the area.

☎ ✎ ♿ Parco/Sinclair Historic District Museum (307-324-3058; http://www.townofsinclair.com/museum.htm), 300 E. Lincoln Avenue, Sinclair. Open 9–noon and 1–4:30 Monday through Friday year-round; free. Part of Sinclair's historic district, this local museum is in the other half of Sinclair's town hall, in a 1924 bank building. Learn more about the history of the local area with a tour through this small-town museum. Also, stop at the nearby **Parco Inn** to read about this historic Wyoming structure with its five-story bell towers, and let the kids play in the playground at **Washington Park,** across the street.

☎ ✎ ♿ Saratoga Museum (307-326-5511; http://www.saratoga-museum.com), 104 Constitution Avenue, Saratoga. Open 1–4 Tuesday through Saturday, Memorial Day through Labor Day; by appointment rest of year; free (donations gladly accepted). Housed in a historic railroad depot, this museum features an extensive Wyoming jade collection in its geology exhibit, American Indian artifacts, hands-on exhibits for children, a collection of Wyoming license plates, pioneer memorabilia, and outdoor exhibits.

☎ ♿ University of Wyoming Art Museum, Geological Museum, and the American Heritage Center. Art Museum (307-766-6622; http://www.uwyo .edu/artmuseum), 2111 Willett Drive (the Centennial Complex), Laramie. Open 10–9 Monday, 10–5 Tuesday through Saturday; free. **Geological Museum** (307-766-2646; http://www.uwyo.edu/geomuseum), in the S. H. Knight Geology Building (northwest corner of campus), Laramie. Closed due to budget cuts in summer 2009 but hopefully it will open again soon; free. **American Heritage Center**

(307-766-4114; http://ahc.uwyo.edu), 2111 Willett Drive (the Centennial Complex), Laramie. Open 8–9 Monday, 8–5 Tuesday through Friday; free. If you visit one of these attractions, you should make an effort to visit the other two, as they are all free, and all explore different aspects of Wyoming's history and heritage. The geological museum's exhibits provide you with an in-depth look at Wyoming's geology, past and present, including dinosaur skeletons (allosaurus and apatosaurus among others), other fossils, mineral specimens, and more. The art museum displays rotating exhibits in nine galleries, with a collection of more than 7,000 pieces of art from around the world, including many works by local and regional artists, past and present. The American Heritage Center strives to preserve Wyoming and western history with exhibits including photographs and artifacts, as well as housing an extensive quantity of reference materials and archives.

See also Wyoming Frontier Prison in *To See*—Historic Landmarks, Places, and Sites.

HISTORIC LANDMARKS, PLACES, AND SITES ❀ Fort Fred Steele State Historic Site (307-320-3013; http://wyoparks.state.wy.us/Site/SiteInfo.asp?siteID=16), north a few miles at Exit 228 off I-80, just east of Sinclair and Rawlins. Open 9–7 daily May 1 through September 15, closed September 16 through April 30; free. Perhaps even more so than the developed historic sites of this region, Fort Fred Steele gives you a real sense of the utter isolation and desolateness that newcomers to this area must have felt when stationed here. Constructed in 1868 to protect the Union Pacific Railroad from Indian attacks, this outpost saw U.S. military occupation for less than two decades. Following that, it experienced brief periods of vibrancy, first with the timber industry, and then with the sheep ranching industry. Today, most of what remains at this undeveloped site are the foundations of the old fort buildings, as well as access to fishing on the North Platte River (see *To Do*—Fishing).

ST. JOSEPH'S CATHOLIC CHURCH

St. Joseph's Catholic Church (307-324-4631; http://www.dioceseof cheyenne.org/history/Rawlins_1867-1928_WCR.html), Third Street and Pine Street, Rawlins. Architecture lovers and those of the Catholic faith both will likely be impressed by this lovely historic structure, constructed in 1916 and situated in downtown Rawlins.

Wyoming Frontier Prison (307-324-4422; http://www.wyomingfrontier prison.org), 500 W. Walnut Street, Rawlins. Open 8–5 daily Memorial Day through Labor Day (by appointment in off-season), with guided tours leaving every hour on the half hour from 8:30–4:30; guided tours are $7 per adult, $6 per child/senior, $30 per family. Step into Wyoming's criminal past at this former state penitentiary that operated for 80 years, from 1901–1981, now listed on the National Register of Historic Places. Affectionately deemed Old Pen, the prison today houses a museum that displays historical exhibits about the prison, including inmate-made weapons and an exhibit about the 1987 movie *Prison,* filmed on the premises. The guided tour takes you through the former prisoners' quarters, the gas chamber, gallows, and the solitary confinement area, among other such cheery locales, as well as through the **Wyoming Peace Officers' Museum.** A short walk on the City of Rawlins' walking path takes you to the prisoners' cemetery. A gift shop is also on the premises.

✔ **Wyoming Territorial Prison State Historic Site** (307-745-6161; http://wyoparks.state.wy.us/Site/SiteInfo.asp?siteID=25), 975 Snowy Range Road, Laramie. Open 9–6 daily May through September; $5 per adult, $2.50 per youth 12–17, children 11 and under free. Constructed in 1872, this former prison is now listed on the National Register of Historic Places. You can take a self-guided tour through the old prison complex, which includes stops at the dining area, guard's quarters, infirmary, women's quarters, and the Lawmen and Outlaw Gallery. Also on the premises, you'll find an extensive ranching exhibit, as well as the warden's house, and a historic boxcar. On weekends costumed volunteers in period dress make your experience that much more authentic. The **Happy Jack Gift Shop** sells souvenirs. See also Butch Cassidy Days in *Special Events.*

See also *To See*—Museums; Saratoga Hobo Hot Pool in *To Do*—Relaxation and Rejuvenation; Brooklyn Lodge Bed and Breakfast and Vee Bar Guest Ranch Bed and Breakfast in *Lodging*—Bed and Breakfasts; Mountain View Historic Hotel, Historic Elk Mountain Hotel, Historic Virginian Hotel, and Historic Wolf Hotel in *Lodging*—Hotels and Motels; Historic Woods Landing Resort in *Lodging*—Other Options; and Historic Downtown Laramie in *Selective Shopping.*

CITY PARKS AND GARDENS ✔

The City of Laramie (see Guidance) has more than 12 city parks (open 8–8 unless otherwise signed), which include everything from playgrounds to fishing ponds, pathways to picnic areas, and more. A complete listing of parks and their amenities can be found on the city's Web site, along with a downloadable map. See also Parco/Sinclair Historic District Museum in *To See*—Museums; Laramie River Greenbelt in *To Do*—Bicycling; and Wyoming Children's Museum and Nature Center in *To Do*—For Families.

✔ **Veterans Island Park,** on Pic Pike Road, Saratoga (near the Saratoga Resort and Spa; see *Lodging*—Hotels and Motels), is a cool park situated on

WYOMING FRONTIER PRISON

an island in the middle of the North Platte River (see *To Do*—Fishing). Here you'll find a walking trail, playground equipment, fishing access, and picnicking areas.

See also Saratoga in *To See*—Towns; Wyoming Frontier Prison in *To See*—Historic Landmarks, Places, and Sites; and Music in the Park in *Special Events*.

SCENIC DRIVES Happy Jack Road, or WY 210, makes for a great, 40-plus-mile scenic drive—so long as the weather's good. Take WY 210 (Exit 323 off I-80), and you're on your way for a tour that will take you first into the Vedauwoo Recreation Area of the Medicine Bow National Forest (see *Green Space*), then past Curt Gowdy State Park (see *Green Space*—State Parks in Cheyenne) and into Cheyenne at Exit 362 on I-80.

Seminoe to Alcova Scenic Backway is a journey of about 70 miles that starts at Alcova, roughly 30 miles southwest of Casper off WY 220. The adventure takes you south from this small town along CR 603/407 to CR 291 to BLM 3159 to CR 351 (Seminoe Road), depositing you at its terminus in Sinclair, near Rawlins. Highlights of this remote, backcountry journey include Fremont Canyon, popular with rock climbers (see *To Do*—Climbing in Central Wyoming: Casper and Douglas); the Miracle Mile of the North Platte River (see *To See*—Natural Wonders); Seminoe State Park (see *Green Space*—State Parks); the Pedro Mountains; and the Seminoe Mountains. This area is rife with streams, springs, and water bodies, making it a tremendous destination for anglers.

Snowy Range Scenic Byway takes you on an awe-inspiring journey through the Snowy Range (also known as the Medicine Bow Mountains) west of Laramie and east of Saratoga along WY 130. Though the byway officially begins about 30 miles west of Laramie, for most travelers this journey is likely to start or end in Laramie, with the other terminus being Saratoga (see *To See*—Towns), for a total distance of about 80 miles. You'll traverse through some of the most breathtaking scenery of the Medicine Bow National Forest (see *Green Space*—National Lands), passing by a range of outdoor recreational opportunities found therein. **Lake Marie,** situated just off the road high in the mountains, makes for a beautiful place to stop and

THE SNOWY RANGE SCENIC BYWAY IN JUNE

take in the scenic vistas surrounding you, including the windswept alpine peaks. This is also where to access Lake Marie Falls Trail (see *To Do—Hiking*), and **Medicine Bow Trail,** a challenging 6-mile round-trip excursion that gains more than 1,500 feet to access the ridgeline.

Wild Horse Tours make for a fun adventure in this region, as you search to see some of Wyoming's bona fide wild horses while traversing windswept prairies and open terrain on back roads. The designated wild horse viewing tour in this region involves taking CR 63 west off US 287 north of Rawlins, and then heading north on CR 23 N to Jeffrey City. This intersection is considered to be the exact center of the Great Divide Basin (see *To See—Natural Wonders*). Please respect the wild horses (it's illegal to chase them), and be sure you are prepared—this means having a spare tire, plenty of water, and paying attention to the weather, since back roads can quickly become quagmires in poor driving conditions. This drive takes place on BLM lands (see *Green Space—National Lands*).

NATURAL WONDERS Great Divide Basin: See listing in Southwest Wyoming: Green River and Rock Springs.

Miracle Mile of the North Platte River—actually about 5.5 miles in length— spans the section of the river that lies between Kortes Reservoir and Pathfinder Reservoir (see *To Do—Boating* in Central Wyoming: Casper and Douglas), and is accessible by driving a portion of the Seminoe to Alcova Scenic Backway (see *To See—Scenic Drives*). If you're an avid fisherman, you probably have already heard of this blue-ribbon trout-fishing stream, which has gained national renown for the high quality of its fishing. This section of river tends to be home to unusually large concentrations of brown, rainbow, and cutthroat trout of unusually large size (both in terms of weight and in terms of length). See also North Platte River in *To Do— Fishing*.

See also Vedauwoo Recreation Area in *Green Space—Recreation Areas*.

✳ To Do

BICYCLING 🚴 ♿ **Laramie River Greenbelt** (307-721-5269; http://www.ci .laramie.wy.us/recreation/parks) is a 5.75-mile trail along the Laramie River in Laramie, offering recreational opportunities for bicycling, as well as for walking, running, skating, and wheelchairs. Along the Greenbelt, you'll find benches where you can stop for a rest or a snack, as well as playground equipment and restroom facilities. **Optimist Park,** located off Cedar Street in southwest Laramie, has a trailhead that provides access to the Greenbelt, as well as playground facilities and fishing access to the Laramie River (see *To Do—Fishing*).

See also *Green Space* and Laramie KOA in *Lodging—Campgrounds*.

THE LARAMIE RIVER GREENBELT

BOATING **Hog Park Reservoir,** accessible by taking Hog Park Road (CR 353 to FR 550) southwest off WY 70 just west of Encampment for about 25 miles to FR 496, lies in the Medicine Bow National Forest (see *Green Space*—National Lands). This small reservoir features a boat ramp and allows motorboats. Fishing for brook trout, brown trout, cutthroat trout, rainbow trout, and splake is popular here, and this is a great place to access the Encampment River (see *To Do*—Fishing). Here you'll also find the **Lake View Campground** (open June 15 through September; $10; http://www.recreation.gov for reservations), as well as access to a portion of the Continental Divide Trail (see *To Do*—Hiking). You can also access the shorter **Hog Park Trail** (#475), about 1.3 miles in length, which links up with the **Encampment River Trail** (see *To Do*—Fishing). Horseback riders are welcome on this trail as well.

Lake Hattie Reservoir lies about 18 miles west of Laramie and is accessible by taking WY 230 7.5 miles southwest to CR 422 (Pahlow Road), and then proceeding west to CR 45 (Lake Hattie Road). Partially managed by the BLM (see *Green Space*—National Lands), Lake Hattie provides opportunities for boaters and anglers alike. Fish species include brown trout, cutthroat trout, and rainbow trout.

See also Saratoga in *To See*—Towns and Seminoe State Park in *Green Space*—State Parks.

CLIMBING **The Infield of Half Acre Gym** (307-766-5586; http://uwadmnweb.uwyo.edu/oap/climbingwall.asp), 1000 E. University Avenue, Laramie. Open 11–1 Monday, Wednesday, Friday; 4 PM–8 PM Tuesday, Thursday (summer; call for winter hours); $5 per person, *plus you must have a current member sponsor you* (equipment rental extra). Inside the University of Wyoming's Half-Acre Gym (a full-service fitness center), you'll find this climbing wall. Beginners are welcome and must complete an introductory climbing wall clinic (usually available whenever the wall is open).

See also Seminoe to Alcova Scenic Backway in *To See*—Scenic Drives; High Plains Outdoor Institute in *To Do*—Unique Adventures; and Vedauwoo Recreation Area in *Green Space*—Recreation Areas.

FISHING **Encampment River** (307-745-4046; http://gf.state.wy.us/fish/fishing/index.asp) flows from the Rockies across the Colorado border north through the Encampment Wilderness of the Medicine Bow National Forest (see *Green Space*—National Lands), eventually joining the North Platte River (see below). You can access the Encampment River via the **Encampment River Trail** (#470) by taking FR 496 south from FR 550 at Hog Park Reservoir (see *To Do*—Boating). This trail, closed to motorized vehicles, takes you through the Encampment Wilderness Area along the banks of the Encampment River, running for about 15 miles to a point just south of the town of Encampment (see *To See*—Towns). At that end, the trail and the river are accessible via BLM 3407 off CR 353. The trailhead departs from the BLM-managed **Encampment River Campground** (open June 1 through November 15; $10), which provides great fishing and floating access. Fish species include brown trout and rainbow trout.

Laramie River (307-745-4046; http://gf.state.wy.us/fish/fishing/index.asp) flows from the Rocky Mountains in Colorado north through Laramie, continuing north to eventually join the North Platte River. Much of the river flows through private land, making access for the most part difficult. In addition to the Laramie River Greenbelt (see *To Do—Bicycling*), you can access the river from several signed Wyoming Game and Fish Department designated access sites off WY 230 and WY 130 southwest of Laramie. Fish species include brown trout and rainbow trout.

Medicine Bow River (307-745-4046; http://gf.state.wy.us/fish/fishing/index.asp) flows from the Medicine Bow Mountains in the south, north to the town of Medicine Bow, where it arcs to the west and flows into Seminoe Reservoir (see Seminoe State Park in *To Do—Boating*). Much of the river flows through private land, making

THE LARAMIE RIVER

access difficult, with the exception of the portions that are found in the Medicine Bow National Forest (see *Green Space*—National Lands). Probably the easiest access comes by taking exit 255 off I-80 and heading south past Elk Mountain, then proceeding south for about 16 miles on FR 101 (Medicine Bow Ranger Station Road) to **Bow River Campground** (open June through October; $10).

North Platte River: See Veterans Island Park in *To See*—City Parks and Gardens; Miracle Mile of the North Platte River in *To See*—Natural Wonders; and listing in *To Do*—Fishing in Central Wyoming: Casper and Douglas.

See also Saratoga in *To See*—Towns; Seminoe to Alcova Scenic Backway in *To See*—Scenic Drives; Laramie River Greenbelt in *To Do*—Bicycling; *To Do*—Boating; and *Green Space*.

FITNESS CENTERS ♿ ✇ **Laramie Community Recreation Center** (307-721-5269; http://www.ci.laramie.wy.us/park&rec/reccenter/index.html), 920 Boulder Drive, Laramie. Open 5 AM–9 PM Monday through Friday, 8–8 Saturday, noon–8 Sunday; $7 per adult, $6.50 per senior 60-plus, $5.50 per youth 13–18, $3.50 per child 3–12, under 3 free. Swimming pools (indoors and outside) plus a leisure pool and water slides are just some of what this full-service recreation center offers. You'll also find an indoor playground, hot tub, fitness equipment, weights, and more.

✇ **Rawlins Family Recreation Center** (307-324-7529; http://www.rawlins-wyoming.com), 1616 Harshman Street, Rawlins. Open 5:30 AM–9 PM Monday through Thursday, 5:30 AM–8 PM Friday, 7–3 Saturday (summer); call for winter hours and current daily rates. This full-service recreation center includes an indoor shooting range, indoor track, gymnasiums, fitness equipment, daycare, and more. See also The Infield of Half Acre Gym in *To Do*—Climbing.

FOR FAMILIES ♿ ✇ **Wyoming Children's Museum and Nature Center** (307-745-6332; http://www.wcmnc.org), 968 N. Ninth Street, Laramie. Open 9–4 Tuesday through Thursday, 10–4 Saturday; $3 per child ages 3 and up, $2 per adult, children under 3 are free. Whether your kids love animals, history, or both, they'll enjoy themselves at this interactive museum and nature center. Exhibits include pioneer-themed fun such as dressing up in old-fashioned clothes, and teepees and cabins to explore. The nature center includes living animal exhibits. The museum is in Laramie's **LaBonte Park,** a perfect place for a family picnic before or after you tour the museum. LaBonte Park also has playground equipment, a short walking and jogging path, and a skateboard park.

See also Parco/Sinclair Historic District Museum and Saratoga Museum in *To See*—Museums; Wyoming Territorial Prison State Historic Site in *To See*—Historic Landmarks, Places, and Sites; *To See*—City Parks and Gardens; Laramie River Greenbelt in *To Do*—Bicycling; *To Do*—Fitness Centers; Saratoga Hobo Hot Pool in *To Do*—Relaxation and Rejuvenation; Ice-skating and Snowy Range Ski Area in *To Do*—Snow Sports; and Seminoe State Park in *Green Space*—State Parks.

GOLF Jacoby Golf Club (307-745-3111; http://www.jacobygc.com), 3501 Willett Drive, Laramie, 18 holes.

Laramie Country Club (307-745-4161), 489 WY 230, Laramie, 9 holes.

Old Baldy Club Golf Course (1-888-777-5303 or 307-326-5706), E. Pic Pike Road, Saratoga, 18 holes.

Rochelle Ranch Golf Club (307-324-7121; http://www.rochelleranch.com), 2808 E. Rochelle Drive, Rawlins, 18 holes.

Saratoga Inn Golf Course (1-800-594-0178 or 307-326-5261; http://www .saratogainn.com), 601 E. Pic Pike Road, 9 holes.

Sinclair Golf Club (307-324-7767), Golf Course Road, Sinclair, 9 holes.

HIKING Continental Divide Trail is a 3,100-mile trail running from the Canadian border to the border with Mexico along the entire Continental Divide, passing through lands managed by a number of different organizations. In this region of Wyoming, you can access a portion of the trail from Hog Park Reservoir (see *To Do*—Boating), where it departs from the campground, heading north through the Sierra Madre Mountains of the Medicine Bow National Forest (see *Green Space*—National Lands). This portion of the trail can also be accessed to the north by taking WY 70 southwest out of Encampment to Battle Pass. The majority of this trail lies in the Huston Park Wilderness, meaning that you won't encounter any motorized vehicles on your journey. You'll also find a large portion of the trail on Wyoming's BLM lands (see *Green Space*—National Lands), as it passes right by Rawlins, and then arcs around the northern edge of the Great Divide Basin (see *To See*—Natural Wonders). For more information about the trail, contact the Continental Divide Trail Alliance (1-888-909-CDTA or 303-838-3760; http://www .cdtrail.org), P.O. Box 628, Pine, CO, 80470.

Lake Marie Falls Trail (#290), an easy, .2-mile loop trail, can be accessed by taking WY 130 south from Saratoga for 7.5 miles, and then going east on WY 130 for almost 27 miles to the parking area along the Snowy Range Scenic Byway (see *To See*—Scenic Drives). This is a lovely place to enjoy a picnic lunch either before or after you explore the gorgeous alpine setting surrounding you.

Platte River Trail (#473), in the Medicine Bow National Forest (see *Green Space*—National Lands), is accessible by taking WY 230 for 26 miles southeast from Riverside to FR 492. Go east for about 2 miles to Six Mile Gap Campground

(open May 15 through October; $10). From here, you can access the North Platte River (see *To Do—Fishing*) for both fishing and floating, as well as hiking along the river's shore in the Platte River Wilderness. The 5-mile trail (one-way) involves a steep descent to the river, but then it is fairly level and moderate as you follow the river's course.

See also Wyoming Frontier Prison in *To See*—Historic Landmarks, Places, and Sites; Veterans Island Park in *To See*—City Parks and Gardens; Laramie River Greenbelt in *To Do*—Bicycling; Encampment River in *To Do*—Fishing; Wyoming Children's Museum and Nature Center in *To Do*—For Families; High Plains Outdoor Institute in *To Do*—Unique Adventures; and *Green Space*.

HORSEBACK RIDING See Hog Park Reservoir in *To Do*—Boating; *Green Space*; Vee Bar Guest Ranch Bed and Breakfast in *Lodging*; and Bit O' Wyo Ranch in *To Do*—Horseback Riding in Cheyenne.

PADDLING/FLOATING See *To Do*—Boating; *To Do*—Fishing; Platte River Trail in *To Do*—Hiking; High Plains Outdoor Institute in *To Do*—Unique Adventures; *Green Space*; BLM Campgrounds in *Lodging*—Campgrounds; and Platte Valley Festival of the Birds in *Special Events*.

RELAXATION AND REJUVENATION Blossom Yoga (307-760-7267; http://www.blossomyogastudio.com), 117 E. Grand Avenue, Laramie. Call or check online for current class schedule; $9 per class. This studio offers Ashtanga, flow, and foundation yoga, among other styles. Also available are Thai yoga massages; call for details.

Hands in Thyme Massage (307-329-6250; http://www.myspace.com/handsinthyme), 204 Fifth Street, Rawlins. Call for an appointment in advance. Situated inside Curves Fitness Center, Hands in Thyme offers a variety of massage services including hot stone, reflexology, and body wraps, among others.

The Herb House (307-742-9696; http://www.elkmountainherbs.com), 214 S. Second Street, Laramie. Open 10–6 Monday through Saturday. This store is your information-rich source for Wyoming-grown herbs and supplements, most of which are cultivated (or grow naturally) and gathered nearby on a private ranch.

❧ **Natural Balance Massage & Spa Therapy** (307-745-8636; http://www.naturalbalancedayspa.com), 220 E. Ivinson Avenue, Laramie. Call for an appointment in advance. This full-service day spa offers a wide range of massage treatments for extremely reasonable prices ($50/hour), as well as facials, manicures and pedicures, body polishes and wraps, and more.

Red Sage Spa (307-326-8066; http://www.redsagespa.com), 106 E. Bridge Street, Saratoga. Open Monday through Saturday; hours vary with season; best to call for an appointment in advance. This full-service day spa offers a range of massages, body wraps and polishes, facials, aromatherapy, waxing, peels, manicures and pedicures, and spa lunch (by appointment), among other offerings.

❧ **Saratoga Hobo Hot Pool** (307-326-8855; http://www.saratogachamber.info/hotpool.html), on Walnut Street. behind the **public swimming pool,** Saratoga. Open seven days a week, 24 hours a day; free. This hot mineral pool and its healing powers were known to numerous tribes of American Indians long before the first pioneers set foot in this area. In the 1930s, the Civilian Conservation Corps constructed the stone pool that you'll find here today. Restrooms and changing areas are located on the premises as well, and the pool welcomes families. Plans are in the works to make an ADA-approved facility and other facility improvements in the near future.

Whole Earth Grainery and Truck Store (307-745-4268), 111 E. Ivinson Avenue, Laramie. Open 11–6 Tuesday through Saturday. If the sign says OPIN, step right into this deliberately irreverent but very resourceful natural/bulk foods store. You'll find all sorts of bargains, from bulk coffee to fresh seafood, nuts and grains to natural beauty products, and more.

Yoga Space (307-742-9461; http://www.yogaspacewyoming.com), 209 S. First Street, Laramie. Call or check online for current class schedule; $8.50 per class. This yoga studio offers a range of classes from beginner to advanced levels in a variety of styles.

See also Mountain View Historic Hotel and Saratoga Resort and Spa in *Lodging—Hotels and Motels*.

SNOW SPORTS Cross-country skiing opportunities can be found throughout this region, particularly in the Medicine Bow National Forest (see *Green Space—National Lands*), which offers a number of groomed trails in wintertime ($5 user fee). These include a trail system with loops of varying distances and varying levels of difficulty that are easily accessed by taking Exit 323 off I-80 east of Laramie. Trails depart from both the Summit Information Center (see Guidance) and from the Tie City Trailhead on WY 210. A snowshoe trail can be found here as well. Go to Medicine Bow Nordic Association (http://www.medbownordic.org) for details and a downloadable map of area ski trails.

Ice fishing opportunities can be found at the lakes and reservoirs in this region. See Saratoga in *To See*—Towns and *To Do*—Boating for ideas of where to go.

✿ **Ice-skating** is available seasonally at the Laramie Community Ice and Events Center (307-721-2161 or 307-721-3530 (events hotline); http://www.ci.laramie.wy.us/park&rec/icerink/index.html), 3510 Garfield Street, Laramie. Call for current schedule/rates. In the off-season, this center hosts community events as well.

Snowmobiling opportunities abound in this region, particularly in the Snowy Mountain Range of the Medicine Bow National Forest (see *Green Space—National Lands*), which includes more than 300 miles of designated trails known as the Snowy Range Trail System. For detailed trail reports, call 307-777-6560 or go to http://wyotrails.state.wy.us/snow, the Wyoming Snow-

THE WHOLE EARTH GRAINERY & TRUCK STORE IN LARAMIE

mobile Trails Web site, which also provides information about rules, rental agencies, trails around the state, and more. You can rent a snowmobile/arrange for a guided tour from Albany Lodge or Snowy Mountain Lodge (see *Lodging*—Lodges)

Snowshoeing is a great way to explore this region in wintertime, particularly in the Medicine Bow National Forest. See *Green Space*—National Lands and Cross-country skiing, above, for details.

✷ **Snowy Range Ski and Recreation Area** (307-745-5750; http://www.snowy range.com) is just west of Centennial off WY 130 in the Medicine Bow National Forest (see *Green Space*—National Lands). Take to the slopes at this lovely local ski area, where you'll find plenty of fun for both skiers and snowboarders, including a half pipe and a terrain park (new in 2004). Lifts: One triple and three double chairlifts, one surface lift. Trails: 27—30 percent beginner, 40 percent intermediate, 30 percent expert. Vertical Drop: 990 feet. Facilities: At the base, you'll find a day lodge with seating for more than 800 people, serving cafeteria-style food. Ski School: Offers both ski and snowboard lessons for all ages and abilities. Rates: $39 adult, $24 child (ages 6–12), $28 senior (ages 60–69), 70 and up and under 6 free (child must be accompanied by paying adult); half-day and multiday rates also available.

See also *Green Space* and Mountain View Historic Hotel in *Lodging*—Hotels and Motels.

UNIQUE ADVENTURES ✷ **High Plains Outdoor Institute** (307-742-0932; http://www.hpoiadventure.com), 1522 Barratt, Laramie. Whether you're interested in rock climbing at Vedauwoo Recreation Area (see *Green Space*—Recreation Areas), learning to kayak, or rafting the North Platte River (see *To Do*—Fishing), High Plains Outdoor offers a lesson for you. Welcoming total novices as well as those with some experience, this outdoor educator provides thorough, top-notch instruction on these and other outdoor adventures in this region. Reasonable prices, small student-to-teacher ratios, and incredible scenery and terrain await those interested in learning the basics of these popular extreme sports. The institute also offers guided hikes and backpacking trips, as well as teen-specific lessons and adventures.

WINERIES AND WINE TASTINGS See Coal Creek Coffee Company, Grand Avenue Pizza, and Sweet Melissa Café in *Where to Eat*—Eating Out.

✳ Green Space

STATE PARKS ✷ **Seminoe State Park** (307-320-3013; http://wyoparks.state.wy .us/Site/SiteInfo.asp?siteID=11), accessible by taking Exit 219 off I-80 at Sinclair, and then proceeding northeast for about 34 miles via CR 351 (Seminoe Road) to the park. Open year-round for both day use $4 (resident), $6 (nonresident); and camping $10 (resident), $17 (nonresident). Here you'll find the enormous Seminoe Reservoir, offering boaters more than 20,000 surface acres of water with almost 200 miles of shoreline—the largest reservoir in the entire state park system. In addition to the park's three boat ramps, you'll also find launching facilities, as well as fuel, supplies, and state fishing licenses, at the nearby marina operated by the Seminoe Boat Club (307-320-3043), 10 miles southeast of the park. Along with boating and water sports, this reservoir is popular for swimming (several sandy beaches), fishing (brown trout, cutthroat trout, rainbow trout, and walleye), and camping (three campgrounds). You'll also find playgrounds and picnicking facilities, as well as ample opportunities for viewing both wildlife and gorgeous natural scenery, including sand dunes. See also Seminoe to Alcova Scenic Backway in *To See*—Scenic Drives.

NATIONAL LANDS Bureau of Land Management (BLM), Rawlins Field Office (307-328-4200; http://www.blm.gov/wy/st/en/field_offices/Rawlins.html), 1300 N. Third, Rawlins. The Rawlins Field Office is responsible for managing 3.5 million acres of public lands and 4.5 million acres of federal mineral estate in this area. Much of the land administered by the BLM is open to recreational pursuits, including bicycling, boating, camping (see *Lodging*—Campgrounds) fishing, hiking, horseback riding, paddling, rock climbing, wildlife viewing (including wild horses) and snow sports, including snowmobiling and cross-country skiing. BLM lands tend to be the most unregulated of public lands, meaning that most typical outdoor recreational pursuits are allowed on most BLM lands, guided by the dictates of Leave No Trace (1-800-332-4100 or 303-442-8222;http://www.lnt.org) outdoor ethics.

Medicine Bow National Forest (307-745-2300; http://www.fs.fed.us/r2/mbr), 2468 Jackson Street, Laramie. With the exception of the area managed by the Douglas Ranger District (see listing in Northeast Wyoming: Gillette and the Devils Tower Area), this region lays claim to the portions of the nearly 3 million acres of land included in the jointly managed Medicine Bow-Routt National Forests that lie north of the Colorado border—the Medicine Bow National Forest. Included in Medicine Bow National Forest are several relatively small wilderness areas—**Encampment River Wilderness, Huston Park Wilderness, Platte River Wilderness,** and **Savage Run Wilderness.** Chief features of the forest in this region include the Snowy Range (part of the Medicine Bow Mountains), the Sierra Madre Mountains, and Vedauwoo Recreation Area (see below). The forest's recreational opportunities include boating, fishing, hiking, mountain biking, camping, paddling/floating, picnicking, rock climbing, off-road vehicle travel (ATVs and snowmobiles), horseback riding, snow sports, hunting, wildlife viewing, and more.

RECREATION AREAS ♿ **Vedauwoo Recreation Area,** located in the Medicine Bow National Forest (see *Green Space*—National Lands), is accessible via Exit 329 off I-80 about 20 miles east of Laramie. This area's chief feature is its remarkable jumble of granite rocks, which range from large to absolutely enormous in size. Vedauwoo means earthborn spirits in Arapaho, and the American Indians believed these rocks were created by fun-loving spirits, both human and animal. You'll see balanced rocks, odd-shaped rocks, and just plain gorgeous rocks here—and perhaps some rock climbers, too, as the area is quite popular with these vertically inclined adventurers. For a short walk amongst the rocks with great views of your surroundings, hike the .6-mile round-trip **Vedauwoo Glen Trail** (#790), accessible from the parking lot by the same name. Camping is also allowed here (early May through late October; $10; handicapped accessible). See also High Plains Outdoor Institute in *To Do*—Unique Adventures.

WILDLIFE REFUGES AND AREAS

🦫 **Pathfinder National Wildlife Refuge:** See listing in Central Wyoming: Casper and Douglas.

OTHER WILD PLACES 🦫 &

Saratoga National Fish Hatchery (307-326-5662; http://saratoga.fws .gov), 4 miles north of town, then 18 miles on CR 207 (very rough); open 8–4 daily Memorial Day through Labor Day; 8–4 Monday through Friday Labor Day through Memorial Day; free. This hatchery invites visitors to explore the grounds and to take a closer look at the nation's process for producing fish. This hatchery alone produces and distributes more than 8 million trout eggs annually.

VEDAUWOO RECREATION AREA

✳ Lodging

BED AND BREAKFASTS

Centennial

🍴 **Brooklyn Lodge Bed and Breakfast** (307-742-6916; http:// www.brooklynlodge.com), 3540 WY 130. Situated in a historic mountain lodge high in the Snowy Mountains of southern Wyoming, this B&B provides luxurious western comfort and personal attention to your every need. The lodge accommodates a maximum of two couples per night in its two guest rooms, each featuring satellite television, king-sized bed, DVD player, western décor, and cedar closets. From the enormous, filling ranch breakfast served each morning to the afternoon's fresh-baked cookies and the delectable chocolates that greet you at bedtime, you will be delighted by the food. As for the views and the solitude, they are simply enchanting—the lodge rests between two trout streams, with views of mountain meadows and ample opportunities for wildlife watching. Constructed by two of Buffalo Bill Cody's sidekicks, this lodge is listed on the National Register of Historic Places. Expensive.

Encampment/Riverside

🍴 **Spirit West River Lodge** (1-888-289-8321 or 307-327-5753; http:// www.spiritwestriverlodge.com), .25 mile east of Riverside, P.O. Box 605, Encampment. On the banks of the Encampment River (see *To Do*—Fishing), you'll find this hidden escape from the daily rat race, which offers you a bed and breakfast experience in a one-of-a-kind setting in a rustic, one-story log lodge. Here you'll stay in one of four rooms, all of which feature carefully chosen western décor and private bathrooms. Not only does a complete breakfast (served outside if the weather allows it) come with your stay, but also you'll be served a delectable selection of hors d'oeuvres every evening. Guests enjoy easy access to the abundant recreational opportunities surrounding this beautiful property. Moderate.

Laramie

"¶" **Mad Carpenter Inn** (307-742-0870; http://www.madcarpenter.com), 353 N. Eighth Street, Laramie. This immaculate inn with its standout woodwork gives you easy access to the University of Wyoming campus. Stay in one of three individually decorated rooms, and enjoy a continental breakfast in the morning, plus access to the game room.

& "¶" ✑ **Vee Bar Guest Ranch Bed and Breakfast** (1-800-483-3227 or 307-745-7036; http://www.veebar.com), 2091 WY 130. The historic Vee Bar Guest Ranch serves as both a bed and breakfast accommodation and an inclusive ranch vacation proprietor. B&B guests stay in one of six riverside suites or one of three cabins, enjoying a full breakfast, access to the hot tub, and catch-and-release fishing privileges. B&B guests can also make reservations to dine at the ranch for lunch and dinner. Horseback riding is extra. Expensive.

Saratoga

"¶" ✑ **The Hood House Bed and Breakfast** (307-326-8901; http://www.hoodhousebnb.com), 214 N. Third Street. Built in 1892, this charming Victorian B&B also happens to be one of the oldest homes in Saratoga. The four comfortably decorated guest bedrooms each come with a private bath, with guests enjoying access to all of the house's facilities, including the kitchen. You are also welcome to play croquet in the yard or go for a bike ride on one of the bicycles. Expensive.

LODGES

Albany

❧ ✑ & **Albany Lodge** (307-745-5782; http://www.albanylodge.com), 1148 WY 11, 35 miles southwest of Laramie and 12 miles south of Centennial. Situated at the foot of the Snowy Moun-
tain Range, this rustic lodge, new in 2003, includes nine comfortable guest rooms with private bathrooms, as well as one cabin with a kitchenette sleeping up to four, and a two-bedroom, two-bathroom house. An on-premises restaurant (open at 8 AM daily year-round) serves up home-cooked fare for breakfast, lunch, and dinner (moderate). Albany lodge also rents snowmobiles and offers guided tours (see *To Do*—Snow Sports), providing easy access to nearby snowmobile trails. Moderate to very expensive.

Centennial

❧ ✑ **Snowy Mountain Lodge** (307-742-SNOW; http://www.snowymountainlodge.com), 3474 WY 130. Constructed in 1927, this historic log lodge features 9,000-square-feet of majestic mountain beauty, harmonizing with its wild surroundings of the Medicine Bow National Forest. Once used as a science camp by the University of Wyoming, this lodge and its surrounding cabins were transformed into comfortable visitor accommodations, beginning in 2001. All of the cabins were newly remodeled and redecorated late in 2004. The lodge rents out snowmobiles, has fueling services, and offers guided snowmobile tours as well. You can also dine at the on-premises restaurant, serving upscale western fare 8–8 daily (moderate to expensive). Moderate to very expensive.

HOTELS AND MOTELS

Centennial

"¶" ❧ & ✑ **Mountain View Historic Hotel** (1-888-400-9953 or 307-742-5476; http://www.themountainviewhotel.com), WY 130 (6 miles from Snowy Range Ski Area and 27 miles west of Laramie), P.O. Box 328. Constructed in 1907, this historic hotel has been fully restored to ensure the comfort of its guests in modern accommodations while retaining its vibrant history. Easy access to the Snowy Range Ski Area (see *To Do*—Snow Sports) is a bonus, as is the access right out your door to more than 300 miles of snowmobile trails in the Medicine Bow National Forest (see *Green Space*—National Lands), as well as plenty of trails for snowshoeing and cross-country skiing. Also on the premises, you can enjoy homemade meals (breakfast and lunch) in the café and coffee shop, which can even pack you a lunch to go. Also available at the hotel is **Healing Mountain Massage** ($60/hour). Moderate to expensive.

See also Prospector Dining Room at the Old Corral Hotel and Steakhouse in *Where to Eat*—Eating Out.

Elk Mountain

☛ ⅖ **Historic Elk Mountain Hotel** (307-348-7774; http://www.elkmountainhotel.com), 102 E. Main Street. Listed on the National Register of Historic Places, this restored 1905 Victorian Folk hotel features luxurious accommodations in each of its 12 uniquely themed guest rooms (adults only, please), all decorated with period antiques, and all with full, private bathrooms. Situated conveniently just off I-80 between Laramie and Rawlins, the hotel affords you a distinctive place to stop and spend the night. The on-premises restaurant offers Cordon Bleu cuisine (complete with a terrific wine list) for breakfast, lunch, and dinner daily for guests; call for hours/reservations if you're not staying at the hotel (expensive). Expensive.

Medicine Bow

🐾 ⅖ **The Historic Virginian Hotel** (307-379-2377), built in 1911 and now on the National Register of Historic Places, pays tribute to Owen Wister's use of this area in his well-known novel. You can still stay there today while you explore the other attractions of the area, including the **Owen Wister Cabin and Monument** and the **Medicine Bow Museum** (307-379-2383), located right across the street from the Virginian. The museum is in the restored Union Pacific railroad depot, which is listed on the National Register of Historic Places. This quirky hotel also has an on-premises restaurant (call for current hours; moderate). Moderate.

Saratoga

✿ **Historic Wolf Hotel** (307-326-5525; http://www.wolfhotel.com), 101 E. Bridge Street. Closed Sunday. This historic property, built in 1893 and listed on the National Register of Historic Places, was once home to a stage stop. Today, it is home to a lovely guest accommodation featuring nine restored rooms/suites for you to choose from, all with private bathrooms. Also on the premises, you'll find a sociable saloon with a pool table, as well as a dining room serving lunch and dinner (reservations recommended for dinner; moderate to expensive). Moderate.

🏵 ☛ ⅖ ✿ 🐾 **Sage and Sand Motel, LLC** (307-326-8339; http://www.sageandsand.net), 311 S. First Street. Centrally located in Saratoga, this is the place to stay if you're visiting Saratoga on a budget but don't want to sacrifice service. A free, continental breakfast is served in summertime. Children 12 and under stay for free. Inexpensive.

☛ ✿ **Saratoga Resort and Spa** (1-800-594-0178 or 307-326-5261; http://www.saratogaresortandspa.com), 601 E. Pic Pike Road. Relax and unwind at this hot springs resort, which allows guests unlimited, complimentary use of its 70-foot hot mineral pool, renowned for its high mineral content. If you like, you can add a spa treatment from the on-premises **Healing Waters Spa,** such as a warm stone massage or a mud wrap. The Saratoga

Inn is also home to the **Silver Saddle Restaurant,** featuring the perfect atmosphere of elegant yet casual dining (expensive); and the **Snowy Mountain Pub,** featuring microbrews made on the premises and pub-style fare (moderate). Moderate to expensive.

CAMPGROUNDS ♿ ⚲ **BLM Campgrounds** (see *Green Space*—National Lands) in this region include six developed campgrounds managed by the Rawlins Field Office. Two of these are **Bennett Peak Campground** (June 1 through November 15; $10) and **Corral Creek Recreation Site** (open June 1 through November 15; free), accessible by taking exit 235 off I-80 and going south on WY 130 about 40 miles to Riverside, and then east on WY 230 for about 4 miles. Go left (northeast) on CR 660 for about 12 miles, and then go left (northwest) on BLM 3404 for about 6 miles to reach Corral Creek and 7 miles to reach Bennett Peak. This beautiful area lies on the banks of the North Platte River (see *To Do*—Fishing), providing great fishing access complete with a boat ramp for floating access, as well as opportunities to hike, horseback ride (bring your own horses—but they're not allowed in Bennett Peak Campground), picnic, and view wildlife. See also Encampment River in *To Do*—Fishing.

♿ ✐ ⁗¶⁗ **Laramie KOA** (1-800-562-4153 or 307-742-6553; http://www.koa kampgrounds.com), 1271 W. Baker Street, Laramie. This full-service RV campground also has cabins and tent sites, as well as a playground and bicycle rentals. Very inexpensive to inexpensive.

♿ **Medicine Bow National Forest** (see *Green Space*—National Lands) has two ranger districts in this region.

The Brush Creek/Hayden Ranger District (307-326-5562) manages 14 developed campgrounds, as well as providing plenty of opportunities for dispersed camping (free). Handicapped-accessible **Lincoln Park Campground** (open June 15 through October; $10), is easily accessed by going east on WY 130 from Saratoga for about 20 miles, and then north on FR 100 for less than 3 miles. Eight more developed campgrounds lie just off WY 130 east of Saratoga (some are in the Laramie Ranger District). A number of additional developed campgrounds can be accessed off WY 70 southwest of Encampment, including **Bottle Creek Campground** (open June through October; $10), accessed by taking WY 70 southwest from Encampment for 7 miles, and then going south on FR 550 for about .25 mile. Visitors can find information about the district, including campgrounds, by calling the **Brush Creek Visitor Center** (307-326-5562). The Laramie Ranger District (307-745-2300), 2468 Jackson Street, Laramie, manages more than 20 developed campgrounds in this region, as well as offering plenty of opportunities for dispersed camping (free). Some of these campgrounds lie along or just off WY 130 (see above). Additional campgrounds lie southwest of Laramie and are accessible off WY 230. You'll also find a couple developed campgrounds just off I-80 at Exit 323, southeast of Laramie, then north on WY 210 or FR 712. Almost all of the campgrounds in this ranger district are open seasonally and charge a $10 per night fee. See also Hog Park Reservoir in *To Do*—Boating; Medicine Bow River in *To Do*—Fishing; Platte River Trail in *To Do*—Hiking; and Vedauwoo Recreation Area in *Green Space*—Recreation Areas.

"ı" ♂ **Rawlins KOA** (1-800-562-7559 or 307-328-2021; http://www.koa.com), 205 E. WY 71, Rawlins. This full-service RV campground also has cabins and tent sites. Also on the premises, you'll find a heated pool, playground, basketball court, and a general store. Very inexpensive to inexpensive.

♂ **"ı"** **Western Hills Campground** (1-888-568-3040 or 307-324-2592; http://www.westernhillscampground.com), 2500 Wagon Circle Road, Rawlins. This RV campground also has tent sites and log cabins that can sleep up to six people, along with a miniature golf course and playground. Very inexpensive to inexpensive.

See also Saratoga in *To See*—Towns; and Seminoe State Park in *Green Space*—State Parks.

OTHER OPTIONS
Jelm
🏛 **"ı"** 🏕 ♂ **Historic Woods Landing Resort** (307-745-9638; http://www.woodslanding.com), #9 WY 10, Jelm, 25 miles southwest of Laramie via WY 230. Stay in one of eight cabins or even a teepee, which include access to a shared bathhouse, or just drive your RV or bring a tent to this rustic and historic resort. It's situated with easy access to the tremendous recreational opportunities found in the Medicine Bow National Forest (see *Green Space*—National Lands). The **Woods Landing Café** serves breakfast, lunch, and dinner daily from Memorial Day through mid-November, serving breakfast on weekends only and lunch and dinner daily during the rest of the year. The dance hall, listed on the National Register of Historic Places, hosts live entertainment (and dancing, of course), on most Saturdays. A country store sells souvenirs and necessities. Children under 12 are free. Inexpensive to moderate.

✳ Where to Eat

EATING OUT
Albany
See Albany Lodge in *Lodging*—Lodges.

Centennial
Prospector Dining Room at the Old Corral Hotel and Steakhouse (1-866-OLD-CORRAL or 307-745-5918; http://www.oldcorral.com), 2750 WY 130. Open 7 AM–9 PM daily. This western restaurant in the Snowy Mountains is renowned for its huge and marvelous creations. If you want to kick back and enjoy a steak after a long day of playing in the snow, you'll find an assortment of sizes and styles on the menu to suit your fancy, right up to a 32-ounce monster steak. If you're looking for a place to stay, you'll also find 35 hotel-style rooms for overnight travelers (moderate to expensive). Moderate to expensive.

See also Mountain View Historic Hotel in *Lodging*.

Jelm
See Historic Woods Landing Resort in *Lodging*—Other Options.

Laramie
Coal Creek Coffee Company (1-800-838-7737 or 307-745-7737; http://www.coalcreekcoffee.com), 108/110 E. Grand Avenue and 2137 Grand Avenue. Open 6 AM–11 PM daily. This local establishment enjoys a well-earned regional reputation for its excellent coffee, which it distributes to numerous locations throughout the American West. Sample some of the stuff right from the source by stepping into the original store in Laramie. Here you'll find expertly prepared coffee beverages made from the finest of beans, as well as teas, hot chocolates, and shakes. If you're hungry, you can order a freshly prepared sandwich, homemade soup, or a salad, or just

nosh on one of the assorted baked goods that tempt patrons daily. Also available are wine by the glass, microbrews, and house cocktails. What else? Well, this cool, high-ceiled hangout features art shows with works by local and regional artists displayed on the walls and a community bulletin board, as well as hosting live entertainment several times each month, usually on Friday and Saturday nights. Inexpensive.

Grand Avenue Pizza (307-721-2909; http://www.grandavenuepizza.com), 301 Grand Avenue. Open for lunch and dinner Tuesday through Saturday. On a busy corner of Laramie's historic downtown, you can sit down at a window table and watch the goings-on outside, if you like, while you peruse the menu. Gourmet pizzas are a favorite here, with original creations such as buffalo chicken, Thai pie, and of course, the Grand Avenue, all of which feature unique combinations of toppings. You can get a more standard pie, too, if you wish. Not a pizza lover? No worries. The menu also includes salads, pasta, sandwiches, and calzones. Be sure to stop in on Wine Wednesday to pick up a half-priced bottle of your favorite and learn more about all things vino. A kids' menu is available. Moderate.

The Library Sports Grill and Brewery (307-742-0500; http://www.librarysportsgrilleandbrewery.com), 1622 E. Grand Avenue. Open for lunch and dinner 11–9 (bar until midnight) Sunday through Wednesday; 11–10 (bar until 2 AM) Thursday through Saturday. This microbrewery makes a fine place to go to catch your favorite sports team on the television while tossin' back a great pub meal and a house-made microbrew. A nice selection of creative salads makes up a big part of the menu, along with just as many sandwiches and wraps, plus hearty burgers and pizza. Moderate.

Sweet Melissa Café (307-742-9607), 213 S. First Street. Open 11–9 Monday through Saturday. Even if you're not a vegetarian, you should probably stop in for a meal at this locals' favorite restaurant. After all, any vegetarian restaurant that's popular in Wyoming is probably pretty darn good—and this one is so good that it just expanded (late 2009) to include more eating space and a wine bar. Organic, freshly prepared and absolutely delicious dishes are creative, proving that there are places that see beyond frozen veggie burgers for vegetarians. Just sit yourself down in the comfy hangout and prepare for a culinary masterpiece, sans meat. Enjoy viewing the local artwork for sale on the walls while you wait. Kids are welcome. Moderate.

Teriyaki Bowl (307-742-0709), 3021 E. Grand Avenue. Open for lunch and dinner; call for current hours. If you're in the mood for Asian food, or you just need something fast—but you can't stomach the idea of fast food—try Teriyaki Bowl, where you can eat in or take out. The entrée menu features a list of bowls, all of which provide a complete and rather healthy meal unto themselves. Choose from a chicken teriyaki bowl, beef teriyaki bowl, combo bowl (both chicken and beef), or vegetable bowl, among others, all of which include rice and an assortment of steamed vegetables. Moderate.

See also Albany Lodge and Snowy Mountain Lodge in *Lodging*—Lodges; and Anong's Thai Cuisine below in Rawlins.

Medicine Bow
See Historic Virginian Hotel in *Lodging*—Hotels and Motels.

Rawlins

☙ **Anong's Thai Cuisine** (307-324-6262), 210 Fifth Street, Rawlins. Open 11–3 and 5–9 Monday through Saturday. The middle of Wyoming might not be where you'd expect to find delicious Thai food, but you will not leave Anong's disappointed. Generous portions and classic dishes (think Pad Thai and Massaman Curry) coupled with fantastic service make this restaurant a great escape from the steakhouse routine. Lunch is a buffet. You can also dine at Anong's in Laramie (307-745-6262), 101 E. Ivinson Avenue. Moderate.

⟨¶⟩ ✿ **Huckleberry's Espresso** (307-324-4758), 509 W. Cedar Street. Open 7 AM–9 PM Monday through Friday, 8 AM–9 PM Saturday, 9 AM–7 PM Sunday (summer), 7:30 AM–7 PM (winter). In the mood for an espresso—or an ice cream cone? Either way, you've come to the right place if you stop at Huckleberry's, where you'll find not only an assortment of specialty coffee drinks and ice cream treats, but also more filling, meal-making options. Breakfast is served all day long, but if you want something else, you'll also find soup, sandwiches, and other light fare on the menu as well. For a cool coffee treat, try a Big Train Blended Ice Rage. Inexpensive.

Kristi's Bakery (307-324-9180), 2350 W. Spruce Street, Rawlins. Open 5 AM–2 PM Tuesday through Friday, 7 AM–2 PM Saturday. Stop in for a cup of Coal Creek Coffee (see listing in Laramie, above), or a fresh-baked pastry or muffin. You can enjoy your light breakfast or snack in the bakery's comfortable dining area, or just take it to go with you. Inexpensive.

Saratoga

✿ **Lazy River Cantina** (307-326-8472), 110 E. Bridge Avenue. Open 2–11 Sunday through Thursday, noon–11:30 Friday through Saturday. Enjoy hearty Mexican fare or just step in for a libation at this establishment. You'll find all your Mexican/Southwestern favorites on the menu, along with more standard American food options for the less spicily inclined among your party. Children are welcome. Olé!

✿ **Lollypop's** (307-326-5020), 107 E. Bridge Avenue. Open 7 AM–11 AM for breakfast and 11 AM–9 PM for lunch, ice cream, coffee, and other treats. IF YOU'RE IN A HURRY, YOU'RE IN THE WRONG TOWN, says the sign at Lollypop's, but if you've got some time to chill, grab a seat on the outdoor patio and relax for a meal at this cute coffee/sandwich shop. You can even grab an ice cream soda at the old-fashioned soda fountain. Inexpensive.

See also Historic Wolf Hotel and Saratoga Resort and Spa in *Lodging—Hotels and Motels*

DINING OUT

Centennial
See Snowy Mountain Lodge in *Lodging—Lodges*.

Elk Mountain
See Historic Elk Mountain Hotel in *Lodging—Hotels and Motels*.

Laramie
✿ **Jeffrey's Bistro** (307-742-7046; http://www.jeffreysbistro.com), 123 E. Ivinson Avenue. Open 11–9 Monday through Saturday. Serving lunch and dinner in a corner location in historic downtown Laramie, Jeffrey's takes pride in offering up deliberately healthy fare, with most of its menu items being meatless, as well as being prepared using heart-healthy canola oil. Creative meal salads, served with bread baked fresh on the premises, include a create-your-own salad option, with 20 add-ins possible to top off the

bistro's special blend of five different leafy greens. Each day features several homemade soups. The menu also includes an array of sandwiches, and entrée items such as potpies, enchiladas, burritos, and pastas. The restaurant even gives you the option of ordering your entrée a la carte, or with all of the yummy extras, which include coffee or tea, soup or salad, and your choice of a homemade dessert (highly recommended). A children's menu is available as well. Moderate to expensive.

Rawlins

Aspen House Restaurant (307-324-4787), 318 Fifth Street. Open 11–2 Monday through Friday and 5 PM–9:30 PM Monday through Saturday. Acclaimed as the finest restaurant in Rawlins, here you'll find a menu with not only expertly prepared, traditional American favorites (steaks, seafood, poultry, and pastas), but also entrées influenced by Cajun cuisine and authentic Singapore cuisine. Great service, a lovely setting, and a fine wine list compliment this excellent dining experience. Expensive.

Saratoga

See Saratoga Resort and Spa in *Lodging*—Hotels and Motels.

✳ Entertainment

Fox Cinema (307-742-2842; http://www.transluxmovies.com), 505 S. 20th Street, Laramie.

Movies 3 (307-324-6624; http://www.rawlinsmovies.com), 1720 Edinburgh Street, Rawlins.

Wyo Theater (307-742-7469), 309 S. Fifth Street, Laramie.

See also University of Wyoming in *Guidance*; Ice-skating in *To Do*—Snow Sports; Historic Woods Landing Resort in *Lodging*—Other Options; Coal Creek Coffee Company and The

Library Sports Grill and Brewery in *Where to Eat*—Eating Out; and *Special Events*.

✳ Selective Shopping

The Brown 'n Gold Outlet (1-800-852-5184 or 307-742-9701; http://www.brownandgold.com), 408 E. University Avenue, Laramie (also has a Cheyenne location). Open 10–7 Monday through Friday, 10–4 Saturday and Sunday, 8–6 on UW football home game days. If you want to take home some University of Wyoming gear or clothing with you, this is where you should go. They sell hoodies, boxers, T-shirts, mugs, and more—pretty much everything you'd expect—emblazoned proudly with the university's colors and emblems.

Historic Downtown Laramie is rife with shopping experiences, including those listed in this section. An avid shopper could easily wile away an entire day—or more—browsing through the downtown area's cool collection of widely varying shops, stopping for every meal at a great restaurant.

2Bazaar, LLC (http://www.2bazaar.com) has two locations: **2Bazaar Gallery/The Mona Lisa Ballroom** (307-742-3864), 404 South Second Street, Laramie, open 11–6 Thursday through Saturday; and **Hart's Jewelry and Gifts** (307-742-9386), 111 E. Grand Avenue, Laramie, open 11–5 Thursday through Saturday and by appointment. At the 2Bazaar Gallery, you'll find an incredible array of unique pieces of art, including lamps, furniture, antiques, pottery, and more. One entire wall of the gallery is reserved for pieces by Wyoming artists. Hart's features unique art pieces as well as jewelry and gifts. You're likely to lose yourself browsing through one or both of these unusual establish-

SHOPPING OPPORTUNITIES ABOUND IN
HISTORIC DOWNTOWN LARAMIE

June: **Woodchopper's Jamboree and Rodeo,** Encampment: An annual event for more than four decades, it includes wood-chopping competitions, rodeo, entertainment, and barbecue.

June: **Platte Valley Festival of the Birds** (307-326-8073), Saratoga: The festivities include a guided scenic float of the North Platte River, speakers, bird-watching, a banquet with a guest speaker, and guided bird-watching hikes.

✍ *June:* **Butch Cassidy Days,** Wyoming Territorial Prison (see *To See*—Historic Landmarks, Places, and Sites): Event includes a tractor display, parade, and pull; educational talks; living history; puppet show; food; and theater.

June and July: **Snowy Range Summer Theatre and Dance Festival** (307-766-2198; http://www.uwyo.edu/ th&d/whats_playing/SnowyRange.asp): This summer arts festival gives a variety of performances featuring students and professional actors/dancers.

June through August: **Music in the Park**, Rawlins: Every Thursday a different musician or band performs at 7 PM in **Washington Park** (15th Street and Walnut Street.); food is available for purchase starting at 5:30.

July: **Grand Encampment Cowboy Gathering** (307-326-8855; http://www .grandencampmentgathering.org), Encampment: This event includes cowboy poetry, music, campfire songs, melodrama, a shootout, cowboy church, and living history demonstrations.

✍ *August:* **Carbon County Fair and Rodeo** (307-328-7811), Rawlins: A traditional county fair including livestock exhibitions, 4-H, rodeo, food, children's activities, demolition derby, a street dance, and more.

ments—and you'll probably walk out with a purchase or two. Special events are held in the Mona Lisa Ballroom.

See also The Laramie Plains Museum at the Historic Ivinson Mansion in *To See*—Museums; Wyoming Frontier Prison and Wyoming Territorial Prison State Historic Site in *To See*—Historic Landmarks, Places, and Sites; The Herb House and Whole Earth Grainery and Truck Store in *To Do*—Relaxation and Rejuvenation; Historic Woods Landing Resort in *Lodging*— Other Options; and Coal Creek Coffee Company and Sweet Melissa Café in *Where to Eat*—Eating Out.

✳ Special Events

✍ *January:* **Ice Fishing Derby,** Saratoga: This family friendly competition includes thousands of dollars in prize money and children's fishing contests as well. See also Saratoga in *To See*—Towns.

February: **Sierra Madre Winter Carnival,** Encampment: The two-day winter celebration includes casino night, snowmobile races, homemade sled races, snow sculpture, and more.

CHEYENNE

I f you're coming from the southeast, you'll enter Wyoming along I-80 in the small border town of Pine Bluffs (see *To See*—Towns), a historic railroad town, and then it's on to Cheyenne. Cheyenne is Wyoming's capital city and its largest city (about 56,000 residents) as well. It owes its very existence to the coming of the transcontinental railroad in the late 1860s. Recognizing the need to provide a hometown for those working on the railroad, the Union Pacific Railroad selected Cheyenne's location in 1867, officially founding the town on the Fourth of July. The establishment of Fort D. A. Russell—today F. E. Warren Air Force Base—followed shortly thereafter, with the Army providing military protection for the railroad construction, mainly against antagonistic American Indians (see *To See*—Historic Landmarks, Places, and Sites).

Cheyenne is full of museums and historical attractions, promising to keep you busy for weeks of exploration if western frontier history interests you. By far the city's most popular annual event is Cheyenne Frontier Days, known as The Daddy of 'Em All, which includes incredible action-packed rodeos, a parade, concerts by famous country stars, free pancake breakfasts, and more—turning the entire city of Cheyenne into one big celebration at the end of July. Each year, the festivities include headlining acts by well-known entertainers that sell out early, so if you're planning on going be sure to check who's playing this year long in advance(see *Special Events*)—and be aware that most lodging accommodations charge premium rates during this popular event. In addition, Cheyenne has nearly 20 municipal parks (see *To See*—City Parks and Gardens), making it easy to find a place for picnicking or other outdoor recreation, among its many other attractions.

GUIDANCE Cheyenne Area Convention and Visitors Bureau (1-800-426-5009 or 307-778-3133; http://www.cheyenne.org), One Depot Square, 121 W. 15th Street, #202, Cheyenne, 82001.

Cheyenne Chamber of Commerce (307-638-3388; http://www.cheyenne chamber.org), One Depot Square, 121 W. 15th Street, #204, Cheyenne, 82003.

Frank Norris Jr. Travel Center (307-777-2883), Exit 7 off I-25 at College Drive, Cheyenne. Open 8–5 daily.

Wyoming Game and Fish Department Headquarters and Visitor Center (307-777-4600; http://gf.state.wy.us/admin/regional/headquarters.asp), 5400 Bishop Boulevard, Cheyenne, 82006.

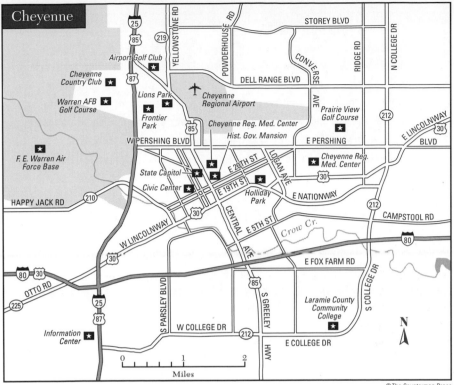

Cheyenne

©The Countryman Press

See also Towns.

GETTING THERE *By car:* Cheyenne lies at the crossroads of Wyoming's two major interstates, I-25 and I-80. US 85 also reaches Cheyenne from the south.

By plane: **Cheyenne Regional Airport** (307-634-7071; http://www.cheyenne airport.com) is at the corner of Eighth Avenue and Evans Avenue in Cheyenne.

GETTING AROUND Though Cheyenne is Wyoming's largest city, you'll still find plenty of opportunities to walk between clustered attractions. However, you may end up footsore and back in your car if you choose to visit attractions that are more spread out within Cheyenne. You can also catch a ride from 6 AM–7 PM Monday through Friday and 10–5 Saturday ($1 per adult, $.75 per student under 18, under 5 free) on one of Cheyenne's handicapped-accessible city buses, part of the Cheyenne Transit Program (307-637-6253; http://www.cheyennenetwork.com/local/bus_schedule/index.asp). Of course, you'll want to drive to those attractions situated outside of the city. See also Cheyenne Street Railway Trolley in *To Do—Unique Adventures.*

MEDICAL EMERGENCY Dial 911.

WYOMING'S RAILROAD PAST

Perhaps more than any other single feature, the transcontinental trans-portation corridor (today better known as I-80) that runs through the entire southern portion of Wyoming has defined and shaped its role and identity in the modern world. This role hearkens back to the emigrant trails that began the massive movement of people west in the early to mid-1800s, when por-tions of the Oregon Trail, Mormon Trail, Pony Express Trail, and other such trails passed through parts of this region. These first trails passed through the far western portion of this region after passing northward over South Pass (see Historic Landmarks, Places, and Sites in Northwest Wyoming: Lander and Riverton), arcing south to the area around present-day Green River. But in 1862, Ben Halladay, a.k.a. the Stagecoach King, created an alternate route that came to be known as the Overland Trail, a route that, though short-lived in its incarnation as a stagecoach route, would nonethe-less have long-lasting repercussions on this desolate, windswept Wyoming landscape.

With the establishment of the Overland Trail as a stagecoach mail route through southern Wyoming in 1862, a precedent for all future trans-state transportation routes was set. The Overland Trail proved to be a safer way to traverse Wyoming than the more northerly trails, both in terms of terrain and in terms of being better protected from the agitated American Indians, who at that point were still struggling wholeheartedly to resist the veritable invasion of pioneers and soldiers attempting to force them off their home-lands and on to reservations. The heyday of the Overland Trail lasted only seven years, but during that time, it became the main route westward for emigrants, despite continued threats of American Indian attacks as well as the general hardships of traveling in those times.

The end of the Overland Trail's precedence as a travel route came about with the completion of the transcontinental railroad in 1869, when the Union Pacific and Central Pacific ends of the railroad met at Promontory Point in Utah. Running the railroad through Wyoming was pretty much a no-

Cheyenne Regional Medical Center (307-634-2273; http://www.crmcwy.org), 214 E. 23rd Street, Cheyenne.

✳ To See

TOWNS ❧ Pine Bluffs welcomes you to Wyoming at the **Pine Bluffs Informa-tion Center** (307-245-3695; http://www.pinebluffs.org), Exit 401 off I-80 in Pine Bluffs. Open daily May through October. You'll see the center just after you cross

brainer for Union Pacific, given not only the suitability of the terrain, but also the discovery of plentiful coal deposits in the vicinity of the railroad's path through the state.

Nonetheless, the railroad was not constructed without difficulties. The American Indians were understandably displeased (to say the least) with this latest invasion of their historic territories, coupled with all of the additional conflicts and unpleasant interactions they'd already had with the newcomers to this land. They did manage to disrupt the railroad's progress on several occasions. Additional military forts followed in the wake of such attacks, helping to further secure the unstoppable progression of the railroad across the landscape. Upon its inevitable completion, the railroad virtually immediately transcended all other forms of transport westward, becoming the preferred and safest mode of travel by emigrants who ventured this way.

Following the precedent set by both the Overland Trail and the transcontinental railroad, the nation's first east west transcontinental highway, the almost 3,400-mile Lincoln Highway, marched into being in the state of Wyoming in 1913. The vision of industrialist Carl Fisher, the Lincoln Highway stretched from New York to San Francisco, passing through 13 states. It would take years for the entirety of the road to be paved, but the official establishment and designation of this road set the tone for America's future interstate roadways, designed to accommodate travel by automobile. The original Lincoln Highway in Wyoming followed the same basic route as today's I-80, with the major exception being the portion of the highway from Laramie to Walcott Junction. That portion originally arced north along the path of today's US 30/287, passing the town of Medicine Bow (see *To See*—Towns in Southeast Wyoming: Rawlins and Laramie).

Though many travelers journey through Wyoming along I-80 today, probably a scant few of them actually realize the historical significance of this travel route not only to the history of the state, but also to the entire nation. As you travel along I-80, delving more deeply into Wyoming's transportation history is as simple as exiting the interstate to visit the cities and their historical and cultural attractions, starting with Wyoming's state capital—Cheyenne.

the border with Nebraska. It provides not only information, but also nature trails that allow the weary traveler an opportunity for some movement and fresh air after long hours in the car, including a trail to view the **High Plains Archaeology Project** (open 9–5 Memorial Day through Labor Day). Here, a helpful guide will gladly walk you through the history of the dig site, and the kids can enjoy hands-on exhibits, too. Like so many towns in this region, Pine Bluffs—formerly known as Rock Ranch—came into being thanks to the arrival of the Union Pacific Railroad in 1867. Before that time, the bluffs that gave the town its name served as favored camping grounds for American Indians, who chose them not only for the tremendous vantage point they gave, but also for their abundance of firewood and close proximity to ample fresh water and food sources. After the coming of the railroad, Pine Bluffs became a hub of the Texas Trail, used to move thousands upon thousands of head of cattle from Texas north to Wyoming for shipping during the 1870s and 80s. Learn more about this at the free, handicapped-accessible **Texas Trail Park and Museum** (307-245-3713; http://www.texastrailmuseumoflaramiecounty .org), in the city park at the corner of Third Street and Market Street; open 11–4 Monday through Saturday, Memorial Day through Labor Day. This museum happens to house one of the nation's largest collections of barbed wire, for all those barbed-wire aficionados out there (say what?). Pine Bluffs is also home to Wyoming's largest sculpture, the 40-foot **Our Lady of Peace Shrine,** by Robert Fida (on US 30 and visible from I-80). Looking for a place to camp? Try **Pine Bluffs RV Park** (307-631-1139), 10 Paintbrush, near the community swimming pool. See also =G (Double Bar G) Rodeo Series in *Special Events*. For more information: **Town of Pine Bluffs** (307-245-3746; http://www.pinebluffs.org), 206 Main Street, P.O. Box 249, Pine Bluffs, 82082.

MUSEUMS ὅ ♪ **Cheyenne Depot Museum** (307-632-3905; http://www .cheyennedepotmuseum.org), One Depot Square, 121 W. 15th Street. Open 9–5 Monday through Saturday, 11–5 Sunday; $5 per adult (ages 13+). A National Historic Landmark, this painstakingly renovated 1929 Union Pacific railroad depot is graced with a beautiful and distinctive clock tower. The museum documents the role played by the railroad both in the establishment of Wyoming's capital city and in the city's ensuing development, as well as the history of the depot building itself. Children will enjoy hands-on exhibits. This museum opened in 2004, and it provides an array of visitor services and information, as well as hosting many community events throughout the year. See also Cheyenne Street Railway Trolley in *To Do*—Unique Adventures; and Cheyenne Depot Garden Festival and Cheyenne Depot Days in *Special Events*.

ὅ ♪ **Cheyenne Frontier Days Old West Museum** (307-778-7290; http:// www.oldwestmuseum.org), 4610 N. Carey Avenue (Frontier Park), P.O. Box 2720. Open 9–5 Monday through Friday, 10–5 Saturday and Sunday; $7 per adult, children under 12 are free. This museum strives to help visitors learn about this area's history from its ties to the Union Pacific Railroad to its legacy of cowboys and rodeos that lives on today during the annual Cheyenne Frontier Days (see *Special Events*). Particular attention is given to western art, ranching history, and the history of the Frontier Days celebration itself. Children can enjoy interactive exhibits (and so can you). The museum hosts

OUR LADY OF PEACE SHRINE, PINE BLUFFS

several art shows and sales throughout the year, among other events. See also Kids'
Cowboy Festival in *Special Events*.

❦ **F. E. Warren Air Force Base Intercontinental Ballistic Missile (ICBM) and Heritage Museum** (307-773-2980; http://www.warrenmuseum.com), 7405 Marne Loop, Bldg. 210, FE Warren AFB. Open 8–4 Monday through Friday; free. Visitors must follow certain procedures to gain entry to this museum, as it's situated on the F. E. Warren Air Force Base, so it's best that you call in advance to ensure that you can gain entry. Housed in the former Army commanders' headquarters used in the early 20th century, this military museum includes exhibits depicting the daily lives of early military personnel, the history of missiles, the 90th Space Wing, and more. This active Air Force Base was originally an Army base (Fort D. A. Russell), established in 1867 to protect the new city of Cheyenne and the workers building the intercontinental railroad. The Air Force took command of the base in 1947, and it retains command of the base today. The base, which still has many of its original red brick buildings, is listed on the National Register of Historic Places.

ৎ **Nelson Museum of the West** (307-635-7670; http://www.nelsonmuseum.com), 1714 Carey Avenue Open 9–4:30 Monday through Saturday, June through August, 9–4:30 Monday through Friday May and September through October; closed November through April; $4 per adult, $3 per senior, children under 12 are free. A must-see for anyone interested in the frontier history of Wyoming, this museum is dedicated to the preservation of all things Western with a capital W. You'll find American Indian and cowboy memorabilia, collectibles, and artifacts as well as a tremendous collection of fine western art on display. Additional exhibits include antique firearms, sculptures, wildlife trophies (both from Wyoming and international), and more.

❦ **Wyoming Arts Council Gallery** (307-777-7742; http://wyoarts.state.wy.us/index.asp), 2320 Capitol Avenue. Open 8–5 Monday through Friday, free. Inside the historic Kendrick Building's restored carriage house, this gallery showcases the work of contemporary artists living and creating artwork in Wyoming. Artwork on exhibit is usually available for purchase as well.

❦ ♪ ৎ **Wyoming State Museum** (307-777-7022; http://wyomuseum.state.wy.us), Barrett Building, 2301 Central Avenue. Open 9–4:30 Monday through Saturday, May through October; 9–4:30 Monday through Friday, 10–2 Saturday, November through April; free. Dedicated to preserving both the human and the natural aspects of Wyoming's history, the official state museum is a treasure trove for history buffs. Here you'll find on display all things Wyoming, with permanent exhibits including a timetable illustrating Wyoming's natural and human past, Wyoming wildlife, Wyoming's mining industry, the state's dinosaur discoveries, and much, much more. Younger visitors will find plenty to keep their little hands busy—and their brains learning—in the Hands-On History Room, an interactive area that encourages kids to engage in learning about the state's history by allowing them to touch and examine relevant items, including a child-sized tipi to explore. In addition to the permanent exhibits, the museum always has numerous temporary and traveling exhibits as well.

See also Pine Bluffs in *To See*—Towns.

HISTORIC GOVERNORS' MANSION

HISTORIC LANDMARKS, PLACES, AND SITES &🕷 Historic Governors' Mansion (307-777-7878; http://wyoparks.state.wy.us/Site/SiteInfo.asp?siteID=18), 300 E. 21st Street. Open 9–5 Monday through Saturday, 1–5 Sunday, June through August; 9–5 Wednesday through Saturday, September through May; free (donations accepted). You'll pass through a doorway framed by four enormous white columns to enter into the brick mansion that served as Wyoming's first official governors' residence. This elegant, three-story home was constructed in 1904 under the guidance of architect Charles Murdock, who designed a Colonial Revival house that segued nicely into the middle-class neighborhood surrounding it. Designed to be large and comfortable—with plenty of room for entertaining guests and comfortable living—the mansion lacked any sense of ostentation or pretentiousness, particularly in comparison with the enormous homes being constructed by the wealthiest Wyomingites of that time period. The mansion continued to serve as the home for a total of 19 of Wyoming's governors until 1976, when a new residence was completed in Frontier Park. You can either take a guided tour of the house, or simply wander through this historic residence on your own.

🕷 & Historic Lakeview Cemetery (307-637-6402; http://www.cheyennecity.org/index.asp?NID=92), 2501 Seymour Avenue, Cheyenne. Grounds open dawn to dusk daily; free (donations accepted). You can take a free, self-guided walking (or driving) tour through this quiet cemetery, a bit off the beaten path but still easily accessed from downtown Cheyenne. Learn interesting bits and pieces of local history during your stroll, which includes stops at 22 different spots on the grounds. Obtain the tour booklet from the cemetery office (open 8–4:30 weekdays).

A TINY GRAVESTONE IN THE HISTORIC LAKEVIEW CEMETERY

🕷 Wyoming State Capitol Building and grounds (307-777-7220; http://wyoming.gov), Capitol Avenue and 24th Street. Open 8:30–4:30 Monday through Friday; free. A National Historic Landmark, Wyoming's State

WYOMING STATE CAPITOL BUILDING

Capitol dates to 1887, when the cornerstone for this majestic architectural masterpiece was laid. The building features sandstone quarried from the area around Fort Collins to the south, as well as around Rawlins to the northwest. Inside, you can view murals and legislative chambers, while outside, the grounds feature lovely landscaping and several statues of note. Guided tours are available (reservations recommended).

See also Pine Bluffs in *To See*—Towns; Cheyenne Depot Museum, F. E. Warren A.F.B. Intercontinental Ballistic Missile (ICBM) and Heritage Museum, and Wyoming Arts Council Gallery in *To See*—Museums; Lions Park in *To See*—City Parks and Gardens; Curt Gowdy State Park in *Green Space*—State Parks; and Nagle Warren Mansion Bed and Breakfast and Historic Plains Hotel in *Lodging*.

CITY PARKS AND GARDENS ♿ ✐ ☙ **Cheyenne Botanic Gardens** (307-637-6458; http://www.botanic.org), 710 S. Lions Park Drive, Cheyenne. Open daily dawn to dusk, conservatory open 8–4:30 weekdays, 11–3:30 weekends (closed Sunday, December through mid-January); free (donations gladly accepted). Both outside and inside, this tribute to all things verdant stimulates your senses with a rainbow of colors and scents. Stroll through perfectly maintained outdoor gardens, including a xeriscape garden, rose garden, herb garden, cactus garden, and a cool interactive sensory garden. The indoor exhibits thrive on renewable energy—the conservatory is heated entirely by solar power, and half of its electricity is derived from solar power as well. A new (2009) **Children's Village** brings botany to life for the little ones with hands-on fun. The majority of the gardens' upkeep comes from the work of volunteers including senior citizens, children, and people with disabilities. See also Lions Park, below.

CHEYENNE BOTANIC GARDENS

 ♿ 📎 🌿 **Lions Park** (307-637-6429; http://www.cheyennecity.org/index .asp?NID=208), 8th Avenue and Carey Avenue, Cheyenne. Lions Park is one of almost 20 municipal parks managed by the City of Cheyenne Parks Division. This showpiece of the parks system includes a bike path, a beach and lake, fishing, boating (canoes and paddleboats for rent), an indoor swimming pool with a waterslide, picnicking facilities, a handicapped-accessible fitness trail, the Cheyenne Botanic Gardens (see above), miniature golf, playground equipment, and athletic facilities. The park is also home to Engine 1242, the oldest locomotive in Wyoming. The engine was built in New Jersey in 1890. Following its retirement in the mid-1950s, it was donated to the city of Cheyenne by the Union Pacific Railroad.

See also Pine Bluffs in *To See*—Towns; and Cheyenne Frontier Days Old West Museum in *To See*—Museums.

SCENIC DRIVES Pine Bluffs to Torrington follows WY 215 to US 85 north for about 70 miles through rolling farmlands and beautiful sandstone bluffs, passing by a cute country church near Albin, and then dropping you into a large and impressive open valley. You'll also go by the small towns of La Grange, Hawk Springs, Huntley, and Yoder as you skirt Wyoming's border with Nebraska.

See also Happy Jack Road in *To See*—Scenic Drives in Rawlins and Laramie.

✱ To Do

BICYCLING ♿ **Greater Cheyenne Greenway** (307-638-4379; http://www .cheyennecity.org/index.asp?nid=207) is an award-winning 24-mile, partially paved pathway that runs along both Crow Creek and Dry Creek in Cheyenne, offering a fun and easy recreational adventure not only for bicyclists, but also for runners, walkers, skaters, and those in wheelchairs. Accessible from a number of parks (see also Lions Park above in City Parks and Gardens), the Greenway also connects neighborhoods, shopping areas, and schools. Along the path you'll discover lovely landscaping, birdhouses and bat boxes, and interpretive signs. Plans are in the works to extend the Greenway's scope in the future, adding more miles of paved trails for the benefit of alternative commuters and outdoor enthusiasts alike.

A COUNTRY CHURCH NEAR ALBIN ALONG THE PINE BLUFFS TO TORRINGTON SCENIC DRIVE

See also Lions Park in *To See*—City Parks and Gardens.

BOATING See Lions Park in *To See*—City Parks and Gardens; and Curt Gowdy State Park in *Green Space*—State Parks.

FISHING See Lions Park in *To See*—City Parks and Gardens; Curt Gowdy State Park in *Green Space*—State Parks; and Terry Bison Ranch Resort in *Lodging*.

FITNESS CENTERS ⟨⟩ ✿ **Cheyenne Family YMCA** (307-634-9622; http:// www.cheyenneymca.org), 1426 E. Lincolnway. Open 5 AM–9 PM Monday through Thursday, 5 AM–8 PM Friday, 7–4 Saturday, noon–4 Sunday; $6 per adult, $3 per child 15 and under, under 3 free. This Y has an indoor swimming pool, hot tub, fitness equipment, a racquetball court, yoga room, stretching area, weights, and more.

⟨⟩ **Cheyenne Regional's Health and Fitness Center** (307-778-5500; http:// www.crmcwy.org), 1620 E. Pershing. Open 5 AM–9:30 PM Monday through Thursday, 5 AM–8 PM Friday, 7–5 Saturday, 11–5 Sunday; $20 to become a member and $10 for each family member after that. This full-service fitness center offers fitness assessments, fitness classes, yoga, personal training, and even an on-premises spa that gives massages ($55/hour).

See Lions Park in *To See*—City Parks and Gardens; and Taco John's Ice and Events Center in *To Do*—For Families.

FOR FAMILIES **Taco John's Ice and Events Center** (307-433-0024; http:// www.cheyennecity.org/index.asp?nid=539), 1530 W. Lincolnway. Open year-round; rates and hours vary according to activity/event. The kids will thank you for a trip to this multi-activity center, a virtual palace of fun. Treat them to a day here for good behavior, and secretly (or maybe openly) enjoy it yourself as well. Activities include laser tag, ice-skating, drop-in ice hockey, and miniature golf on a course that features some of Wyoming's top attractions in miniature, including Devils Tower and Old Faithful. The facility also hosts numerous events throughout the year; call to find out what's happening now.

See also Pine Bluffs in *To See*—Towns; Cheyenne Depot Museum, Cheyenne Frontier Days™ Old West Museum, and Wyoming State Museum in *To See*— Museums; Cheyenne Botanic Gardens and Lions Park in *To See*—City Parks and Gardens; Cheyenne Family YMCA in *To Do*—Fitness Centers; Bit O' Wyo Ranch in *To Do*—Horseback Riding; Curt Gowdy State Park in *Green Space*—State Parks; Terry Bison Ranch Resort in *Lodging*; and Kids' Cowboy Festival in *Special Events*.

GOLF **Airport Golf Course** (307-637-6418; http://www.cheyennecity.org), 4801 Central Avenue, 18 holes.

Cheyenne Country Club (307-637-2200; http://www.cheyennecountryclub.com), 800 Stinner Road, 18 holes.

F. E. Warren AFB Golf Club (307-773-3556), 6110 Clubhouse Drive, Bldg. 2111, 18 holes.

Kingham Prairie View (307-637-6420; http://www.cheyennecity.org), 3601 Windmill Road, 9 holes.

Leaning Rock Golf Course (307-245-3236), 1200 S. Beech Street, Pine Bluffs, 9 holes.

Little America Cheyenne Golf Course (307-775-8500; http://www.littleamerica .com/cheyenne), 2800 W. Lincolnway, 9 holes.

HIKING See Greater Cheyenne Greenway in *To Do*—Bicycling and Curt Gowdy State Park in *Green Space*—State Parks.

HORSEBACK RIDING ❀ **Bit O' Wyo Ranch** (307-638-6924; http://www.bito wyoranch.com), 470 Happy Jack Road. Trail rides depart daily at 10 and 2; $35/hour (rides last one to three hours). Children are welcome on rides and reservations are recommended. The Bit O' Wyo also offers old-fashioned cowboy entertainment for the whole family with their rollicking two-hour **Cowboy Dinner Show** ($40 per person; under 7 free; reservations required).

See also Curt Gowdy State Park in *Green Space*—State Parks; and Terry Bison Ranch Resort in *Lodging*.

PADDLING/FLOATING See Lions Park in *To See*—City Parks and Gardens; and Curt Gowdy State Park in *Green Space*—State Parks.

RELAXATION AND REJUVENATION **Noah's Ark Nutrition Center** (307-778-2088; http://www.noahsarknutritioncenter.com), 1900 Thomes Avenue. Open 9–6 Monday through Friday, 9–4 Saturday. One-stop shopping for all of your on-the-road nutritional needs is what you'll find at Noah's Ark. Find your favorite brands of natural/organic food providers here, along with health and beauty products and gift items.

❀ **Yoga Zion Studios** (307-221-3585; http://www.yogazionstudios.com), 218 W. 17th Street. Call or check online for a current class schedule; $6 per class. Hatha yoga, freestyle yoga, and more await you at this positive-thinking yoga studio. Life coaching services are also available.

See also Cheyenne Regional's Health and Fitness Center in *To Do*—Fitness Centers; and Windy Hills Bed and Breakfast and Historic Plains Hotel in *Lodging*.

SNOW SPORTS See Taco John's Ice and Events Center in *To Do*—For Families.

UNIQUE ADVENTURES **Cheyenne Street Railway Trolley** (1-800-426-5009 or 307-778-3133; http://www.cheyenne.org), departs from Cheyenne Depot Museum (see *To See*—Museums). Tours are 90 minutes, departing at 10, 11:30, 1, 2:30, and 4 (weekdays), 10:30 and 1:30 Saturday, and 1:30 Sunday; $10 per adult, $5 per child ages 2–12. Whether you don't have a ton of time, or you just want to get a quick overview of Cheyenne's historical attractions before exploring them more on your own, this narrated trolley tour provides you with a convenient introduction to the city. Stops include the Big Boy Steam Engine (the world's largest steam engine), Cheyenne Botanic Gardens, Cheyenne Frontier Days Old West Museum, Nelson Museum of the West, Wyoming State Capitol building, and the Wyoming State Museum.

See also Terry Bison Ranch Resort in *Lodging*.

WINERIES AND WINE TASTINGS See Nagle Warren Mansion Bed and Breakfast and The Historic Plains Hotel in *Lodging*—Hotels and Motels.

✳ Green Space

STATE PARKS ✏ ♿ **Curt Gowdy State Park** (307-632-7946; http://wyoparks
.state.wy.us/Site/SiteInfo.asp?siteID=4), 1351 Hynds Lodge Road, 24 miles west of
Cheyenne and 23 miles east of Laramie via WY 210 (Happy Jack Road). Open
year-round for both day use $4 (resident), $6 (nonresident); and camping $10 (resident), $17 (nonresident). This state park sits on grounds long-used by multiple
American Indian tribes as camping grounds when scouting for buffalo. In addition
to this historical tie, the park is also home to **Hynds Lodge,** listed on the National
Register of Historic Places, which was built in 1922–23 for the Boy Scouts. Today
the structure can be reserved for group events, as it includes a kitchen, sleeping
facilities, a dining area, and a covered porch (contact the park for information and
reservations). The park has opportunities for boating (two ramps), fishing (handicapped-accessible pier), paddling, and swimming on Granite Lake Reservoir and
Crystal Lake Reservoir. Additional attractions include hiking trails (6.2 miles), two
playgrounds, picnicking, horseback riding trails, camping, and wildlife watching,
among others. See also Happy Jack Bluegrass Festival in *Special Events.*

NATIONAL LANDS Bureau of Land Management (BLM) (307-775-6256;
http://www.wy.blm.gov), State Office, 5353 Yellowstone, P.O. Box 1828, Cheyenne.
Responsible for managing more than 18 million surface acres of land in the state of
Wyoming, along with more than 23 million acres of federal mineral estate, the
Wyoming BLM is headquartered in this region. The Wyoming Information Desk
(phone number above) operates 7:45–4:30 Monday through Friday. Also on the
premises is the Public Room, open 9–4 Monday through Friday.

✳ Lodging

BED AND BREAKFASTS ✏ 🐾

Howdy Pardner Bed and Breakfast
(307-634-6493; http://www.howdy
pardner.net), 1920 Tranquility Road.
Just 10 minutes from the hustle and
bustle of downtown Cheyenne, you'll
find this hillside retreat, promising you
the best of both worlds. Enjoy quick
access to all of the capital city's attractions, but start and end each day of
your vacation in the comfort and peace
of the Howdy Pardner. The three guest
rooms all include queen-sized beds,
private baths, and western décor
throughout. For the more adventurous
of spirit, an Old West sheepherder's
wagon can provide your overnight
accommodation as well, with easy
access to restroom facilities in the
main house. A full ranch breakfast is
served daily. Moderate to expensive.

"♀" 🐾 ♿ **Nagle Warren Mansion
Bed and Breakfast** (1-800-811-2610
or 307-637-3333; http://www.nagle
warrenmansion.com), 222 E. 17th
Street. Built in 1888 for Erasmus
Nagle, this incredible Victorian mansion also served as the home for
Wyoming notable Francis E. Warren,
who served as the state's governor and
as a U.S. Senator. A complete renovation and restoration of this architectural icon was finished in 1999. Today it
provides a full range of modern amenities to its guests while retaining a historic authenticity throughout. The
luxuriously furnished guest rooms—six
in the main house and six in the adjacent carriage house—all include private baths, private phones, televisions,
and access to a hot tub. Guests enjoy a

full gourmet breakfast served daily. Afternoon tea is served Friday and Saturday. Murder mystery dinners and wine pairing dinners also take place regularly. Expensive.

& ♂ **Windy Hills Bed and Breakfast** (1-877-946-3944 or 307-632-6423; http://www.windyhillswyo.com), 393 Happy Jack Road. Overlooking Granite Lake, this lovely mountain retreat lies at an elevation of 7,200 feet, between Cheyenne and Laramie. You'll have a number of options about where you sleep, ranging from multi-bedroom private homes to suites in the main house (which all feature private entrances as well). Two unique spa rooms include private steam rooms, outdoor Jacuzzis, and see-through ceiling domes that make for a romantic place to sleep under the stars in cozy comfort. Whatever accommodation you choose, you'll enjoy access right outside your door to numerous recreational opportunities, including hiking and mountain biking trails, fishing, cross-country skiing, paddling, boating, ice-skating, and more. Expensive to very expensive.

HOTELS AND MOTELS & **"¡" Historic Plains Hotel** (1-866-275-2467 or 307-638-3311; http://www.theplains hotel.com), 1600 Central Avenue. This historic hotel, constructed in 1911, once housed cattle barons and other upscale visitors passing through the city. Today you can revisit the splendor in the remodeled (2003) version of this mainstay of Cheyenne's lodging facilities, situated right in the heart of Cheyenne's historic downtown. Across the street from the hotel, you can start your explorations with Cheyenne Depot Museum (see *To See*—Museums), housed in the old Union Pacific Railroad Depot. Stay in one of 100 luxurious hotel rooms with custom-designed western décor, or choose

from the 30 suites and spread out a little more. Package deals, including bed and breakfast packages, spa packages, and theatre packages, are available. You'll enjoy access to an on-site fitness center and business center, a gift shop, **Adora Spa** (a full-service day spa), **The Trail Coffee Shoppe** (inexpensive), and the **Capitol Grille,** serving fine, western cuisine for breakfast, lunch, and dinner (expensive). The hotel also hosts wine dinners, musical entertainment, and other community events. Expensive.

CAMPGROUNDS ♂ **"¡" Cheyenne KOA** (1-800-562-1507 or 307-638-8840; http://www.cheyennekoa.com), 8800 Archer Frontage Road. This full-service RV park includes sites for tents as well as cabins. It also has a swimming pool, miniature golf, and a game room. Very inexpensive to inexpensive.

"¡" ❀ Last Chance Camp (307-640-0697; http://www.lastchancecamp .com), 11234 Coorod Road. This basic RV park boasts close proximity to the Cheyenne Frontier Days event. Tent campers and RVs are welcome, and horse-boarding facilities are available as well (but no sewage for RVs). They do have electric hookups. Showers cost extra. Very inexpensive.

See also Pine Bluffs in *To See*—Towns; Curt Gowdy State Park in *Green Space*—State Parks; and Terry Bison Ranch Resort (below).

OTHER OPTIONS & ♂ **Terry Bison Ranch Resort** (307-634-4171; http:// www.terrybisonranch.com), 51 I-25 Service Road E. Not your typical vacation destination, the Terry Bison Ranch offers you the unique, year-round opportunity to stay and play on a 27,500-acre working buffalo ranch. Accommodation options include cabins, a bunkhouse, RV campsites, and tent campsites. The ranch's amenities and attractions include the **Brass Buffalo Saloon** and **Senator's Steakhouse** (open for lunch and dinner April through October) specializing in—appropriately—buffalo entrées (with other menu items featuring steaks, seafood, poultry, and more; expensive), horseback riding, a kid corral (with amusement park rides), train/driving tours of the ranch, and trout fishing on a private lake. The **Terry Trading Post** (open 8–5) sells bison meat, among other items, and it's where you go to sign up for all of the fun activities. Very inexpensive to expensive.

✴ Where to Eat

EATING OUT ✎ ✦ **Avanti Ristorante Italiano** (307-634-3432; http://www.avanticheyenne.com), 4620 Grandview Avenue. Open 11–2 and 4–9 Monday through Saturday. This Italian restaurant just might be what you're looking for if you're in the mood for some spaghetti, lasagna, fettuccine alfredo, or other classic Italian entrées. You can choose to order an individual item off the menu, such as gnocchi, spicy shrimp alfredo, or chicken abruzzo, among other offerings, or you can choose to sample a number of entrées by ordering the buffet (available for both lunch and dinner, Monday through Saturday). This is a great option for families with children, as the kids can partake of the buffet as well—but at special, reduced rates. Inexpensive to moderate.

✦ ✎ **Casa de Trujillo** (307-635-1227), 122 W. Sixth Street. Open for lunch and dinner 11–2 and 4:30–8 Tuesday through Thursday, 11–2 and 4:30–9 Friday, 11–9 Saturday. Popular with locals, this Mexican restaurant has all of the favorites you would expect to find on the menu—plus some interesting creations and combination plates of its own. Broaden your south-of-the-border horizons by ordering the red chili burger, a chili relleno or chorizo omelet, or a stuffed sopapilla—or if you like, stick with an old standby like a platter including tacos, burritos, guacamole, or tostadas. Most dinner entrées come with Mexican refried beans and rice as well. The prices at Casa de Trujillo are extremely reasonable, while the serving sizes are generous. A children's menu is available. Inexpensive.

✦ **Korean House Restaurant** (307-638-7938), 3219 Snyder Avenue. Open 11–7:30 (8 for takeout) Monday through Friday. A standout Asian restaurant awaits you here in Cheyenne, with the convenience of takeout if you prefer. Authentic dishes such as chicken bulgogi and Korean dumplings (mondoo) will make your taste buds happy, while the prices just might make you sing with joy. Individual entrées come with shared sides. Inexpensive.

✎ **The Pie Lady** (307-637-8838), 3515 E. Lincolnway (in Cheyenne Plaza). Open for lunch and dinner; call for current hours. This restaurant's name conjures up images of the welcoming, grandmotherly type, baking up a storm in preparation for the arrival of her grandkids—and really, that isn't too far from the truth of what you'll discover at this family friendly diner. A menu of down-home cooking selections features an array of homemade soups, incredible chili and cornbread, sandwiches, quiche, cinnamon rolls, pot pies, salads, and of course, pies, pies, and more pies, with the selection varying daily. Devour a slice—a la mode if you like—or take home a whole pie (you may find yourself doing both) to enjoy later. Inexpensive to moderate.

Synergy Café (307-778-3838; http://www.synergycafe.com), 459 Vandehei Avenue #100. Open 6 AM–9 PM Monday through Thursday, 6 AM–10 PM Friday, 7 AM–10 PM Saturday, 10–6 Sunday. For coffee from an independent source, this is a good choice in Cheyenne. In addition to serving specialty coffee drinks and other coffee-shop beverages (tea, smoothies, Italian crème sodas, bubble tea), Synergy also has an array of soups, salads, sandwiches, and baked goods. The shop regularly hosts community concerts and events, so call or check the online schedule to get the scoop on what's coming up. Inexpensive.

See also The Plains Hotel and Terry Bison Ranch Resort in *Lodging*.

DINING OUT & **Little Bear Inn** (307-634-3684; http://www.littlebearinn.com), 1700 Little Bear Road. Open 5 PM–9 PM Tuesday through Thursday and Sunday, 5 PM–10 PM Friday through Saturday. Treat yourself to an authentic, western-style, fine-dining experience at this locally owned and operated establishment, a Cheyenne fixture since 1958. In a world rife with chain steakhouses, this restaurant is an original, one-of-a-kind destination, featuring top-notch cuisine in an unsurpassable atmosphere of cozy and elegant western hospitality. But be forewarned: You might find it hard to select just one of the chef's creations from the menu, with choices such as buffalo top sirloin, northern walleye pike, salmon in parchment paper, or bourbon blackjack steak, to name a few. For the more adventurous palate, the restaurant also has offbeat selections including fried frog legs and Rocky Mountain oysters. Weekends bring live entertainment and dancing. Expensive to very expensive.

See also The Plains Hotel and Terry Bison Ranch Resort in *Lodging*.

✳ Entertainment

Cheyenne Little Theatre (307-638-6543; http://www.cheyennelittletheatre.com), P.O. Box 20087. This theatre troupe offers a variety of dramatic performances; call or check the Web site for what's currently playing.

Cheyenne Symphony Orchestra (307-778-8561; http://www.cheyennesymphony.org), 1904 Thomes Avenue.

& **Cheyenne Civic Center** (307-637-6363; http://www.cheyenneciviccenter.org), 2101 O'Neil Avenue. Cheyenne's premier arts venue hosts performers and entertainers from all over the world, from traveling Broadway shows to famous ballet companies, plus concerts by today's hottest stars.

Frontier 9 (307-634-9499; http://www.carmike.com), 1400 Del Range Boulevard, #21.

Cole Square 3 (307-635-2923; http://www.carmike.com), 517 Cole Square Shopping Center.

Lincoln Movie Theaters (307-637-7469), 1615 Central Avenue.

See also Cheyenne Depot Museum and Cheyenne Frontier Days Old West Museum in *To See*—Museums; Taco John's Ice and Events Center in *To Do*—For Families; Bit O' Wyo Ranch in *To Do*—Horseback Riding; Nagle Warren Mansion Bed and Breakfast and Historic Plains Hotel in *Lodging*; Synergy Café in *Where to Eat*—Eating Out; and Little Bear Inn in *Where to Eat*—Dining Out.

✳ Selective Shopping

Manitou Galleries (307-635-0019; http://www.manitouartbrokers.com), 1715 Carey Avenue. Call for current hours. At this gallery you can look at/purchase original fine art (contemporary and historic), bronze sculptures, and prints, but that's not all. You'll also find western antiques, especially old firearms, cowboy memorabilia and items, and American Indian collectible items (beadwork, weaving, baskets, weapons, jewelry, pottery, and more).

Sierra Trading Post (307-775-0850; http://www.sierratradingpost.com), 5025 Campstool Avenue. See listing in Northwest Wyoming: Cody and Powell.

Wyoming Home (1-877-754-8855 or 307-632-2222; http://www.wyoming home.com), 216 W. Lincolnway. Open 9–7 Monday through Friday, 9–5 Saturday, noon–5 Sunday (summer); 10–6 Monday through Friday, 10–5 Saturday (winter). For all things western, turn to Wyoming Home, whether you're in search of home décor or the perfect gift item to bring back for someone special. An enormous selection of items ranges from foodstuff to cowboy/cowgirl clothing and gear, books and mugs, jewelry and even spa products—and that's not nearly all.

See also *To See*—Museums (almost all have gift shops); Noah's Ark Nutrition Center in *To Do*—Relaxation and Rejuvenation; Historic Plains Hotel in *Lodging*; and Brown 'n Gold Outlet in Rawlins and Laramie.

✳ Special Events

🌱 *May:* **Cheyenne Depot Garden Festival,** Cheyenne: This annual free event includes free lectures and plant sales. See also Cheyenne Depot Museum in *To See*—Museums.

May: **Cheyenne Depot Days:** An annual celebration of Cheyenne's railroad roots is at the Cheyenne Depot Museum (see *To See*—Museums).

🐎 *June:* **Kids' Cowboy Festival:** The annual festival for children is held at the Cheyenne Frontier Days Old West Museum (see *To See*—Museums).

June: **Wyoming Brewer's Festival** (307-432-5395; http://www.wyoming brewersfestival.com): Sample more than 40 microbrews brewed in the state of Wyoming and the Front Range area during this two-day festival.

🌱 🐎 *June through July:* **Cheyenne Gunslingers** (307-778-3133): Monday through Friday at 6 PM and Saturday at noon; Witness old-time western fun at Old Town Square with skits, gunfights, and more.

June and July: **=G (Double Bar G) Rodeo Series** (307-632-3626; http://www.outlawrodeo.com) Pine Bluffs: Almost every Friday at 7 PM, you can catch the buckin' broncos in action, as well as all of the other exciting rodeo events.

🐎 *July:* **Cheyenne Frontier Days** (1-800-227-6336 or 307-778-7222; http://www.cfdrodeo.com): Known as The Daddy of 'Em All, this annual 10-day celebration running since 1897 includes rodeos, a parade, free pancake breakfasts, and big-name entertainers.

♪ ✿ *August:* **Happy Jack Music Festival** (303-638-3725; http://www.hj musicfestival.com), Curt Gowdy State Park (see *Green Space*—State Parks): This free festival includes bluegrass, folk, old-time, gospel, and country music.

✿ *September:* **Cheyenne Greek Festival** (307-635-5929; http://www .cheyennegoc.org/GreekFestival.dsp), Cheyenne: This two-day festival includes Greek food, dancing, and entertainment.

INDEX